MEXICAN WORKERS AND THE MAKING OF ARIZONA

Edited by
LUIS F. B. PLASCENCIA
and GLORIA H. CUÁDRAZ

MEXICAN WORKERS AND THE MAKING OF ARIZONA

★

THE UNIVERSITY OF
ARIZONA PRESS
TUCSON

The University of Arizona Press
www.uapress.arizona.edu

First paperback edition 2019

ISBN-13: 978-0-8165-3186-8 (cloth)
ISBN-13: 978-0-8165-4067-9 (paper)

Cover design by Leigh McDonald
Cover photo by Philip Decker, courtesy of the Philip Decker Photographs, Arizona Collection, Arizona State University Libraries

Publication of this book is made possible in part by funding from the Center for Critical Inquiry and Cultural Studies at Arizona State University, and by the proceeds of a permanent endowment created with the assistance of a Challenge Grant from the National Endowment for the Humanities, a federal agency.

Library of Congress Cataloging-in-Publication Data
Names: Plascencia, Luis F. B., editor. | Cuádraz, Gloria, editor.
Title: Mexican workers and the making of Arizona / edited by Luis F. B. Plascencia and Gloria H. Cuádraz.
Description: Tucson : The University of Arizona Press, 2018 | Includes bibliographical references and index.
Identifiers: LCCN 2018008711 | ISBN 9780816531868 (cloth : alk. paper)
Subjects: LCSH: Foreign workers, Mexican—Arizona—Social conditions. | Foreign workers, Mexican—Arizona—Economic conditions. | Foreign workers, Mexican—Arizona—History.
Classification: LCC HD8081.M6 M48 2018 | DDC 331.6/27209791—dc23 LC record available at https://lccn.loc.gov/2018008711

Printed in the United States of America
♾ This paper meets the requirements of ANSI/NISO Z39.48-1992 (Permanence of Paper).

Dedicated
to
F. Arturo Rosales
Beloved historian and scholar
of
Arizona's Chicana/o history

And
in honor of
Arizona's Mexican people
and their struggles to improve their lives

★

CONTENTS

Prologue: Contextualizing Mexican Labor and Arizona's National Importance 3

Introduction: Arizona's Six Cs and Mexicana/o Labor 23

1. Lost Land and México Lindo: Origins of Mexicans in Arizona's Salt River Valley, 1865–1910 61
Jaime R. Águila and F. Arturo Rosales

2. The Mobilization and Immobilization of "Legally Imported Aliens": Cotton in the Salt River Valley, 1917–1921 90
Gloria H. Cuádraz

3. "Get Us Our Privilege of Bringing in Mexican Labor": Recruitment and Desire for Mexican Labor in Arizona, 1917–2016 124
Luis F. B. Plascencia

PHOTO ESSAY 179

4. Mexicano Miners, Dual Wage, and the Pursuit of Wage Equality in Miami, Arizona 203
Christine Marin and Luis F. B. Plascencia

5. Mexican American Women Workers in Mid-Twentieth-Century Phoenix 227
Jean Reynolds

6. **The Morenci Miners Women's Auxiliary during the Great Arizona Copper Strike, 1983–1986** **248**
Anna Ochoa O'Leary

7. **Constructing Arizona: The Lives and Labor of Mexicans in the Valley of the Sun** **270**
Cristina Gallardo-Sanidad

Epilogue *301*
Acknowledgments *311*
References *315*
Contributors *375*
Index *379*

MEXICAN WORKERS
AND THE MAKING OF ARIZONA

MAP 1 Map of Arizona. Courtesy of the Arizona Historical Society

PROLOGUE

★

Contextualizing Mexican Labor and Arizona's National Importance

Thus in the face of the greatest demand for labor the world has ever seen, with the country at the highest point of prosperity it has ever known, the cotton growers of the Salt River Valley maintained as perfectly an elastic supply of labor as the world has ever seen and maintained an even low level of prices for wages throughout its territory. Outsiders looked, studied, and went away amazed at the accomplishment of such an organization.

ANONYMOUS ARIZONA COTTON GROWERS ASSOCIATION REPRESENTATIVE

ON ANY GIVEN DAY IN ARIZONA, residents encounter a common circumstance. Thousands of workers of Mexican descent labor each day to make our lives possible in urban and rural areas. The majority of such workers are largely invisible. Their work as child caretakers, dishwashers or cooks in restaurants, hotel housekeeping staff, caretakers of the elderly, and in many other settings, remains in the shadows of an economy dependent on their labor. Their presence and labor sustain conveniences and consumer prices we have grown accustomed to, as well as key economic activities that benefit the state economy. To visit Yuma in the winter for the harvesting of lettuce or a Home Depot in the suburbs, to drive by a new residential construction area, or to see the myriad landscapers as one drives through residential areas, one sees Mexican-descent workers performing numerous work activities. Mexican-origin workers, both invisible and visible, whether in public or private spheres, are essential to our standard of living. Paradoxically, however, both historically and contemporarily, Mexican workers occupy a space where employers classify them as a needed low-wage "elastic supply of labor" because, on the one hand, U.S. workers are allegedly not available, and, on the other hand, segments of the public perceive them as an unwanted foreign group harming the economy and society. This anthology aims to expand our understanding of this paradox.

The uncertain future status and well-being of Mexican households in Arizona under the Trump administration augments the importance of understanding the aforementioned paradox. Efforts to encourage the deportation of individuals subject to removal, build an eighteen- to thirty-foot border wall on the Mexico-U.S. boundary, greatly shrink access to medical care for low-income households, and reduce protective labor and environmental regulations affecting workers can be labeled "solutions" by those with an incomplete or limited understanding of the history of the region or the nation.[1] Reality, however, is more complex. A salient constraint to all concocted solutions, from the Reagan administration to the current administration, is the second part of the paradox: historically, the U.S. economy has actively fostered the recruitment of, and benefitted from, a low-wage elastic supply of labor composed of Mexicanas/os.[2] It is easy to promote a populist or nativist interpretation of migration and migrants and to call for creating jobs for "Americans" (a coded term for white U.S. nationals). It is another matter to actually transform all economic activities sustained by undocumented workers or foreign contract workers who are granted employment-based visas precisely because employers, such as The Trump Organization, attest they cannot find U.S. workers.[3] As discussed in chapter 3, Arizona elected officials and employers sustained a "labor shortage" argument for over a century—1917 to the present.

President Trump has for several years relied on H-2A (temporary agricultural workers) for his two-hundred-acre Trump Winery in Virginia, and H-2B (temporary nonagricultural workers) for the operation of his exclusive Mar-a-Lago Resort in Palm Beach, Florida. He also has utilized undocumented workers for construction projects—a violation of the 1986 employer sanctions provision enacted by President Reagan. The premise of using such labor is that "American" workers are not available—or more correctly but not acknowledged—are not available under the wages, working conditions, and production levels demanded.

To date, neither President Trump nor The Trump Organization have announced that they will Make America Great Again and create jobs for "Americans" by replacing all contract workers at Trump properties with U.S. workers or publicly pledged to no longer use undocumented workers directly or indirectly (i.e., subcontracting) in all future construction projects in the United States. Such a change does not require a presidential executive order or Congressional action—it can easily be made on any day chosen by the president. It is ironic that among the easiest actions that President Trump could take to model how U.S. employers could create jobs for U.S. workers is one that he has not taken. Presumably Trump does not want to forego the capital accumulation made possible by undocumented and contract workers. This suggests that the touted concepts of "economic nationalism" and Make America Great Again may seem appealing on the surface, but instead may be floating signifiers deployed to foster the perception that he seeks a populist public policy.

The unnamed representative of the Arizona Cotton Growers Association (ACGA), who in the early 1900s made the statement noted in the epigraph, indexes an important employer-worker dynamic that is not limited to the hand harvesting of cotton. There are two critical dimensions in the dynamic. First, that the ACGA was able to advantageously regulate the volume of workers needed to meet estimated labor needs in cotton plantations in Arizona—even when estimates were inflated. In other words, the ACGA was able to recruit what it estimated were the appropriate number of needed and surplus workers, and then terminate their employment when no longer needed. Chapter 3 discusses the presence of this process in the boom-bust period at the end of World War I. Second, that cotton planters collectively imposed low wages on workers recruited. The concept of low-wage elastic labor supply provides a framework for understanding the historiography of Mexicana/o labor in Arizona and beyond. We also argue that the process is evident in the contemporary period in Arizona.

Arizona's own importance to the nation is also paradoxical. Since the early 2000s, Arizona has been at the center of media coverage. International and national media allocated much time and space to covering events and people in Arizona. News media covered a long list of stories such as Governor Napolitano's 2007 enactment of the state's employer sanctions law; Senator John McCain's 2008 presidential campaign; the enactment of Arizona's SB 1070 in 2010; the 2011 Tucson shooting that killed six individuals, including a federal judge, and injured U.S. Representative Gabrielle Giffords and eighteen other persons; the racial profiling lawsuit against Sheriff Joseph M. Arpaio; and the more recent fiasco in the March 2016 primary presidential election, particularly in Maricopa County, where Democrats alleged multiple irregularities surfaced that disenfranchised "minority" voters. Despite the international and national attention, Arizona's prominence and historical importance to the economic growth of the West and the nation, and its role in shaping the national political discourse are commonly overlooked in contemporary media accounts.

While a notable academic literature examines Mexican labor in California and Texas, the scholarly literature on Mexican workers in the Grand Canyon State is one that remains limited. This book aims to reduce this gap in the history of the Southwest and enhance our knowledge of the presence and contributions of Mexican-descent individuals to the wealth and infrastructure of Arizona's economy. Historically, for the majority of the nineteenth and twentieth century, Mexican labor was instrumental in the establishment and profitability of the state's five Cs: cattle, citrus, climate, copper, and cotton. In the contemporary period, with the expansion and growth of real estate speculation in housing construction, Mexican labor has been essential to what we would add as Arizona's sixth C: construction. The combined capital and labor in these six sectors are central to the past and present economic growth of the region and the nation.

Arizona is a spectacular state. The state not only counts with internationally known tourism sites such as the Grand Canyon, Hoover Dam, Lake Havasu's London Bridge, Canyon de Chelly, Monument Valley in the Diné (Navajo) Nation, and Saguaro

National Park, but also lesser-known wonders such as Montezuma's Castle, Barringer Crater, and others. Arizona's spectacularity, however, is not limited to natural or human-made tourist sites. Its resplendency is also located in its historical importance in the electrification of the nation based on copper deposits in the state, its production of cotton for the auto industry and essential military goods in World Wars I and II, as the site of multiple military operations and installations dating back to the 1800s, as well as other events and resources of national importance.[4]

Although not often noted, its national impact is greater than more populous states. According to the Bureau of the Census, Arizona ranked fifteen in total population in 2014. Its estimated total of 6.73 million residents represents a fraction of the totals found in California (17.3 percent), Texas (25 percent), and Florida (33 percent). Nationally, only 2.1 percent of the total U.S. population resides in Arizona. Correspondingly, Arizona holds 11 of the total 538 national Electoral College votes, or 4.1 percent of the 270 needed to win the presidency. Led by California's 55 Electoral College votes, 13 other states hold more votes than Arizona. Yet despite fewer residents and Electoral College votes than Georgia, North Carolina, Michigan, New Jersey, and Washington, its historical and contemporary national political significance cannot be ignored.

Arizona's substantial population growth that emerged in the mid-1980s captured national attention. Arizona and other states such as Nevada underwent an unprecedented demographic transition. However, it was not simply the growth of the European-descent population due to native births and migration from midwestern states and Canada—it was also growth in the diversity of the state. Between 1980 and 2000, the overall population increased by 88.8 percent. This overall growth was made possible by a 191.7 percent growth of Latinos, a 44.9 percent growth of European descent, a 102.2 percent growth in the African-descent community, and a 53.2 percent growth in Indigenous communities. In short, in two decades Arizona became a more diverse state, one where Latinos were central to its growth and diversification.

According to the 2014 American Community Survey, Latinos comprise 30.5 percent of the state's 6.73 million residents. Nationally, the Bureau of the Census estimates that the Latino 17.4 percent of the total U.S. population will reach 20.5 percent by 2060. If Arizona's growth between 2014 and 2060 was equal to the national rate, this means that in 2060, 41.6 percent of the state will be of Latino origin—the reality is that Latino growth has consistently exceeded the national rate and hence may exceed 50 percent before 2060. The importance of such a demographic transition to the economy, society, and politics of the state has yet to be fully examined or understood by state leaders as a whole. Arizona's leaders will need to reconceptualize the state's historical narrative and its horizon, in the context of the growing Latino population, and the role and importance of Mexicana/o labor to the continued prosperity of the state.

It also should be acknowledged that Arizona has always been a diverse state. It was a diverse area before the Spanish Empire asserted its presence in what became Arizona. Currently, Arizona includes the single largest Native American nation—the Diné with its large semiautonomous territory (over twenty-seven square miles)—and is a state with one of the most diverse Indian populations. There are a total of twenty-one federally recognized Indian tribes. These communities encompass slightly more than 350,000 individuals (2010), and thirteen language groups.

During World War II, Arizona was an important site for "solving national security" anxieties. Arizona was second only to California in the number of detention facilities for Japanese-descent individuals, including U.S. citizens of Japanese descent.[5] A total of seven facilities were in operation in Arizona, accounting for close to 45,000 internees; this represented about 35 percent of the approximately 127,000 adults and children involuntarily imprisoned. While the largest war relocation center, Tule Lake in California, held a maximum population of 18,789, the Poston and Gila River War Relocation Centers were the second- and third-largest facilities with 17,814 and 13,348 maximum capacity, respectively.

Over the long run, the more important question was the scale of military-related expenditures in Arizona. Federal expenditures during and after the war for military bases, military contractors, the GI Bill, veteran housing assistance, and veteran's health care were essential to not only increasing the population, but also to stimulating the economic growth accompanying the population growth. The Dwight D. Eisenhower National System of Interstate and Defense Highways was not simply a plan for civilian motor vehicle roads—it was envisioned as part of the nation's military defense system. In Arizona, as well as in most other states, the interstate highway system made possible the formation of suburbs, and the suburbs stimulated the growth in population, as well as the speculation in land and housing construction.

Most U.S. residents who have seen a law-and-order television show or movie can probably recite what federal, state, or local police agents are supposed to say as they arrest someone: "You have the right to remain silent. . . ." Yet what is less known by most audiences is that the recitation—Miranda rights—emerged because of the legal challenge brought forth by Ernesto Arturo Miranda, a Mexican American resident of Phoenix. His challenge to his arrest by the Phoenix Police Department reached the U.S. Supreme Court (*Miranda v. Arizona*, 384 U.S. 436, 1966), and the court issued its guidance on what should be communicated to an individual who has been seized and is not free to go on their way.

The contemporary political climate and its marked partisan divide at the state and federal level cannot be understood without taking into account the rise of conservatism in the United States. And while President Reagan is commonly represented as the actor who ushered in the conservative revolution, scholarship on five-term Republican

U.S. senator Barry M. Goldwater positions Goldwater as the more central figure in founding the conservative political movement—an ideological position Reagan followed and used in rising to national prominence.[6] Senator Goldwater's views on Soviet Union communism, organized labor, law and order, public assistance, and the New Deal are core elements in contemporary arguments for smaller federal government, states' rights, lower taxes, rule of law, personal responsibility, and the promotion of the free market and trickle-down prosperity. President Reagan is more quotable, but Senator Goldwater's political intervention has been more durable.

The presence and impact of Arizona leaders in the U.S. Senate is imposing. Five-term senator Goldwater was preceded by seven-term Democratic senator Carl T. Hayden and followed by six-term Republican senator John McCain. Stated differently, for close to a century, three men from Arizona held senior positions in Senate actions related to major national policies, including federal government expenditures benefiting Arizona. More recently, the two Republican senators from Arizona (John McCain and Jeff Flake) made up half of the four Republicans on the bipartisan Gang of Eight, which negotiated the 2013 immigration reform bill approved by the Senate. Neither Democratic nor Republican senators from the two most populous states and ones where migration policies are prominent (California and Texas) were members in the bipartisan group. More recently, Senator Flake and Senator McCain have garnered media attention due to their unshrinking critiques of actions and policy statements by President Trump, and have been vocal critics of some of President Trump's nominees for cabinet positions and the federal courts. These public positions stand in clear contrast to other Republican senators.

Arizonans also occupied key roles in the U.S. Supreme Court, and thus shaped the nation's jurisprudence on multiple Constitutional issues related to the Fourth Amendment, the 1964 Civil Rights Act, the 1965 Voting Rights Act, affirmative action, the outcome of *Bush v. Gore* (531 U.S. 98, 2000), and others. President Nixon appointed a young conservative attorney from Arizona—William Hubbs Rehnquist—as associate justice in January 1972.[7] Subsequently, President Reagan appointed Rehnquist as chief justice in 1986. Five years earlier, President Reagan named the first woman to the Supreme Court: Sandra Day O'Connor.[8] For close to a quarter of a century (1981–2005), two of the nine justices were conservative Republicans from Arizona.[9] Goldwater's conservatism constituted part of their political foundations. Ironically, although Arizona is now considered a red state, Arizona's earlier history represents one where labor rights were more central, and white women had rights that other white women did not have in other states. Arizona granted women the right to vote in November 1912, eight years before the Nineteenth Amendment was ratified.[10]

Arizona's general contribution to the United States' prosperity is known by the general public, but the contribution of Mexicans to the state's social, political, and economic prosperity is less known. One commonly finds that these contributions are excluded from historical narratives of the state. This anthology focuses on one dimension of the broader impact—paid wage labor.[11] It focuses on the economic activities of men and women who struggled to achieve what most other households were also seeking to achieve: economic security that would allow them to meet parental responsibilities, provide sustenance and adequate housing for household members, and aspirations to reduce the economic hardships they experienced from being repeated in the lives of their children. They hoped their children could benefit from education, pursue less arduous occupations, and achieve what their generation struggled to reach.

In this anthology, we want to make clear that when we talk about Mexican laborers, we refer to both men and women, cognizant of the fact that all too often the operating assumption in the scholarly literature on Mexican labor is that men predominate. Indeed, men have occupied a majority of laborer positions in various sectors, such as construction, day labor, landscape services, and cooks. In other sectors, such as hotel housekeeping, private domestic services, and care of the elderly and children, women are the preferred labor force. Far too often, however, data is not collected on the extent to which women were part of given workforces or crews in male-dominated occupations and, more often than not, their presence in agricultural production was counted in terms of their participation in a "family unit," which as scholars have established, was the primary and preferred unit of production for agricultural commodities such as citrus, cotton, onions, sugar beets, as well as in copper mines and railroads.[12]

Children often worked alongside their parents. The enactment of the Fair Labor Standards Act (FLSA) in 1938 set in place some protections for child workers.[13] However, agribusiness interests received some exemptions within the law, and subsequent amendments expanded these. The outcome of these is that states are provided flexibility in reducing child labor protections. Arizona, for example, in parallel manner to federal law, does not require certification of the age or employment certificate proving the age of the child. In contrast, California requires an employment certificate showing the person is eighteen years of age or older. Children continue to be found toiling in the agricultural fields of the United States during school days, as well as on nonschool days.

It is fair to reiterate, for this point has certainly been made by Chicana scholars in history and the social sciences, that a paucity of research exists about Mexicana women in the agricultural industry, the sector in which the vast majority of Mexicans were able to economically provide for their families in the southwestern economy in the twentieth century.[14] To date, a full-length monograph is yet to be written that focuses specifically on Mexican women farmworkers within the production process, although a number of critical and groundbreaking studies that focus on Chicanas, work, and family do abound.[15] The one notable exception to the above is the oral history of María Elena Lucas—a Mexicana agricultural worker who became an organizer with the Farm

Labor Organizing Committee (FLOC) in Ohio, and later under the United Farm Workers Union (UFW) in Illinois (Buss 1993).

Lastly, we want to acknowledge that this anthology does not examine the important segment of Mexicana/o business owners in Arizona. The analysis of Mexicana/o entrepreneurs merits a separate volume. It is a diverse cohort encompassing from single owner/operators who work on their own or may employ additional workers based on the size of projects (e.g., hair stylist, makers of tamales, street vendor, *yarderos*, carpet layers, painters, barbers, etc.), to professionals operating small businesses (e.g., bookkeepers, dentist, medical doctor, nail- or hair-salon owners, etc.), and midsize businesses (e.g., small grocery stores, general contractors, etc.).

This omission means that the stories and experiences of Mexicanas/os who struggled to remain self-employed and be their own bosses are unfortunately not captured, even in cases where we met and/or knew such entrepreneurs. The full story of Mr. Martínez and his family (see photos on pages 200 and 201), for example, are excluded because of our decision to focus on paid wage work. In brief, Mr. Martínez was born in León, Guanajuato, Mexico, and by age seven he was recognized as a talented shoemaker. Guanajuato is one of the four Mexican states that historically dominated the flow of migrants to the United States, and León is one of Mexico's principal shoe-production sites. In 1939 Mr. Martínez, his wife, and their two daughters migrated to El Paso, Texas. After working for a few years at the Tony Lama boot factory, the family relocated to Phoenix. In Phoenix he had the good fortune to have been employed by a kindhearted employer, Mr. Gregory, and when Mr. Gregory decided to close his shoe-repair business, he allowed Mr. Martínez to buy the equipment without requiring an immediate payment. Over time Mr. Martínez and his sons and daughters came to specialize in repairing shoes, purses, and other leather items. The family venture led to the establishment of five shops and, for a short while, a restaurant. One of the shops has been at the same location in Phoenix for close to fifty years. Moreover, even though we tend to create a binary between urban and agricultural industries, in the past some family members sought work harvesting onions in the Phoenix area to make ends meet. It also should be noted that it is not only his sons who learned skills from their father—Mr. Martínez's daughters are also skilled at repairing shoes, leather items, and running the business. When he is not in the main shop, Mr. Martínez, who is now in his eighties, can still be seen operating the heavy equipment in the shop (Guerra and Washington, 2015).

ORIENTATION OF THE BOOK

This anthology seeks to intervene in the production of knowledge about Mexicans in Arizona, as well as the Southwest more generally. As noted earlier, the book has a narrow focus: the labor Mexicanas/os perform in Arizona. To comprehensively examine the total social, legal, political, religious, and family dynamics of Mexicans in Arizona would require a much larger tome, most likely a multivolume edition. Our intent is not to reify or fetishize the human activity of work, or to suggest that Mexicans or other groups in the state can be understood solely as expressions of *homo economicus*—subjects who are solely driven by and act in relation to economic factors and cost-benefit material calculations. To the contrary, the communities we are part of and study are like most other human communities. They pursue dreams, work, education, careers, fall in love, marry/cohabitate/divorce/remarry, raise children, possess contradictions, embrace humor, pursue religious/spiritual ends, enjoy music and friends, assist neighbors, observe ironies in their own lives, and pursue civil rights and social justice in the broader society.

They, like most of us, however, live in a capitalist economy wherein they must sell their labor power to obtain wages and then use those wages to meet their everyday material needs. Mexican parents, like other parents, try to do the best they can. Their ability to provide more is contingent on the cycles of the economy and the opportunities and exclusions in the labor market. In a capitalist economy, work is the primary means to meet the economic and social needs of households. Consequently, our aim in this book is to capture a narrow slice of the broad spectrum of labor performed by wage workers. The limited scholarship on historical and contemporary types of labor meant that we as editors searched widely for unpublished original essays on Mexican labor that captured some of the diversity of paid work activities. The contributions included provide a sample of work activities covering the approximate period from the 1910s to the present.

The book represents a transdisciplinary analysis of the socioeconomic experience of Mexican laborers. One way to highlight our focus is to note what it is not. It is not a traditional labor history of a particular occupation or industrial sector (e.g., Gilbert González's analysis of citrus workers in Southern California, 1994). It is also not a conventional social history of a geographic community revolving around a particular firm or type of work (e.g., Monica Perales's examination of the community and workers employed at the American Smelting and Refining Company in El Paso, 2010), nor of the production of a particular regional commodity (e.g., Roberto R. Calderón's *Mexican Coal Mining Labor in Texas and Coahuila, 1880–1930*, 2000). It is also not a community case study of an urban area (e.g., Zaragosa Vargas's investigation of Mexican workers in Detroit and surrounding area, 1993). It is also not a history of intercommunity relations (e.g., the impressive work of the historian Eric Meeks on the relations between Anglos, Indians, and Mexicans in Arizona, 2007a). Instead, it is an effort to bridge conventional historical and social science approaches to examine a sample of the work experience of Mexicanas/os in Arizona across a significant time period.

It is important to also note that the anthology is not a Mexico-U.S. borderlands book or, using the construct suggested by Professor Vélez-Ibáñez, a book about the Southwest North American Region (2017). More concretely, we acknowledge that the labor, capital, and commodities noted in this work have an intrinsic transnational dimension, but our focus was not on examining the processes that fostered and sustained their transnationalism or transcontinental mobility. Readers interested in the broader borderlands can turn to the excellent recent scholarship directly engaging transnational dimensions that shape the Mexico-U.S. borderlands.[16]

The research in this volume resonates with themes commonly found in Chicana/o labor history in the Southwest, such as (a) the targeted discrimination directed toward Mexican workers—one intricately tied to corporate interests to maximize profit—hence, how the organizing principle of race served the interests of capital; (b) how the intensive penetration of capital turned traditional stratification along class lines (with alliances that crossed ethnic lines) into a more racially stratified social order that rendered the Mexican subject as subaltern; (c) how Mexican elite lost land and elite economic status such that by the early twentieth century they, along with Mexicans of various strata were effectively proletarianized; (d) how the expansion of the West required a Mexican labor force in unprecedented volumes; (e) how Mexican men, women, and children, both foreign-born and U.S. citizens, were incorporated to labor in the low-wage sector of agriculture; (f) how women's labor or involvement in labor conflicts remain largely invisible in historical accounts, and whose paid and unpaid labor are rarely addressed; (g) how multiple stakeholders/interests colluded to create the conditions under which Mexicans would participate in the labor market. In these ways, our study of Mexicana/o workers in Arizona builds on the scholarship of Chicana/o labor in the Southwest.[17] Arizona is unique to the extent that its rich mineral supply of copper positioned it to be essential to national interests. The extent to which Arizona, through the Arizona Cotton Growers Association were responsible for bringing in half of all the officially recruited workers under the temporary admissions program during World War I suggests, once again, how central capital interests in Arizona, with the aid of the federal government, were to the larger expansion of the West.

To reiterate, there currently exists no single monograph whose primary focus is the study of Mexican labor in Arizona. Several monographs, however, do render significant the population of Mexican workers and incorporate it into broader accounts. Of single monographs that incorporate the issue of labor in Arizona, two have been especially useful to our work. Benton-Cohen's (2009) *Borderline Americans: Racial Divisions and Labor War in the Arizona Borderlands* provides one of the more detailed and analytically rich accounts of Mexicans' incorporation into the mining and copper industry and the racial divides ensuing from those processes. In *Border Citizen: The Making of Indians, Mexicans, and Anglos in Arizona*, Eric Meeks (2007) meticulously delineates the complex terrain of racial classifications (all too often problematically monolithic), shaping identities, and interethnic relations in the context of Arizona's incorporation into the U.S. political economy in the early decades of the twentieth century. In the tradition of E. P. Thompson's (1964) emphasis on the processes of formation, Meeks directs our attention to the "making" of racial and ethnic identities, enabling us to more fully grasp the extent to which "race" and processes of racial formation were intricately tied "from the state's inception, to racial, economic, and political inequality" (43). Of other single monographs on Arizona whose primary focus is on Mexican Americans, some scholarly attention has been given to case studies of discrimination at social and community levels, or to social relations between Mexicans and Anglos, and other white and nonwhite ethnic groups.[18]

In this book, we bring together a spectrum of scholars and practitioners with a deep desire to expand our understanding of Mexicanas and Mexicanos as they labored in different historical periods, and multiple economic sectors, and occupations. The contributors to this anthology, as noted in the short biographies included, encompass three historians, a sociologist, two social anthropologists, a civil/labor rights advocate, and a public archivist. Chronologically, the chapters cover the period from the late 1800s to the present. The reader will note several notable gaps in the coverage. The absence of scholarship regarding important sectors, such as the cattle industry, citrus production, the lumber industry in the Flagstaff area, the use of Mexican "commuter" labor in the Yuma Valley, sugar-beet processing in Glendale, or the participation of Mexicanas/os in Arizona's major railroad corporations, is a reflection of the many gaps that exist regarding the labor by Mexicanas/os in Arizona. As editors, we made a concerted effort to locate scholarly analyses of work within Arizona, but unfortunately much research has yet to be carried out in order to produce a comprehensive picture of the range of work activities and specifics about the work and life experiences of those whose sweat and blood contributed to the making of Arizona.

A NOTE ON GEOGRAPHIC COVERAGE

The reader will note that although our overall focus is Arizona, four chapters focus on experiences in the Salt River Valley/El Salado, one chapter focuses on the Clifton and Morenci area in the southeastern portion of the state, a second chapter is grounded in central eastern Arizona (Miami), and one chapter focuses on the state as a whole. As editors, we sought to locate original unpublished works in other parts of the state that focused on Mexican labor. Some of the scholarly works identified examined multiple important issues such as education, intermarriage, voting, politics, etc., but were excluded because the primary focus was not Mexican labor. In addition, a sizable scholarship has been produced about the settlement and cultural history of the Mexican community in Tucson, but little has been published on the labor or working-class experience of Mexicanas/os in that city.[19] Lastly, this anthology aspires to provide a partial list of the many gaps in the scholarly research regarding the presence and experience of Mexicana/o labor in Arizona. We anticipate that the lengthy bibliography can serve as a starting point for undergraduate and graduate students interested in examining a question of interest related to the central role that Mexican labor has played in the making of Arizona.

A NOTE ON LABELS

Critical discussion of group labels is complex and involves examining the articulation between history and social theory. The reader will note that the editors of this anthology and the contributors do not deploy the exact same group labels. As editors, we left the issue of which labels to use to the contributors but asked them to provide an explanation for their choices. The final result is that the anthology reflects the variation that exists regarding labels used in discussing people of Mexican descent, a diverse community with multiple identifications.[20]

The first significant engagement with the question of what label to apply to persons of Mexican descent is the 1949 foreword by the attorney/journalist/civil rights advocate Carey McWilliams, in his classic *North from Mexico: The Spanish-Speaking People of the United States*. McWilliams struggled with the title and the subtitle to his book about a community in the United States that predated the establishment of the United States, expanded by the significant migration that began in the late 1880s, and was accelerated between 1910 and 1920 and again after 1965. McWilliams insightfully noted in 1949:

> Titles have always bothered me and never more so than in selecting a title for this book. . . . There can be no doubt that the Spanish-speaking constitute a clearly delineated ethnic group. But one must also recognize that there is no more heterogeneous ethnic group in the United States than the Spanish-speaking. Hence it is quite impossible to hit upon a phrase that aptly characterizes all the people now living in this country who by national origin, appearance, speech, or background might be called and probably are called, "Mexican" or "Mexican-American" . . . Any phrase selected to characterize the Spanish-speaking will necessarily prove to be misleading, inaccurate, or possibly libelous. (McWilliams 1949, 7)

Although one can quibble with specifics raised by McWilliams, what is more important is his larger point. Any single label used to name the broad community of persons who trace their ancestry to individuals who settled in the United States during the Spanish Empire or the Estados Unidos Mexicanos (Mexico) period prior to 1853, or are part of the diverse migration initiated in the nineteenth century and continuing to the present, will be problematic. McWilliams also raises parallel issues related to the label *Anglo*—another social group that is neither monolithic nor homogeneous. In thinking about group labels one must also keep in mind important linguistic insights, particularly the observation of Russian linguist Mikhail M. Bakhtin, who in his 1934 essay reminds us that "As a result of the work done by all these stratifying forces in language, there are no 'neutral' words or forms—words and forms that can belong to 'no one'; language has been completely taken over, shot through with intentions and accents" (Bakhtin 1998, 293). Bakhtin's insight suggests that Hispanic, Latino, Latinx, Chicano, Xicano, La Raza, Raza, Mexican American, Mexican, American of Mexican descent, Hispano, Hispano Americano, Spanish American, Latin American, etc., are not neutral labels, nor is there a consensus on the preferred term.

We believe that the fairly wide use of Mexicana and Mexicano, in its Spanish-language form, allows us to index the Mexican-origin community. It is not uncommon for an individual of Mexican descent in the Southwest and beyond to indicate that they identify as a Mexican American in a conversation taking place in English but indicate Mexicana/o if the conversation is in Spanish.[21]

Secondly, we use the term *white* or *European descent* to refer to non-Latino-descent individuals. These labels are, as suggested earlier, also "misleading, inaccurate," and "shot through with intentions and accents." The juridical question of who is a white person is at the center of over fifty federal naturalization cases between 1878 and 1944, some of which reached the U.S. Supreme Court, and did not produce a consistent construction across cases (Haney López 1996).

OVERVIEW OF CHAPTERS

The introduction, "Arizona's Six Cs and Mexicana/o Labor," introduces and contextualizes the volume and chapters by presenting an overview of the Mexican-origin experience in the state, and a synthesis of the literature regarding Mexicana/o labor in Arizona. While the primary focus is to summarize the existing published and unpublished literature, it also notes some of the important gaps in the scholarly literature. The chapter frames the discussion within the construct of six Cs: cattle, citrus, climate, copper, cotton, and construction. The section makes clear that our knowledge of labor in general, and Mexican labor specifically, within the six Cs is uneven.

In chapter 1, "Lost Land and México Lindo: Origins of Mexicans in Arizona's Salt River Valley, 1865–1910," Jaime Águila and the late F. Arturo Rosales explore the social and labor history of the Mexican-origin community of the Salt River Valley, arguing for an examination of the transitional period of the late nineteenth century and a generational approach that contextualizes the settlement and dynamics that shaped the presence and status of that community. The aim of including the chapter is to provide a historical profile for the settlement of the Mexican community in the Salt River Valley. It should be read as supplementary to the well-known discussion of the settlement of Tucson by the anthropologist Thomas E. Sheridan.

Águila and Rosales trace the first generation of Mexican Americans who lived in a fragile symbiosis with European Americans, Native Americans, Chinese, and other communities in the late nineteenth and early twentieth centuries in the Salt River Valley. With the coming of railroads, outside capital and entrepreneurs with new visions, the economic, political, and cultural arrangements forged by Phoenix-area Mexicans in the first years of United States' domination were disrupted, and the blueprint for the processes by which they would become second-class citizens became firmly established. Águila and Rosales, in contrast to Sheridan, give greater attention to Mexicano-Anglo conflicts.[22] They also document the early foundation that constructed Mexican labor as an elastic supply of labor that could be recruited to meet expanding capitalist desires for low-wage workers.

In chapter 2, "The Mobilization and Immobilization of 'Legally Imported Aliens': Cotton in the Salt River Valley, 1917–1921," Gloria H. Cuádraz examines the confluence of forces that bring together the stories of cotton, Mexican labor, and the Goodyear Tire & Rubber Corporation. Her essay chronicles how the constellation of federal laws and corporate and agribusiness interests coalesced to radically transform a once arid desert region into one of the most productive agricultural areas in Arizona, while fortifying Goodyear Tire & Rubber's national preeminence in the tire manufacturing and international rubber industries. Cuádraz documents the cotton industry's boom and bust years, between 1917 and 1921, when thousands of "legally imported aliens," as noted in official accounts, were recruited to work under waivers sanctioned by the Immigration Act of 1917's ninth proviso. Over the period in question, the Arizona Cotton Growers Association (ACGA) alone brought in a reported 33,460 workers to the Salt River Valley. In keeping with scholarly interpretations that examine how workers are "mobilized" and, subsequently, "immobilized" for the benefit of capitalists' enterprise and profit, she investigates the roles of the ACGA, government officials, the Mexican consulate, labor unions, and workers' efforts to organize during the initial boom and bust period demarcating cotton's entry into Arizona's economy. When the cotton market collapsed shortly after the end of World War I, the ACGA violated their contractual agreement with the Department of Labor and abandoned thousands of Mexican workers, leaving them homeless, without wages, or transportation to return to Mexico. Cuádraz reveals how Arizona growers conspired to guarantee for themselves a low-wage elastic supply of labor—one that also relied on a gendering of elasticity with respect to Mexican women, who either officially or unofficially comprised the workforce.

In chapter 3, "'Get Us Our Privilege of Bringing in Mexican Labor': Recruitment and Desire for Mexican Labor in Arizona, 1917–2017," Luis F. B. Plascencia turns attention to the period from the first Congressional hearing that explicitly addressed Mexican migration to the United States (1920) to multiple Congressional and commission hearings related to indentured migrant labor for agricultural and nonagricultural enterprises in the contemporary period. In the series of Congressional hearings, agribusiness interests and state and federal elected officials repeatedly called on Congress to come to the aid of the struggling agricultural sector and address the serious "labor shortage" confronting the sector. Their plea varied somewhat over time, but the essence remained consistent. This can be summarized as "Please let us have our Mexicans, we cannot survive without them, and without them not only will local economies collapse, but the nation will also suffer." World War I, World War II, and the Korean War allowed agribusiness to point out that their ability to produce the volume of food and fiber demanded by the war machine depended on Congress's ability to aid in allowing a sufficient number of indentured contract workers to enter the United States. Plascencia illustrates the importance of arguments about alleged "labor shortages" to the formation of a low-wage elastic supply of labor, and how these continue and now encompass agricultural and nonagricultural interests.

In chapter 4, "Mexicano Miners, Dual Wage, and the Pursuit of Wage Equality in Miami, Arizona," Christine Marin and Luis F. B. Plascencia examine a period during World War II when Mexican Americans of the copper mining community of Miami, Arizona, challenged the discriminatory labor practice known as the dual-wage system. The dual-wage system—the practice of paying a group of workers, in this case Mexican Americans and Mexicans, less than their white counterparts, while classifying their work as unskilled—is but one among a plethora of discriminatory labor practices that worked against the ability of the Mexican population to be as economically mobile as non-Mexicans. The dual-wage system, with its complex and multilayered history contributed to the racialization of the Mexican population and firmly situated them in the secondary labor market, while aiding the formation of hierarchies that privileged their white counterparts. Marin and Plascencia establish the intensely hostile and negative perceptions toward Mexican workers in the mining industry and chronicle efforts by Mexican workers in the 1940s to abolish the dual-wage system. Ultimately unsuccessful in the aftermath of war, this case study underscores the limitations of federal and state powers to protect a class of workers against discrimination and enforce and reverse inequitable practices. The chapter also reinforces the importance of understanding the complexity of wage hierarchies, and the difficulty of determining when they may have ended. Unequal wage systems reinforced the notion that Mexican workers were part of the low-wage elastic supply of labor that copper mines relied on.

In chapter 5, "Mexican American Women Workers in Mid-Twentieth-Century Phoenix," Jean Reynolds examines Mexican American women's labor force participation and work experiences in the Salt River Valley economy of the 1930s and 1940s. Based on archival sources and oral histories of women who worked in retail, laundry, clerical, banking, defense factories, domestic, and service work, Reynolds offers a rare glimpse into the work experiences of Mexican women whose very presence in these sectors often signified mobility from work in the fields and agriculture to jobs that offered slightly higher wages and improved work conditions. Driven by economic needs at home and by outside labor demands, Mexican American women were drawn into the paid-labor force in Phoenix in greater numbers, particularly in the service industry, in response to fewer male workers. Women in effect were part of the elastic supply of labor that employers created and drew upon. As the Great Depression waned, the growth of retail and tourism industries opened up job opportunities for women of Mexican descent. By the 1940s, a high school diploma, wartime labor needs, and an upturn in Phoenix's economy opened a path for some women to rise into higher-status white-collar jobs. Reynolds demonstrates how the work women do fluctuates with the economy, whether during wartime, economic recessions, or legislation that shapes the nature of the opportunity structures they encounter. Chapter 5 also illustrates the linkage between economic expansion and fostering of an elastic supply of labor.

In chapter 6, "The Morenci Miners Women's Auxiliary during the Great Arizona Copper Strike, 1983–1986," Anna Ochoa O'Leary documents Mexican women's participation in the Morenci Miners Women's Auxiliary (MMWA) and how their mobilizations during the great copper strike of 1983–1986—one of the longest strikes in the history of Arizona's mining industry—led to heightened political consciousness and gendered forms of empowerment. This case is unique, O'Leary argues, because women's activities went beyond women's traditional forms of auxiliary-based participation (e.g., supporting workers on strike, feeding workers) to political mobilizing, strategizing, and outreach that altered workers' plans for action and brought national attention to their plight. The Phelps Dodge Corporation ultimately succeeded in defeating the unions, leaving many of the Mexican workers and their families little choice but to leave their respective mining communities, where generations of their families had lived, in search of more viable employment. While the defeat, in effect, signified the end of labor struggles in Arizona's copper industry, it illuminates the potential impact that women's activism and women's unpaid labor can bring to bear in the labor struggles of the future. While Mexicano males were part of the lower-wage elastic supply of labor that the Phelps Dodge Corporation depended on, the female family members were central to sustaining the social reproduction associated with mine workers, and thus occupied a position related to but not the same as the male wage workers.

In chapter 7, "Constructing Arizona: The Lives and Labor of Mexicans in the Valley of the Sun," Cristina Gallardo-Sanidad draws our attention to the prominence of a new C—that of a bustling construction and real estate industry that now firmly situates Phoenix as the twelfth largest metropolitan city in the United States. The availability of thousands of Mexicano workers, U.S.-born, recent immigrant, and undocumented, contribute immensely to the construction industry's speculative actions to meet the accelerated pace of growth and demand for new housing and commercial development that began with a doubling of the state's population in the mid-1980s. At the peak of the construction boom in 2006, Latinos accounted for 46.7 percent of construction workers but composed about a third of the state's total population. With the collapse of the prime and subprime mortgage loan and broader capitalist markets, then followed by the Great Recession of 2007–2008, Gallardo-Sanidad presents a critical look at the structural violence within Arizona's construction industry and the disproportionate impact on Mexican workers and their families, unveiling how inequalities are reinforced as risks are shifted from contractors to a workforce increasingly dispensable during downward shifts of the economy, while deemed indispensable during periods of market growth and demand. Arizona's sixth C is the most recent and visible formation of how capitalist enterprises create a low-wage elastic supply of labor when the housing market booms, but then banish the same workers when the bust cycle inevitably arrives.

NOTES

The epigraph is quoted in Brown and Cassmore (1939, 65).

1. Multiple examples can be provided regarding the limitations of these and similar proposals. A particular idea may sound like a solution, but in reality ignores the existing research-based evidence and hides the dimensions of race and class in the proposal. The often-made call by President Trump for the need to build a Mexico-U.S. wall, which (some believe) will eliminate or reduce the population subject to removal and the entry of illicit drugs demanded by U.S. residents, is one of the many illusionary solutions. It is an illusion for two important reasons. One, for over a decade we have known that approximately half of the population subject to removal, from China, Ireland, Mexico, Poland, and other nations, entered through a formal port of entry with a visa in hand. The most recent examination of undocumented migrants (2014) reports that about 66 percent of the total fell into that category (Warren and Kerwin 2017). In other words, a thirty-, sixty-, or one-hundred-foot wall will not eliminate the population subject to deportation; at best, it only impacts about 40 percent of those present without formal authorization. Two, most illicit drugs enter through ports of entry, and multiple Customs, Border Patrol, Immigration and Customs Enforcement, and FBI agents have been convicted of taking bribes or assisting in the drug trade. A thirty-foot wall does not eliminate the illicit

drug trade or the temptation or greed that may lead a federal agent to participate in the smuggling of humans or drugs.

2. It should be noted that the text capitalizes the term *Mexicano/s*. Although in Mexican Spanish grammar, the terms are lowercase, we wanted to reduce the potential awkwardness for U.S. readers, who expect proper nouns to be capitalized.
3. The term *U.S. workers* is used to refer to U.S. nationals and nonnationals authorized to work in the United States. It is not limited to U.S. citizens.
4. It is worth noting that despite the strong discourse in Arizona against the federal government (i.e., "big government"), the large and prominent footprint of the federal government from the Indian Wars waged against Apaches in the late 1800s and the establishment of military forts, to the 1902 Reclamation Act that built the Roosevelt Dam, the latter funding of the most expensive and largest aqueduct irrigation systems in the United States (the Central Arizona Project), and federal investment in important military bases during and after World War II (e.g., Luke Air Force Base), is one that was dominant in creating present-day Arizona. Without the munificent flow of federal dollars, Arizona would be a radically different state.
5. The facilities included War Relocation Centers, Citizen Isolation Centers, Civilian Assembly Centers, Federal Bureau of Prison facilities, Department of Justice facilities, and U.S. Army facilities. It also should be noted that these facilities do not include prisoner of war camps specifically for Germans and Italians. The United States operated four such sites in Arizona: Camp Florence, Camp Papago Park, Camp Pima, and Imperial Dam (Yuma).
6. See, for example, LaBau (2010), Larkin (2008, 2013), McGirr (2001), Dylan Rodríguez (2014), and Shermer (2008, 2009a, 2009b, 2013a, 2013b). Although these authors place different emphases on the importance of race in Senator Goldwater's political career, they all concur that Senator Goldwater was central in the political movement that made conservatism salient to national and state political debates.
7. At his 1971 Senate nomination hearing, Rehnquist indicated that he personally did not intimidate voters in Arizona. However, as has been reported by journalists and others, "Bill" was one of the Republican activists that participated in Operation Eagle Eye in 1964 (Cohen 1986; Dershowitz 2005; Roddy 2000; Ruha circa 2000). The aim of Operation Eagle Eye was to prevent African American and other racial/ethnic groups in the Phoenix area from voting in the 1964 elections. The operation's aim was to garner support for Senator Goldwater's presidential run. Thirty-year Arizona legislator Manuel Lito Peña, a Democratic poll watcher in 1964, however remembers the events differently. According to Peña, Rehnquist had to be forcefully removed from the Bethune Elementary School polling site in South Phoenix for his efforts to discourage and prevent minority voters (likely Democrat voters) from voting. Rehnquist placed himself at the entrance to the polling site and demanded that voters arriving at the site prove to him their residence and understanding of the Constitution before entering the building. He, as a local attorney,

positioned himself as the sole arbiter of who could be allowed to vote. Some individuals in the long line decided to forego voting. In addition, one of the four attorney generals appointed by President Nixon, Richard G. Kleindienst (June 1972–April 1973) was also from Arizona.

8. Although Associate Justice O'Connor was born in El Paso, Texas, after graduating from Stanford University Law School, she established her legal and political career in Arizona starting in the mid-1960s. Justice O'Connor's views on the court frequently aligned with those of her fellow classmate from Stanford: William H. Rehnquist.
9. It is safe to argue that both generally supported conservative views, though Justice O'Connor in several important cases took a moderate conservative position. When she served on the Supreme Court, the media tended to label her political views as moderate conservative.
10. Arizona's progressiveness was not uniform for all social groups. In the case of Native Americans, the road to suffrage was long. Under the Treaty of Guadalupe Hidalgo (1848), at the end of Mexican-American War, individuals remaining in the ceded territory were to be recognized as U.S. citizens; and under the Indian Citizenship Act of 1924 (43 Stat. 253), all remaining Native Americans who had not been previously granted citizenship under special treaties were to be recognized as U.S. citizens. In the case of Arizona, however, Native Americans were not granted the right to vote until July 1948. The favorable ruling by the Arizona Supreme Court in *Harrison v. Laveen* (67 Ariz. 337, 1948) finally granted U.S. citizens of Native American ancestry the right to vote. Using the 1848 date, it took one hundred years to gain suffrage, or twenty-four years after being recognized by Congress as U.S. citizens.
11. An important general limitation in this book and in most accounts of Mexican labor in the Southwest is the even more limited scholarship on unpaid work performed by persons of Mexican descent, particularly Mexicanas. The maintenance of a household requires a high level of work, from feeding and caring for children, to housecleaning, laundry, etc., all of which is performed without remuneration. For a useful summary of the historical debate related to unpaid work, see Ellen Malos (1980).
12. By unit of production we are not suggesting that women and men labored equally in the production of these commodities or the building of the railroads, but rather for different reasons the presence of women and families was encouraged. In the production of cotton or citrus, families were encouraged because they provided multiple workers; but in mines and railroads families were encouraged because they aided in creating a stable workforce (i.e., men with wives and children tended not to pick up and leave on short notice), and because corporations viewed women as playing an important role in "domesticating" men. "Domesticated" men were perceived as more controllable workers.
13. In 1935 Congress passed and President Franklin Roosevelt enacted the National Labor Relations Act. Agribusiness obtained an important concession: the law's effort to provide collective bargaining to workers did not apply to agriculture.

14. See, for example, Weber (1994), DeCierdo (1999); for a broader overview of women of color with respect to western history, see Castañeda (1992).
15. See, for example, DeCierdo (1999), Hondagneu-Sotelo (2007), Romero (1992), Ruiz (1987, 1998), Zavella (1987).
16. The University of Arizona Press anthology edited by Vélez-Ibáñez and Heyman, *The U.S.-Mexico Transborder Region: Cultural Dynamics and Historical Interactions* (2017), is a recent effort that examines the social and historical dimensions of the region. Two complementary discussions of "Chinese Mexicans" encompassing Sonora, Arizona, and China are the impressive books by Delgado (2012) and Schiavone Camacho (2012); the historian Kelly Lytle Hernandez (2010) has written the best overall discussion of the development of the Border Patrol; and six books have made important contributions to our rethinking of the North American borderlands—Truett and Young (2004), Hämäläinen and Johnson (2012), Lattanzi Shutika (2011), McCrossen (2009), Truett (2008), Overmyer-Velásquez (2011).
17. See, for example, Acuña (1972, 2007), Alamillo (2006), Almaguer (1994), Barrera (1979), Calderón (2000), Camarillo (1979), Cortes (1976), Corwin and Cardoso (1978), Daniel (1991), Fernández Kelley (1984), Neil Foley (1997), Mario García (1981), Matt García (2001), Garcilazo (2013), Gómez-Quiñones (1994), González (1994), Guerín-Gonzales (1994), McWilliams (1941 [1967]), Meeks (2007a); Mize and Swords (2011); Montejano (1987), Peña (1997), Perales (2010); Reisler (1976a), Romero (1992), Ruíz (1998), Servín (1970), Taylor (1931–32 [1968], 1970), Vargas (1993, 2005), Weber (1994), Zamora (1993), Zavella (1987).
18. See, for example, Linda Gordon (1999), Dimas (1999), Martin (1992, 2004), Otero (2010).
19. The historian Geraldo L. Cadava's social history of Tucson and the Sonora-Arizona border (2013) is an important contribution to transnational borderlands history, but does not address the history of labor or means of production in the area.
20. Our use of the concept of "identification" rather than "identity" or "identities" follows the critique raised by Stuart Hall (1996). Hall's criticism of the concept "identity" centers on the suggestion that the latter suggests a "finished thing" rather than "an ongoing process." For Hall, "identity arises, not so much from the fullness of identity which is already inside us as individuals, but from a *lack* of wholeness which is 'filled' from *outside of us*" (1996).
21. It is also important to foreground that a significant segment of migrants from Mexico have primary identifications with indigenous communities such as Purépecha, Mayos (Yoremes), Yaqui (Yoéme/Yoemen), Mixteco, etc.
22. The historian Deena J. González offers a close reading of Sheridan's classic text, and points out that there appears to be a disinterest on Sheridan's part to discuss Mexican versus Anglo/white conflict in Tucson (1992).

INTRODUCTION

Arizona's Six Cs and Mexicana/o Labor

Although the Mexican-American is not the most deprived or the most oppressed minority in the United States, nevertheless he is the most historically neglected and ignored group.

MANUEL SERVÍN, *THE MEXICAN AMERICANS: AN AWAKENING MINORITY* (1970)

INTRODUCTION

THE 2004 RELEASE OF SERGIO ARAU'S satirical film *Un Día sin Mexicanos* (*A Day Without a Mexican*) stirred mixed responses from Latino and non-Latino viewers. Arau's film relies on stereotypical representations of Mexicans and white residents in California. The premise of the film is that a mysterious fog descends on California, and in the process individuals of Mexican descent disappear. White employers and individuals accustomed to the services of such workers find themselves in chaotic circumstances. While film critics found the characters in the film overly stereotyped and the narrative simplistic, there was little reflection on the merits of Arau's storyline: California's historical and contemporary economy is dependent on the labor of Mexicanas/os, and without that labor the economy and standard of living enjoyed in California would be dramatically different. The dependency is not limited to California. Arizona's six Cs are also made possible by the labor of Mexicanas/os. The popular and academic historical narrative of Arizona shares something with Arau's fog: it is often a historiography that socially and symbolically erases the labor of a working-class community that was central to its history. One could characterize this as a historiography of work without workers, and as one that reifies the history of commodities but disavows the labor that produced them—what some would refer to as a form of commodity fetishism.

An example of historiographic lapse is the otherwise informative volume on Phoenix's history in the twentieth century (Johnson Jr. 1993). G. Wesley Johnson Jr.'s anthology offers a broad historical discussion of the forces, leaders, and issues that

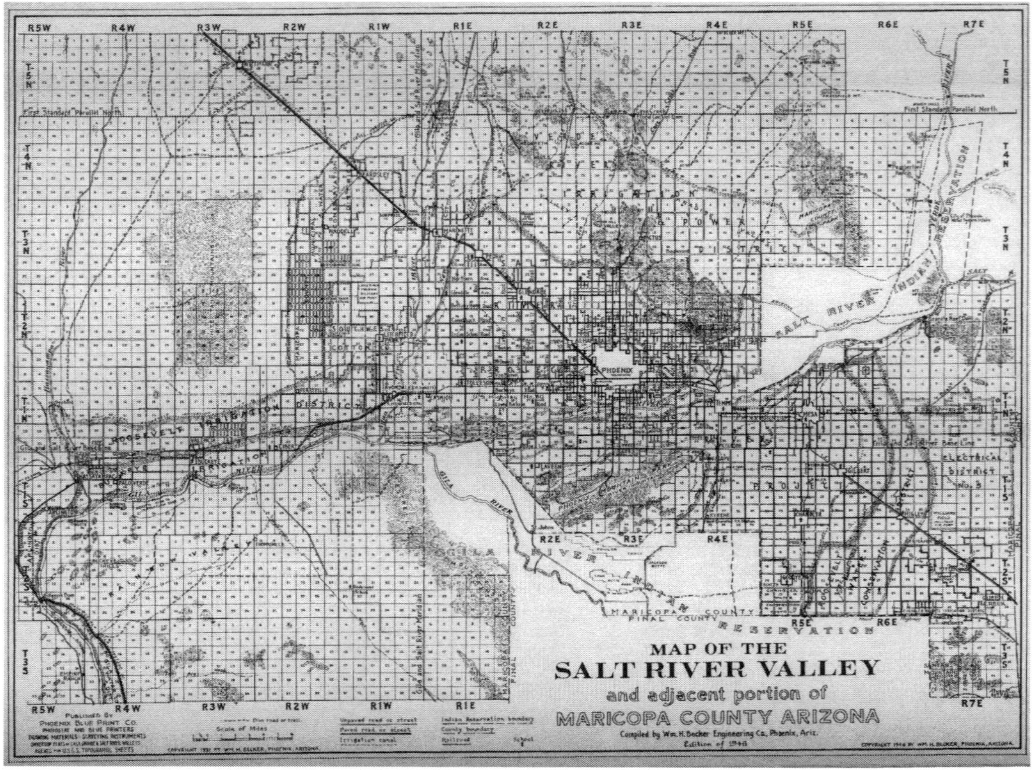

MAP 2 Map of the Salt River Valley, 1946. Courtesy of the Arizona Historical Society

shaped Phoenix's formation. A reader unfamiliar with Phoenix or Arizona, based on the text of the fifteen chapters, would conclude that Mexicans did not have a prominent role in building wealth in the city.[1] The nine passing references to Mexicans/Hispanics in the 276-page book imply that Mexicans are marginal to Phoenix.[2] In contrast to Johnson Jr.'s anthology, the present anthology foregrounds the central position of Mexicanas/os in Arizona's economic development.

Our effort to expand the historical record regarding Mexicans in Arizona is not unprecedented. In 1970 the historian Manuel Servín authored the anthology *The Mexican-Americans: An Awakening Minority*. The book's preface notes: "It is to overcome this lack of historical study, which is so necessary to understand the present-day Mexican-American, that this textbook is published" (1970, viii). It is unfortunate that forty-eight years later, we find ourselves repeating Servin's observation. Two years after the publication of Servín's anthology, the historian Rodolfo Acuña articulated a similar observation regarding Arizona in the first edition of *Occupied America*. Acuña asserts, "More words have been written about the shootout at the OK Corral than have been written in all combined works on the Mexican in Arizona" (Acuña 1972, 80). Although a good number of theses and dissertations have been written regarding the Mexican experience in Arizona since 1972, the list of published books and journal articles explicitly focusing on Mexican labor in Arizona remains limited.[3]

One aim of this anthology is to offer a partial corrective to the academic and popular representation of Arizona's history. It is partial because the scholarship is also partial. We cannot present the history of Mexicanas/os in railroads in Arizona, for example, because that research has not been carried out. We know that Mexicans became the dominant workforce in all Southwest railroad corporations by 1910, but we do not know much about labor arrangements, racialized wage hierarchies, labor conflicts, or working conditions of Mexicanas and Mexicanos employed by the railroad corporations operating in Arizona.

As insightfully discussed by the late historian Jeffrey Garcilazo, in order to grasp the central role of the principal form of transportation that made the socioeconomic development of the Southwest (including Arizona) possible, one has to comprehend the active recruitment of Mexican *traqueros* (railroad workers) by the railroads in the establishment and operation of railroad lines (1995, 2013). In 1911, to cite one example, the Santa Fe Railway employed 2,672 common laborers; 2,599 of these were Mexicans (Garcílazo 1995, 100–101).[4] Workers performing higher-paid and less physically demanding tasks were smaller in number and were classified as "white labor." David F. Myrick's classic, *Railroads of Arizona* (1981), offers many important details regarding railroad owners and investors, number of locomotives, engineering difficulties encountered, the establishment of railroad hotels, and freight transported. However, there is only passing reference to workers who carried out arduous tasks in difficult conditions. Mexican laborers who made the Arizona railroads possible are manifestly absent.[5]

REFLECTIONS ON THE MAKING OF AN ELASTIC SUPPLY OF LABOR

The epigraph in the prologue represents the frank observation of an official of the Arizona Cotton Growers Association regarding the 1919–20 harvests. We draw upon that observation not because it is a novel theoretical construct regarding labor control, production, or the externalization of social reproduction costs, but because it highlights an important labor process that has received limited scholarly attention. Although the term *elastic supply of labor* is drawn from the general study of labor economics and its formulation of labor-supply curves, what is relevant for understanding the position of Mexican workers is that it discursively captures an important dynamic in Arizona.[6] The concept names a strategy within capital accumulation. It indexes how cotton planters in Arizona achieved an important level of success in maximizing a net profit in the production of cotton in the early 1900s. The strategy is not limited to the hand harvesting of cotton—we suggest that it can aid our understanding of other commodities or services.

Like other discourses about labor, the notion of an elastic supply of labor both reveals and obscures important power relations and the role of the state in aiding the position of corporations vis-à-vis labor in producing wealth. The concept encompasses the following elements. One, it asserts how cotton planters managed the recruitment of "as perfectly an elastic supply of labor as the world has ever seen," though does not mention that part of the recruitment involved the illegal recruitment of labor, the lack of enforcement of federal laws by immigration officials, and the direct role of the state in aiding employers meet unproven "labor shortages." Two, it obscures that the labor arrangements involved the transnational mobility of workers and the indirect support of the Mexican State. Three, it integrated a conception that workers were subjects whose mobility and immobility could be controlled, at times with the aid of local police. Four, as explicitly noted in the epigraph, that the strategy was not simply about access to a sufficient supply but, of equal importance, that it could be fostered at a collectively determined low wage as possible. The ability of associations to fix wages (even if not legal) "throughout its territory" largely eliminated the possibility of employers competing for workers—in this sense it eliminated the freedom of workers in a capitalist democracy. Lastly, though not noted, the foundation of the supply of labor was the perception of Mexico as the location of an "inexhaustible" supply of labor, and of Mexicana/o workers as a racialized ideal cohort of workers. The long list of "positive" attributes assumed to exist among Mexicans, such as a biopolitical argument about ability to work in hot climates, preference to work close to the ground (e.g., using the short hoe), and ability to survive on very little, transformed Mexicanas/os into "preferred" workers.[7]

We believe that the deployment of such strategies to control labor and minimize wages allows us to move away from simplistic analyses that merely argue that white racism explains the exploitation of Mexican workers, whether in agriculture, manufacturing, mining, construction, etc. Instead, it suggests the need to examine how capital deploys such strategies in the accumulation of capital and also the need to pay close attention to the racialization of a particular community as preferred workers. The concept allows us to integrate standard political economic analyses of labor and the labor process with the central importance of racialization. In other words, it is not simply that capitalist enterprises seek to maximize profits through the exploitation of workers, but that the capitalist processes integrate notions of race, and that once established, the labor process is normalized as one about labor economics and capital accumulation.

In varying degrees, the chapters in this anthology document some of the specific processes in the production of an elastic supply of labor, though may not explicitly integrate the construct.

ARIZONA'S SIX Cs

The following discussion is organized around six Cs. We deploy this framework as a heuristic device and not as a reification of the five Cs mnemonic. The reader should note that the division of economic activities into five or six categories should not be interpreted as indicating that these are isolatable sectors. To the contrary, all of the Cs overlapped or articulated closely with each other. The expansion of copper mining, for example, was good news for cattle producers because it translated to an increased demand for beef in mining districts. On the other hand, the cyclical downturns in the copper market negatively impacted capital accumulation among livestock producers. In addition, other activities not included in the five Cs narrative, such as railroad and federal government expenditures in Arizona, were key in making most of the Cs profitable, though they are not integrated as Cs in the popular mnemonic. Railroads made the shipping of cattle, citrus, copper, and cotton to urban markets and out-of-state processing facilities possible. Federal beneficence made possible the irrigation of the Salt River Valley and the Yuma Valley. This in turn allowed the speculative expansion of acreage for citrus, cotton, and vegetable production, and the consonant demand for additional Mexican labor to meet the federally stimulated shortage of low-wage labor. The expansion of house ownership and the building of the interstate highway system fostered the creation of suburbs in Tucson and Phoenix and the competition for land between housing speculators and agricultural/ranch landowners. As observed by the anthropologist Thomas E. Sheridan, "More than most places, modern Arizona would not exist without federal support" (2012, 3).[8]

Moreover, Sheridan captures the tension between housing speculators willing to pay top dollar for agricultural/ranch land as one between "cows and condos" and "embattled ranchers" and "urban sprawl" (2001, 2007). Long-term residents in Tucson, Flagstaff, Phoenix, and Yuma readily remember cattle ranches, citrus orchards, vegetable farms, timber operations, or cotton fields converted to gated communities with water features, golf courses, prominent lawns, and Spanish-style homes designed for professional couples in search of good schools for their children, away from central-city areas. Farm and ranch owners are attracted to lucrative purchase offers, particularly in agricultural markets with declining prices and rising operating costs, children not interested in pursuing farm/ranch operations, and high credit debts owed to lenders. Suburban sprawl depends on the availability of lower-cost land for building the next housing development. Low-wage construction workers aided in the realization of larger margins of profit for housing speculators and related suppliers of building materials, kitchen equipment, as well as financial institutions, insurance, and real estate firms.

The following discussion is organized into six sections: cattle, citrus, climate, copper, cotton, and construction. The aim in each section is to provide a background to the sector/commodity, present the overall importance of the sector/commodity to the Grand Canyon State, and summarize the scholarly knowledge generated to date on the contribution of Mexicana/o labor to the respective sector/commodity.

FIRST C—CATTLE: LIVESTOCK, CAPITAL, AND PARADISE LOST[9]

The presence and importance of Mexican labor to managing cattle in Arizona are factors generally absent from historical accounts of the cattle (and sheep) industry. The story of Mexicana/o labor in the care of cattle and livestock in Arizona is one that remains largely untold. It is a story that is difficult to tell. The care of cattle is not a centralized productive activity, and the work activity is not confined to a single geographic space. While we seek to present the history of cattle in Arizona within a narrative about the state, the actual story, like that of copper, cotton, service sector, construction, and other capital formation activities, is a transnational one. It is a story about global capitalism (e.g., British surplus capital) and the inherent drive of capital to expand into increasingly distant markets and capitalists seeking to maximize returns on their capital. Lopes and Riguzzi, for example, in a detailed analysis of the Mexico-U.S. cattle market, point out that between 1880 and 1946, over a million cattle were moved from the United States to Mexico, and about ten million heads of cattle were moved from Mexico to the United States (2012, 603).

Arizona's history of cattle is one that was made possible by unconstrained access given to cattle owners by state officials in the late 1800s and early 1900s, short-lived fortuitous weather (climate), and a surplus of capital in Great Britain.[10] Arizona's first C (cattle) is a story of how East Coast, Midwest, and European capital fostered speculation on a commodity of high demand that produced high returns, and the eventual ecological damage brought about by the industry. Consumer demand for beef on the West and East Coasts, as well as earlier demand within Arizona due to military forts, Native American reservations dependent on federal rations, the expansion of mining, and the proliferation of railroad lines linking Arizona to California and to the East Coast stimulated major capital investments in cattle production in the late 1800s. The depletion of grazing land in Texas and New Mexico and damaging weather in the Great Plains fostered a vision of Arizona as cattle paradise for investors—low-cost cattle and land and a presumed infinite abundance of free grazing land. An 1885 report on Arizona promoted the following: "In Arizona a day without bright sunshine is so rare as to be remarkable, and every month of the year cattle run on their ranges and find no lack of feed. These favorable climatic conditions make Arizona the stock-raisers' paradise" (Sayre 1999b, 257). The promotion of Arizona as a cattle paradise, and aspirations among some individuals to get-rich-quick-without-much-work, produced a cattle bubble.

INTRODUCTION OF CATTLE IN THE PIMERÍA ALTA

The introduction and presence of cattle in Arizona is due to two agents of the Spanish Empire. Francisco Vásquez de Coronado, as part of his 1540 exploration in search of a fantasized place of great wealth in the Southwest, traveled with soldiers and Indian allies from central Mexico. He brought horses and cattle in his exploration. Most of the cattle brought by Coronado to Arizona perished.

The more important introduction of cattle took place between 1687 and 1710. The Jesuit missionary Eusebio Francisco Kino imagined that indigenous communities in Sonora and Arizona (Pimería Alta) would more readily convert to Catholicism and Spanish ways with the adoption of livestock production—*ganado mayor* (cattle) and *ganado menor* (sheep). Cattle were central to his "civilizing" mission, and the broader Spanish hegemonic project. Kino allocated cattle and sheep to Indians within the missions and *visitas* (smaller settlements) established. The gradual growth of Spanish outposts and land grants awarded in northern Sonora and southern Arizona relied on two principal economic enterprises: mining and cattle production. Lieutenant Ignacio Pérez, for example, received over 73,000 acres as part of the San Bernardino Grant to stock his over 4,000 heads of cattle.

ARIZONA'S CATTLE BOOM AND COLLAPSE (1873-1893)

Although there is general agreement that the period between 1873 and 1893 marks Arizona's cattle boom, there is less agreement about the exact number of cattle, and even less knowledge about the number of workers involved. Scholars note that prior to 1934, the enumeration of cattle herd sizes are estimates. It has been noted that even cattle owners during the period did not have exact counts of their herds. Cattle corporations, similar to the accounting books maintained by railroad corporations, were largely wishes recorded on paper. The historian Richard White, in his meticulous book *Railroaded* (2011) on the history of the railroad industry and its impact beyond railroads, notes that cattle corporations formulated fanciful records. White observes:

> So to estimate their herds, cattle companies created a book count. Book count cattle were just numbers on a ledger, ideally existing on a one-to-one ratio with the animals turning grass into meat. . . . Real cattle died in much larger numbers than book cattle. (2011, 473)

During the two decades, significant movement of cattle from Sonora, Texas, Oklahoma, California, and Utah took place. Arizona cattle producers were able to secure cattle within the state for relatively low prices and supplemented these with the purchase of cattle from Mexico and other U.S. states. In addition, some stock raisers formed partnerships with cattle owners in other states and managed the grazing of their cattle in Arizona.

Between 1873 and 1893, Arizona cattle producers experienced high profits. In general, it is reported that in Texas in 1865, cattle could be purchased for $3 to $4 per head and sold in northern markets for $30 to $40 (Sayre 1999b, 71).[11] In the late 1870s and early 1880s, prices rose. Investors in Great Britain and in eastern banks recognized the potential of the West as a capital-reproduction paradise. Sayre notes that at the start of the cattle boom, Arizona and other western cattle producers were accepting investment capital with interest rates averaging 1.5 and 2 percent per month, allowing for the potential of 12.5 to 15 percent per annum for investors. According to an 1882 report by British Royal Commission, which traveled to the United States and reviewed the cattle industry, some investors could earn 33 percent return per year (Sayre 1999b, 74). With such glowing reports about the reproduction of capital, British investors were eager to invest in Arizona's cattle paradise.

A key production factor was the cost of grazing. The imagined infinite supply of a wide variety of native grasses at no or minimal cost, due to local political arrangements that linked water "ownership" (meaning customary control as well as actual legal ownership) with surrounding grazing areas, greatly reduced the cost of raising/feeding cattle, and allowed for added profit from selling access to "owned" water. Arizona government officials and influential cattle owners colluded to ensure free access to public lands for cattle producers, as well as a low tax rate for cattle. Although some cattle producers foresaw the future possibility of overgrazing and the depletion of grasses, the majority of stock raisers were optimistic that Arizona would remain a cattle paradise and cattle producing a highly profitable activity. Investors naïvely shared this optimism.

An important factor that increased the number of cattle in the state was negative conditions in other cattle-producing areas. In Texas overgrazing led to difficult conditions and the need to salvage cattle investments by relocating cattle to other locations; Arizona was one of these. Additionally, harsh winter conditions in the Great Plains also prompted cattle producers to transfer cattle to Arizona. Many cattle perished in the drives overland to Arizona. Larger cattle enterprises in Texas and the Great Plains were able to relocate the cattle via railroads, and most of these cattle survived the trip. A second important factor is the heavier rains experienced prior to 1873 and during the 1870s. The rains stimulated the growth of grasses and this produced the illusion that Arizona's imagined climate (one of the Cs) was the norm and that it would generate the bounty needed for low-cost/high-profit cattle production. Droughts, the depletion of grasses due to overgrazing, summer monsoon rains, and accompanying soil erosion that prevented the return of the waist-high grasses reported in earlier times, were excluded from more careful assessment of potential cattle to available grazing, and possible returns on capital. An "irrational exuberance" sustained a vision of Arizona as a cattle paradise with great potential for capital accumulation.[12]

J. J. Wagoner's estimates of the number of cattle in Arizona remain the most commonly cited (1949, 232–33). Unfortunately, Wagoner's estimates start in 1880, thus the number of cattle in the state between 1873 and 1879 is less certain. Though several sources estimate that in 1870 there were approximately 40,000 heads of cattle in the state. Arizona experienced a marked increase in the number of cattle between 1880 and a peak in 1891. The increase of 340,894 cattle represented a 1,672 percent growth over the total for 1880.

Arizona's third C (climate) brought an end to the 1873–93 cattle boom. Drought conditions between 1891 and 1893 created havoc for all cattle producers, though larger enterprises had the capital to relocate Arizona cattle starting in 1892, via land or train, to Montana, Kansas, California, Texas, Indian Territory (Oklahoma), and Sonora. Smaller firms were likely the ones most affected by the cattle bust. Several sources note that 50 to 75 percent of Arizona cattle perished during the 1891–93 drought. Descriptions of cattle areas such as south and southeast of Tucson make reference to dead cattle throughout the area—on roads, ditches, farms, public land, and multiple other spaces.

Cattle production in Arizona gradually recovered. The number of cattle estimated for 1910 exceeded the peak number in 1891. According to the United States Department of Agriculture's Census of Agriculture for 2007 and 2012 (the most recent year), there were a total of 1,000,038 cattle and calves in the earlier census, and 911,334 for 2012. Despite these seemingly large numbers of cattle, Arizona's total volume in 2007 and 2012 represented .01 percent of the national total; this places Arizona behind thirty-one other states. Texas leads the nation with about 11 million cattle (USDA 2014b).

LOCATING MEXICAN VAQUERAS/OS

Although literature on cattle in Arizona is noteworthy, the labor that facilitated the flourishing of the cattle industry and made the profits in the industry possible has not been a primary concern for scholars.[13] In several of the published works one finds an occasional passing reference to Mexicans carrying out some task, but not much beyond this. Our review of the literature did not locate a single published book or journal article, or dissertation or thesis that focused explicitly on Mexican vaqueras/os in the cattle industry in Arizona. A few photographs of vaqueras and vaqueros in Arizona were found, but no scholarly analysis of their contribution, the conditions of their work, wage hierarchies, strikes, conflicts/cooperation among Mexican and non-Mexican workers, or experiences in the cattle industry were found.[14]

The three most notable discussions of Arizona's cattle production (Haskett 1935; Sheridan 2012, 131–50; Sayre 1999b) present important insights regarding the broad contours of cattle ranching. However, they share similar limitations, though for different reasons. Haskett's account seeks to present a comprehensive history of the development of cattle production, and some of the prominent pioneers that established the foundation of the sector. He makes passing references to the presence of workers who carried out some tasks, but nothing is said about the actual composition of cattle workers, wages, or conditions of production. Sheridan and Sayre, on the other hand, are concerned with the ecological impact of that history. As scholars oriented to examining questions related to political ecology/cultural ecology (i.e., the overall human impact on a local ecology), they focus on examining the ecological devastation produced by the cattle sector on large sections of the state. Their excellent discussions, nonetheless, occlude the examination of the workforce that made the sector profitable for the cattle owners and investors. Such an emphasis means that political economic factors related to capital-labor relationships are not of primary concern. Hence, our knowledge of the role of Mexicanas/os in cattle production is quite limited.

SECOND C—CITRUS: CLIMATE, CAPITAL, LAND, AND LABOR

When Padfield and Martin (1965) were financed by the Department of Labor in the early 1960s to undertake a study of the lettuce, citrus, and cotton industries in Arizona, their intent was twofold: to document the changing technology of agricultural production in the aforementioned industries and to understand how agricultural workers were affected by these changes. Of citrus, one feature was abundantly clear, "Our technology has propelled humans into space and instruments to Mars, but we pick oranges the same way the Ancient Malaysians picked them—by hand" (1965, 9). Indeed, Arizona's citrus industry is based on grapefruit, orange, lemon, and tangerine production, all of which require workers to skillfully handpick the fruit and handle it in such a way that does not damage it. One should also foreground that citrus harvesting is arduous and dangerous. Citrus trees contain thorns near the fruit, and these commonly injure harvesters' hands. Additionally, citrus workers must use ladders to reach the fruit while holding a bag with the fruit already picked (the weight of which will vary depending on the amount of fruit harvested); they then must climb down, move the ladder, and climb up the ladder to a new spot. The photograph on the cover of this book offers a glimpse of grapefruit hand harvesting in Arizona. The repetitive climbing up and down the ladder frequently results in falls and serious injuries to workers. Depending on the worker's migration status, the extent of the injury, and whether the employer carries worker's compensation insurance and makes it available to injured workers, a fall may end an individual's ability to earn wages harvesting citrus.

Like the other Cs important to Arizona's early economy, climatic conditions in the Valley of the Sun and the harnessing of water provided the necessary conditions for the planting of citrus.[15] The earliest groves date back to the mid-1890s and grew from an initial 1,500 acres to 80,000 acres, at its peak, in 1970.

Arizona's citrus industry flourished and waned over the years, depending on a variety of factors, which included periodic freezing temperatures or drought conditions, increases or declines in market prices, and changes to methods and manner in the harvesting and packing of fruit. Until transportation facilitated the distribution of citrus, the growth of the citrus industry in Arizona was gradual and did not experience the kind of boom-and-bust growth found in other industries. The local market limited the speculative desires to rapidly expand citrus acreage and trees, as well as the related expansion of needed labor. Moreover, the competition from citrus on the East

Coast (Florida) and West Coast (California) also tampered the interests of Arizona producers or investors to achieve monopoly or monopsony conditions.

Central to the success of the citrus industry was the availability of seasonal and migrant Mexican laborers, both domestic and Mexican nationals, whether formally authorized as was the case during the World War II Bracero Program, "undocumented migrants," or citizens. Yet very little is known about the workers and their families in Arizona who toiled in this industry. What is generally known, from scholarly works based in California's citrus industry, is that the ideal production unit was the family. It would not be unusual to find child labor being used during picking season, where it was customary for wages to be folded into the father's wages. While men were more represented among the workers, women were more likely to be employed in citrus-packing sheds, where wages were low but slightly higher than that of pickers.[16]

Between 1890 and 1940 citrus became California's most important agricultural product; thus it is not surprising that the most in-depth studies of the citrus industry and Mexican workers are studies based in Southern California (Alamillo 2006; García 2001; González 1994). Entire towns and, in some cases, company towns, sprung up around the citrus industry. Gilbert G. González (1994) provides one of the most comprehensive discussions about the history, labor, and social relations of the citrus industry, of which several similarities and differences with respect to Arizona are worth noting.

In California Mexicans did not become the preferred labor force until, first, the Chinese through the Chinese Exclusion Act of 1882 and subsequent restrictions, and then the Japanese (1907 Gentleman's Agreement), were excluded and driven away from working in the citrus industry. In Arizona hand harvesting citrus relied from its incipience on a predominantly Mexican labor force that, with an increase in acreage and commercial production of citrus, became a largely recruited workforce during World War I, due to the passage of the Immigration Act of 1917 and subsequent legislation; the 1927 General Order 86, which created the commuter labor program (greatly important to Yuma agribusiness); the World War II Bracero Program; and later the H-2 (later revised as H-2A) visa program, which guaranteed growers a steady government-managed supply of laborers to meet alleged perennial labor shortages. Whites that worked in the citrus industry were more likely to be employed as supervisors or in sales and management positions.

Unlike California, where citrus production created entire race- and class-stratified company towns such as Corona, the "lemon capital of the world," so aptly captured in José Alamillo's (2006) *Making Lemonade out of Lemons*, Arizona's citrus industry was not sufficiently expansive that entire company towns were built around it as they were for mining. Instead, citrus-growing areas and orchards could be found dispersed from what became central Phoenix to Mesa and the northwest valley, such as the 22,000 trees that were planted along Camelback Mountain in 1888, or the now-historic Arcadia neighborhood, where rural, wealthy estates were designed to attract homeowners interested in growing citrus, or the 5,000 acres of citrus at Arrowhead Ranch (a portion of which were owned by the Goldwater family and relied on undocumented Mexican migrant workers), which were supplanted by the development of residential subdivisions in the 1980s. Yuma, which began with a mere 20 acres of citrus in 1892, grew to 1,954 acres in 1948, and 17,600 acres by 1962; today Yuma County is considered the largest citrus-growing region in Arizona. Workers from Sonora, commuter workers, are a major component of the labor force used by agribusiness in Yuma to harvest citrus and vegetable crops.[17] A strong and steady demand for lemons places Arizona second only to California in lemon production, and in fourth place in grapefruit and orange production (USDA 2014a).

Similar to their California counterparts, Arizona citrus growers organized themselves into cooperatives or associations, and in 1928 formed the Arizona Citrus Growers Association (ACGA). Like their counterparts, in addition to transportation issues, the availability of sufficient labor during harvest was a central concern, as was collectively controlling the wages workers would be paid. Arizona growers benefited from lobbying efforts undertaken by the California Fruit Growers Exchange to relax immigration restrictions before and during World War I and became part of the "voluntary association" form of collective organizations that came to define how Arizona's business elite conducted business (González 1994; Larkin 2008). Ironically, these employer collective organizations strongly opposed the creation of parallel collective associations of workers, and the ability of workers to collectively bargain.

For citrus workers, handpicking fruit, much like cotton picking, is grueling and labor-intensive. González (1994) summed it up in the following way.

> Thus the picker, standing on a twelve-foot ladder, hauling a bulky canvas bag capable of holding fifty pounds of fruit, and working with tress that were often thirty to thirty-five feet high and had rough and thorny branches, was required to work delicately and quickly, to measure an orange, and pick it. (29)

In the citrus industry's social hierarchy of workers, pickers were not only the lowest paid, but they were also more vulnerable to the unpredictable circumstances during harvest, which fluctuated according to weather and grove conditions. It was through the persistently low wages paid to Mexican workers that race and class converged to create a social and economic stratification in the Yuma and Salt River Valleys that continues to the present.

Throughout the twentieth century, housing and living conditions for citrus workers were less than ideal, especially for migrant seasonal workers, who would live in camps or makeshift shelters that were often unsanitary and unsafe. One example of deplorable living conditions was reported as recently as the 1970s at Glendale Arrowhead Ranch, a citrus farm partially owned by Senator Barry Goldwater's brother. Following an investigation of crime and corruption in Arizona, a team of reporters documented the widespread use of undocumented Mexican workers, referred to in the article as "illegal aliens," and among the infractions described that striking workers at the ranch "lived amid their own excrement and garbage in orange crate shelters and fly-infested camps shielded from curious eyes by black plastic sheets hung on trees," and "worked from dawn to dusk for as little as $5 a day, a pittance bled down by phony Social Security deductions and food prices inflated by their overseers" (*United Press International* 1977; Morin 1977).

In 2012 Arizona reported 17,830 acres dedicated to citrus production, with 13,202 of those acres planted in Yuma County, followed by Maricopa County (USDA 2014a). Citrus now ranks eighth in sales for Arizona, replaced by the top three sellers of vegetables, melons, potatoes, sweet potatoes, cow's milk, and cattle and calves. Farm sales of Arizona's agricultural products generated $3,732,113,000 in revenue, 78 percent of which derive from Maricopa, Yuma, and Pinal Counties.[18] Over time the need for Mexican workers in the citrus industry as a whole declined but continues to be salient in areas with high production, such as Yuma County. As the shifts in agricultural crop production occur, a corresponding variation in the locations where Mexican workers may be found persists.

THIRD C—CLIMATE: HEALTH, SERVICES, AND LABOR

Of the five Cs, climate is the only nonmaterial commodity that was central to the early growth of Arizona's economy. It remains critically important to Arizona's current economic well-being, both as a place whose year-round climate make possible the success of the other Cs, and as a selling point to attract new residents, winter visitors, and those in the tourism industry. Like the other Cs, the issue of who works in this sphere is largely overlooked in the industries for which climate is central.

The broad historical narratives about Arizona's climate establish that climate initially became part of a promotional campaign in the late nineteenth century to attract health-seekers.[19] The spread of tuberculosis and pulmonary illnesses led many to seek out, in keeping with the medical knowledge of the day, places that were arid, warm, and sunny. Private businessmen and government officials in Arizona went out of their way to attract those afflicted with such illnesses. A number of sanatoriums and hospitals were built in the periphery of Phoenix well into the 1920s and through the 1930s, but as research refuted the role of climate in curing such illnesses, new approaches were put in place. By the time the cotton market collapsed in 1921, concerns developed that an overemphasis on recruiting ill persons to the state would deter new residents from Arizona, whether as visitors or prospective residents. Hence businessmen and promoters shifted strategies and directed their efforts to diversifying their approach to climate, and instead waged a campaign to build on Arizona's sunny climate to boost tourism and cast a broad net to capture a variety of different needs and interests.

An entire tourism industry began to flourish, beginning with the development of luxurious resorts. A. J. Chandler, who was involved in establishing Goodyear Tire & Rubber's first cotton company town, built the San Marcos Hotel in 1912. As the tourist industry began to grow, efforts to change the advertisement from "Salt River Valley" to the "Valley of the Sun" commenced, the latter of which eventually became the moniker by which the region would be known.

Winter visitors by the end of the 1920s could choose to stay in a number of winter resorts or hotels throughout Arizona, including the Jokake Inn, the Hotel Westward Ho, the refurbished Adams Hotel, the San Carlos Hotel in downtown Phoenix, the Hotel Monte Vista in Flagstaff, the Hotel Congress in Tucson, and by 1929 the Arizona Biltmore Hotel in Phoenix, and the Wigwam Resort in Litchfield Park in the West Valley. Guest, or dude, ranches also proliferated, built along the lines of the Southern Pacific Railroad.[20]

In Tucson, town elites rediscovered their city's romantic Spanish heritage while in the process of constructing an image of a modern mainstream American city. From the 1880s to 1929, the use of pressed bricks, rather than mud-and-straw blocks (i.e., adobe; principally produced by Mexicans), symbolized a transition to modernity. Bricks were the future—adobe, the past. In 1892 an editorial in the *Arizona Daily Star* noted, "The Future building material for Tucson will be brick and stone. The adobe must go, likewise the mud roof. They belong in the past and with the past they must remain" (Diehl and Diehl 2001, 436). Within the drive to create a modern Tucson, the same elites foresaw the importance of tourism and sought to revive an idyllic, sanitized old Pueblo that would stimulate tourism.[21] It was a strategy to create a positive imaginary of the charming Spanish/Mexican past with respectable caballeros and fair-skinned and modest señoritas. It was a strategy that fostered a distinction between a socially acceptable class of Mexicans and a stereotypical mestizo peon class that could offend white tourists.[22]

With the exception of one year during the Great Depression, the hotel and resort industry thrived and construction continued, expanding development for a tourist industry that would serve people of different economic means. Kotlanger (1983, 251) notes, "By 1949, tourism had grown to become Arizona's third fundamental industry behind agriculture and mining. In the growth process Phoenix became the regional center for tourist services."

In one allusion to the workforce, Kotlanger (1983, 237) notes that in the very design of the Arizona Biltmore Hotel, the architect for the project included in his plans "a large guest building, a 'discreet Mexican village' in which the 'carefully selected members of Mexican employees will be housed.'" The building of separate quarters and living residences was not new. When Goodyear Tire & Rubber leased land from A. J. Chandler to build Ocotillo in the East Valley, separate and lesser quality accommodations for Mexican cotton workers and their families were built into the plans (Hill 2007; Lucio 2007). Similarly, the building of the Wigwam Resort in Litchfield Park in 1929 entailed moving a number of Mexican families that had once lived in a camp in the center of town. It was in the context of the building of the Wigwam Resort that Mexicans were moved to the periphery of Litchfield Park's city limits and provided dwellings in what became known as *los campos* of Litchfield Park. In an oral history interview with Marie López Rogers, former mayor of Avondale, she remembers how both of her grandmothers worked as laundresses for the Wigwam Resort, while living in the camps.[23]

> They would do all the laundry for the executives—the sheets. I remember they would have a big, almost a bonfire, where the job was to mix the water and the sheets to make sure they were clean . . . and that was our job [as children], we got to do that and turn the clothes and the sheets in the tubs. (López-Rogers)

Indeed, sustaining a vibrant tourism industry in Arizona required, and still does, a large array of workers, including housekeeping staff, cooks, gardeners, attendants, golf caddies, drivers, waitstaff, dishwashers, landscape workers (*yarderos*), and many others. The elder seasonal winter migration (popularly labeled *snowbirds*), stimulated by climate and the hospitality industry that attracts them, also requires an array of eldercare workers to maintain a quality of life. Such workers are part of the inherently elastic supply of labor that, like agricultural workers, must cope with the seasonality of employment. Moreover, as personal service workers they, for the most part, are classified as self-employed/independent contractors liable for the employer and employee portion of federal and Medicare taxes, and not eligible for unemployment insurance. Consequently, they absorb the economic and social reproduction costs of their households.

Climate is also important in the development of military installations such as the Airplane Graveyard/Boneyard at the Davis-Monthan Air Force Base to benefit from the warmer, drier weather; Luke Air Force Base, where non-U.S. pilots are trained to fly F-16s and F-35s, due to the three-hundred-plus days of clear weather. Additionally, the establishment of the army's Yuma Proving Ground on over 1,300 square miles of the Sonoran Desert was also based on a favorable climate rationale. The site is used to test a wide variety of weapon systems, bombs, munitions, and artillery, as well as desert training for the wars in Afghanistan and Iraq. Lower-income neighborhoods surrounding the Proving Grounds face multiple health hazards associated with their proximity to the installation.

There is no doubt that Arizona's ability to market its three-hundred-plus days of clear weather stimulated the development of tourism, and this in turn fostered the expansion of the service sector. The service economy is solidly rooted in Arizona. Unfortunately, the long-term emphasis on service jobs has simultaneously rooted lower wages in the state.[24] An economic development strategy that emphasizes a low tax-base and business-friendly environment (i.e., a Right-to-Work law, strong anti-labor-union view, low-wage labor) are key factors in the relatively low minimum wage and mean hourly wage in the state. It is also part of what fostered the need for a large number of individuals, particularly young couples, to work two jobs at the same time. A single, full-time job earning Arizona's minimum wage makes it impossible for individuals to enter the aspired middle class.

Lastly, the boosterism related to climate and the paradise-like environment for young couples and active adults to enjoy—hiking, bicycling, quaint towns with antique stores, a vibrant nightlife in Scottsdale, an abundance of golf courses, etc.—represent a selected portion of reality. The paradise associated with climate excludes much of the reality in Arizona: recurring droughts, dust storms, snow in the higher elevations, freezes, unbearable summer heat, monsoon rains, high desert winds that knock down trees and risk public safety; the presence of valley fever and the possibility of contracting the desert fungus; multiple forms of skin cancer due to continuous exposure to the sun; and others. The Arizona agencies promoting tourism and relocation to the state carefully eschew mentioning these real elements in Arizona. Like the issue of "book cattle," the alleged three hundred days of clear weather is more solidly fixed on paper than experienced by those living in the Grand Canyon State. Mexican labor, though also not mentioned in the state's boosterism, is part of what of makes the many amenities found in Arizona possible. Arizona boosters knowingly continue to promote climate-related enterprises that are dependent on a low-wage labor sector that makes possible the relaxation and natural beauty promised. As noted on several billboards in Maricopa, Arizona is the place where you can retire and "live like you mean it."

FOURTH C—COPPER: EXTERNAL CAPITAL, LABOR, AND CONFLICT[25]

Chapters 4 and 6 address two consequential historical issues related to Mexicanas/os and copper production in Arizona. The former examines a long-standing practice in copper production in Arizona known as the dual-wage pay scale in the Miami-Globe area,[26] and the latter chapter focuses on the last major confrontation in Arizona between labor (mostly of Mexican descent) and the copper giant Phelps Dodge Corporation in the Clifton-Morenci area—the corporation won the battle and the war.[27] In this section we focus on highlighting issues and questions not examined in the two chapters that are useful to understand the complexity of the copper industry and the position of Mexican workers in making copper a commodity central to Arizona's economic formation, as well as enriched many individual owners, managers, bankers, and investors.

Similar to cotton, the scholarly literature on copper mining in Arizona is extensive. It encompasses works describing the migration of capitalist entrepreneurs from Canada, other U.S. states, and Europe to Arizona, and development of corporate interests that produced the major mines (this segment of writings pay tribute to the pioneers, technological innovations, and leadership of the larger mines); writings related to key historical events (e.g., the 1917 Bisbee Deportation); analyses of multiple management-labor conflicts and strikes (i.e., from the 1896 Globe strike, to the 1983 strike against the Phelps Dodge Corporation); a smaller number of discussions on the importance of gender and masculinity in understanding the articulation of race and class[28]; and some autobiographical accounts related to work in Arizona copper mines.[29]

Again, similar to the academic writings on cotton, significant facts and insights regarding Mexicana/o labor are found in the extensive literature on copper mining in Arizona. However, like cotton, a comprehensive scholarly book focused on the labor experience of Mexican miners in a major or smaller copper mine does not exist.[30] What we are suggesting here is that despite the large volume of writings on copper, one does not find comparable works to those written by historians and social scientists that make labor in general, or Mexican workers more specifically, the central focus. We do not have a single model in mind, but rather a diversity of approaches to understanding the lives of workers selling their labor-power in exchange for wages in the production process, and their everyday lives related to earning a wage. Multiple examples have been published that examine the labor process.[31] Our point here is that there remains a long-standing need to examine the experience of Mexicano copper miners in Arizona; such an endeavor can reflect upon and improve on published works that have examined the labor process.

The extensive scholarly literature on copper in Arizona has expanded our knowledge and understanding of four broad topics: (1) the development and organization of copper mining in the state; (2) the recurring tensions between owners/managers of mines and workers; (3) the importance of race and class in understanding the divisions and alliances within workers, within organized labor unions, and between some unions and Mexican workers; and (4) the economic marginalization of Mexicans and the making of the Mexican working class (i.e., the proletarianization of Mexicanas/os). With reference to the development and organization of copper mining, the combined descriptions in multiple sources highlight several key elements in the sector, and stand in contrast to our common perception of the fourth C. According to these, most of the initial pioneers were not from Arizona, and the major portion of capital was from East Coast and European sources (similar to the flow of capital that stimulated railroads and cattle production).

In addition, while most of the literature focuses on the large enterprises such as the Phelps Dodge Copper Queen mine in Bisbee, or the United Verde Copper Company mine in Jerome, less is known about the smaller mines (particularly before many of them were acquired by the larger mines). Form of ownership also varied: Phelps Dodge, with its multiple large mines, was a publicly traded corporation; however, other important mines, such as "the Big Hole"—the United Verde Copper Company mine in Jerome—was privately owned by William A. Clark during its peak years. Larger mines were more capitalized and had access to larger credit and so could invest in building railroad lines that would link to lines of the larger railroad corporations such as Southern Pacific or Santa Fe Railway.

Between 1896 and 1983, the copper mines experienced various degrees of worker protests (e.g., walkouts, sabotage, strikes). In 1917, the year that the well-known Bisbee Deportation took place, Arizona copper mines were confronted with twenty strikes. Some of these were more violent than others, and the response on the part of mine owners/managers also varied. In most of these, mine managers collaborated and relied on the assistance of the local sheriff, and in a smaller number of strikes state officials became involved in seeking to end the impasse in copper production. Governor George W. P. Hunt, Governor Thomas E. Campbell, and Governor Bruce Babbitt visited striking areas and made efforts to end the respective strikes. One strategy adopted by larger mines was to contract with detective agencies to infiltrate and/or assume the role of agent provocateurs in local unions. For the most part these proved to be an effective way to monitor what union organizers were discussing and planning, as well as identify ringleaders; such persons could then be targeted for threats, direct violence, or possible deportation by migration officials. As discussed in greater detail by Anna Ochoa O'Leary in chapter 6, the 1983 strike at the Phelps Dodge mine in the Clifton-Morenci area marks the end of the over eight-decade confrontation between labor and mine owners/managers. No copper strike has taken place since the 1983 strike.

The third prominent topic in the literature is the analyses and discussions of how race and class have been salient issues in the organization of copper mining (e.g., Mexican work versus non-Mexican work); underground skilled work and unskilled surface work, housing segregation in mining camps, division of camps into "white man's" camp (e.g., Bisbee) and Mexican camp (Clifton-Morenci), the development of a differential wage scale (i.e., the commonly labeled dual-wage system), and the exclusion of Mexicans from the larger unions such as the Western Federation of Miners. There is a general consensus that race and racialization are central to the entire organization of the copper production process through most of its history in Arizona. Scholar of political science Andrés E. Jiménez Montoya, in a short working paper, was one of the earliest scholars to give prominence to race as a paramount construct in the production of copper in Arizona (1977).[32] Subsequent scholars have refined and expanded his descriptions and insights—four notable works include those by Boswell (1984), Huginnie (1991), Mellinger (1995), and Parrish (1979).[33]

Multiple scholars, including the authors of chapters 4 and 6, note the economic marginalization of Mexican copper workers. The description of the marginalization has focused on four elements: the imposition of a dual-wage system, residential segregation (e.g., Little Sonora, Chihuahuita), the bifurcation of work into underground and surface work, and the arbitrary division of labor into "skilled" and "unskilled" work tasks. The latter two elements are important because they were implemented through a prism of race: Whites (and to a large degree, European migrants) were deemed to be skilled, and then allocated to underground or aboveground jobs—this distinction in production was arbitrary, in some whites were assigned to one category, and in another assigned to the other. Surface or underground "Mexican" workers received a lower wage. "Mexicans" (including Indigenous workers and, in some locations, Italians) were assigned to perform "Mexican work." The result was a tautological matrix. Mexicans were assigned to perform Mexican work because it matched their presumed skill level, and Mexican work was by definition lower-skilled work; consequently, Mexicans, and those categorized as such, "naturally" were paid a lower wage.

Although race was unquestionably fundamental in the organization of copper production, it is not often acknowledged that the exclusion and segregation of Mexicans did not emerge with copper mining, but rather was present in the prior mining speculation regarding gold and silver. The historian Robert L. Spude presents an insightful discussion of the formal exclusion and expulsion of Mexicans from the Walker-Weaver mining area (1975).[34] Not unlike contemporary legislative efforts in Arizona aimed at promoting self-deportation (also referred to as attrition through enforcement), local ordinances were enacted that prohibited Mexicans from filing placer (surface) claims on public land.[35] This ensured that Mexicans would provide the needed labor, but not interfere with the enrichment of white placer miners.

Gender, class, and race also impacted the earnings of Mexicans. In larger mines, whites were often provided, or assisted with, better built and solid housing and were encouraged to live in heterosexual, nuclear households. The family served to domesticate male miners. Because whites were considered family men, it was thought as natural that they should receive a decent family wage. Mexicans, because they were excluded from the better residential section were forced to live in the Chihuahuitas/

Little Sonoras. And because Mexicans lived in such poor conditions, it was clear that they could easily live with a lower wage, even if they also were domesticated family men.

With reference to dual-wage hierarchies, most authors deploy this label to refer to the differential wage system that created a higher wage scale for Native Americans (also referred to as Americans, or whites) and a lower wage for Mexicans. In a general sense, this is largely correct. However, in some instances the wage hierarchy was more nuanced. The historian Philip J. Mellinger notes that the wage hierarchy was more differentiated in some cases. He points out that Italians (who later would be labeled white) earned less than the Anglo-Irish, were excluded from skilled tasks, and so may have earned wages closer to the "Mexican wage" (1995, 170). Along similar lines, the historian Linda Gordon observes, "The copper companies delineated three formal wage groups: Mexican, Italian and Spaniard, and whites, but there was slippage between the nonwhite groups and some Italians earned the Mexican rate" (1999, 102). The historian Eric V. Meeks goes a step further and suggests that discussions of the dual wage in copper production need greater scholarly reflection.

> Still, even by the turn of the century, it would be inaccurate to characterize the racialized class structure in the mining towns as a binary system. . . . Wage stratification was not based simply on different skill levels but on race and nationality. . . . Racial classification, rather than nationality, language, or degree of skill, structured the wage hierarchy. Moreover, this was a multitiered rather than a binary or dual-wage system. . . . Indigenous workers—a group almost whole ignored by most historians of Arizona labor—were often relegated to the lowest-paid manual jobs . . . below . . . ethnic Mexicans. (Meeks 2007a, 28–29)

In order to arrive at a better understanding of the issue of dual wage what is needed is to concretize the presence of a differentiated wage scale by mining area, mine (and type of ownership), the racio-ethnic composition of the workforce, and historical period. The implication of this is that in some mines with a particular worker composition during a specific time period, a binary wage scale was fully implemented; in others, it may have existed in more than two wage categories.

It also should not be assumed that whites and Mexicans were always in opposition to each other and that they did not share common interests. In Jerome, the Jerome Miners Union, oddly enough supported by William A. Clark (the mine owner), enrolled all interested miners; this stands in contrast to the earlier position of the Western Federation of Miners, which excluded Mexicans. Moreover, in the early phase of copper mining, prior to 1880s, there are reported incidents of Mexicans aligning themselves with whites to eliminate the presence of the Chinese. Chinese workers earned lower wages than their Mexican counterparts, but nonetheless, Mexicans held anti-Chinese views like those of whites.[36] Additionally, in mining towns defined as "white man's camp," some towns enacted restrictions to eradicate the presence of Chinese persons from the town, or deployed local ordinances that placed a sunset curfew on the Chinese. Chinese business owners, fruit and vegetable vendors, and those operating a laundry or other entrepreneurial capitalist enterprises had to banish from the town by sunset. This meant they had to live outside the town's boundaries.

A final issue related to marginalization, though not often discussed, is the importance of company stores in copper company towns, and the use of scrip to pay workers—scrip for use in the company store and other approved vendors. The sociologist Terry E. Boswell (1984) presents an insightful discussion of the importance of the company store. Boswell notes that company stores with profits of 50 to 300 percent played key roles in creating debt (ultimately a form of debt peonage, a relationship outlawed in 1865 by the Thirteenth Amendment), and thus served as a mechanism to recover labor costs and ensure an elastic and tractable supply of labor. An individual with a debt to the copper company was an unfree laborer. Within Arizona's peculiar history, one of the early mining ventures began with debt peonage. Charles D. Poston (the "Father of Arizona") bought the debt of workers indebted to a wealthy Sonora hacienda owner, and in doing so the workers became Poston's workers—in essence he owned the workers because he held their debt, though illegal (Meeks 2007a, 26).

This suggests the presence of a dual-labor process. On the one hand, Mexican mine workers underwent a process of proletarianization in the transition from placer miners (a form of petty commodity producers) to full-time wage-workers dependent on the wages to meet their material needs. Secondly, the company store fostered the deproletarianization of workers—workers became unfree workers who did not have the freedom to seek the highest wage for their labor power. They could not leave the company until they had cleared their debt to it. Copper-company stores were similar to the *tiendas de raya* (company stores) in nineteenth- and twentieth-century haciendas in Mexico prior to the Mexican Revolution. Exorbitant prices on items sold in company stores, granting of credit to workers, and loans provided by employers to workers assured the immobility of workers. Worker debts to employers produced a form of indentured labor.

FIFTH C—COTTON: CAPITAL, LAND, AND AN ELASTIC SUPPLY OF LABOR

One of the most important Cs to significantly impact and fortify Arizona's economy in the twentieth century was cotton. Similar to discussions of the other Cs, mainstream accounts present narratives and imagery that describe the product, the form and sources of capital investment required to produce said commodity, the nature of the technology necessary for its production, profit calculations, and what it meant for the well-being of Arizona's economy.[37] Little attention is given to the laborers or the conditions for workers that made cotton production possible.

Were a consensus about the story of cotton in Arizona to exist, several declarations could be named. First, the advent of large-scale cotton production in the Salt River Valley, in particular, placed Arizona's agricultural economy on the national landscape. Second, the federal government, both in terms of legislation and resources, played a critical role in cotton's success. On the one hand, the harnessing of water made irrigated agriculture the norm in Arizona and, on the other hand, the federal government's early investment in the experimentation of cotton production in Arizona facilitated the possibility for private capital to benefit and profit and fortified cotton's future in Arizona, albeit eventually in a diversified agricultural economy.[38] Third, the production of cotton on a large-scale basis in Arizona simply would not have been possible without the availability of thousands of both U.S.-born and recruited Mexican workers—men, women, and children—that labored to plant, till, weed, pick, and hand harvest the cotton.

Of the five Cs, cotton production required not only the mobilization of the largest number of workers at any given time but also required the availability of both a permanent and seasonal workforce, the latter of which required mobilizing thousands of workers to ensure its production. Fourth, large-scale cotton production in Arizona and throughout the Southwest was incumbent on legislation, at the federal level, that ensured for agricultural growers that federal law would sanction the massive recruitment of many workers for agricultural interests. That marriage of immigration legislation with corporate agricultural interests would set a blueprint—one adversarial at times, and harmonious at other times—that set the stage for twentieth-century policy, which opportunistically looked to Mexico in times of need and, contradictorily, banished and deported Mexican workers during economic recessions.

Of the scholarly works written about cotton in relation to Mexican labor, two of the most significant are Devra Weber's (1994), and Neil Foley's (1997) work in California and Texas, respectively. With respect to Arizona, Herbert B. Peterson's (1974, 1975) provides one of the earliest accounts of Mexican labor with respect to cotton, while Mark Reisler's (1976a) and Eric Meek's (2007a) works each address a section or chapter of their books to the topic of cotton and Mexican labor. A rich source of data may be found in a number of dissertations and theses that have been written about cotton from a number of disciplinary perspectives.[39] A full-length monograph about cotton, Arizona, and Mexican labor is yet to be written, although works by Marsha Weisiger (1995) and Geta LeSeur (2000) do address the role and history of African Americans and Oklahomans with respect to cotton production in Arizona. That a paucity of scholarship exists is somewhat surprising, given the extent to which the production of cotton was among the most important crops produced throughout much of the twentieth century and which, to this day, is among "the most lucrative field crops" grown in Arizona, California, and New Mexico, and Texas generating $924 million in 2012.[40]

Despite how critically important Mexican workers were to the success of Arizona's agricultural economy, two themes prevail in primary and secondary sources with respect to Mexican labor. First, Mexican labor is characterized as a "problem," whether from growers' points of view, newspaper accounts, editorials, or official government reports, and simultaneously were subject to racialization processes that confronted other "non-Anglo-Saxon" groups.[41] With that, inferences about cultural inferiority, backwardness, and dehumanizing attributions were directed at people of Mexican descent (Clark 1908). About the growing sentiment towards Mexican workers, a 1908 report noted:

> Cotton picking suits the Mexican for several reasons: It requires nimble fingers rather than physical strength, in which he can not compete with the white man or the Negro; it employs his whole family; he can follow it from place to place, living out of doors, which seems to suit the half-subdued nomadic instinct of a part of the Mexican race; it is a seasonal occupation conveniently with the demands of labor and leisure in his own country, and it is well paid, and paid by the piece. (Clark 1908, 482)

The Dillingham Commission (1907–1911), one of the first comprehensive reports on immigration, encompassing forty-one volumes, allocated thirteen pages to the subject of Mexican immigrants, captured the growing number of Mexicans working in railroad and agriculture, while incorrectly projecting they would cease to be important (U.S. Immigration Commission 1911). Negative characterizations of Mexican workers have been amply covered in labor history scholarship and need not be repeated here; suffice it to say that with the passage of time, relations between Mexicans and whites became increasingly acrimonious with the desperate and growing need for labor to satisfy large-scale agricultural production in Arizona.

Second, Mexican labor, and the "problem" of Mexican labor in agriculture was persistently construed and presented as a labor shortage—one so severe that not having sufficient laborers risked the solvency of the agricultural empire in the making. The formation of the unsubstantiated labor-shortage argument is discussed more fully in chapter 3. It was cotton production that catapulted this argument to the forefront and persists to the present in Arizona and beyond.[42] No entity argued more vehemently than growers and the associations designed to protect their interests for the need to bring Mexican labor to Arizona; similarly, no entity was more responsible for creating the harsh conditions, low wages, and broken contractual agreements than those very same growers and associations. While corporate owners, growers, associations, and governmental officials are amply credited for their role in the story of cotton in Arizona, laborers metaphorically and materially occupy but a footnote in the historical production of Arizona's cotton plantations. Mexican labor is a bothersome side note that, more often than not, is insufficiently recognized as the critical variable whose absence of availability would have rendered the entire agricultural enterprise moot.

The story of cotton, in the context of the broader story of Arizona's agriculture and that tied to Mexican labor, is best understood in terms of the critical role the federal government played to enact key legislation and bring its resources to bear in fortifying Arizona's economy and, by caveat, the West.[43] Four pieces of legislation directly and indirectly benefited the production of cotton. The Reclamation Land Act of 1902 and the building and completion of the Roosevelt Dam in 1911 provided the water to support large-scale agriculture in Arizona. Earlier, the Desert Land Act of 1877 although intended to support a Jeffersonian notion of the family farm, encouraged white migration to the desert by guaranteeing 160 acres of land in which to settle and farm. The passage of the Immigration Act of 1917, designed to curb immigration from largely Southern and Eastern European countries, became important to the Mexico-U.S. borderlands economy after the United States' involvement in World War I.[44] A peculiar interpretation of the Immigration Act's ninth proviso allowed for the conditions to legally recruit thousands of Mexican workers for the burgeoning cotton industry during the war years and led to a pattern that encouraged migration and stemmed migration in accordance with the needs of agribusiness.[45] More than any other piece of legislation, the "organization and structure" of the ninth proviso established the juridical basis for the contracting of migrant laborers for the remainder of the twentieth century and well into the present debates on guest workers. Finally, the passage and implementation of the World War II Bracero Program (1942–1968) effectively guaranteed that Mexicans would remain the elastic supply of labor for a significant portion of the twentieth century.[46]

The story of cotton in Arizona often begins with the Goodyear Tire & Rubber Company's entry onto the scene in 1916. Indeed, Goodyear's decision to pursue the production of long-staple cotton in Arizona brought an unprecedented amount of capital, financing, and investment to the Salt River Valley, securing a place among the influential factors that led to Phoenix becoming the twelfth largest metropolitan city in the country. This story, however, could not be told without speaking to the role of the Arizona Cotton Growers Association (ACGA), one worthy of its own scholarly investigation. In brief, the ACGA organized growers throughout the Salt River Valley into an organization designed to represent and protect growers' interests. The ACGA became the means by which growers would obtain the vast numbers of

Mexican laborers needed for cotton production. They were responsible for recruiting and transporting the vast number of laborers; they lobbied Washington and governmental officials, fixed the abysmally low wages to be paid at harvest, and pursued whatever means necessary to quell any attempts by workers to organize on their own behalf (Weisiger 1995).

The initial large-scale production of cotton in Arizona began with a boom and bust period, which lasted from 1917 to 1921. During this period the demand for cotton, particularly long-staple cotton, grew in part due to World War I and in part to the burgeoning automobile industry. The labor force for the growing season of long-staple cotton required a steady but smaller workforce from March until August, and a large temporary workforce once handpicking began in September and concluded in February. One estimate reported that ten to fifteen times as many workers were needed during picking season, above and beyond the year-round workers. Pima cotton, earlier classified as American Egyptian cotton, was considered to be more arduous and painstaking because the cotton is shorter and removed from a narrower opening of the boll of the plant (Christy 1920, 21–27). The ACGA hired *enganchadores*, known as labor recruiters or middlemen, to station themselves at key border or metropolitan locations such as Nogales, Los Angeles, El Paso, and San Antonio to recruit the number of labors required. When demand surged, recruiters traveled deep into Mexican villages, with promises of good wages and housing. The latter was carried out despite the federal prohibition of such recruiting under the 1885 Alien Contract Labor Law (also known as the Foran Act). Annually, the ACGA would pronounce an impending crisis in the form of a "labor shortage," establishing a pattern of frenzied recruitment practices that brought in more laborers than were actually needed and, simultaneously, attracted a large number of workers who immigrated to the United States on their own in response to a labor market that appeared to have an insatiable need for laborers.

From 1917 to 1921, the commissioner general of immigration reported a total of 72,862 work contracts principally for agriculture. The authorized flow of Mexican workers under the ninth proviso would gradually decline following the 1921 bust, even though some exceptions continued to be made for Arizona cotton growers. By the mid-1920s Arizona growers turned to Puerto Rico, and throughout the Great Depression recruited white workers from Texas and Oklahoma to fulfill their labor needs. By World War II, the Bracero Program, which officially began in August 1942, signified the first time the federal government would become directly involved in the direct recruitment and management of foreign migrant contract labor. As Plascencia (2016) argues, however, "the Ninth Proviso was the juridical basis that migration officials used to admit migrant contract laborers at the start of WWII," noting that workers were admitted between 1942 and 1943, and after the war, 1948 to 1952, under the ninth proviso. It was not supplanted until the enactment of the H-2 provision in the 1952 Immigration and Nationality Act (also known as the McCarran-Walter Act). Over five million worker contracts were approved (approximately two million individual workers) over the course of its duration and subjected to inhumane and discriminatory practices now well documented in scholarly literature. Despite the peaks and valleys of cotton production, and the changes mechanization and machine-picked cotton meant for the volume of laborers needed during harvest, growers remained steadfast in their need and preference for Mexican laborers.

The future of cotton production in Arizona fluctuates and remains tenuous, as global competition from China's control of the cotton market supply poses a formidable challenge to the U.S. cotton industry. In the past two decades Arizona cotton acreage declined, while encroaching residential development further threatens dedicated farmlands.[47] The 2012 Census of Agriculture reports that total cotton acreage in Arizona amounts to 197,455, and places Arizona twelfth in the United States for the production of cotton (USDA 2014c). According to National Cotton Council of America data, approximately $258 million in revenue contribute to Arizona's economy from the "farms, cotton gins, merchants, warehouses and mills," leaving cotton production as one of the crops critical to Arizona's economy.[48]

SIXTH C—CONSTRUCTION: CAPITAL, LAND, AND LABOR

Eight years after the end of the Great Recession (December 2007–June 2009), Arizona's economy has experienced some improvement, but overall it lags behind the national recovery pattern. Unemployment rates, employment growth, and median wage incomes, for example, suggest that the Great Recession had a deeper impact than state leaders anticipated. At the center of the current post–Great Recession period, as well as previous recessions, is the central importance of residential housing (single- and multi-family units) sector within Arizona's economy. Beginning in the post–World War II period, housing gradually became the presumed safety net of the economy. Housing, and the multiplicity of industries and workers involved, was thought of as the one solid foundation that could weather a downturn, and then quickly rebound. It was the one economic driver that would shorten the impact of any recession in the horizon.

The highly speculative market of house building produced a housing bubble that could not be sustained under the best of scenarios. House builders, like cattle raisers in the late 1800s and cotton producers in the early 1900s, imagined Arizona as an exceptional state—a housing paradise—that would support the building of a surplus of houses that would quickly be sold to prospective buyers. It was a boom dating back to the post–World War II era, but accelerated around 2000. Cristina Gallardo-Sanidad (chapter 7) focuses her analysis on the 2000–2012 time period.

The boom reversed the economic principle of supply and demand—demand emerges and then is satisfied with a supply of the desired commodity. Instead, it focused on producing an abundant supply of houses, and hoped that a robust housing demand would surface to consume the speculated commodity. Arizona economic development agencies, business schools, and chambers of commerce imagined an unbroken chain of in-migration. The migration chimera relied on several assumptions: (a) job growth in Arizona would continue to expand and serve to attract working-age migrants and retirees; (b) prospective migrants experienced a wage growth that gave them a financial cushion to absorb the migration costs; (c) prospective migrants would easily sell their houses elsewhere (i.e., a strong housing demand); and (d) the attraction of low taxes, business-friendly environment, and plenty of water and sun (i.e., climate) would foster a perpetual flow of new residents from California, the Midwest, Canada, and other points.

While some observers readily note the long-standing presence of Mexican labor in Arizona's agricultural sector (such as citrus, cotton, or winter vegetables), the participation of Mexicana/o labor in construction is thought of as a more recent phenomenon. Although this is generally correct, Mexicans actually have a longer association with construction in the Grand Canyon State. As part of the negotiations for the establishment of temporary agricultural contract labor under World War I, part of the 1917 Immigration Act's ninth proviso, the U.S. Army requested that contract labor from Mexico be allowed entry in order to construct barracks in Arizona because of an alleged labor shortage available to build barracks. Secondly, based on the forced deportations/repatriations in the late 1920s to 1931 involving over a million individuals principally from urban areas, the deportations included Mexican workers who worked in construction in the Southwest and Midwest (Balderrama and Rodríguez 1995). Thus, it is evident that by the late 1920s and early 1930s, Mexicano males had sought higher wages in construction work in the larger cities. However, the exact proportion performing construction work in Arizona in the 1920s and 1930s is not known for certain.

An important figure that initiated the conversation regarding the importance of house ownership and the national economy was President Herbert Hoover. He insightfully linked the idea that an increase in homeownership would directly impact consumer spending, and consumer spending in housing would benefit local and state revenues, and these in turn would benefit the U.S. economy. He envisioned the need to expand the ownership base and the financial practices at the time. In the late 1920s, buyers would need to make a down payment of 40 to 50 percent and assume a five- to ten-year mortgage. These terms made house ownership a privilege for a fraction of the population. The Great Depression, however, displaced Hoover's grand idea.

Hoover's aspirations regarding house ownership materialized after World War II. Again, federal actions and subsidies made Hoover's dream possible. The GI Bill not only allowed veterans to attend college, it also stimulated a desire for the "good life" and fostered the dream of house ownership. Federal approval of the VA Home Loan Guaranty program, part of the Servicemen's Readjustment Act of 1944 (PL 78–346), made it possible for veterans to purchase a house. Housebuilders and financial institutions, of course, supported such public assistance; the federal government guaranteed the mortgage loans. Veterans were assisted with the down payment and provided a low interest rate, and the federal government allowed the stretching of mortgages to thirty years. The federal government stimulated the housing construction sector. A new demand, and available financing, made housing construction a highly profitable venture. The suburbanization experienced in Tucson and Phoenix in the post–World War II era was fostered by the momentous action of the federal government. Accompanying suburbanization was the innovation of planned retirement communities for "active adults." Del Webb's Sun City, west of Phoenix, and Green Valley, south of Tucson, are early examples of such communities.

A second important major federal expenditure was the commitment to build an interstate highway system. Its importance is best appreciated in the context of the suburbanization process. Building a transportation system that readily connected distant geographic sections (emerging and future suburbs) and central parts of cities made suburbanization possible. Working-age residents of suburbs could relatively easily commute to work in downtown Tucson or Phoenix because federally sponsored highways made it possible. Without the interstate system most cities in the United States would be configured significantly differently from what now exists.

Contemporary discussions of housing construction in Arizona explicitly or implicitly acknowledge the importance and prominence of Latino labor (Central American, Mexican, and Mexican American), including a sizable proportion of Mexican undocumented migrant workers, in most construction tasks. In the building of single-family houses, for example, Latino labor is visible in the preparation, setting, and finishing of the foundation; the framing of outside and inside walls; roofing; setting and finishing Sheetrock; installing baths, sinks, shower stalls, and kitchen cabinets; installing windows; installing carpeting, linoleum, tile, or wood flooring; installing molding and painting; and completing the landscape option selected by the purchaser. On the other hand, Latino labor is less visible in tasks requiring a license and subsequent government inspection, such as the installation of electrical systems.

Arizona Daily Star reporters Brady McCombs and Thomas Stauffer authored an impressive news story about housing construction in the Tucson area. According to their investigation, they were able to calculate the savings/price reduction based on the use of undocumented migrant workers. McCombs and Stauffer calculated that as much as $38,000 on an average-price house in Tucson ($267,000) was attributable to the workers preferred by housebuilders (McCombs and Stauffer 2006b, 2006c). Such employers employed individuals not authorized to work in the United States, despite the 1986 Immigration Reform and Control Act, which made it illegal to employ such persons. McCombs and Stauffer also note that this level of savings/price reduction ultimately made average-priced houses affordable to many households with limited savings and assets.

Despite the importance of construction to Arizona and the prominent role of Mexican labor, and similar to the other Cs, scholars have largely ignored this issue. There is no comprehensive scholarly book examining an area of construction and the relations of production involved. With reference to academic journals, one of the few published works focusing on Mexican labor is Denisse Roca-Servat's excellent discussion of Latino (principally Mexican) roofers (2009). Although the focus of her discussion is the organizing activities sponsored by the AFL-CIO Organizing Institute, the context for the organizing efforts are the difficult and exploitative conditions that Latino roofers endure at the hands of contractors/subcontractors. Additionally, a useful discussion of day labor in Phoenix is that by Jacob Fisher (2006) and Francisco Lara-Valencia and Jacob Fisher (2013). Fischer's research offers a noteworthy description of the geographic dispersion of day labor recruitment sites and makes brief reference to some of the experiences of workers. It would have been greatly valuable had Fisher broadened his investigation to capture more of the work experiences of day laborers at the eighteen sites examined.

The presence and contribution of Mexicanas/os to the construction sector in Arizona remains one for which we do not have a solid understanding. There is no shortage of business/economic reports about the decline or growth of individual components of the construction sector, but ultimately the status of the workers who make construction possible receive almost no attention. We are informed, for example, of an increased trend in house construction permits issued by Tucson or Peoria, but nothing about the implications of these for the Mexican American and undocumented Mexican migrants who will participate in building the single- and multi-family units being proposed.[49]

At the end of 2015, media and business school reports began to furnish the good news that state leaders were longing for: existing house prices were rising, the existing housing inventory was gradually decreasing and, more importantly, the construction industry was projected to soon rebound based on small surveys of contractors. The contractors were projecting an apparent shortage of skilled workers, and increased hiring in 2016. Representatives of lending firms, real estate corporations, general contractors, and journalists avoided the central question: If all previous housing booms in recent times increased and relied on the presence of undocumented migrant labor from Mexico, will the projected rebound in 2016 and thereafter also lead to the recruitment of the same labor in order to reduce the overall costs of building, and increase housebuilders' profits? If it is projected to be different, who will constitute the bulk of construction workers? Who will be recruited to meet the alleged shortage of skilled workers? Lastly, how will the widespread fraud, avarice, and, borrowing a phrase from Alan Greenspan, "infectious greed" that characterized the housing market bubble leading to the Great Recession be eliminated or controlled in 2016 and subsequent years of recovery?

DISCUSSION

This anthology's editors do not take credit for being the first to foreground the historical marginalization and erasure of salient Mexican labor to economic development in Arizona, or the Southwest more broadly. Few would contest that the history of Mexicans in Arizona and the United States is complex and contradictory. It was carved from colonization processes, industrialization, global capitalism, patriarchal, racist, xenophobic, and heteronormative forces that have simultaneously included and excluded its members, and has positioned Mexicans in Arizona as "essential outsiders."[50] Arizona, like its counterpart southwestern states has built its "empires" on the backs of Mexican-origin people. It is a most paradoxical relationship, one cemented in a reluctant but necessary interdependence.

As scholars have established, the Mexican-origin population has resisted and organized against the debilitating and often violent forces. Well-documented by Bada, Fox, and Steele (2006), over a million migrants and supporters marched nationwide to oppose antimigrant proposals in 2006, and in Phoenix 100,000 to 250,000 marched. The actual number of participants caught the organizers, and the Phoenix Police Department, by surprise. Organizers had projected a much smaller number of participants.

Undoubtedly, strides have been made, even as setbacks and patterns of inequality, persistent discriminatory laws, and practices continue. From the Mexican miners who organized strikes against copper corporations in the late 1800s, to the Mexican deportees in the Jerome and Bisbee Deportations of 1917, to the cotton, copper, and citrus workers whose efforts to unionize were repeatedly stymied by conjoined efforts of government, police agencies, and private corporate leaders and investors, to the women who valiantly organized, as blue-collar or pink-collar workers, against low wages and poor working conditions in an array of service-sector jobs, Mexicans in Arizona have claimed and fought for their civil and human rights and their right to be recognized as belonging. The historians Pete Dimas (1991, 1999) and James

McBride (1974, 1975, 1978, 1999) provide important foundations for understanding the experience and resistance of Mexican communities to their social and political marginalization.

They joined unions even when unions did not want them; they filed lawsuits when their children were placed in inferior or separate schools; they founded new organizations, small and large, such as Liga Protectora Latina, Chicanos Por La Causa, Los Bomberos, and countless others, to advocate and fill in gaps to services otherwise absent. While Mexicans may now be found distributed throughout the social class structure, they are overwhelmingly over-represented in the lower-wage sectors. While a small number of Mexicans have occupied seats in Arizona's House of Representatives, served as senators and congressmen, and even once in the governor's seat, the quality of their lives, whether as workers, citizens, and noncitizens, remains precarious, not knowing when the next shoe will drop.

For yesterday, and today, Mexicans may vacillate from being the preferred labor force to being despised and ridiculed across the national media to assuage a sector of the nation intent to hold onto a perspective that vilifies Mexicans.

NOTES

1. Ten of the twelve contributors to the anthology are practicing historians or were trained in history.
2. The most encompassing reference to Mexicans is found in Johnson Jr.'s introduction: "In prewar [WWII] Phoenix, Hispanics and poor whites dominated the migrant labor market; farmers in the Phoenix area long had used not only Mexican Americans but also Mexican workers legally and illegally brought in from across the border. Phoenix society might rail against so-called wetbacks, but the reality was that local prosperity was intimately tied to the availability of cheap migrant labor working the vast farmlands of the valley" (Johnson Jr. 1993, 5).
3. It should be noted that a good number of master's theses and doctoral dissertations have been written, but most of these, unfortunately, remain unpublished. Although we searched and compiled over four file boxes of unpublished theses and dissertations on Mexicans in Arizona, most of these do not explicitly focus on the production-related experience of Mexicanas/os. Moreover, because they remain unpublished they are marginal to the broader knowledge about the Mexican laborer experience in Arizona. Some notable exceptions include Michael E. Casilla's insightful thesis on Mexican labor conflicts in Arizona (1979); Joseph F. Park's excellent thesis in history on Mexican labor in Arizona (1961); Edwin C. Pendleton's unmatched dissertation on irrigated agriculture in Arizona (1950); and Andrea Yvette Huginnie's high-quality dissertation on copper mining in Arizona (1991).

4. The shift from Italian, Japanese, Greek, and white labor to Mexican labor is discussed in Victor S. Clark's classic Department of Labor report (Clark 1908). Clark not only notes the widespread presence of Mexican labor in most major railroad lines, but also their wide geographic distribution within the Southwest and beyond.
5. Patrick W. O'Bannon presents a detailed description of the construction of the San Diego and Arizona Railway, which connected San Diego, via Mexico, to Seeley, California (in the Imperial Valley), and then joined the Southern Pacific track to Yuma and continuing to Tucson and beyond. Similar to Myrick, workers are noted in passing and thus appear to be minor factors in the construction of the railroad (1979).
6. See Freeman, chapter 2 (1972), specifically the description of "infinitely elastic supply" of labor curve.
7. Such biopolitical arguments can be thought of as part of what Anibal Quijano labels the "coloniality of power" (2000). In short, the legacy of empires, colonial relations, and settler colonialism patterns that shaped the contemporary world system of political and labor relations, including the enactment and management of transnational contract labor regimes. They are power relations that intrinsically rely on racialized distinctions.
8. Although not noted by Sheridan, his observation is ironic. It is ironic insofar as contemporary Arizona Republican Party leaders take the position that the federal government (i.e., big government) has no role meddling in state business, or is "the problem," and that smaller federal government is ideal. Yet it was federal largesse that made possible the capital accumulation and wealth of modern Arizona. Many scholars of Arizona history have noted this point. See also Larkin (2008), Mawn (1979), Pendleton (1950), Smith (1982).
9. In order to make the section more readable, we limited the number of in-text citations. The discussion regarding the development of cattle and livestock in Arizona relies significantly on the following sources: Dowell (1978), Haskett (1935, 1936), Mattison (1946), Sayre (1999a, 1999b), Sheridan (2001, 2007, 2012), Spicer (1967), Wagoner (1949). Readers interested in the important development of cattle production in Arizona should review Sayre's dissertation (1999b), and the excellent shorter discussion by Sheridan, chapter 7 (2012).
10. The surplus capital in Great Britain, as briefly noted by Sayres (1999b, 87), was the product of the expansion of the British Empire and its gradual global domination. The military and economic control of a wide set of commodities and the trade related to these, as well as the large populations, including enslaved persons, that labored to benefit the empire, made possible large returns to investors in Great Britain.
11. In the late 1880s individuals could buy a steer for $3 to $6 and sell it for $25 to $45; however, the cattle accounting was based on rosy mathematics. Interim costs between original purchase and final sale were excluded. The dreamy "dividends" of 15 to 30 percent between 1881 and 1883 excluded: (a) the cost of capital (which could reach 10 percent

compounded every three to six months); (b) loss of animals to weather; (c) deaths due to predators; (d) taxes; and (e) transportation costs to deliver cattle to market.

12. We borrow the phrase from Alan Greenspan, former chairman of the Federal Reserve. Greenspan suggested that "irrational exuberance" was at the core of the Dotcom bubble (Greenspan 1996).
13. Although vaqueras/os are not the primary focus of the historian Armando C. Alonzo's analysis of cattle ranches in South Texas, he provides a glimpse into the internal separation of cattle-related activities (e.g., branding, driving stock to market, gathering), and the presence of a dual-wage system. In the early 1880s Mexican sheepherders and vaqueros averaged $12 per month and $15 for "American" cowboys (1998, 199).
14. The inclusion of the topic of strikes, though odd sounding, is in reference to the multiple cowboy strikes that took place in the 1880s across the Great Plains and Mountain West. See, for example, Ruth Allen's classic description of the 1883 Texas strike (1941), and the more recent fuller account of the strikes in the region by Mark Lause (2018).
15. For scholarly sources about the citrus industry in relation to Mexican labor, see Alamillo (2006), García (2001), González (1994), and Padfield and Martin (1965). For work on Arizona's associations, see Larkin (2008).
16. It is thus not surprising that among the earliest full-length works done on Chicanas and labor were based on Chicanas' work in California's canneries (Ruiz 1987; Zavella 1987).
17. The Bureau of Immigration, a unit within the U.S. Department of Labor, without approval from Congress issued General Order 86 in 1927. The Bureau's order created the original green card and classified commuters as permanent residents. Legal scholars have dubbed the permanent resident/commuter classification as an "amiable fiction" (Gordon 1969). Commuters from Sonora travel to the Yuma Valley on a daily, weekly, or seasonal basis to harvest winter vegetables, particularly lettuce.
18. See https://www.azeconomy.org/2014/09/featured/the-changing-face-of-agriculture-in-arizona/.
19. Our discussion of climate and hospitality industry relies on discussions in Kotlanger (1985) and Mawn (1979), in addition to other secondary sources in the form of government documents, hospitality industry reports, and website searches.
20. Ranches (1935).
21. Diehl and Diehl's (2001) informative discussion of the major brick producers in Tucson provides an important insight about architectural styles. They observe that starting in the 1950s the construction of houses replaced brick with the cheaper concrete blocks, and then were stuccoed. Multiple housing tracts in the Tucson area and Maricopa County were constructed with the aim of "lending an appearance of Southwestern folk architecture to mass-produced neighborhoods" (2001, 433). Although not noted by the authors, stucco exteriors can be thought of as a contemporary form that duplicates the visual

image and texture of adobe walls—the building material that was alleged to represent the past.

22. A similar process is found in the redevelopment of Olvera Street in downtown Los Angeles, and El Mercado (Market Square) in San Antonio, Texas. Each of these spaces was, in a sense, sanitized to increase their tourist value to visitors.
23. Interview with Marie López Rogers, April 17. Mexican Americans of Litchfield Park Oral History Project, 2007.
24. To the surprise of many, in November 2016 Arizona voters approved Proposition 206. The law raised the minimum wage from $8.05 to $10 in 2017, and then gradually to $12 by 2020. The Goldwater Institute, Senate president Steve Yarborough and, along with the Arizona Chamber of Commerce, Tucson Hispanic Chamber of Commerce, and other business interests filed suit, challenging the measure. On March 14, 2017, the Arizona Supreme Court ruled that Proposition 206 was constitutional and would remain.
25. Due to the sizable scholarly literature on copper, and the aim to make the subsection easier to read, we limited the citation of works examined. Moreover, the listing of scholarly works reviewed in this footnote would result in a very long footnote. The reader is referred to the seventy-five citations related to copper in the references section. Secondly, we want to acknowledge that although the production of copper Arizona is certainly part of transnational and global factors, to fully explore these for each of the six Cs would produce a more diffused and much longer manuscript. Those interested in understanding some of the transnational links can read the excellent historical analysis of the dynamics that linked railroads and mines in northern Mexico and Arizona (and the broader Southwest) by Kenneth Dale Underwood (2009).
26. It is worth noting that U.S.-owned copper mining interest in Mexico, such as that owned by William C. Greene in Cananea, Sonora (the Green Consolidated Copper Company), also operated with a dual wage.
27. The Freeport-McMoRan Corporation acquired Phelps Dodge in March 2007 for $25.9 billion in cash and stock. After Freeport-McMoRan acquired Phelps Dodge, the company relocated its headquarters to Phoenix (the building previously known as the Phelps Dodge Building).
28. See, for example, Benton-Cohen (2002), Johnson (1982, 1984, 1987), and O'Neill (1993).
29. An example of such writings is Tafoya (2006). A clear limitation of Tafoya's and similar writings is that they tend to be broadly descriptive and avoid examining the actual labor-relations process, and avoid discussing conflictive or internally contradictory worker dynamics.
30. See, for example, Parrish's short booklet on Mexican workers in copper mining in Arizona (1979), Mellinger's discussion of Mexican mining districts in the early 1900s (1992), Ríos-Bustamante's outstanding effort to understand the presence in seven mining districts

with a sizable Mexican American population (1998), and Spude's important work on Mexican gold/silver *placeros* in the Walker and Weaver mining districts (1975).

31. Some of the more notable examples include the following works: Roberto R. Calderón (2000), Neil Foley (1997), Gilbert González (1994), Josiah McC. Heyman (1991), Aihwa Ong (2010), Devon Peña (1997), Monica Perales (2010), Paul Taylor (1934), and Anthony F. C. Wallace (1978). These examples reflect diverse academic specialties. The scholars listed include two anthropologists (Ong and Wallace), an economist (Taylor), four historians (Calderón, Foley, González, and Perales), and a sociologist (Peña).
32. Boswell and Bush (1984) offer an insightful close reading of Jiménez Montoya's working paper. They are correct in noting that in 1977 Jiménez Montoya did not carry out the extensive archival research needed on Clifton-Morenci and other major mining locations in Arizona; consequently, they argue that he makes race/racism the overriding factor without the necessary historical research. However, they overlook contextualizing what they were critiquing: Jiménez Montoya appears to be the first scholar to make race/racism central to examining a copper mine, and no comprehensive scholarly work has since been published that makes race and Mexican labor across all major mines the primary focus of analysis.
33. Phyllis Cancilia Martinelli's discussion of the social position of Italians and Spaniards in copper camps in Arizona is an important complement to understanding how copper mine owners/managers understood and manipulated the notion of race among workers (2009).
34. See also Gillespie and Farrell (2002) for a discussion of the clear segregation of Mexicans in the Santa Rita Water and Mining Company mine (south of Tucson). The Mexican section of the camp consisted of tents, in contrast to the housing made available to white workers.
35. For a discussion of the development and use of the concept of attrition through enforcement, see Plascencia (2013).
36. The Camp Grant Massacre also involved the alignment of prominent Mexicans with whites in the spree to kill "Apaches." Additionally, the sad chapter in Mexico's history, particularly in Sonora, regarding the fervent anti-Chinese movement that took place between 1910 and the 1930s, reminds us that forms of Mexican supremacy can erupt against needed but unwanted migrants, including Mexican citizens of Chinese descent.
37. See, for example, Christy (1920), Shapiro (1989), McGowan (1961), Padfield and Martin (1965).
38. For sources regarding the role of the federal government, see Smith (1982).
39. For additional works pertaining specifically to cotton industry in Arizona, see Brown and Cassmore (1939), Christy (1920), Nancy Hill (2007), McGowan (1961), Meeks (2007a), Hill (2007), Peterson (1974, 1975), Shapiro (1989), Walker (2012).
40. http://swclimatehub.info/bulletin/cotton-southwestern-us.

41. For illustrative examples of culturally biased views of Mexicans, see Padfield and Martin (1965, 187–97), Meeks (2006, 91–113), Reisler (1976b, 231–54).
42. Sugar-beet producers were also important in the development of arguments about labor shortages and the need for the federal government to aid in providing needed labor. At the meeting between Presidents Taft and Díaz in 1909, Taft requested that Mexico provide "one thousand" workers to aid sugar-beet growers in Colorado and Nebraska (Garcia y Griego 1983, 55; 1988, 43).
43. See, for example, Sheridan (1995a).
44. For a discussion of this issue, see Plascencia (2016). For one of the most thorough discussions of the Immigration Act of 1917 and the temporary admissions program that developed as a result of the reinterpretation of the ninth proviso, see Reisler (1976a, 24–48).
45. For the impact in Arizona of the Immigration Act of 1917, the ninth proviso, and how it shaped Mexican labor between 1917 and 1921, see Peterson (1974, 113–32; 1975), Brown and Cassmore (1939, 63–66), Weisiger (1995, 40–44), Meeks (2007a, 78–80, 109–113), Pendleton (1950, 105–59), Walker (2012, 162–66).
46. Although standard accounts record the ending of the Bracero Program in 1964, our preference is to use the 1968 date to highlight that the state continued to authorize workers for select growers until 1968. A fuller discussion can be found in chapter 3.
47. http://kjzz.org/content/238904/facing-low-prices-and-urbanization-west-valley-cotton-farmers-turn-other-crops.
48. U.S. exports of cotton are expected to expand by as much as 25 percent within the next five years, according to the USDA, http://cronkitenewsonline.com/2010/09/arizona-cotton-farmers-benefiting-from-global-demand-high-prices.
49. See, for example, Brodie (2015), Goldstein (2016).
50. We borrow the phrase from Chirot and Reid (1997).

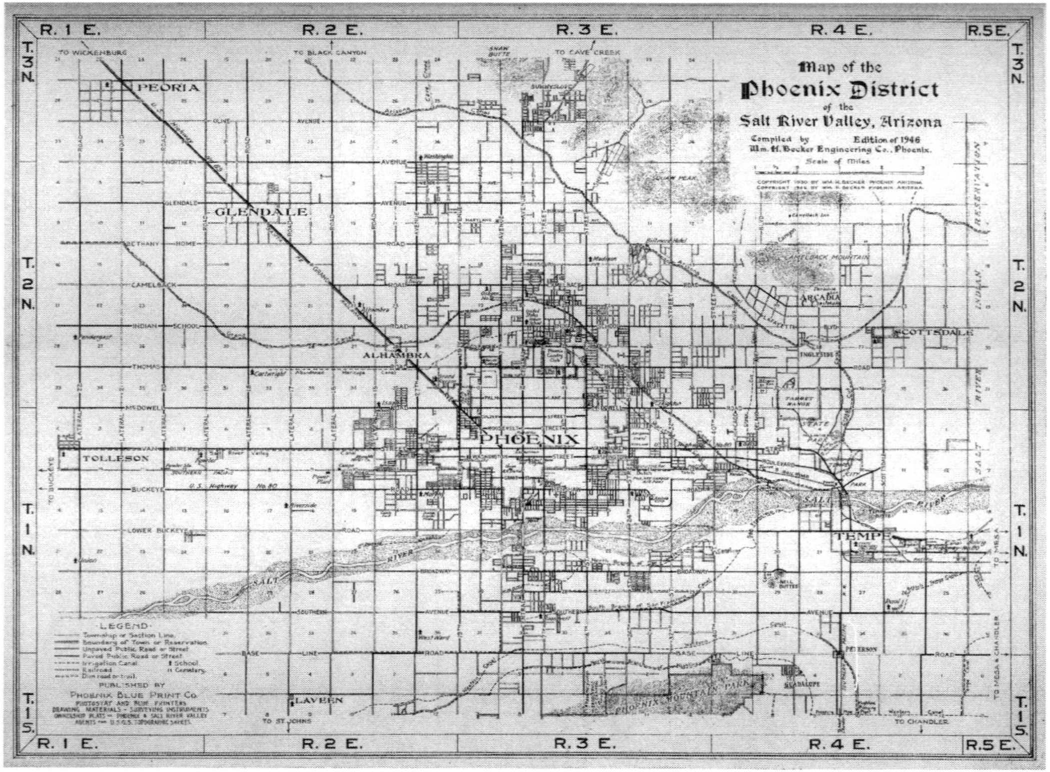

MAP 3 Map of the Phoenix District of the Salt River Valley, 1946. Courtesy of the Arizona Historical Society

1

LOST LAND AND MÉXICO LINDO

★

Origins of Mexicans in Arizona's Salt River Valley, 1865–1910

JAIME R. ÁGUILA AND F. ARTURO ROSALES

TODAY ARIZONA'S VAST SALT RIVER VALLEY has one of the largest concentrations of Latinos and Mexican origin peoples (Mexicans)[1] in the United States; 1,204,092 Latinos or Hispanics estimated by the 2013 U.S. Census. Besides Phoenix, the Valley embraces most towns within Maricopa County, including eastern communities such as Mesa, Tempe, Chandler, and Gilbert (Marin 2015). According to estimates from the 2010 U.S. Census, the Mexican origin population was 975,622. They live in barrios (Mexican neighborhoods) and integrated neighborhoods throughout Phoenix and its numerous suburban communities. Some are descendants of nineteenth-century pioneers who settled as farmers in the Valley itself, or as miners from various locations in Arizona. A larger number trace their ancestry to agricultural workers' communities, which spread across the central Valley in the beginning of this century. The majority, however, are post–World War II arrivals or their descendants from Mexico, from other Spanish American countries, and from southwestern states such as Texas and New Mexico.[2]

Since the late nineteenth century, as was true throughout the American Southwest, Mexicans laboring in the Salt River Valley simultaneously filled short-term labor gaps while suffering from racial discrimination. Migration during this initial phase was a causal process primarily across the Sonoran Desert region. However, over the course of the twentieth century, transnational industrialization brought laborers from central Mexico northward in large numbers. The 1965 Border Industrialization Program was another major milestone as it created the modern Mexican maquiladora industry, which emerged after the large-scale portion of the Bracero Program was terminated in 1964. Its effect expanded the Mexican migration stream to include the entire nation, but especially from southern Mexico, with industries throughout the continental United States.[3]

This chapter historically delineates the roots of this significant but understudied Mexican community within the Salt River Valley. In comparison to Tucson's richer historiography, this project seeks to begin filling the gap of other areas in Arizona (Flagstaff, Prescott, and Yuma are examples of other regions in need of published historical studies). While books such as Thomas Sheridan's 1986 *Los Tucsonenses* present a detailed description of the settlement of Tucson, a parallel scholarly discussion regarding the settlement of Mexicans in the greater Phoenix area has not been published. This chapter aims to begin filling this important omission regarding our knowledge of Mexicans in Arizona.

The emergence of the first significant Spanish- and Mexican-origin communities anywhere in the United States fall within a historical spectrum that is divided by the Lost Land stage beginning in 1848 and concludes with the México Lindo phase in the 1930s. The determining dynamic separating each time frame was driven by two divergent communal identities and their relationship with the dominant Anglo hierarchy. In 1848 the Lost Land ideal pertains to thousands of people left in the territories conquered from Mexico and annexed by the United States after the Texas Rebellion (1835–1836), the Mexican-American War (1846–1848) and the Gadsden Purchase (1854); in essence, the first Latinos in this country who were overwhelmingly of Mexican origin. Their identity was largely based on a perception that they had lost their homeland and were cut off from their Mexican roots. John R. Chávez's pioneering work demonstrated that the Mexicano identification as a conquered people has remained a salient theme within this community to the present (Chávez 1984, 4).

The application of México Lindo is more adequate to early twentieth-century immigrant colonias made up of workers who came directly from Mexico. Political postures were shaped by survival and adaptation strategies and identity rested on an idealized and romanticized memory of the old country. The immigrants in this historical pattern were segregated and subordinated in a society where their value was measured primarily in the labor marketplace. Moreover, the barrios where these immigrant workers lived had little influence in shaping the image of the larger host communities. Political postures were shaped by survival and adaptation strategies and identity rested on an idealized and romanticized memory of the old country.

Prior to 1848 the Mexican population of the northern frontier wanted closer ties with their metropolis. However, the Mexican-American War completely cut them off from their capital. Subsequently, the Lost Land construct emerged from a broad sense of social and economic displacement where they now resided in the U.S. Southwest, a region that used to belong to them, but now their position, regardless of their social standing, was one of a displaced community in a lost homeland.

Nonetheless, the coming of railroads, outside capital, and entrepreneurs with new visions disrupted or eliminated the economic, political, and cultural arrangements forged by Hispanics[4] of Spanish and then Mexican descent in the first years of U.S. domination. By the end of the nineteenth century, southwest Mexicans saw their efforts to slow this decline fail. Ironically, Anglos and Europeans who mixed with Mexicans in the transitional period often identified or sympathized with the Lost Land perspective, and some even joined political movements to stem the losses. Likewise, for southwest Mexicans, the loss was not just felt for the Spanish and Mexican periods. The perspective of Lost Land adherents was that much of the dispossession did not take place until after transitional era and early cultural and economic contacts with Anglos came to an end. However, according to Samuel Truett, where the aspirations of the Spanish and Mexican governments failed, for the local population these outcomes, "were also symbols of a fugitive landscape, one characterized by mobility and flexibility that survived . . . by resisting incorporation" (Truett 2006, 15).

During the initial contact years, in spite of the Lost Land community's resistance to Anglo[5] domination and a marked reluctance on the part of Anglo Americans to incorporate them, a fragile symbiosis evolved in which the two groups cooperated at different levels of the economic and societal structures. Moreover, some Mexicans amassed political and economic power within the total community, as well as a degree of prestige and respect. An important feature of the cooperative structure was marriage between Mexican women and non-Mexican adventurers, entrepreneurs, farmers, and workers. Such marriages tended to bind economic relationships between newcomers and resident Mexicans.

Another salient feature of the Lost Land is that prior to the 1910s, the southwest Mexican population never acquired a strong link to Mexico. Their community identification did not "grow up," as it were, with the evolution of modern *mexicanidad* during the Porfiriato and the years of the Mexican Revolution. Immigration from northern Mexico to a preindustrial, in great part subsistent Southwest was constant in the early transitional years (ca. 1848–1880). But these newcomers, who migrated just north of the U.S. border where many had relatives, found familiar surroundings and preindustrial economic activity that fit into their own experience. Others were reentries or the offspring of Mexicans who, in an earlier period, had abandoned those same areas. As a consequence, they, too, felt the loss. Finally, México Lindo consciousness did emerge in many communities alongside the Lost Land memories, either complementing or inundating this source of identity (see García 1989, for a discussion on generational model and its application in studying Mexican Americans). Chávez (1984) provides a discussion of the evolution of Lost Land identity. Other studies that delineate the Lost Land model are Pitt (1970), Griswold del Castillo (1980), and de León (1985).

F. Arturo Rosales's work has delineated the México Lindo concept. Mexican consuls and Mexican expatriate community leaders promoted a nationalistic loyalty to their native country as a means of unifying and empowering the immigrant community in the face of discrimination and rejection by U.S. society. During the late nineteenth century, México Lindo impressions began appearing in communities that experienced increased levels of immigration, such as in Tucson and San Antonio. However, such feelings waned within these communities when the Mexican Revolution as the major push factor and the economic growth related to World War I drove mass immigration northward to more economically dynamic regions such as Southern California and Chicago (Rosales 1999, 5–6). However, it must be noted that cultural and linguistic characteristics reinforced by extended familial relationships created significant intersection between older and more recent Mexican communities. For example, "the older Hispanics with weaker ties to the old country (Mexico) were in a significantly better position to help immigrants if they chose to do so" (ibid., 194). An example of the overlap between the two ideologies is the self-perception of the Mexican American educator and *político* George I. Sánchez. Throughout his life he claimed that he descended from seventeenth-century pioneers of New Mexico. This self-perception, which empowered his reformist agenda, emerged from his nostalgic projection about a past that did not stigmatize Mexicanos proudly speaking Spanish and constructing a new frontier way of life (Blanton 2014, 14). Throughout his career, Sánchez sought to advance the entire Mexican community's position, regardless of its member's nationality.

In the epilogue to his study of Spanish and Mexican Arizona, James Officer offers characteristics in the Tucson experience that are remarkably similar to the Lost Land concept delineated earlier. Intermarriage between Anglos and Mexicans was common and Anglo men who were parties to these marriages—both formal and common law—were often the community's social, economic, and political leaders. Mexican merchants prospered during the 1870s, sometimes in partnership with Anglos (Officer 1989, 5; Acuña 1988, 88–93). From 1890 to 1920 in Albuquerque, New Mexico, the intermarriage between Anglos and Mexicans remained steady at 6 to 11 percent, which was similar to other settings in the Southwest. Albuquerque's population changed from four times as many men as women in 1885, to a ratio of 3:2 in 1910, to near parity in 1920. Intermarriage between Anglo men and Hispanas outnumbered marriages between Anglo women and Hispanos. In 1890 ten Hispanas married Anglo men, while only two Hispanos married Anglo women. In 1920 fifteen marriages involved Hispanas and Anglo men, while eleven marriages between Hispanas and Anglo women occurred (Mitchell 2005, 8, 10–11).

Officer finishes by stating that the ability to acquire political power by Mexicans is an ultimate qualification for determining whether Mexican influence was significant.

But with the coming of the railroad came a new Anglo-European influx, and "the pattern of intermarriage in Tucson would change dramatically, and the partnerships involving Anglo and Mexican merchants and teamsters would come to an end" (Officer 1989, 311).

Like other historians, Officer believes that Lost Land identity traits present in southern Arizona did not extend to areas north of the Gila River. He tells us: "Phoenix, which was established under American rule, was always an Anglo stronghold. Of the major Arizona towns in existence by 1875, the Mexican lifestyle was most influential in Tucson, Florence, with Yuma a distant third" (ibid., 311). The contours of these assertions are correct but the assessment is too general and consequently overstated. With little substantiation, a popular myth has persisted that Mexicans are better off in Tucson than Phoenix (Luckingham 1988, 9).

Certainly the experience of Mexicans in the Salt River Valley has been one of subordination and segregation, but we suspect that a comparative study would bear out that this has been the case in Tucson as well. Thomas Sheridan's in-depth study of Tucson's Mexican community in the nineteenth and twentieth centuries demonstrates many aspects of the subordination of Tucson's Mexican community but does not draw comparisons to the Phoenix area (Sheridan 1986). The differences are only a matter of degree. Because so little research has been done on the history of Mexicans in the Valley, their more recent experience as agricultural workers during the early twentieth century is what stands out historically. This essay demonstrates that Phoenix-area Mexican communities in the late nineteenth century contained much of the criteria applied by Officer, which, according to him, made Tucson distinct. Unless this first period is properly understood, any attempt to produce a history of the immigrant generation (México Lindo), will run into major obstacles, and the myths will continue to cloud our perceptions and result in simplistic assessments. For an example of how rooted this belief is, see Alba (1988). Other historians have argued the opposite, but their research remains preliminary, unpublished, or in limited circulation (Dimas 1991, 1999; Marin 2005; Solliday 1993).

EARLY MEXICAN HISTORY NORTH OF THE GILA RIVER

Arizona was sparsely populated in both the Spanish (1513–1821) and Mexican (1821–1846) periods, and because of Apache domination most Mexicans were limited to the narrow Santa Cruz Valley or the adjoining Altar Valley in present-day Sonora.[6] Apache and Pima tribes along the Gila and Salt Rivers inhabited areas to the north. In the seventeenth century, Jesuits, who proselytized among Pima and Tohono O'odham natives south of the Gila River, called it Pimería Alta. Northern Pimería Alta was incorporated into the United States by the Gadsden Purchase in 1854. The inhabitants of the southern portion, who remained in the Mexican state of Sonora, continued to maintain economic, cultural, and family ties with former compatriots in southern Arizona. For an account of early Spanish settlement in southern Arizona, see Officer (1989).

A major difference between Hispanicization of areas south and north of the Gila is that after the 1850s an Anglo American, rather than a Spanish or Mexican colonization policy, unwittingly allowed migrating *sonorenses* (natives of the Mexican state of Sonora) to carry the cultural and economic frontier of Sonora into central Arizona. Federal militarization of Arizona diminished the Apache threat, and the ability to obtain land within the new political system was facilitated by the Homestead Act of 1862 and the Desert Land Act of 1877. By the 1860s, in spite of opposition by some Anglo civilians, but under the watchful eye of U.S. officials, sonorenses began developing a cultural underpinning, highlighted by such as an increase in the number of marriages in Phoenix, which fulfilled an ambition that had eluded and frustrated them for more than a generation (see table 1.1).

Some of these early Mexican pioneers migrated directly to El Salado, as they called the Phoenix area, from the Altar and the Santa Cruz Valleys. For example, in the 1860s a bloody civil conflict between Sonoran caudillos compelled some of the first emigrants to leave Sonora. Tucson and Tubac became the primary destinations, but poorer sonorenses could not make a living in those communities crowded with refugees. Fortuitously, by the 1860s opportunities in the Salt River Valley opened up with the building of Fort McDowell. This prospect prompted Tiburcio Sotelo and

Table 1.1 Origins of Mexican Immigrants Married at St. Mary's Catholic Church in Phoenix*

	1882-1890	1913-1920	1920-1926
Total	249	172	282
Sonora	94%	70	47
Sinaloa	2	5	14
Jalisco	2	—	10
Chihuahua	2	8	9
Zacatecas	—	11	1
Durango	—	6	6
Guanuajuato	—	—	5
Baja Calif.	—	—	3
Other	—	—	5

Source: St Mary's Church Marriage Records. Only those identified as Mexican-born were enumerated.
*Does not include Asians or Indians.

his sons to leave Tucson in 1871 for Tempe. Born in Tubac, where his father served as an officer during the Spanish and Mexican periods, Sotelo and his family moved to the Altar Valley in 1849 because of Apache raids. Political conditions in Sonora, however, prompted him to move again in 1867, and he took his family on a wagon train headed for Tubac. When they arrived they found the old presidio economically devastated and in the throes of a cholera epidemic, so they continued on to Tucson. The Sotelos's economic position in Tucson was precarious, however. A biographical interview of Tiburcio's daughter María tells us what happened next. "During that year 1871 Tempe began to be heard of with the digging of an irrigation canal which would open up much land. María's father and brothers went to learn about it and remained to assist in the work of this canal" (U.S. Bureau of the Census 1880b; Officer 1989, 305).

Tiburcio Sotelo filed for land through provisions of the Homestead Act in an area that became known as the Sotelo Addition once Tempe began to grow. His brother Pedro had already preceded him and obtained land near the Gila Indian Reservation, and later in Tempe. Other early Tempe residents who made their way up from Tucson and Tubac via the Santa Cruz River were the Bojórquez family, the Acedos, and the Romeros. Like Sotelo, they were former soldiers or farmers at the presidios in Tucson and Tubac. In 1873 Mexicans started their own town and called it San Pablo. Anglos lived in a separate part of present-day Tempe in a section called Hayden's Ferry. Many other Mexicans arrived during the 1880s, settling primarily near the throat of the Tempe Canal in a sonorense-type cluster of adobe homes rather than the isolated farmsteads of Anglo Americans. The area became the barrio known as *la cremería* (the creamery) by the early twentieth century (U.S. Bureau of the Census 1880b; Solliday 1993; *Arizona Citizen* 1873; Officer 1989, 332, 400 n61).

Since sonorenses initially reached the Salt River Valley in larger numbers than other ethnic groups, they put their preindustrial stamp on Valley economic and cultural modes. Anglos and Europeans not experienced with the Sonoran Desert's severe aridity adapted many Mexican methods of survival to their own needs. By the mid-1860s Anglos began establishing farms. Within the next ten years this would accelerate for two reasons. The demand for agricultural products grew due to the military and mining towns. By 1870, 240 inhabitants, including 115 Mexicans, had cultivated only 1,500 acres. "That same year, however, the federal government opened the Salt River Valley to homesteading, and in February 1871 Phoenix became the seat of Maricopa County, which encompassed the entire river basin" (Meeks 2007b, 33).

Other destinations in central Arizona besides El Salado were equally sought after by sonorenses. But by the late 1870s, the Salt River Valley began attracting settlers from previously more important communities such as Wickenburg. There were roughly four of these temporary areas: the Upper Gila Valley (Solomonsville), the Florence region, the Hassayampa Valley (Wickenburg), and the Lower Gila Valley

(Yuma), where the Gila and Colorado Rivers intersect. These regions also served Anglos and Europeans who traveled beside Mexicans, engaged in the same economic endeavors, and who often married Mexican women.

Sonorenses settled the first area, the Upper Gila Valley, in the late 1850s by following the San Pedro River from the Santa Cruz and the Sonoita Valleys. Like the settlers in the Tempe area, many were ex-soldiers, ranchers, and miners who decided to move northward after the Gadsden Purchase instead of retreating south of the border. Farmers and their families congregated in sonorense clusters. They emerged daily to gather mesquite wood for fuel, to tend cattle, and on adjacent plots to plant vegetables, corn, and chili for family subsistence. But wheat and barley were also grown for the emerging military and mining markets. Joining the sonorenses in the Upper Gila were a few Mexicans from New Mexico, Chihuahua, Durango, and Zacatecas. In fact, early non-Sonoran immigration from Mexico, albeit sparse, continued to follow this route for many years. Mormons arriving in the late 1870s pursued a more commercial form of agriculture, and many Mexicans became day laborers on Mormon farms while still maintaining a resilient link to their own land and preindustrial pursuits (Tetreau 1939, 294–336).

A westward migratory drift along the river reached the periphery of the Upper Pima Indian congregations in what is now Florence, and from there settlers could easily bridge the short desert space to the southern bank of the Salt River. Two farmers, Juan and Plácido Soza, had lived first in the Upper Gila Valley before settling in Tempe during the 1870s. In the Solomonsville area they farmed and worked with a freighter and merchant, W. H. Kirkland, an Anglo who also moved his operations to the Tempe area (Solliday 1894–1900; U.S. Bureau of the Census 1880b).

In the second staging area, near present-day Florence, homesteading by Mexicans and Anglo Europeans provoked Pima and Maricopa Indians to resist the invasion of their ancestral lands by sabotaging the crops of the newcomers (*Arizona Weekly Miner* 1871b). In 1869 preparations were made to expand the Gila Indian Reservation in order to defuse the hostility, and the federal government surveyed the homesteaders' properties so they could be compensated if their claims were valid. U.S. Army surveyors believed that 2,500 acres belonging to twenty farmers and speculators were affected; seventeen were Mexicans. In a gesture of marked sympathy for the Indians, many of the Mexicans were described in the report as interlopers whose bids were not legitimate because they were opportunistically claiming land for its compensation value. The surveyors, however, portrayed Anglos and Europeans as more deserving. Pedro Sotelo, Tiburcio's brother, and a former private at the Mexican presidio in Tucson during the 1850s, owned 160 acres on part of the proposed expansion. It is probable that because he lost this land during the enlargement of the reservation he and other Mexicans moved farther north to El Salado. In the 1870s and 1880s Sotelo filed for and received other land in the Tempe area (U.S. House of Representatives 1871, 1–17).

A third area of settlement emerged along what became a well-traveled stagecoach route from the Colorado River along the banks of the Gila River. The settlers in this region were probably headed for the gold fields northwest of Phoenix but were drawn by the opportunity of supplying miners and the stagecoach stations with foodstuffs along the irrigated riverbanks. Many of these were former forty-niners from Sonora, from other parts of the United States, and from Europe, who abandoned California after spending a number of years in that state. They were joined by *californios* (Mexicans native to California) who left their homeland because of a severe drought and a subsequent economic crisis that devastated the Southern California economy in the 1860s. In the 1850s José Eligio Amabisca, a returned sonorense from California, homesteaded in Agua Caliente (Hot Spring—near present-day Buckeye) next to the hot springs that gave the area its name. His brother Felipe, upon returning from California, remained in Arizona City (Yuma), and established a mercantile store. His partner, Antonio Contreras, on the other hand, eventually moved to Phoenix (*Arizona Citizen* 1873; *El Observador* 1897b; Jose Eligio n.d., 78; Acuña 1988, 91).

Just two years after José Eligio settled in Agua Caliente, King S. Woolsey became his neighbor. Woolsey, an Alabama native and an adventurer, had spent time in a Cuban jail before venturing out to California's gold mines as a freighter. That business brought him to Yuma, where he hauled supplies for the army in the 1850s. Anglos like Woolsey, while usually in positions of power, depended heavily on Mexicans and their skills in farming, mining, handling livestock, and irrigation. His Mexican workers raised large crops of barley and vegetables to supply freighting, stagecoach stations, and mines along the Gila (*Arizona Citizen* 1873).

A fourth staging area for entry into the Valley was the mining region northwest of Phoenix (Hassayampa Valley). Sonorenses arrived first and were the majority of miners for a number of years until mining declined in the 1870s (see table 1.2). According to one source:

> The Black Canyon mines (30 miles north of Phoenix) were first discovered in 1864 by Mexicans, who were working placers in Turkey Creek, on which Black Canyon is situated, and they at once built arrastres and worked the mine for two years during which they extracted . . . over $35,000 in gold. (Peralta 1870; U.S. Bureau of the Census 1870)

But when Anglo and other competitors came in, considerable violence ensued, and many Mexican miners were probably driven from the diggings, as had taken place during the California gold rush. A significant amount of interethnic cooperation existed, however. Non-Mexicans depended on Mexican freighters, merchants, and

Table 1.2 Occupations in Maricopa County

	1870		1880		1900	
	Mexican	White	Mexican	White	Mexican	White
Laborer	49	4	430	330	880	740
Service	14	9	90	80	40	390
Agri Equipment	0	0	20	90	0	20
Mining	56	54	30	130	10	220
Artisan	0	0	40	50	30	350
Farmer	79	61	70	240	30	1,180
Mechanical	0	3	20	60	10	240
Transportation	0	0	10	50	20	180
White Collar	0	0	0	40	0	470
Building Trades	0	4	0	40	50	330
Merchant	0	5	30	50	10	520
Hotel & Saloons	0	0	0	60	10	130
Professional	0	0	0	90	0	450
Total	198	140	740	1,310	1,090	5,220

Source: 1870, 1880, 1900 U.S. Bureau of the Census schedules; 1880 and 1900 computed from 10 percent sample.

craftsmen who arrived early enough to establish businesses. Most of the settlers in this area were a backwash from the gold and silver rushes in California and Nevada. They entered the mines first from the Colorado River town of Ehrenberg, which served as a destination of steamship traffic bringing in passengers and supplies and shipping out gold. Since the boats sailed out on the Sonoran Coast around the Baja Peninsula to San Francisco, many Mexicans, who had never been in California, came directly from ports in Guaymas and La Paz. A multiethnic collection of at least two thousand men made the mining communities east of the Colorado River their home within a few short years. The few women and children living in the mining communities were mainly Mexican. At the same time settlers, who found that the Valley's mainstay of farming was just as lucrative as mining, filled up the Salt River Valley. Moreover, the mining regions provided Phoenix agriculturists alternative markets, apart from military and Indian installations (*Arizona Weekly Miner* 1872b, September 1872c; *Arizona Sentinel* 1874a; Pamphlet n.d.).

A national depression affecting Arizona in the early 1870s caused a decline in both mining and agriculture and simultaneous cuts in military spending. Once again sonorenses, californios, Anglos, and Europeans pulled up stakes from various central Arizona communities. But a few enterprising merchants and farmers remained in the

Salt River Valley. Some came from the nearby failing settlements, riding out the crisis until it subsided after 1876. They then profited from a renewed demand for goods in mining centers, reinstated under more modern conditions, and the growing needs of Fort McDowell and the Indian reservations. They raised cotton, grapes, tobacco, figs, oranges, lemons, sugarcane, sweet potatoes, wheat, barley, and hay. Many young fruit trees and grape cuttings were brought in from California or Sonora by Anglo and Mexican farmers (*Arizona Weekly Miner* 1871a, 1871b; *Arizona Citizen* 1873).

Other farmers and merchants from outside the Valley, both Mexicans and non-Mexicans, were quick to see similar opportunities. Frederick and David Balsz, two brothers whose fortunes were intimately intertwined with those of Mexicans, came to Phoenix with the new arrivals and became cattle dealers. Born in Germany, they grew up in St. Louis and, as youths, migrated to California in the 1850s. In 1865 David established a cattle and butchering business in Yuma with his former employer, Jose María Redondo, a sonorense who had also been in California. The business folded during the depression, but in 1875 the Balszes came to Phoenix, where they received lucrative contracts to supply the military and Indian installations. Even though David Balsz broke with Redondo when he left Yuma, he maintained Mexican ties. Married to one of Redondo's daughters, he often traveled to Sonora, where he personally bought most of his cattle. (Balsz n.d.; *Arizona Gazette* 1882; *Phoenix Herald* 1882d).

Similarly, Miguel L. Peralta, a successful miner and merchant in Wickenburg and the town's first postmaster in 1878, transferred his merchandise to Phoenix in 1880 and established a general store. It is not clear whether he abandoned Wickenburg because of the faltering economy, but when he arrived in the Valley, the *Phoenix Herald* welcomed him with the plaudits "Work was commenced last Monday morning on . . . M. L. Peralta's new building. . . . It will cost . . . $6,000 and be one of the handsomest buildings in our midst." Unfortunately, Peralta seems to have been a compulsive gambler. He eventually sold out and moved to Nogales, where he lost all his holdings in a gambling spree and ended up committing suicide (Peralta 1870).

By the 1870s the majority of Mexicans attracted to the Salt River Valley migrated directly from south of the border, bypassing the areas of temporary residence. Political violence and Indian raids pushed them out. U.S. military campaigns to subdue Apaches in Arizona during the 1860s and 1870s drove them south across the border, where they made life difficult for sonorenses. In addition, a civil war ravaging Mexico after Porfirio Díaz's violent rise to power extended into Sonora, creating unwelcome conscription and political instability (Acuña 1988, 86–87; *Arizona Weekly Miner* 1875). Many sonorenses left via steamship either to Yuma or California, while others chose the Salt River Valley, where many compatriots had preceded them. Jacobo González came to Tempe in 1875 after Apache raids made it impossible to pursue farming and ranching around San Miguel Horcasitas, a town in central Sonora. He left Guaymas, bringing with him a number of peach tree seedlings, and established orchards in the Valley. His widowed daughter, whose husband had been killed by Apaches, married an Anglo sugarcane farmer, William Osborne. Osborne boiled sugarcane squeezings into panocha (brown sugar cakes) and in cooperation with González, marketed peaches preserved with syrup made from the raw sugar (Clayton n.d.).

THE ROLE OF THE MEXICAN WORKING CLASS

Unlike the Sotelos, Jacobo González and Miguel Peralta, who came with an explicit desire to engage in capitalistic ventures such as farming, mining or trade, a larger number of sonorenses streamed into Arizona in the 1870s and 1880s as laborers. Post-Depression development in Arizona required larger numbers of workers in agriculture, digging canals, and laying railroad track. Economic development during the 1876–1911 dictatorship of Porfirio Díaz (Porfiriato) created dislocations among Sonoran farmers, as haciendas encroached on their land. Many became day laborers or *gambusinos* (scavenger miners), either in Sonora or in Arizona. Even if they had not been usurped of their lands, many Sonoran peasants opted for mining or working for someone else because they could not survive on earnings from their meager farms. Joining these Mexican laborers were a sizable group of Chinese workers recruited in California (Heyman 1991, 48–49; Tinker Salas 1992).

In the Salt River Valley itself Mexican workers, skilled and unskilled, filled the needs of various labor sectors. For example, sonorenses who possessed an intimate knowledge of irrigation methods, alongside local Indians who had a similar experience, dug most of the main trunk canals and also became contractors in charge of the projects. In Tempe the San Francisco Canal, one of the most crucial on the south side of the river, was dug up by Pedro Sotelo and other Mexican farmers who homesteaded the land opened up by irrigation. Larger water projects were left to non-Mexican entrepreneurs with more capital, but the bulk of the labor force remained Mexican. In 1870 a group of developers led by W. B. Hardy initiated the Hardy Irrigating Canal Company. They hired nine labor contractors to carve out the channel, which became the foundation of Tempe farming and commerce. Three of those contractors—Ines Jotires, Mariano Carrión, and Acimiro Candelaria—were Mexicans, as were their crews. The developers, however, had to contend with the earlier presence of Mexicans. When the ditch was completed, Miguel López won a lawsuit over property infringement, which forced all of the stockholders to decide whether to pay the plaintiff López, or to appeal the case to a higher court (Solliday Personal Files n.d.; Solliday Files 1894–1900).

On the north side of the river, other early canals were cut out by Mexicans in the late 1860s. A Pima, Juan Chavarí, was in charge of constructing a canal that bore his name on the north side of the river near Phoenix founder Jack Swilling's larger irrigation system. Its worth was estimated at $10,000, and the canal could irrigate up to 1,300 acres of farmland. Other canals, known simply as the Mexican ditches, combined with those of Swilling's and other Anglos to irrigate another 7,000 acres. During this initial building era, Antonio Contreras, Amabisca's partner in Arizona City during the 1850s, constructed the Contreras ditch in league with four Mexican partners, north of the river (*Arizona Weekly Miner* 1872a, 1872f; *Arizona Sentinel* 1883).

Canals led to further economic expansion, which in turn stimulated a labor market demand that could only be met with Mexican immigrants. In Tempe, during this expansion period, Mexicans were involved from beginning to end, in the planting and picking of crops such as hay, and various vegetables along the length of the Salt River (Lamb 1870–1930). When Charles T. Hayden started his ferrying service across the Salt River in the 1870s, Mexicans and Indians built his rafts from "great logs from the cotton woods that lined river bank. The dry, rough bark was shaved off and the logs fitted closely together in an awkward-appearing but substantial raft" (*Phoenix Gazette* 1941). Dependence on Mexican labor is patent in the following statement made by an Anglo farmer in the 1880s. "The Mexican population did much of the hard work. On account of their large numbers and constant intercourse, our people learn to speak Spanish as well as Indian" (Solliday Files 1894–1900).

Along with other sonorense laborers came Yaqui Indians (their own societal identification being Yoéme or Yoéme Noki). This group, more than any other, suffered depredations in Sonora during the Porfiriato and thousands fled seeking asylum north of the border in Arizona. According to Theodore Ramos, a Yaqui who arrived in the Valley in 1882, about thirty of his compatriots already lived there working on various farms and ranches with other Mexicans. Later, a few families settled one mile north of the present-day village of Guadalupe, south of the Salt River, in a place known as the Cemetery. Yaquis established another village between Phoenix and Scottsdale along the Arizona Canal on the old Phoenix-Scottsdale highway (Yaqui Indians n.d.).

Labor demands during the initial railroad construction in the 1880s surpassed the need during the initial years of development, however. Thousands of Mexicans worked alongside hundreds of Chinese on the Southern Pacific Railroad, which crossed southern Arizona through Tucson from California in late 1870s. When the route was finished in 1879 to Casa Grande, over one thousand newly unemployed Mexicans and Chinese railroad workers migrated to the Phoenix area. They worked in the growing agricultural economy, and on the Maricopa and Phoenix Railroad that eventually connected the Valley to the town of Maricopa, thirty miles south of Phoenix. In Phoenix most of these workers congregated south of Washington Street near the round house on Fourth Avenue, an area that by the 1920s was the most densely populated barrio in the Salt River Valley. This new influx of workers included many Mexicans from outside of Sonora. Now workers could enter the United States at El Paso and, via the faster mode of railroad travel that reached all the way to Mexico City, spanned distances that had taken weeks by wagon in just a few days (*Arizona Sentinel* 1874b, 1878, 1880; Luckingham 1988, 29–30).

With the exception of railroad construction, the work of nineteenth-century Mexican laborers, however, was not as labor-intensive or deskilling as it was in twentieth-century commercial agriculture. As a consequence, the "laborer" category to which Mexicans were relegated is misleading. For example, in the 1870 census schedule, only three persons in Maricopa County are identified as working in the building trades, and none were Mexican. Yet this was a time when Mexicans practically constructed all buildings, from start to finish, out of adobe. Charles T. Hayden, father of future U.S. senator Carl T. Hayden, who first arrived in Tempe in 1872, remembered it as a congregation of adobe homes. Similar descriptions are given about Phoenix buildings during this time as well. Besides adobe making, another underestimated craft, prevalent among Mexicans in Phoenix, was woodcutting. This occupation was extremely important since slow-burning mesquite during this era was a crucial source of fuel (Solliday Files 1894–1900; Luckingham 1988, 21–22). A harbinger of the future role of Mexican workers is their exclusion from the operation of farm machinery when equipment such as threshers, reapers, and headers were first brought into the Valley in the 1870s. Consequently, the only form of employment that was most often open to them fell within the "laborer" category (see table 1.2).

The story of Pedro Pérez is a good case study of an immigrant who came to the Valley to work as a day laborer, not to homestead. He entered the Salt River Valley on three different occasions from his native Pitiquito in Sonora's Altar Valley. He was but a boy in 1870 when his parents brought him by wagon and worked as farm laborer for a year. They returned to Pitiquito, but in 1875 Pedro, now aged fifteen, returned, bypassing the Valley because he heard of the El Vocho (Vulture) gold diggings near Wickenburg. In his own words: "and there I made a living lots of money, for a year and four months, and then I decided to go back to my folks at Pitiquito and in 1877 . . . we all left Pitiquito never to return. . . . we established ourselves in El SALADO . . . on a ranch at that time owned by a Mr. Henshaw . . ." (Pedro Pérez 1938). Pérez, over the period of his working life, was a farmer, a teamster, and, finally, a street maintenance worker for the city of Phoenix before he retired in the 1920s.

ANTIPATHY TOWARD MEXICANS

The interethnic cooperation described earlier existed within a framework of hostility, competition, and tension between Anglos and Mexicans. Many non-Mexicans, perhaps a majority, resented having to depend on Mexicans or felt that they should not have to compete with them as farmers and miners. Racism was evident from the very beginning, but it was particularly acute during the depression of the 1870s, which stalled central Arizona's economy. Additionally, there was a fivefold increase in the Salt River Valley's population during the decade, and many of the newcomers did not share the more benign view of Mexicans held by the earlier Anglos and European settlers. Arizona newspapers are replete with stories of this warfare, which was interpreted as simple banditry by Mexicans from Sonora. In 1872 one newspaper writer declared "the Indian is now a nuisance and the Sonoran a decided annoyance, but both of these are sure to disappear before civilization as sure as the noonday sun" (*Arizona Weekly Miner* 1872e).

Vigilante committees sprang up throughout Arizona. One of their main objectives was to deal with Mexican banditry, and in the 1870s a number of Mexicans were lynched throughout Arizona. The persistence of outlaw raids regardless of their nationality reinforced Anglo prejudices against the Mexican people's innate lawlessness. Widespread rumors accused Mexicans of secretly conspiring with insurrectionists across the border, which prompted Anglos to threaten Mexicans to check such criminality or risked brutal reprisals. The *Arizona Weekly Miner* exclaimed in September 1873: "Cut throats from Mexico have commenced another bloody crusade against American citizens, and we call upon our Government to take measures that will, forever, put a stop to the diabolical crimes of the half-civilized, semi-devils of the accursed land of Montezuma" (Carrigan and Webb 2003, 423). From 1848 to 1928, such hostile attitudes undoubtedly contributed to the lynching of 579 Mexicans by mobs within the Southwest (ibid., 413).[7]

At a mass meeting in Phoenix on April 19, 1872, citizens organized for protection against Sonorans and elected County Sheriff T. C. Warden as captain of the Safety Committee. All suspicious Mexicans deemed not to have legitimate business in the Valley were to be run out of town (Luckingham 1988, 19–20). While on the surface it seemed that a distinction was made between "good" and "bad" Mexicans, according to Pedro Pérez the vigilantes were indiscriminate in deciding which ones were unwelcome strangers.

> From 1875 to 1880 a lot of people were hanged for small steals [*sic*] of any kind and a lot of them were framed in horse stealing, cattle . . . When this was happening most of the early Mexican families besides ours, that were residing here left town and for awhile [*sic*] it looked like the future of the town was done for, but after quite a while the people began to come back. (Pérez 1938)

The proportionate decline in the ratio of Mexican miners and farmers to non-Mexicans between 1870 and 1880 as well as a decline in real numbers confirms this exodus, suggesting that Mexicans could have been run out because of competition (see table 1.2). Paradoxically, while the word *Mexican* or *Sonoran* became synonymous with outsiders and criminality, Mexican merchants, artisans, and necessary laborers were tolerated or disassociated from the negative images projected by real and imagined Sonoran bandits. At times, in fact, alliances were made between Mexicans and non-Mexicans in order to deal with outlaws whether they were Mexicans, Anglos, or Indians. Tempe's first constable, for example, was J. Andrade. In 1872 town residents selected him informally since the community was not yet incorporated (*Arizona Weekly Miner* 1872). Similarly, in Phoenix, Enrique Garfias, a member of a prominent californio family, became the first elected marshal and, more than once, he campaigned against what was considered Mexican banditry. In Agua Caliente members of the Amabisca family served "as captains for King Woolsey . . . who pursued outlaws and Indians on both sides of the international boundary" (Eligio n.d.).

Even though law-abiding Mexicans supported Anglos in condemning criminality, they protested and acted out against extreme application of frontier justice. In 1879 Jesús Romero, incarcerated for driving his horse into a crowd during a race and wounding several people with a saber, was shot while trying to escape. Many in the Mexican community saw this killing as orchestrated and objected. The following week, when Phoenix Anglos were busy lynching two Anglo drifters for unrelated murders, they threatened to hang two of the Mexicans that were protesting the previous week's jailhouse killing of Romero. "They were . . . two Mexican merchants who had for several days been preaching a crusade against the 'Gringo'" (Widman n.d.).

As can be expected, versions as to why Mexicans were lynched vary according to factors such as each ethnic group's point of view, local politics, interethnic relations, etc. For example, in 1873 Mariano Tisnado was lynched after he stole an Anglo widow's cow, but he was also suspected of murdering an Anglo farmer. Yet the Mexican version of this incident is that Tisnado, a young rancher of considerable wealth, took a cow from a Texas family while he was on a drinking spree and was, at the same time, paying too much attention to a girl in the same family (Pérez 1938; Paredes 1992).

MARRIAGE AND FAMILY

During early settlement in Phoenix and Tempe, Mexican economic cooperation with Anglos and Europeans continued to be bolstered by intermarriage. Then, as table 1.4 demonstrates, this mixing tapers off in the 1890s. Most of these liaisons were legally consummated, but others were common law. In 1896 a newly arrived Franciscan priest complained: "The number of practicing Catholics is very low, among both the English speaking and the Mexicans. The Parish has more than forty mixed marriages between Mexican and English speaking. Many of them are not married at all or live in civil marriages only" (Corley 1992, 21).[8] Regardless of the legal or religious status of the

Table 1.3 Marriages between Mexican-Origin* and Non-Mexican Persons Married at St. Mary's Catholic Church in Phoenix, 1882–1926

Origin of Non-Mexican Spouse	1882–1899	1910–1919	1920–1926
United States	9	18	3
Italy	8	7	1
Ireland	1	1	0
Scotland	1	0	0
Spain	1	3	1
England	2	0	0
France	1	0	0
Canada	0	1	0
Lebanon-Syria	0	2	1
Philippines	0	1	0
Greece	0	1	0
India	0	1	1
Portugal	0	1	0
Afghanistan	0	0	1
Japan	0	0	1
Total	23	36	9

*Does not include Asians or Indians.

Table 1.4 Percentage of Mixed Marriages to Total Number of Marriages at St. Mary's Catholic Church in Phoenix 1882–1926

	1882–1899	1910–1919	1920–1926
Total Number of Marriages	464	937	525
Percentage of Mexican Mixed Marriages to Total Marriages	4.7	3.8	1.5

marriages, the vast majority produced children who came to be known as mestizos, a term that in Mexico and the rest of Spanish America was applied to the offspring of Indian and European couples.

Symbolic of this early mingling is that Trinidad Escalante married the developer Jack Swilling in 1867. Some accounts consider her to have been the first woman from Mexico in the Valley when she arrived that year. She was probably also the first to marry a non-Mexican. By 1880 her husband died ignominiously in the Yuma prison,

Table 1.5 Age and Marital Status of Economically Active Population 1880 Maricopa County, 10 Percent Sample

Average Age		Percent Married		With Total Family in Arizona	
Mexican	Other	Mexican	Other	Mexican	Other
34	35	59	33	74	131

Source: 1880 Census schedule.

where he was incarcerated for robbing a stagecoach (U.S. Bureau of the Census 1880a; Widman n.d., 40–41). In Tempe, Winchester Miller, an Ohio native, married María Sotelo in 1873; María was the daughter of Tiburcio Sotelo, the Tempe pioneer discussed earlier. Miller was a freighter who came to the Valley in 1871 after working in California. Selected as superintendent of the Tempe Canal system on which the Sotelos were dependent, he was in a position to woo the attractive teenage María even though he was thirty-seven at the time. According to María, all her suitors were Anglos (U.S. Bureau of the Census 1880b).

A similar case involves Juanita González, granddaughter of the Tempe pioneer Jacobo González. In 1882 she married William Fellows, "a man much older than herself," when she was only seventeen. Juanita's mother, Eulalia, who was widowed in Sonora, moved with her father to Tempe in 1871, and herself married an Anglo farmer named William Osborne, who had previously married two Mexican women. Juanita was taken to Vulture by her husband, but she returned to the Valley, and in 1900 she was a widow with six children (Clayton n.d.).

An interesting case, perhaps not an uncommon one, is the arrangement between King Woolsey and a Yaqui woman named Lucía Martínez. Woolsey, who died in Phoenix in 1879, was one of Arizona's most powerful citizens. He made his fortune by controlling significant amounts of water that he sold for irrigation and was elected multiple times to the state legislature (*Los Angeles Times* 1903). In 1864 Woolsey and his Anglo common-law wife, Mary, adopted a ten-year-old Yaqui girl, Lucía Martinez, after he rescued her while she was fleeing from Gila Apache slavers. He had found the girl while tracking Gila Apaches who local ranchers had accused of cattle rustling (Adams and DeLuzio 2010, 255; Wyllys 1950, 154).

Some years later, Woolsey set her up as his concubine in an adobe house next door to his family home. Lucía had two daughters by him, Clara and Johanna (Swenson 1988: 6–10; St. Mary's Church 1882–1926). This example demonstrates the complexity of borderland culture and family men, rendering nonwhite sexual assault victims silent if their attackers were white.

The same year, the state senate, of which Woolsey was a member, passed the Howell Code, "a five-hundred-page legal code addressing the civil and criminal conduct of all men and women, minors and adults, citizens and subjects." It "codified racial and gender hierarchies that were widely contested throughout the ethnically diverse and demographically imbalanced territory" allowing Woolsey and other white men to control "the body and labor" of their nonwhite concubines. As in many other western and southern states, the fixed age of sexual consent for all females was ten years but set girls' marriageable age at sixteen. And worse, females had to prove sexual assault through evidence of physical injury, could not deny sex to their husbands, and could be imprisoned for five years if they aborted their pregnancy. Specifically, during the 1864–1871 period, which Lucía spent under Woolsey's reign, she had no hope of protection from their courts because nonwhite Arizonans could not testify in criminal cases against whites (Adams and DeLuzio 2012, 257–58). Despite Woolsey's bondage-like control over Lucía, he financially supported his illegitimate children. He could not legally leave them an inheritance, but because he had indentured them as laborers, they were eligible for $1,000 from his estate (ibid., 255).

The Balszes brothers' marital history is the most intricate example of the intermarriage pattern that emerged in the Valley. As indicated earlier, in 1875 David married Luz, the daughter of José María Redondo, his partner in the Yuma business. He was associated with this family in California before both the Redondos and David moved to Yuma. Frederick was married to a Chilean in California but in Phoenix he married a Mexican, Soledad Bracamonte. Both brothers were much older than their brides. Frederick, for example, was fifty-two, and his wife seventeen. In 1880, when they first married, the couple lived in the same household with Frederick's teenaged children from the previous marriage and Soledad's father and older brother. The Yuma-California-Phoenix linkage is also demonstrated by other marriage patterns. Henry Garfias, the Phoenix lawman, who came from California via Yuma and Wickenburg married Delores Redondo, the sister of David Balsz's wife, Luz (Adams and DeLuzio 2012, 255; *Phoenix Herald* 1882a; Balsz 1939; Phoenix City Directories, 1895, 1905–06, 1918, 1928; U.S. Bureau of the Census 1880a).

Early Italian pioneers tended to take Mexican women as wives more than any other group, probably because of ethnic affinity. Stefano Daneri, a saloonkeeper in his early twenties who came to Phoenix in the 1870s, married Juana Domínguez in 1888, and was a member of the first lodge of the Alianza Hispano Americana in Phoenix. Similarly, Joseph Righetti, who was born in Switzerland of Italian ancestry, came to Phoenix in the 1870s, started a general merchandise store, and married Gertrudes Baldonado (Phoenix City Directory 1895; St. Mary's Church 1882–1926; *El Ocasional* 1898e; U.S. Bureau of the Census 1880a).

The main reason for intermarriage was the scarcity of non-Mexican women. Fifty-nine percent of the employed Mexican adults in 1880 were married, in contrast to only 33 percent of non-Mexicans (see table 1.3). In 1870 Mexican women dramatically outnumbered white women, and while the number of white females increased in the ensuing decade, a large number of those were Mormons, who lived in relative isolation from the mainstream population and were not available as partners to non-Mormons. According to one claim, the first white woman (i.e., non-Mexican) was Mrs. C. H. Gray, and it was not until 1870 that another woman who was considered white arrived (before the Mormon influx) (*Phoenix Herald* 1882a).

There is a strong possibility that Mexican women preferred non-Mexicans as marriage partners. James Officer indicates that in Tucson, Mexicans seemed to defer to Anglo Americans, especially when it came to selection of the few available women. He cites a letter written by an Anglo to his sister in the east indicating that "'native women' have a great fancy for Americans and a greaser stands no chance with a white man" (Officer 1989, 310). This could have been wishful thinking on the writer's part, but the fact that many of these young girls married non-Mexicans who were much older than themselves suggests that social mobility was a factor in marital decisions. In the Phoenix area, while most of the men who married Mexicans were not prominent men, they certainly held positions to which most Mexicans could not aspire.

Although the orthodox claim about Mexican women's preferences based on class has some merit, recent scholarship has created a more complex picture. Antonia I. Castañeda argues that influential scholars, such as Herbert Eugene Bolton, uncritically reinforced the notion made by European males of the period that Mexican women preferred them over Mexican males. (Castañeda 1990, 8–20). Census records for central Arizona indicate that many Mexican women cohabitated with a higher percentage of Mexican males despite living alongside a large Anglo community with very few women. In the Prescott mining camps, 19 or 61 percent of the Mexican women lived with Mexican companions, which included two marriages. Accordingly, "For Mexican women informal union existed as a cultural category in a way that it did not for Anglo women" (Johnson 1984, 37).

Considering the number of mixed liaisons, there were probably close to five hundred mestizo children growing up in the Valley during the second half of the nineteenth century. For example, by 1880 Trinidad Swilling, symbolic as she is of the women who married non-Mexicans, was a widow fending for herself, possibly as a housekeeper, with her four children, aged two to fifteen. Her youngest son, John, married a non-Mexican in 1902, Harriet Amantha De Vilbiss. Winchester and María Sotelo-Miller of Tempe had six children. They attended school at 8th Street and Mill Avenue in the 1880s, long before that building became the Mexican school. One of the daughters of this union became a teacher in the same school. Frederick Balsz's two marriages produced the largest progeny of mestizo children living under one house. Balsz sired sixteen children between his first wife in California and Soledad Bracamonte.

Table 1.6 History of Balsz Marriages at St. Mary's Church in Phoenix

Males		
Date	Groom	Bride
01/26/1891	Nicolás Balsz	Carmela Bracamonte
06/25/1892	Alejandro Balsz	Antonia Moreno
05/17/1894	José M. Balsz	Carmela M. Duarte
03/05/1896	Nicólas Balsz	Cruz Chretín
03/16/1901	Bartholomew Balsz	Belén (María) Vindiola

Females		
Date	Bride	Groom
04/06/1896	María Piedad Balsz	John Baggiore
02/13/1899	Luz Balsz	Manuel Zepeda

The offspring of mixed marriages sometimes arrived from elsewhere and joined the middle-class Mexican group already tied by marriage or business to Anglos and Europeans. Samuel Brown, for instance, whose father was from Maine, had a Mexican-born mother, and was born in California. He and his adolescent brother, Alfred, came to Tempe in the 1870s, and there Samuel married Bertha González. What is significant about Brown, who was a blacksmith upon arriving in the Valley, is that he became a large property owner, a member of the Tempe City Council, and in the 1920s was elected president of the nationwide Alianza Hispano Americana when he was sixty-seven years old. Similarly, Ricardo Painter, who came to Phoenix during the 1870s from his native California as a *fayuquero* (peddler), had an English father and Mexican mother. In 1885 he married Gregoria Contreras from Hermosillo, and went to work in Vulture (U.S. Census Bureau 1880a; St. Mary's Church n.d.).

It was rare through the late nineteenth century for a mestizo male to marry a non-Mexican, which either demonstrates identification with their Hispanic heritage or discrimination on the part of Anglo women against mestizos. Judging by the parish records at St. Mary's Church, Frederick Balsz's numerous male offspring married Mexican females, while one of his daughters took an Italian as a spouse and the other a Mexican (see table 1.6). Mestizos grew up with "full-blooded" Mexican children, were exposed to Spanish-language institutions such as the church, and were raised by Mexican mothers. As a consequence, they became Mexican in culture and identity and were bilingual. Moreover, mixed-race couples tended to live in close proximity with other mixed-race couples and middle-class Mexican families (Phoenix City Directory 1914, 1930; Maricopa County 1876, 1894).

That mestizos identified with their Mexican heritage is manifested by their sustained participation in the Hispanic community's political and cultural life. José, for example, the son of Frederick Balsz, was involved with Mexican Americans in starting Democratic Party organizations to deliver the Mexican vote. Juanita González Fellows' son, William J. Fellows, ran for Maricopa County Attorney in the 1930s and was a member of the Latin American Club. Albert, the son of María González and Winchester Miller, was offered by the Democratic Party as a Mexican American candidate for county office in 1898 on the same ticket as José Balsz. Mestizos were held accountable for adherence to Hispanic identity by nonmestizos, however. When Democrats ran Balsz and Miller as Mexicans, Pedro B. de Salazar, Republican publisher of *El Observador Mexicano*, approved of Balsz's claim to being Hispanic, even though he was part Chilean, not half-Mexican, but denounced Miller, asserting "that *mesclán* (half-breed) has never ever been seen among Mexicans" [author's translation] (*El Observador Mexicano* 1898b).

POLITICAL PARTICIPATION OF MEXICANS

In 1912 Samuel Bryan, a Stanford University professor, wrote an article in the *Survey* designed to alert Americans to the perils of Mexican immigration. After reeling off a litany of undesirable traits, he berated them for lack of political involvement. "In some cases, however," he continued, "they have been organized to serve the purpose of political bosses, as for example in Phoenix, Arizona." That this accusation was leveled at Phoenician Mexican Americans is an indication that their block vote was one to be reckoned with, even at a time when their political power was considerably diminished. They were much more active in the nineteenth century. In 1876 over 20 percent of the registered voters were Mexican and the importance of their role was evident even earlier (see table 1.7). In the controversial election of 1871, held to decide where the county seat would be located, all sides vied for the Mexican vote. Jack Swilling, who wanted the seat located next to his properties heard that his opponents "were bribing and intimidating Mexicans and using Papago Indians (Tohono O'odham) posing as Mexicans to vote . . . retaliated by acting in a similar fashion" (Luckingham 1988, 19–20). Another version has a Mexican leader betraying Swilling, forcing his faction to lose the election. According to this source, Swilling was so enraged that he sought out the Mexican and shot him (Widman n.d.).

Mexican voters, however, had more to gain in these early elections than a bribe or the insurance that they would not be bullied by Anglos. Considering the heavy investment that Mexican farmers, merchants, and even workers had in the canal systems, local government, and justice issues, they voted to protect or promote their interests as

Table 1.7 Voters in Maricopa County, 1876 and 1894

Year Registered	Total Voters	Total Mexican Voters	Regional Origins of Mexican Voters in Percent: Arizona	Mexico	New Mexico	California
1876	2,112	398	25	69	2	3
1894	4,973	276	32	45	7	16

Source: Maricopa County Great Registrar of Voters, 1876 and 1894 Arizona state archives.

property owners and citizens. Take, for example, the case of Henry Garfias, the highest elected Mexican American official in any town in the Valley during the nineteenth century. He came to Phoenix from California in 1875 and operated a freighting business, then in 1881 was elected town marshal of Phoenix. After serving his full term as marshal he went on to a number of other city offices: constable, town assessor and tax collector, and street superintendent. In these positions he was able to provide patronage and protection for his constituents. He also published *El Progreso*, a newspaper in Spanish, which helped him garner the Mexican vote (*El Latino Americano* 1934, 8).

Old-timer Pedro Pérez proudly recounted a story of how Garfias subdued seven Texas cowboys who were shooting up the town, but he most appreciated the former marshal because "he used to help everybody in solving their everyday problems. I, myself for one appreciate the fact that he helped me . . . get my citizenship . . . now as an Old Timer [*sic*] I am getting the benefit of that affair" (Pérez 1938). During a fight in 1898, Pérez killed a man who would not marry his daughter after she became pregnant. Democratic Party activist Jesús Meléndrez, editor of *El Ocasional*, campaigned to get him as light a sentence as possible and to pay Pérez's bail. Pérez spent his last years working as a city street employee, a job he probably obtained because of his political affiliation (*El Ocasional* 1898g).

Tempe Mexicans were able to get similar concessions because they were a force at the ballot box. Joe Encinas, a Mexican Democratic Party activist in Tempe, registered 138 voters in 1895, the year after the city was incorporated. The effort paid off because in 1898 Samuel Brown was elected to the city council with one of the biggest margins received by any of the candidates. The city council, indebted to the Mexican vote, appointed G. G. González as constable who, in turn, hired Marcos Pacho as his deputy. Both González's and Pacho's fathers were early pioneer farmers in Tempe (*Tempe News* 1895, 1897; Solliday Files 1894–1900).

Mexican Americans were not monolithically under the umbrella of one party, however. Pedro Bonillas y Salazar, for example, editor of *El Observador* in Phoenix, was a promoter of the Republican Party in the 1890s, and in 1898 he ran for office public on that party's ticket. The same year in Tempe, a young Republican Club for Mexicans was formed to support Brown's successful candidacy for city council. The majority of Mexicans were Democrats, however, and very much influenced by the populist ideology of the era. During April, a pro-silver club was formed in Tempe by Mexican farmers and small merchants who were aware that a national inflationist policy would be to their benefit. Through his newspaper, Bonillas y Salazar charged that Democrats took Mexicans for granted while Republicans were really serious about including Mexican candidates such as himself on the ticket, unlike Democrats, who tried to pass off Albert Miller as a Mexican (*El Observador Mexicano* 1898a, 1898c). The Democratic newspaper *El Ocasional*, edited by Meléndrez, countered by affirming the ethnic credentials of Balsz and Miller, both candidates on the ticket, and expressing the pro-silver ideal. Mexican Democrats, however, found an issue that was even closer to the hearts of Mexicans in that election year. In 1898 the federal government made cutting mesquite trees without a proper license a crime because the wood was classified as lumber. Mesquite gathering was a crucial economic endeavor for hundreds of Valley Mexicans, and *El Ocasional* immediately blamed Republicans for the ban. Meléndrez warned Mexicans to stay away from the opposition because they are trying to take away "*el pan de cada día*" (our daily bread) (*El Observador Mexicano* 1898b; *El Ocasional* 1898b, 1898d, 1898f).

RELIGIOSITY AND THE CHURCH

Because there were no churches in the early years, Catholicism was introduced and maintained by the Mexican people in the Valley, even if their practices did not meet with the approval of the mainstream church. Bereft of priests and the trappings of formal church doctrine, they brought sonorense folk practices, where families carefully maintained ritual calendars usually based on saints' days. For the December 12 Feast of Our Lady of Guadalupe, Mexican women in the Valley created altars, adorning them according to their means, and worshiped as they were taught by their mothers. However, El Día de San Juan, celebrated on June 24, was the most important of holy observations. For many Anglos and Europeans, the observation only meant days on end of merriment in which they either participated or voiced their objections on puritanical grounds. But the celebrations had profound religious meaning for Mexicans. Because it signaled the start of the rainy season, it was also significant for the farmers and their families (Widman n.d., 14–15; *Arizona Weekly Miner* 1872b; *Phoenix Herald* 1882c, 1897).

To hear Mass, Mexicans opened their homes to itinerant priests, a practice that was the same in priest-scarce Sonora. Trinidad Escalante Swilling was doing this as early as 1870, but Catholic Masses were also said regularly at the Tempe home of farmer and businessman Jesús L. Otero. Eventually, these practices gave way to church building, and plans for the first Catholic Church in the Tempe area were underway as early as 1873. To raise the funds, lots in the new town of San Pablo were subdivided and sold, with the proceeds slated for the building of the church. When Mt. Carmel finally opened in Tempe in 1881, it served primarily Mexicans and services were provided by a priest who came from Florence. Mexicans from throughout the East Valley attended Mass or obtain their sacraments regularly if they lived close by. A chapel was built in the 1890s to serve the Yaqui Indians in Guadalupe (Yaqui Indians n.d.; Corley 1992, 20–21). In Phoenix La Imaculada Concepción de Santa María—or St. Mary's as it came to be known—was built in 1881. It ministered to the largest number of Mexican Catholics in the Valley. Mexicans provided most of the labor to build the church, were practically the only parishioners, and the land on which it stood was donated by Miguel Peralta, Jesús Otero, and an Italian merchant, Paulo Perazzo. The same priest from Florence who inaugurated Mt. Carmel, Father Gerard, dedicated the small adobe building (Yaqui Indians n.d.; Corley 1992, 16–46).

EVERYDAY LIFE AND ENTERTAINMENT

Early Valley homes were built of adobe with slits instead of windows serving as protection against Indians. They were small and consisted of one or two rooms and a door. In this early milieu, Mexicans and Anglos banded together for defense purposes and were committed to the ideology of the yeoman farmer. In 1878 farmers from both ethnic groups cultivated 10,000 acres mostly on 160-acre spreads. In a romantic allusion to this ideal, a writer for the *Arizona Weekly Miner* wrote in 1878:

> It is well that for Phoenix that some of the land comorants of California were not among the first settlers in the Salt River Valley for instead of beholding, as you do now, on every quarter- section a neat adobe cottage, with the family of the peasant proprietor or small farmer; about half a dozen elegant residences, with their bloated and pampered inmates would constitute the population, with hordes of Chinamen to make it more revolting. (Pendleton 1950, 65)

Daily life for women consisted of making huge quantities of flour tortillas, *carne seca* (jerked beef), churning butter, making cheese, and wrapping these perishables in hay, a method by which they were transported and sold in the mining towns. There was a great amount of interaction among neighbors in house raisings, *tertulias* where people entertained each other with musical instruments, *declamaciones* (parlor recitals), and picnics. Maintaining cultural awareness was important. María González-Fellows remembers that as a child in Tempe she and other children were given lessons on Mexican culture by a private tutor (U.S. Bureau of the Census 1880b).

Dances during this era, if only to mark special celebrations, were held often. In 1880 forty-two-year-old Dionicio Carrasco had a small ensemble and actually made a living by playing at weddings, baptisms, and funerals in the 1870s and 1880s. By 1905 there were more formal dance halls, such as Chris Sigala's dancing pavilion in Tempe. Sigala was also a constable and able therefore to maintain order at his functions, which tended to get out of control at times (U.S. Bureau of the Census 1880a; Solliday Files 1894–1900).

While El Día de San Juan was religious, the day marked the beginning of a fiesta that lasted until the Fourth of July. Among Valley residents there was mutual association between the two holidays. Two acres on David Balsz's ranch, west of Phoenix, were outfitted with makeshift tents where Mexicans operated food stands, played in the music ensembles known as *orquestas de cuero* (rawhide orchestras), and ran faro casinos. The most important event during the festivities was horse racing, which Mexican horsemen dominated (Widman n.d., 14–15; *Arizona Weekly Miner* 1872b; *Phoenix Herald* 1882c, 1897).

By the turn of the century, Mexican cultural life and economic activity became increasingly separate from that of Anglos. At the same time, because of the arrival of more educated immigrants during the 1890s, entertainment and interests in the arts was much more varied and sophisticated. In 1897 D. Manuel Manzo and his daughter came from Los Angeles and established a music school in downtown Phoenix. Mexicans also maintained the Yucatec Fire Hose Company, which sponsored social and recreational activity in Spanish as well as plays at the Phoenix Opera House. The Mexican volunteer firemen also manned a formidable baseball team, often beating teams from other firehouses. The company was, in reality, made up primarily of Phoenix's Mexican businessmen and non-Mexicans married to Mexican women, such as William Scott, C. Ceschetti, and F. Cerrino. Julio Marrón, a blacksmith, who married one of King Woolsey's daughters and a founder of the Alianza Hispano Americana (Hispanic American Alliance), was elected president in 1898 (*El Observador* 1897a, 1897b, 1898a; *El Ocasional* 1898e). In 1897 La Sociedad Literaria Hispano Americana (Hispanic American Literary Society) was organized by Tempe Mexicans. The group met to read works in Spanish and promote cultural awareness. Additionally, a number of Spanish-language newspapers emerged in Phoenix. The first known one is *La Guardia*, which was initially published in 1881. In the same decade, two others, *El Progreso* and *La Verdad*, appeared. By the close of the century *El Observador* and *El Ocasional* were published with a strong political orientation.

Lost Land sentiments were intensified by rapid land loss among Valley Mexican farmers. Between 1870 and 1900 the number of Mexican farmers in Maricopa County declined from seventy-nine to about thirty even though the Mexican population increased twelvefold during the three decades. The most dramatic example of land loss was the takeover of large tracts of irrigated properties in west Tempe by W. Wormser in the 1890s. Wormser, a merchant, obtained a seven-thousand-acre farm south of the Salt River by foreclosing on a number of farmers after they could not pay for seed, tools, and other supplies that were advanced at an earlier date. Many of these usurped farmers were the Mexicans who built the San Francisco Canal. Making this unhappy turn of events even more symbolic is that Pedro Sotelo, the former Tucson Presidio soldier and one of the earliest pioneers in the Valley, was among those who were affected. As late as 1901, at an advanced age, he was still litigating in Maricopa County courts to retain 110 acres, which he thought were his (Goldman and Sotelo 1901–1904: 114; Kupel 1992).

By 1910 the original Mexican settlements in Phoenix and Tempe were now barrios, isolated from the growing and more prosperous Anglo community. As Salt River Valley economic activity reflected the new industrial age, many of the preindustrial activities providing Mexicans a more diverse social and economic base disappeared. Increasingly, Mexicans became subordinated laborers in commercial agriculture. Furthermore, the voluntary and coerced repatriation of Mexican laborers during the 1907 and 1919 recessions revealed U.S. employer's inconsistent and exploitive demand for this vital segment of the economy. During such periods of commercial stagnation the Mexican-origin labor force was the first to be eliminated. Furthermore, as has been the case throughout the twentieth and into the twenty-first century, immigrant workers have served as scapegoats for public discontent. But, in times of high demand for labor, the same population is counted on to meet increased production. The example of the Salt River Valley demonstrates the early formation of agriculture (particularly cotton), and later more broadly the construction of railroads, and copper mining, where Mexicanos were recruited to meet the expansion of capital. However, responding to multiple slumps, employers protected themselves by fostering their labor's expulsion. This oft-repeated process was an essential component for the formation of the creation of an elastic supply of Mexicano labor.

Today, the evolution from Lost Land into México Lindo is taken for granted as if its progression was somehow an evitable natural process. Consequently, it is worth clarifying that the transition from Lost Land into México Lindo was not preordained. During the 1880s various factors reinforced the Anglo-induced subordination of native Mexicano elite and recently arrived Mexican immigrants. This sense of loss and physical marginalization making barrios out of former Mexican towns gradually merged into the Lost Land generation. The accelerating economic dynamism greatly reduced their cultural prominence and sociopolitical position over the Salt River Valley. Simultaneously, as in other parts of the Southwest, industries such as commercial agriculture and the railroads drover this transition, but it had multiple effects over the evolving Mexicano society. Mexican industrialization drew central Mexicans northward and then into southern Arizona. But, inadequate opportunities in and around Tucson caused these laborers to continue on towards the Salt River Valley. Once there, the expanding industries came to rely increasingly on their manual/stoop labor along with the native Mexicano population. This progression accelerated into the twentieth century powering the overlap between Lost Land and México Lindo.

Later, in the 1920s, immigrants developed their own leadership, and formed their own organizations. Unlike the native Mexican Americans, who were deeply rooted to the Valley, they perceived their needs to be different and expected to return to Mexico. For the first time, Lost Land esthetics existed alongside the México Lindo mind-set of a generation of immigrants who had no connection to Phoenix's early Spanish-sonorense history. Both groups were forced to interact in an intensely Anglo milieu that was indifferent and even hostile to the present and the past of its people of Mexican origin. Mexican pioneers to the Valley and their descendants must have viewed all these drastic changes with dismay and anxiety lamenting the loss and decline of their status, prestige, and influence.

NOTES

1. The following terminology is used for the sake of simplicity and clarity: Latino broadly refers to all peoples of Latin American descent. Mexican refers to all people of Mexican origin regardless of citizenship including those with Mexican citizenship and U.S. citizenship. Mexican is conceptualized as a reference to "cultural citizenship" as described by Eric V. Meeks (2007, 10–11). It allows for a fluid social identity that evolves as Mexicans struggle to maintain a distinct view of themselves and their community, with respect to the norms of the dominant national community, "without compromising [their] right to belong, in the sense of participating in the nation-state's democratic processes." Mexican American will be used when the distinction between U.S. and Mexican citizenship is required.
2. For a general overview of the history of Phoenix, see "Settlement of the Salt River Valley," chapter 4 in the History of Arizona, University of Arizona Library, http://southwest.library.arizona.edu/hav6/body.1_div.4.html. According to the U.S. Census, in 2013 Arizona's population was 6,731,484 and Maricopa County's was 4,013,164. The Hispanic or Latino population made up 30 percent of the state's population. See U.S. Census, Maricopa, AZ, http://quickfacts.census.gov/qfd/states/04/04013.html.

3. Numerous scholars have examined in detail the issue of how Mexico-U.S. relations have fostered the out migration from Mexico to the United States, including Arizona. For two examples, see Juan Gómez-Quiñones, *Mexican American Labor, 1790–1990* (Albuquerque: University of New Mexico Press, 1994) and Ron Mize and Alicia Swords, *Consuming Mexican Labor: From the Bracero Program to NAFTA* (Toronto: University of Toronto Press, 2010).
4. Hispanic generally stresses the Latino population's Spanish heritage (as separate from its Indigenous or sub-Saharan African roots). It can also serve as a term of inclusivity amongst the various Latin American nationalities residing within the United States; see Mellinger (1995, 14, n20).
5. The terms *Anglo*, *white*, and *European* broadly refer to U.S. citizens and immigrants who are descended from Europe as distinct from Latinos and Indigenous peoples.
6. There is no one Apache community or identity. According to Myla Vicenti Carpio, my colleague in American Indian Studies at Arizona State University, "In Arizona there are now on reservations the Tonto Apache, White Mountain Apache, and San Carlos Apache. Previously, there were the Chiricahua Apache and Lipan Apache. All are very different, but historically and still today viewed as one homogeneous people; a misconception that is rooted in the Spanish and Mexican periods." For more information, see Haley (1997, 3–13), Kiser (2012, 37–53), and Griffin-Pierce (2006, 17–27).
7. According to the authors, no amount of historical research will ever reveal every single lynching victim—no matter their race and ethnicity—that is anywhere near the actual number of victims. In most publications and data summaries the lynching victims are divided into only two categories: black and white. This neat binary division belies historical reality since the list of white victims actually included Native Americans, Chinese immigrants, Italians, and Mexicans. For more information about individual lynchings, see appendix A, "Confirmed Cases of Mob Violence against Persons of Mexican Origin and Descent in the United States, 1848–1928" (Carrigan 2013, 180–221).
8. It is difficult to determine which Mexican–non-Mexican couples were legally married. We were unable to find any marriage records in Maricopa County for some of the couples that were shown as living together in the 1870 or 1880 census manuscripts—whether they were Mexican or non-Mexican. A great many probably received some kind of legal vows elsewhere.

2

THE MOBILIZATION AND IMMOBILIZATION OF "LEGALLY IMPORTED ALIENS"

★

Cotton in the Salt River Valley, 1917–1921

GLORIA H. CUÁDRAZ

LOCATED IN THE FAR SOUTHWEST portion of the Salt River Valley is the City of Litchfield Park, a former cotton company town of the Southwest Cotton Company, once a Goodyear Tire & Rubber Company subsidiary. Not far from the center of town, tucked into what is now a residential area, is the entrance to the Goodyear Farms Historic Cemetery. As one enters the grounds one sees to the south a graveyard of resting places, crosses, monuments, some named, others unnamed, that stretch to the cemetery's cinder-block walls; flanking the north edge of the cemetery is a self-standing concrete wall that depicts a pastoral agricultural scene that includes workers in the fields, with families and children nearby (figure 2.1). Just below the mural wall is a commemorative stone monument with the following etched inscription:

> This historical monument is dedicated to the early farming pioneers who traveled from afar in search of life's blessings. Litchfield was founded around 1916 and was originally established as a labor camp. This cemetery was founded by Paul W. Litchfield in 1917 for private use by hundreds of legally imported aliens and other employees whose services were to convert raw desert into cleaned fields for planting cotton and other crops. A serious influenza epidemic claimed more lives than WWI. Here in memory lie those and their families who dedicated their lives. This cemetery was once located in the heart of the labor camps and played a very important role in Arizona history.[1]

Several observations come to mind in the framing of this tribute. First, while the monument is dedicated to those who labored to clear the land, the description effectively alludes to a group of people in whose honor this monument was built, but chooses

FIGURE 2.1 Goodyear Farms Historic Cemetery, Mural, Litchfield Park. Photo by Sarina E. Guerra and Derick Douglas Washington.

to have them remain nameless. In its place, visitors to this site are offered a more legalistic description of this workforce—one ensconced in a legal classification tied to one's status. *Alien*, derived from the Latin term *alienus*, means stranger or foreigner.[2] Thus, we quickly gather the people who cleared this land were from somewhere else—foreigners—who belong somewhere else but for the purpose of "life's blessings," were brought to this land to provide the services to fulfill this goal. That they were legally brought here suggests perhaps the possibility they could have been illegally brought here, at the same time that it invokes the existence of a state—an entity designed to sanction by law the importation of these "aliens." The use of the term *importation* implies not only the movement of but, more insidiously, the commodification of humans into goods—as if they were products shipped from place to place. When placed in the contemporary context of Southwest history and demographics, the descriptive phrase *legally imported aliens* immediately conjures an image, knowledge of who these aliens are, namely—people of Mexican descent.[3] Why use the phrase *legally imported aliens* to describe members and families of this Mexican workforce? In the context of the social relations of power, what are the stories to be unpacked? How do the events of the 1917–1921 time period index the processes that set a foundation for how Mexican labor would be integrated into capitalist production in Arizona and the Southwest?

My interest in the history of the Goodyear Farms Cemetery and the City of Litchfield Park began with my copartnership in an oral history project with the Litchfield Park Historical Society.[4] An interesting historical irony is that I discovered my father's migration story began during the 1917–1921 time period and that he was among the thousands of workers recruited by the Arizona Cotton Growers Association to come to the United States under the Immigration Act of 1917's ninth proviso. In my effort to better contextualize and analyze the fifty-plus oral histories we conducted with former Mexican American residents of the labor camps once located on the periphery of Litchfield Park, I began to investigate the history of the town, the history of cotton in Arizona, and the Mexican community in this region. In addition to a number of secondary sources, my research draws from archives in the following collections: Goodyear Rubber & Tire Company Collection at the University of Akron, Ohio; the Seiberling Collection at the Ohio Historical Society, Columbus, Ohio; the Campbell Papers at Arizona State Library, Archives and Public Records. At Arizona State University I utilized the Hudson Cotton Company Collection, the Litchfield Park Collection in the Department of Archives and Special Collections, the Chicano Research Collection, and the Carl T. Hayden Collection.

I begin this chapter with an overview of how cotton became central to the borderlands economy, the Goodyear Tire & Rubber Company's status in the world economy and its role in cotton production, and what Goodyear's entry meant to Arizona's developing economy. Next, I examine U.S. laws surrounding the recruitment of foreign labor, followed by a consideration of the conditions of Mexican workers on both sides of the border, but also the ways in which the social and racialized construction of the Mexican worker on the U.S. side of the border served corporate and state interests. I then briefly consider the outcome of events between 1917 and 1921, what has been characterized as the boom-and-bust period for the cotton industry to consider the ways in which workers were "mobilized and immobilized"—a construct used by scholars of labor history to illustrate the "intricate use of permissions and denials as mechanisms of control through which foreign labor becomes incorporated into social relations of production as unfree labor."[5] In other words, once mobilized, what are the processes by which labor is regulated and controlled, and hence immobilized? I follow select actions undertaken by the Southwest Cotton Company (SWCC) and the Arizona Cotton Growers Association (ACGA) with respect to legally imported aliens and the sequence of events that took place when the market for cotton declined.

The concepts of *labor repression* and the construct of *mobilizing to immobilize* are particularly useful to analyze the cotton industry's boom-and-bust period of 1917–1921 in Arizona and how Mexican workers were central to these events. In his analysis of south Texas labor relations between Anglos and Mexicans, Montejano's (1987) concept of "labor repression" encapsulates "the use of compulsion for organizing the recruitment, work activity, and compensation of wage labor" (197). The concept of labor repression is useful to reframe the early years of Arizona's cotton industry—a period, I argue, that established the seeds for: (a) the manner in which legislation, state intervention, and private capital interests colluded; (b) the kinds of labor controls that were put in place to regulate the use and expulsion of Mexican workers; and (c) establishing the social relations that would govern twentieth-century relations between Mexican workers and Anglos in Arizona.

With respect to the cotton industry in Arizona and the role of Mexican labor, The Goodyear Company's entry into Arizona in 1916 and its investment in cotton production integrated Arizona into a borderlands' global system of textile production, challenging the largely U.S.-centric framework that dominates discussions of the cotton industry in Arizona. Second, to achieve their interests pertaining to cotton, Goodyear, a conglomerate of agricultural interests, and the state "mobilized to immobilize"; that is, Mexican workers as a "foreign labor force" were massively recruited and mobilized to fulfill the labor needs of large-scale agriculture in Arizona—one centered around cotton—yet were subsequently "immobilized" once in the United States (Smith 2013). Third, evidence for this immobilization includes the policies and activities of the SWCC and the ACGA and the restrictions and repressions they imposed on their recruited workforce. With the decline of the cotton boom, and the subsequent abandonment and mistreatment of Mexican workers, the stage was set for a pattern of racialization and mobilization/immobilization of Mexican workers that carries us right into the present day.

COTTON, THE BORDERLANDS, AND MEXICAN LABOR

A U.S. lieutenant scouting the Salt River Valley on behalf of the federal government in 1858 would report, "The region is altogether valueless. After entering it, there is nothing to do but leave."[6] What the lieutenant could not have predicted was the impact the advent of the Civil War in 1861 would have worldwide, but especially in the web of domestic and international markets tied to cotton. Among several contributing factors, the U.S. federal government would play a critical role in the late nineteenth through early the twentieth century to create the conditions that made not only Arizona's development possible, but that brought Arizona into larger processes of what Walsh describes as, "integrating the borderlands into a global system of industrial textile production" (Walsh 2001, 49).

Cotton production became possible in the borderlands with the advent of railroads, irrigation, and colonization (ibid., 49). Due in part to federally subsidized grants, the building of the transcontinental railroad system in the 1880s connected Arizona to the rest of the country (McGinnis 1930, 6). Industrial capitalists began what Sheridan (1995a) named the "extractive phase" of Arizona's resources—which at that point consisted of copper, cattle, and citrus—to develop for national and international markets.

The international railroad, built in a north-south direction into Mexico, provided a critical linkage to the vast number of laborers needed for the industrialization of the borderlands.[7] Garcilazo (1995) posits that the railroad industry was the "nation's first big business" in both the United States and Mexico and "made it the largest and often first employer of Mexican labor in the United States" (1995, 9). Indeed, the 1911 Dillingham Commission, in the most comprehensive investigation into immigrant populations in the United States, at the time found that Mexican railroad laborers comprised one-sixth of the labor force in the Western Division (made up of eleven states), constituted the majority of workers for other lines, and were the lowest-paid railroad laborers in the West.[8]

Moreover, the massive undertaking by the U.S. federal government to harness water, such that "irrigated agriculture" was able to prevail in creating a "regional process of industrial capital formation" essentially ensured that the once desert wastelands would transform into a highly productive and profitable region. Meanwhile, the Mexican federal government also facilitated the penetration and concentration of foreign capital into northern Mexico and passed water laws that favored its centralization at the expense of local use water rights—all in an effort to support cotton production (Kerig 1988).

With respect to the political ecology and economy of the borderlands, which encompasses the modern states on both sides of the international border, Walsh (2001,

2008) argues that cotton and cotton production, "cultivated by an army of migratory workers, was central to the formation of borderlands society," of which the Salt River Valley was but one part.[9] He further argues that the establishment of "irrigated cotton zones" in the borderlands, which was certainly the case in the Salt River Valley, was "a process of state formation" (Walsh 2001, 48). To understand how and the extent to which the Salt River Valley became part of this global system related to the commodity of cotton, it is necessary to understand how it became a cotton agricultural zone, its relationship to cotton markets, industrial centers, and to capital entities with global reach.

To argue the Salt River Valley's transformation into a cotton agricultural zone began with the Goodyear Tire & Rubber Company's entry into the area would not be overstated, for Goodyear represented a scale of capital enterprise and investment unprecedented in Arizona's agricultural industry. To understand the landscape into which Goodyear Tire & Rubber eventually came to invest in cotton production in Arizona, establish the company town of Litchfield Park, and the role of Mexican labor requires taking the elements posited by Walsh into account, in addition to the passage of immigration and labor laws, and the role of race and racial ideologies in shaping the stratification that ultimately became a blueprint for the Southwest.

GOODYEAR TIRE & RUBBER AND COTTON

By 1916, when Goodyear Tire & Rubber first turned to Arizona to investigate whether growing long-staple cotton would be feasible, the company was already considered the world's largest manufacturer. To guarantee their place in the world market, long-staple cotton was critical to their production of pneumatic tires, and hence to their entire enterprise. Achieving the milestone as the world's largest manufacturer had not been without its challenges. Incorporated in 1898, Frank A. Seiberling founded the Goodyear Tire & Rubber Company with limited knowledge of the rubber and tire business. The company was named in honor of Charles Goodyear, considered the founder of the commercial rubber industry, whose accidental discovery of the hot vulcanization of rubber in 1839 provided the innovative component that led to its commercial application and use. A chance opportunity for Seiberling to purchase a plant in Akron, Ohio, during an economic downturn in the 1890s led Seiberling and family members to direct their investments toward tire production. Coinciding with the accelerated expansion of the automobile industry, it took less than two decades for Goodyear to become the largest tire producer in the world.

One fact was certain about cotton in the first two decades of the century and that was that its production was essential. "There is no regnant plant in all the world that supplies so many needs of the world as the cotton plant" noted Secretary of the Navy Daniels at a meeting of the Cotton Manufacturer's Association held in Washington, D.C., in 1917.[10] Indeed, the United States was a chief exporter of cotton in 1916, exporting 2,760,890 bales of cotton to the United Kingdom, 890,376 bales to France, 836,915 to Italy, 173,449 to Russia, and a total of 6,168,140 bales to countries around the world (ibid., 8). With the advent of World War I in 1914 and the United States' entry into the war in 1917, the need for cotton multiplied. Cotton was necessary not only for the production of clothing and uniforms, but was also critical to manufacturing guncotton and explosives. By way of evidence, Secretary Daniels recorded that 583,710 cotton bales were used for war-related goods in 1917, as compared to 244,003 bales in the prior year. The demand for cotton would only grow, and American farmers and industries for which cotton was essential lined up to ensure its production.

The availability of cotton became increasingly important to Goodyear's success as it entered its second decade of operations. During its first decade of business Goodyear had struggled to stay afloat, with competitors far better financed, and with bigger operations than the fledgling, smaller company. With a carefully chosen group of men to lead the company, itself a different model from the one-man business model that prevailed, Goodyear diversified its production. Bicycle tires, carriage tires, and automobile tires—the latter as yet a new arena not quite predictable, but with the greatest potential in terms of the company's growth—comprised the products that Goodyear focused on to establish its name. More strategically vital, however, was Goodyear's decision to contest the patent blockade—an association of companies that owned patents and licensees for bicycle and automobile tires and were able to dictate who would be granted a license or manufacturing rights, thereby thwarting serious competitors from the market. While Goodyear awaited a decision, it continued with production and sales and focused on improving its product line and developing its own patents. The strategy worked. The courts ruled in Goodyear's favor. As Goodyear's company historian would later remark, "It made Goodyear" (Allen 1949, 17).

Meanwhile, Goodyear proceeded to improve and develop the straight-side tire, which proved to be a breakthrough for the tire industry and placed Goodyear squarely among the industry's top leaders. It increased its tire production from ninety tires per day in 1905 to nine hundred per day by 1908 (ibid., 28). As one of the supporting industries to the automobile industry, Goodyear expanded in accordance with an industry that was changing the way in which Americans would be mobile. Its ability to meet the growing demand, improve its products, and develop the equipment to increase the production rate allowed Goodyear to flourish during the "automobile age"—when automobile ownership for American individuals and families became the norm (ibid., 50).

In 1913 Goodyear's release of the cord tire catapulted it into first place in the industry, and its development of a pneumatic tire for trucks, according to Goodyear's company historian, "changed the whole course of transportation in America" (Allen 1949, 31). Goodyear's production of truck tires, both solid and pneumatic, was so important that it made World War I the first motorized war. Hence, by 1916, when Goodyear entertained the prospect of growing cotton in Arizona, Goodyear's sales had gone from $2,189,749 in 1907–1908 to $63,950,399 in 1916–1917 (ibid., 50).

Accounts of why and how Goodyear came to Arizona to grow long-staple cotton are most often attributed to two things—a boll weevil infestation in the south, and the British embargo of cotton from Egypt due to World War I—both of which created a critical shortage for centers of textile production. These accounts trace the evolution of long-staple cotton and the discovery it would grow well in Arizona's semiarid climate. For Goodyear, the demand for cotton was initially driven by its use in the production of the newly patented pneumatic tire, which promised to be lucrative in the context of the burgeoning automobile industry; by chance, this coincided with increased demand for cotton-dependent goods, such as clothing for uniforms, tents, and military equipment, stimulated by World War I.

Initially, Goodyear sent Paul W. Litchfield to visit the Salt River Valley in the fall of 1916 to interest a sufficient number of farmers to produce the amount of cotton needed, offering to finance and purchase the cotton they produced. Unsuccessful, the Goodyear Tire & Rubber Company could ill afford to proceed without the necessary raw materials. Intent on keeping their lead in the industry, Goodyear decided to enter the cotton-producing business in the Salt River Valley. For the most part, the official stories center solely on Arizona and the development of cotton in the Salt River Valley, providing a U.S.-centric model and one that, at best, considers it only from its relevance to the Southwest (Schetter 1976; "The Story of Goodyear Farms" n.d.).

However, wild cotton predates the entry of Europeans into the borderlands, and had long been a part of the ecology of the area. Nomadic groups inhabited the area, as well as "sedentary, complex societies that practiced irrigated agriculture, built urban centers, and engaged in trade with Mexico" (Walsh 2001, 52). The small-scale and flood-recession agriculture practiced by these populations enabled cotton agriculture to flourish in Mexico following their independence from Spain in 1821. With state support and linkages to European capital, markets, and manufacturers, the fate of Mexico's cotton industry became intricately tied to a global system of production—a system that relied heavily on cotton exports from the U.S. South—one long rendered profitable by the institution of slavery.

With the outbreak of the Civil War in the United States (1861–1865), an awareness of Europe's dependence on U.S. Southern markets gradually led them to seek alternative cotton sources. The English turned to colonized areas such as Egypt, Sudan, and India for their cotton supply, while the French, with 93 percent of its cotton fiber coming from the United States, looked to Mexico as a source for raw cotton (ibid., 61). France's invasion of Mexico in 1862 signified their attempt to control cotton production in Mexico, but also to prevent it from developing its own textile manufacturing industry (ibid., 64). Nonetheless, when the North blockaded cotton exports from the South to Europe's industrial and manufacturing centers, Mexico's cotton industry participated in increased trade with the South and a highly profitable "cotton contraband" that found its way via Mexican ports to central Mexico and global centers in Europe. These profits allowed Mexico to build their own textile manufacturing centers in Sonora and the Laguna region in north-central Mexico, such that by 1885 the first irrigated cotton zone of the Mexico-U.S. borderlands was actually in the Laguna region.[11]

MEXICANS, MIGRATION, AND COTTON

Scholars of Mexican immigration, labor, and early twentieth-century Southwest have long pointed to the Mexican Revolution of 1910 and the land policies of the Díaz regime that displaced thousands of workers and their families and led to one of the first massive waves of Mexican immigration to the United States (Acuña 2007; Cardoso 1976, 1980; Corwin and Cardoso 1978; Foster 1982; Gamio 1930 [1971]; Gómez-Quiñones 1994; Guerín-Gonzales 1994; Gutiérrez 1995, 1996; Martínez 1957 [1971]; McWilliams 1949 [1968]; Reisler 1976a; Ruiz 1998; Taylor 1931–1932 [1968], 1970; Zamora 1993). Among these were workers who had been involved in cotton production in the borderlands and whose relationship to these processes positioned them very differently. Cotton production has two seasons, each of which requires different volumes of workers. The preparation of the soil, tilling, and planting can be completed with a relatively small labor force, but it is the harvesting season—manually picking the cotton—that constitutes the labor-intensive component or dimension of cotton production. The larger the acreage of cotton under plow, the greater the number of workers to be mobilized for the harvesting phase alone. This seasonal demand and intensification of labor in cotton production in the borderlands, Walsh (2001) argues, resulted in "a new, socially unstable migrant worker class" (72). Walsh draws on William Meyers's (1994, 1998) research in Laguna, Mexico, where three types of agricultural workers were identified: "resident workers; temporary workers (*trabajadores eventuales*); and migrant workers." The resident workers were the most stable, living on the plantation, as they held the jobs that not only paid better but were also year-round. The trabajadores eventuales consisted of workers who lived on the periphery of the plantations, sought full-time work during cotton-picking season, and worked part time in other industries in between. With the advent of the railroad in the 1880s, workers migrated into northern Mexico and the Southwest, seeking work in the large cotton plantations and hacendados that dominated the landscape. Walsh notes that "by 1910, the Laguna had become just one stop on international migrant labor circuits that included the cotton harvest of Texas and the harvests of California. These migrant movements would swell with the violence and disruption of the Mexican Revolution in 1910" (ibid., 76).

Meyers (1994) and Walsh (2008) argue that it was the trabajadores eventuales and the migrant workers whose disenfranchisement, periodic employment and unemployment, and their vulnerability to exploitation sparked the rebellions leading to the Mexican Revolution. For at least two decades, families left Sonora, fleeing villages and haciendas and the turmoil caused by the warring factions.[12] Thousands are reported to have flocked across the border, looking for work and new places to settle.

This confluence of factors on both sides of the border created optimal conditions for the moment that Goodyear Tire & Rubber would bring its capital investments to Arizona and look to Mexico to meet the volume of laborers it would need for its own cotton production. In doing so, Goodyear forever changed Arizona's economy, bringing Arizona into the global production of cotton already underway in the region; they brought unprecedented capital and large-scale commercial production to the state and fortified the ceaseless quest and reliance on Mexican labor that would define the U.S.-Mexico borderlands for most of the twentieth century.

ARIZONA AND THE ADVENT OF COMMERCIAL AGRICULTURE

By the turn of twentieth century, the struggle for land and the harnessing of water defined the prestatehood years of Arizona's Salt River Valley. The Hohokam—"the people who have gone"—whose system of canals and irrigation agricultural methods sustained the Hohokam culture for over five centuries provided the blueprint for the irrigation system and canals later developed by Anglos and where the state's capital of Phoenix would eventually thrive (Kotlanger 1983; Marin 1987; Mawn 1979; Vander Meer 2010). A model of "corporate canal development" became the trademark for the Salt River Valley, as quarter sections of land were sold to raise capital for the building of canals (Weisiger 1995, 33).[13] Within twenty years, the Arizona Improvement Company had a "virtual monopoly" over early water rights, making it "possible for the Arizona Improvement Company to control the development of desert land by selling and leasing access to water, resulting in the development of joint-stock companies and the financing of canals and water rights. The company then embarked on a national campaign to promote the potential of the Salt River Valley for commercial agriculture, particularly for high value crops like citrus, in an effort to attract investors and settlers" (ibid., 35).

Throughout the 1890s, with significant pressure from California, the idea that unusable, desert lands could be converted for agricultural production gained hold (Hill 2007). Beyond the means of either local government or funds from private capital, the federal government was viewed as the entity most able to finance reclamation. Thomas Sheridan (1995a) duly noted, "More than most places, modern Arizona would not exist without federal support" (xvi). Massive irrigation projects would be required to harness and stabilize the water supply for the development of the West.

Under Theodore Roosevelt's administration, the Reclamation Act of 1902 created the U.S. Reclamation Service, carving the way for the development of the vast western agricultural empire of which Arizona would be a part (Smith 1986). The Roosevelt Dam was built and completed by the Salt River Project in 1911, becoming the first reclamation project developed under the Reclamation Act. American Indian and Mexican workers helped build the Roosevelt Dam and later, along with Yaquis, were vital to the maintenance of the canal systems throughout the Salt River Valley (Dimas 1999; Smith 1982). Although agriculture had long been a part of the Salt River Valley, it was the completion of the Roosevelt Dam that enabled Arizona to develop into one of the "most capitalized industrial agricultural systems the world had known" (Weisiger 1995, 31). At its dedication, President Roosevelt projected that the Salt River Valley would become "one of the richest agricultural areas in the world" (Sheridan 1995a, 211). This system, no less than six years later, would be in a position to join the global system of production tied to the commodity of cotton and, in sharing a border with northern Mexico, in an advantageous position to utilize its already migratory "semi-industrial, semi-agricultural labor force" in search of refuge and work.

Since the 1880s Arizona had relied upon and grown increasingly dependent on the ability to attract foreign investors from midwestern and eastern capitalists, as well as European investors, for its growth, providing an ideal context for the Goodyear Tire & Rubber Company to invest in their agricultural enterprise. The agricultural industry in Arizona at the dawn of Goodyear's entrance into the state was one fairly diversified in its production of vegetables, fruit, alfalfa, wheat, and barley. Dairy and flour mills, hay and grain companies, dotted the landscape. Cotton production was already taking place in the Salt River Valley, but on a much smaller scale. Unlike other agricultural products raw cotton is not sold directly to the consumer, and instead requires processing. As agriculture expanded in the Salt River Valley, railroad lines and spurs were built to towns from Mesa, Chandler, Tempe, Phoenix, Glendale, and later to the West Valley town of Litchfield to facilitate the transport of imports and exports to outside markets.

The Desert Land Act of 1877, an amendment to the Homestead Act of 1862, undergirded the structure of Arizona's agricultural industry, as it encouraged settlement in the West's desert lands by granting a maximum of 640 acres to individuals willing to irrigate and cultivate these lands. A loophole in the law did not require owners to live on the lands, leaving considerable room for abuses and for large-scale enterprises to be established and the family farm to subside. In accordance with the new reclamation laws, individual owners could irrigate only 160 acres with water from Roosevelt Dam. Thus, for the thousands of acres Goodyear purchased in the West Valley, their major source of water came from wells tapping groundwater not too far below the surface.

Edwin Pendleton (1950), whose voluminous dissertation outlines the history of "irrigated agriculture in Arizona," reported that from 1910 to 1920, "the total number of people engaged in agricultural pursuits increased from 22,416 to 36,199, or about 60 percent. Over one-half of the farm laborers were foreign-born white, undoubtedly, Mexicans" (105).

The Goodyear Rubber & Tire Company purchased a total of twenty-four thousand acres of Arizonan desert land in 1916 in the southeastern and southwestern portions of the Salt River Valley.[14] By January 1917 it established the Southwest Cotton Company as its subsidiary and committed $1 million of capital to the venture, leased land in the vicinity of Chandler, set up headquarters in central Phoenix, and began to build the infrastructure that would support the purchased acreage in the southwest valley.

A January 1917 article in *Arizona Magazine* titled "Goodyear Plantation" captures the anticipation and significance of the corporation's entry into the Salt River Valley.

> During the last three months the Salt River Valley has lived in a state of ecstasy over the promised realities of the cotton industry. . . . Rumors have been current for two or three months of large corporations leasing or buying lands for cotton growing, and guarantees of high prices to those who would contract to market their crops in certain quarters have been rife. The *Arizona Magazine* is now pleased to make the announcement of a specific fact, which is a beginning of this realization—and is an incident of no mean importance. ("Goodyear Cotton Plantation" 1917)

Meanwhile, Phoenix more than doubled its population from 1910, with 11,134 inhabitants to 29,053 by 1920. The Mexican population residing in Phoenix during this time went from 1,100 in 1910 to 2,323 in 1920, comprising approximately 8 percent of the city's population, a far cry from the 1870s, when Mexicans comprised half of the city's population.[15] As more and more Anglos settled in Phoenix during the final decades of the nineteenth century, what had once been a mutually dependent relationship between Mexicans and Anglos during the territorial period gradually diminished into a racially stratified social order that rendered Mexicans as second-class citizens (Casillas 1979; Dean and Reynolds 2006, 26; Dimas, 1999; Meeks 2001; Park 1961).

"LESS DESIRABLE AS A CITIZEN THAN AS A LABORER"

The individuals and families that would end up working for Southwest Cotton Company when the Goodyear Tire & Rubber Company first came into Arizona would find a structuring of inequality undergirded by an ideological terrain that used skin color and racial/ethnic membership as a basis for differential treatment. As noted by Montejano (1987), "the notion of race does not just consist of ideas and sentiments; it comes into being when these ideas and sentiments are publicly articulated and institutionalized."[16]

Two of the earliest sources pertaining to Mexican labor in the United States illustrate how race and class intertwined in the views about people of Mexican descent. "The Mexican who comes to the United States as a laborer is from the peon or tramp labor class in Mexico," wrote Victor Clark (1908). He described an impoverished, displaced, Indigenous population coming out of a debt peonage system in Mexico's northern Sonoran states. "The Mexican is docile, patient, usually orderly in camp, fairly intelligent under competent supervision, obedient, and cheap. If he were active and ambitious he would be less tractable, and would cost more. His strongest point is that he is willing to work for a lower wage" (1908, 496). But the words used to describe their impoverished conditions very quickly became associated with behavioral characteristics, such as "docile, indolent, and backward," which were then used to justify either a pro- or anti-immigrant position.

Three years later, in 1911 the Dillingham Commission reported that although Mexican workers in the railroad, mining, smelter, sugar beet, and agricultural industries of the West were considered "satisfactory" laborers, largely migratory, employed in unskilled jobs, possessed "limited" competitive abilities, and were likely to remain in southwestern states so they could return to Mexico—they were also the lowest-paid workers of any ethnic group. The commission concluded, "It is evident that in the case of the Mexican he is less desirable as a citizen than as a laborer" (U.S. Immigration Commission 1911, 690).

THE MOBILIZATION AND IMMOBILIZATION OF LEGALLY IMPORTED ALIENS: 1917–1921

Several descriptive accounts exist about the initial boom-and-bust period of Arizona's cotton industry (Hill 2007; Lucio 2007; Pendleton 1950; Peterson 1974, 1975; Reisler 1976a; Walker 2012). Combined, these works provide a sequence of the events that unfolded from 1917 to 1921, and the key actors and entities involved.[17] My interest here is not so much to offer another iteration of these events as it is to propose a conceptual framework that speaks to a broader understanding of these events in the context of the development and penetration of capitalism in the Southwest with respect to Mexican labor, and to elucidate the social relations of power as they evolved for Mexican workers and their eventual place in society. Scholars who interrogate the distinction between free and unfree labor utilize the construct of "mobilizing to immobilize" to illustrate the "intricate use of permissions and denials as mechanisms of control through which foreign labor becomes incorporated into social relations of production as unfree labor" (Smith 2013, 20; see also Bhattacharya and Lucassen 2005; Mohapatra 2005; Montejano 1987; Standing 2008). Once mobilized, what are the processes by which labor is regulated and controlled, and hence immobilized?

In Arizona, between 1917 and 1921, the legally sanctioned and massive recruitment of Mexican workers—"legally imported aliens"—signified a regulatory role on the part of the state to ensure a steady supply of cheap labor for the capitalist expansion of commercial farming in Arizona and the Southwest. This lens stands in juxtaposition to a historiography of Arizona that depicts and celebrates the growth of the cotton industry largely in terms of its contributions to the economy—one that ignores how a local capitalist labor market, albeit with global ties, incorporates a foreign labor force into the social relations of production, and how, through a web of repressive measures immobilizes the very workforce they mobilized. Integral to these processes, as argued, for example, by Smith (2013) in his analysis of the sugar workers imported into the Caribbean and Montejano (1987) of Mexican workers in south Texas, are the processes of racialization and racism whereby workers are subject to differential and discriminatory treatment as wage laborers on the basis of their assignment to a racial classification deemed inferior and subordinate.

By focusing on the "intricate use of permissions and denials as mechanism of control" we may better understand the ways in which Mexican workers were recruited and mobilized and almost immediately immobilized through mechanisms that extracted, commodified, and exploited their labor power, including that of women and children. It potentially rewrites a master narrative that glamorizes the history of the cotton industry in Arizona, renders invisible the labor of Mexican workers in that endeavor, and fails to critically examine the ways in which these processes established a pattern of stratification and social relations that would, in effect, dominate twentieth-century Mexico-U.S. relations.[18] In the following sections I present both sides of the mobilization and immobilization continuum during the period in question and delineate how Mexican workers became part of the racialized elastic supply of labor that continues to the present.

THE SOUTHWEST COTTON COMPANY, LEGISLATION, AND THE RECRUITMENT OF LABOR

The Southwest Cotton Company (SWCC) faced what employers of the railroad industry and growers in California, Texas, and Colorado confronted when irrigation made large-scale commercial agribusiness possible. With thousands of acres expected to come under cultivation, how could they be guaranteed an adequate supply of laborers? Before the arrival of the Goodyear Tire & Rubber Company, the Salt River Valley met its need for workers by relying on the local workforce and by using private labor agencies to surreptitiously recruit workers from Mexico to fill their respective labor needs. Such actions operated below the radar of U.S. Immigration, who neither fully regulated immigration from the southern border, nor provided the personnel at the two-thousand-miles-long border to enforce it (Reisler 1976a, 1–23).

But the magnitude of the large-scale agricultural enterprise required a more strategic approach as thousands of acres needed to be prepared to cultivate and an unprecedented number of workers needed to be mobilized for the labor processes involved in planting and harvesting cotton. To grow cotton in the Salt River Valley, cultivation and preparation of the land begins almost eight months before picking season arrives. Once the ground is evenly distributed, cotton is planted between mid-March and the first week in April. Once the plants have germinated and reached a height of two inches, weeding begins. Cotton rows are spaced three to four feet apart and thinned when the plants have reached a height of four to twelve inches. It was common throughout the southwest for workers to use a short hoe (*el cortito, mano del diablo*) for the thinning process, a practice that was eventually banned in 1984 because of the injuries it caused workers. Thinning, which takes place twice during a season, can also take place by uprooting the plant entirely. Meanwhile, assuming the ground has been constantly cultivated and properly irrigated, the crop is ready to be harvested by early September, subject to three pickings by a season that ends in February (Christy 1920, 21–27).

The labor force for the growing season of long-staple cotton requires a steady but smaller workforce from March until August, and a large seasonal workforce once picking begins in September and concludes in February. The picking of long-staple cotton is done manually. Classified as American Egyptian cotton and later labeled Pima cotton, it is considered to be more arduous and painstaking because the cotton is shorter and removed from a narrower opening of the boll of the plant.

Two laws were in place that made the importation of foreign workers illegal. The Alien Contract Labor Law of 1885, known as the Foran Act, prohibited the recruitment of all foreign workers for jobs in the United States (Plascencia 2013a). The

Immigration Act of 1917, which was passed on February 5, 1917, and incorporated the Foran Act, was scheduled to go into effect on May 5. It restricted immigration by establishing a literacy requirement, increased a head tax to $8, and continued to mandate a visa fee—provisions that reflected nativist sentiments to curb immigration from Eastern and Southern Europe and the interests of unions to restrict the flow of foreign workers in order to enhance bargaining negotiations for American workers.[19]

Meanwhile, the news of the passage of the Immigration Act of 1917 could not have come at a worse time for the Goodyear Tire & Rubber Company.[20] The SWCC had already broken ground in its West Valley acreage. Paul Litchfield's (1954) account of the first day of plowing captures the significance of the day.

> Time literally meant money. . . . Almost overnight an army of men started moving in, hundreds of Mexicans who threw up brushwood and adobe shelters and a still larger force of adventurers drawn from all over the West by the lure of good pay, men who went from one big construction job to the next. We soon had 2,000 men on the job—and 1,300 mules at the peak, more than half the mule population of the state.[21]

Growers and politicians from Arizona and across the Southwest lobbied intensively for a reinterpretation of the Immigration Act of 1917; among them was Goodyear's president, Frank A. Seiberling, and a host of Arizona officials. Two letters between Seiberling to Edward F. Parker, newly appointed vice president of the SWCC in charge of managing operations, reveal their lobbying activities and an acute awareness of the critical importance Mexican labor posed to their enterprise.

Edward F. Parker, a lawyer from California who had first advised another client regarding the lucrativeness of a contract with the Goodyear Tire & Rubber Company to grow cotton, was himself contracted by the SWCC to serve as manager of operations.[22] His lengthy letters to Goodyear president Seiberling reveal a great deal about the SWCC's day-to-day operations, and even more about the character of the individual primarily responsible for the company's operations during its more critical period.[23] Parker eventually became president of the ACGA—a position that, in effect, ensured that the SWCC's interests were vetted, in an entity billed to represent the growers of the Salt River Valley through the association's business.

In a letter dated May 11, 1917, Seiberling encourages Parker to organize "prominent" Arizona people to visit Washington, D.C., stating they could do a "better job of logrolling" than he could. He continues, "should it finally develop that we have to bring American labor, or that standard of wage, to the Arizona cotton proposition, it will become as dead as Julius Caesar."[24] In a subsequent letter, dated May 19, 1917, Seiberling writes:

> In the matter of our labor situation, I was in Washington three days the past week and am going there for the same time next week. I talked with our Congressman Bathrick and he says that he will get Secretary (William B.) Wilson to send a special representative to look into the situation, anticipation that a provision may be had that will give us the labor we require. . . . My impression is that we shall never make a success of our project without Mexican labor; that to depend upon the whites, blacks or Indians leaves us on very unstable ground.[25]

Dwight Heard, chairman of Arizona's State Council of Defense, could also be found in Washington, D.C., meeting with Secretary of Labor Wilson and Assistant Secretary Louis Post. In a May 19, 1917, letter to Wilson, Heard reported on the resolution passed by the executive committee of the Council of Defense, requesting the suspension of the literacy test and the head tax, noting that 240,000 acres of crops were under cultivation in the Salt River Valley, 25,000 of which were planted in cotton alone, requiring an additional ten thousand seasonal laborers for the anticipated fall harvest (*Arizona Republican* May 26, 1917).

Intense lobbying by agricultural interests in the midst of United States' participation in World War I provided the opening for Secretary of Labor William Wilson to waive the 1885 Contract Labor Law and accept a peculiar interpretation of the Immigration Act of 1917's ninth proviso. To justify challenges to the waiver by members of Congress, Wilson argued it was an emergency suspension due to the war, emphasizing that workers admitted through the waiver were "temporary," with no interest to remain in the United States permanently, at the same time that he "headed off the suspension of the Chinese Exclusion Law." As Mark Reisler (1976a) outlines, the argument that it was more "convenient" and "easy" to return Mexican workers to Mexico held more sway, given the prospect of a more "permanent race problem" were Chinese persons allowed to regain entry in the United States, pointing to the racialization undergirding their efforts with respect to foreign workers (28–29).

Shortly thereafter, the official bulletin of the U.S. Congress dated May 23, 1917, "Will Admit Aliens from Mexico to U.S. to Provide against Farm-labor Shortage," announced that Secretary of Labor Wilson "has issued orders for the admission to the United States of aliens from Mexico otherwise barred by the literacy test or the contract-labor clause of the Immigration Law."[26] Hence, the first set of regulations were established that would govern the terms under which the temporary admission of Mexican workers would occur, and that until its official termination in 1921,[27] would fluctuate with pressures from growers and nonagricultural interests, labor unions, and congressional disputes.[28] In short, the head tax and literacy requirements were waived; workers were to be admitted only for a six-month period; employers would be responsible for transportation costs from and to Mexico and provide adequate shelter and minimal care for their needs through the duration of their stay. Workers were obligated to work solely for agricultural employers, and employers were granted permission to withhold a fraction of their wages which, at the end of their stay, would be released upon their return to Mexico.

On September 5, 1917, the *Arizona Republican*, in an article titled "Cotton Pickers Coming from Mexico," announced: "The Mexicans are coming! A whole trainload of them—men, women, and children—will arrive in the valley tomorrow, the very first importation by the cotton growers of the valley of labor to help harvest cotton this season."[29]

The recruitment of Mexican workers, by the thousands, is indeed what took place. As the amount of acreage in cotton grew from 33,000 acres in 1917 to 230,000 acres by the 1920–1921 season, so did the increasing urgency and reliance on a Mexican workforce recruited for temporary admission.

THE ARIZONA COTTON GROWERS ASSOCIATION AND THE GENDERING OF ELASTICITY

The Arizona Cotton Growers Association (ACGA) became the chief and centralized entity responsible for recruiting and transporting workers to the Salt River Valley. The mobilization of Mexican workers to Arizona's cotton fields represented the first full-scale unilateral effort, sanctioned by the federal government, to bring foreign labor into the United States. The enterprise involved cooperation between officials in the U.S. Department of Labor, lawmakers and politicians at the state level, law enforcement, U.S. Immigration, city boosters and, subsequently, Mexican government officials.

The formation of the Arizona Cotton Growers Association dates back to 1912, when growers from Tempe, Mesa, and Chandler formed the Salt River Valley Egyptian Cotton Growers Association, deeming themselves a "cooperative" that would oversee "marketing, promoted varietal purity, and lobbied for protective legislation" (Weisiger 1995, 40). Immigration before the Goodyear Tire & Rubber Company arrived in Arizona was hardly a matter of great concern, as the border between Mexico and United States was rather fluid. Those who wished to cross the border from Mexico did so without much impunity or risk. Growers in need of laborers were already in the custom of hiring middlemen (*enganchadores*) often comprised of bilingual English- and Spanish-speaking Mexicans who traveled the rail lines into Mexico to recruit laborers from throughout Sonora and villages as far south as Nayarit, Tepic. As the need for laborers intensified, these *enganchadores* became the means by which thousands of workers, with promises of great fortunes to be made, gained entry into the United States (Peterson 1974, 1975).

The ACGA was comprised of growers that were selected from twenty-four farm bureaus located throughout the Salt River Valley (cited in Pendleton 1950, 112). They became part of the "associational culture" that Larkin (2008) argues valued "cooperation, camaraderie, and the sharing of technical resources (especially information) between individual farmers and merchants" (71). In Arizona this culture came to dominate the way in which entities under a highly organized structure positioned themselves to protect their organizational and profit-making interests in relation to local, state, and federal governments; external capital; and foreign trade. How their "anti-labor rhetoric and practices" unfolded lead Larkin to conclude that the roots of modern conservatism in Arizona can be traced to this period. As will become evident later, it is in the protection of their profit margins and the ways in which they collectively "mobilized to immobilize" Mexican workers that also reveals the contradictory nature of their enterprise.

With the ninth proviso in place, the ACGA launched a relentless campaign to meet the labor needs of the growers it served and manage what they came to characterize as "the labor problem." Characterized by the increased seasonal demand for workers during harvest, growers needed "an elastic supply of labor" that would expand and retract in accordance with production specific to the cultivation, planting, harvesting, and ginning of cotton (Pendleton 1950, 107).

The task of documenting the number of workers that were brought in to the United States during this period is muddled with contradictory evidence and conditions. Between 1917 and 1921 the official statewide count of workers brought under the temporary admissions program was 72,862—33,460 of these were reportedly brought in by the ACGA (Pendleton 1950, 113). The actual number of workers that came under the auspices of ACGA, however, is unknown because family members accompanied many of the workers.[30] Of the portion that came in through the efforts of the ACGA, the official total better reflects the number whom they designated as individual, admitted workers, but not necessarily how many individuals were physically admitted that accompanied each individual worker or that joined their respective family members to work in the fields.[31]

Early on, growers articulated a preference for family men, under the notion that a breadwinner would be more motivated to work in order to provide for his family and less likely to engage in labor-organizing activities of a dissenting nature. While a preference for family men was not unusual during the early part of the twentieth century, this preference within the cotton industry played out quite differently from that of the mining industry. Benton-Cohen (2009) talks about the preference in mining for family men in terms of a "family wage"—the practice being that white men, and white men only, were considered deserving of a wage tied to a standard of living capable of sustaining an entire family unit. In mining this did not apply to the wages paid to

Mexican men, whom employers, conveniently relying on racial ideology that depicted Mexicans as an inferior race, argued did not need or deserve a comparable compensation for their work. The establishment of a racial hierarchy within the mining industry's workforce set up the terms and rationale under which workers from different racial and ethnic groups would receive different wages—most commonly referred to as a *dual wage*, despite, in some cases, doing similar kinds of work. In cotton, particularly during this intensified period of recruitment of Mexican workers, a primarily Mexican workforce accomplished the production processes related to the harvesting of cotton. Hence, a dual-wage structure was deemed unnecessary in the cotton industry since Mexicans were the preferred labor force to whom growers could also, in their self-designated authority, pay the abysmally low wages. Even though growers actively sought out family units, they chose not to pay a family wage to individual Mexican workers, reproducing a racialized, gendered construct to be exclusively applied only to white men.[32] Insidiously, however, they relied on families to serve as the primary production units from which to have their work conducted.

The idea of supporting a family man also suited growers' paternalism toward Mexican workers, allowing them to control the workforce, while portending to extend to them the rights and privileges afforded other men. In defining the family as the preferred production unit, the ACGA was also able to utilize the labor of women and children who entered the country with their husbands and fathers, without counting either as part of their official workforce. It became common practice not to pay women or children as formal individual employees for their work, but instead added the fruits of their labor into the calculations of poundage that was paid to the male head of household.[33]

The participation of women in agricultural work is not as widely studied as one might expect, given the focus on work by scholars of Chicana/o labor history and the extent to which Mexicans' labor force participation rates in agricultural dominated for a significant part of the twentieth century. Devra Weber aptly notes that "the upheavals in migration and revolution led Mexican working-class women to shoulder increased responsibilities, migrate, and survive on their own," leading to her observation that, "in the United States, Mexican women worked" (Weber 1994, 58). Contrary to the prominent depiction of the Mexican single-male immigrant laborer, Mexican women have occupied a nebulous position as individual paid laborers, on the one hand, and unpaid (and invisible) laborers in the context of a family unit, on the other. Both operated simultaneously and were contingent on arrangements specific to time and place. In the case of the ninth proviso, nothing in the language forbade adult women from being admitted as temporary workers, although the preference and operating assumption was that the male worker would be the target for recruitment. In the context of the 1917–1921 time period, women were admitted as

FIGURE 2.2 Cotton pickers, Maricopa County, Arizona. Courtesy of José Villela Photographs, Chicano Research Collection, Arizona State University Libraries.

temporary workers under the Department of Labor's ninth proviso implementation provisions, granted identification numbers, photographed, and subject to the processes of other male workers. Equally important, however, women were also incorporated into the labor force but not officially counted, and their labor power instead became part of the production of the family unit, with wages being paid to the male head of household. The latter rendered the work that women did in the production processes as formally unpaid work. It also rendered the work that children did as formally unpaid work. While their labor was extracted and commodified it was not fully recognized as wage work and instead relied upon indirect payments through a male head of household (one formally admitted through the ninth proviso). The ability of women and children to exchange their labor power for wages was rendered invisible, creating a hierarchy of unremunerated workers, and employers ideally situated to benefit from that cushion and the profits made possible by the labor of the family unit.[34] Thus, the additional family members available for work provided a gendered elasticity to the labor force that ACGA and the vested interests came to rely on, bringing new meaning to how we understand the making and workings of an elastic supply of labor.

LABOR REPRESSION AND IMMOBILIZATION

One of the first courses of action undertaken by the ACGA was to establish as fact among the general public and the federal government that a "labor shortage" existed.[35] This allowed ACGA to recruit in large numbers and to provide, essentially, an oversupply of laborers which, in turn, completed two objectives. First, it created a sense of urgency to "the labor problem," such that practices or adherence to the laws and conditions of the ninth proviso could be subject to state practices that waived infractions and instead, heeded the urgent call for more workers. Second, it created a situation where an abundance of workers would, in effect, serve to quell any proclivities on the part of workers to organize on their own behalf, knowing full well a surplus of laborers remained ready to replace them. In doing so, the seeds were sown to ensure that a steady and elastic supply of labor—one that could both be drawn from and returned to Mexico as needed—and pliable in its political vulnerability to the agricultural interests of the state.

The third course of action was to fix wages growers would pay across the board to cotton workers. Workers were paid 2 cents per pound from 1912 to 1916, when acreage went from 350 acres in 1912 to 7,300 acres in 1916. In 1917 and 1918 workers were paid 2.5 cents per pound, when acreage went from 33,000 acres in 1917 to 72,000 acres by 1918. Not until 1919, when acreage reached 85,000 acres, were workers paid 3 cents per pound, increasing to 3.5 cents in 1920, when acreage increased to 186,000 acres. For the 1921 season, when acreage had ballooned to 230,000 acres, but when the cotton market went bust, workers' wages were reduced to 2 cents, and remained such for the 1922 season, when acreage was reduced to 78,000 acres (Walker 2012, 181). By fixing wages, the ACGA prevented workers from exercising their rights to sell their labor power to employers willing to pay a higher wage and prevented competition among growers that could benefit workers' earnings. This structuring of their exploitation immobilized workers' mobility and thwarted their efforts to protect their interests as workers. Moreover, the ACGA maintained the practice of withholding a percentage of workers' wages until their return, another measure designed to disincentivize workers from leaving without going through arrangements made by the ACGA. The Department of Labor established regulations so as to restrict workers' mobility by denying them the ability to move from grower to grower, and instead obligated them to remain with whatever employer was assigned. Restricting workers to a single employer, in effect, immobilized workers who chose to violate these regulations, thereby making them more susceptible to deportation—a policy, Plascencia (2016) argues, created conditions more similar to indentured servitude than to wage workers.

Yet a fourth course of action undertaken by the ACGA, with the assistance of county and local law enforcement agencies, was to repress any attempts by workers to organize. Labor unions typically opposed nonrestrictive immigration policies so there was little concern that mainstream unions would direct their efforts to organize Mexican workers brought in through the temporary admissions program. The first incident occurred as early as February 1917 and reveals how the ACGA, SWCC, and related interests responded to early efforts to organize cotton workers. The waiver to the ninth proviso had not yet been decided, but operations in Chandler, which relied on a predominantly Mexican labor force, were well underway.[36] The International Workers of the World (IWW), whose aim had been to organize miners in Arizona's mining communities, decided that organizing agricultural workers and immigrants would be in keeping with their philosophy and efforts to organize workers as wage workers (i.e., working class), and not necessarily by trade or craft, as had been the practice by the American Federation of Labor. When the IWW attempted to organize six hundred cotton workers at the Shattuck and Mimo ranch south of Chandler in a quest for higher wages, the response was immediate. Law enforcement moved quickly to "protect" nonstriking workers, while Governor Campbell's office called a meeting of IWW organizers, after which he concluded to "do all in my power to thwart your efforts to confiscate and destroy property of any kinds in state of Arizona. I consider yours an outlaw labor organization and will act accordingly."[37] Indeed, by the time the Southwest Cotton Company held their first company picnic, Edward F. Parker declared in a speech to the audience:

> I frankly confess that it is not wholly clear to me what our duty is toward these I.W.W.'s at this time, but on one thing I am clear, and that is that the Salt River Valley of Arizona is not large enough, peacefully, to contain the Southwest Cotton company organization and the I.W.W.'s at one and the same time. It seems to me this problem can be met along two lines; one is to fight these people from the start and the other is to import good Mexican families to this valley.[38]

Despite renewed efforts by the IWW to organize workers during harvest season, correspondence between Seiberling and Parker divulges the SWCC's direct involvement to obstruct any efforts by the IWW to organize cotton workers, including the firing of "agitators," infiltrating the labor camps with individuals to "listen to the 'secret' talk," and garnering the support of local sheriffs to deputize men who would provoke labor organizers into resisting arrest.[39] Their efforts to rid themselves of the IWW were successful, and workers, who had hoped for wages of 3 cents per pound of cotton, continued to earn the 2.5 cents established by the ACGA.

By the end of 1917 Frank A. Seiberling addressed stockholders at the annual meeting with a cache of good news, indicative of a company positioning itself to be the number one company worldwide in rubber and tire production. Over the past ten years of growth, the Goodyear Tire & Rubber Company went from net earnings of $120,000 to $14 million. Seiberling calculated that business over this ten-year period amounted to over $230 million, with a net profit of over $38 million. Earnings from their Arizona "cotton plantation" brought $5 million in revenue.[40]

EFFORTS TO UNIONIZE, THE END OF THE BOOM, AND "ACTS OF CRUELTY"

For three consecutive years the cotton harvests of 1917, 1918, and 1919 brought increased acreage, unprecedented capital, wealth, and prosperity to the Goodyear Tire & Rubber Company, Arizona cotton growers, the banks, and related businesses profiting from the cotton boom. Towns comprising the Salt River Valley logged record revenues as new roads, buildings, and commerce expanded during the industry's incline. The heightened prosperity did not go unnoticed by workers, nor by unions whose own interests for self-preservation were at stake.

Scholars aptly note that thousands of Mexican and Mexican American workers in northern Mexico and the Southwest organized to fight for higher wages and better working conditions in the latter part of the nineteenth century and first two decades of the twentieth century (Casillas 1979; Gómez-Quiñones 1972 [also cited in Peterson 1975]; Zamora 1993). Workers faced two giant obstacles—labor unions in the United States that viewed any kind of immigrant workforce as threatening to their unionizing efforts for higher wages for the American worker—and industrial and agricultural employers who did everything in their power to maximize profits and suppress dissent. Casillas (1979) argues that each side "used Mexican labor to enhance its position" and left workers "exploited, denigrated, and manipulated by both management and organized labor" (37). Even with the formation of the Liga Protectora Latina, concerns articulated by the organization in 1919 over workers' conditions and contractual breaches over wages, were facilely dismissed by the ACGA and government officials (Peterson 1975, 39–44).

While the national office of the Federation of Labor lobbied against the ninth proviso and "the adverse effects of Mexican immigration on the AFL" (Peterson 1975, 44), the Arizona State Federation of Labor (AFL) effectively reversed its initial anti-immigrant stance such that by mid-1920 eleven federal labor union locals comprised primarily of cotton workers were in place (Peterson 1975). From these concerted efforts to organize cotton workers, the ACGA agreed with the AFL to raise wages for cotton pickers of long-staple cotton to four cents a pound for the 1920 harvest season.

The optimistic belief that cotton, in conjunction with alfalfa, assured prosperity for "decades to come" (McClintock 1918, 7) was shaken off its course when market prices for cotton began to decline in May 1920. The end of World War 1, the persistent pressure on extensions to the waivers under the ninth proviso, and the reopening of previously embargoed markets resulted in a market value for Pima cotton that went from $1.25 per pound to 12 cents a pound by mid-October (Peterson 1975, 53). The entire cotton industry went into crisis, and Arizona, with so much at stake, spiraled into economic and political crisis.

As the market declined, the higher wages previously agreed to stood on tenuous grounds. Instead, the ACGA fortified its union-busting activities and used their alliances with law enforcement to criminalize workers and deport them accordingly (Peterson 1975, 55–68; Walker 2012, 201–7). Peterson (1975) notes three strategies undertaken by ACGA were particularly successful in thwarting workers' efforts to unionize: "jailing activists on trumped-up charges, stepped up recruitment of new immigrants to dilute the labor unionists' forces, and deportation" (55). In one instance, for his attempts to organize cotton workers, the president of the Litchfield Federal Labor Union was arrested and thrown in jail for disturbing the peace. In the fall of 1920, another key organizer of cotton workers was held for the length of the cotton-harvesting season,[41] while three Mexican union leaders were deported by local police who, three years into the cotton industry's boom, were fully familiar with the tactics necessary to impede dissent (57).

In her analysis of Mexican workers, unions, and conservatism in Arizona, Larkin (2008) documents how Arizona's business elite organized themselves into voluntaristic associations to protect their profit-making and powerful interests, while suppressing any and all efforts on the part of workers to organize (i.e., mobilize) on their own behalf. In doing so, they relied on the cooperation of lawmakers and law enforcement.

> Viewing themselves as protectors of society and progress, Arizona's entrepreneurial elite saw their efforts to constrain unions as a way of protecting individual workers and society from the dangers of radicalism. The irony is that while these businessmen feared small groups of laboring men dictating government policies, they put in place the structures to enable small groups of businessmen to do the same. In addition, as businessmen pursuing a profit, they utilized their associations to ensure their supply of Mexican labor.[42]

Indeed, the ability to suppress dissent relied upon the cooperation and joint efforts of these voluntaristic associations, business leaders, and law enforcement at every level of government.

The ACGA, with William H. Knox at the helm (who testified before the congressional hearing on temporary admission of illiterate Mexican workers, 1926) proposed to growers for a second time to cut workers' wages to three cents per pound by November 1920. With 230,000 acres of cotton in the process of being harvested, and pressure from bankers, "who feared a strike and resulting chaos," the growers refused to follow Knox's advice and voted to pay the four cents a pound agreed to in earlier negotiations (Peterson 1975, 57–58). The decision would be short-lived as the cotton market crashed by early December 1920, and the Salt River Valley plummeted into chaos. By January 1921, thousands of workers were left penniless and homeless.

Growers reneged on wages for work already done and for wages withheld from workers that were to be payable in Nogales, Arizona, upon their return to Mexico. Meanwhile, the ACGA continued to bring in workers, even as circumstances unraveled before them. In case after case, from Chandler to Glendale, Avondale, and Litchfield Park, workers reported growers' refusals to pay the wages due them or to provide the conditions to which they were under contractual agreement to comply, leaving Mexican officials with no recourse but to depict their actions as acts of cruelty to Governor Campbell and render the ACGA responsible for the crisis at hand.

In a letter dated January 7, 1921, Edward Parker communicated with Goodyear Tire & Rubber Company president Seiberling about possible plans for the SWCC to go into receivership; of the labor situation, he notes:

> There is a great deal of unemployment here and a lot of the Mexicans are getting hungry. They now find that silk shirts are a poor substitute for food. These poor people really cannot be blamed as they are like a lot of ignorant children. What with some thousands of hungry Mexicans in this valley, we are in a somewhat dangerous situation. Thefts, hold-ups and other crimes are increasing daily. We shall be obliged either to establish concentration camps and feed some of these people or else finance their transportation back to Mexico, or both. This matter will have to be a community proposition and handled probably through the Labor Association.[43]

On February 5, 1921, special envoy from the Mexican Republic, Eduardo Ruiz, and Mexican consul to Phoenix, Gonzalo Córdoba, addressed a letter to the Honorable Thomas E. Campbell, governor of Arizona, calling upon him to "do what is right" and "devise some means by which this situation can be cleared." Attached to the letter, a forty-plus-pages document details conditions in which Mexican cotton pickers found themselves following the bust of the cotton market, which four years prior been deemed the "crowning crop" of the "royal valley." The document records the names of 161 cases of individuals—a majority with family, children, and in some cases extended family members—who were effectively abandoned by the ACGA and the growers, leaving workers "penniless," "destitute," "living out in the open," "at the mercy of the public," and cheated out of deductions and wages owed to them. The report establishes the refusal of growers and the ACGA to meet with the terms of the contract stipulated by the Department of Labor. Workers were repeatedly refused receipts by growers for funds they had deducted from their pay (typically $15) and payable upon their return to Mexico through Nogales. It also reveals the extent to which workers were still being brought in to work as late as mid-November 1920, despite the ACGA having ample knowledge of the market downturn. Workers reported having been underemployed or unemployed and looking for any kinds of employment prior to the crash. Moreover, workers pleaded to be returned to Mexico, a key component of the contract with the Department of Labor.

The following excerpts illustrate the nature and conditions of the displaced workers:

> Jesús Machado is a man that has six children and his wife to support. There is due him from Mr. John Kudeshoff the sum of Forty-eight and 63/100 ($48.62) Dollars. This man informs us that he has tried on many occasions to get Mr. Kudeshoff to pay him but he is now living out in the open with his wife and children and is absolutely without one penny.

> Gregorio C. Martínez, Number 9, was brought here by the Arizona Cotton Growers Association within the last three months and he was deducted Twenty-five ($.25) cents per day from his wages to make up the Fifteen ($15.00) Dollar deposit to be delivered to him upon reaching the Mexican boundary, and for some unknown reason, Mr. Banes, for whom he was working under the orders and directions of the Arizona Cotton Growers' Association, will not give him his receipt for the Fifteen ($15.00) Dollars to which he was legally entitled.

> Francisco V. Moreno, No. 21459, was recruited September 21, 1920, by the Arizona Cotton Growers Association and ordered to work for the West Avondale Ranch. He now has $36.54 due from them, which he is having trouble to collect. This man has a wife and six children and is in destitute circumstances. He urges to us to get his pass to the Mexican border.

> Alejandra Ramírez was brought here by the Arizona Cotton Growers' Association, we are informed, something like two or three months ago. She is a widow and has a boy and a girl. She was last employed by the Chandler Improvement Company and on the 2nd day of February, 1921, she was ordered to leave the tent and seek shelter elsewhere.

> She immediately proceeded to move out her belongings, as well as a great many others who were moving out from other tents nearby, but before she was able to get her belongings out of the tent the tent was pulled down under the orders and directions of one Mr. Cook, and thereafter the tent was removed from the place and she was left out in the open in company with a great many others.[44]

The report describes the evolving crisis, noting that approximately four thousand Mexican workers were "roaming the streets" after being abandoned by their employers and the ACGA, creating havoc among all involved in the once-booming cotton industry. Although numbers vary, a reported thirty-five thousand workers awaited deportation and transportation to Mexico.[45]

On January 20, 1921, the *Labor Journal* featured an editorial condemning the ACGA for breaching their contract with the Department of Labor and failing to provide transportation for the workers' return to Mexico. "They [workers] are being treated villainously and inhumanely. Hundreds are starving and freezing. They are becoming desperate and dangerous to the community and themselves" (cited in Pendleton 1950, 132).

With thousands of workers wandering the streets of Phoenix and surrounding communities, the Arizona Federation of Labor and other union locals gathered resources to provide meals to the workers and their families in downtown Phoenix. The ACGA was now subject to pressure from multiple entities, including the Arizona 5th State Legislature, the Department of Labor, unions, the Mexican government, the county board of supervisors, and neighboring citizenry. A poignant example of the latter is found in a letter from an unlikely source, the conservative editor of the *Arizona Record* in Globe, Arizona, who wrote, "the shameful treatment of the Mexican cotton picker in the Salt River Valley surpasses in heartlessness anything that has occurred in Arizona since its organization as a territory 57 years ago" (cited in Peterson 1975, 75).

Even after the ACGA assured the Mexican consul they would pay for the transportation of all workers in need of transport, the ACGA, only after concerted pressure, partially honored its agreement, claiming it paid for the costs to repatriate 20,651 contract workers (Peterson 1975, 90). The ACGA later testified in 1926 at congressional hearings (despite evidence to the contrary) that it "never allowed any one of these aliens so imported to become public charges" (cited in Peterson 1975, 79).

The Mexican government, working through their consuls, also bore a significant share of the costs to transport workers, allocating $17,000 toward this effort (Peterson 1975, 79).[46] By late May 1921 the last and largest number of workers arrived in Nogales, overwhelming the rail lines, leaving thousands stranded on both sides of the border as they awaited transportation.

While some workers did manage to return to Mexico, others waited the crisis out, while others went in search of work in other southwestern states, thereby joining the ranks of undocumented migrant workers.

CONCLUSION

To return to the "legally imported aliens" inscribed into the headstone, it is difficult to know whether the Mexican workers that initially broke ground for the Southwest Cotton Company in January 1917 were those to be found among the local labor force, or whether they were possibly brought in illegally prior to the official date of the waiver in May. A chronology of Litchfield's history indicates 1917 as the year in which Mexican workers were first brought in, "First laborers, Mexican aliens obtained for six-month period under bond by authority of immigration authority. $1 to $2.50 day wage scales,"[47] but records in the voluminous Goodyear Tire & Rubber Company archives held at Arizona State University fail to definitively answer the origins of the initial crew that broke ground. What is known is that the SWCC and the array of growers and agricultural interests that worked through the ACGA ensured that the execution of the mobilization of thousands of Mexican workers would take place, and that the profits overwhelmingly benefitted growers. The era of utilizing cheap labor, at all costs, had arrived, and the pattern of systematically immobilizing the workforce was also set in place. The very structure put in place by the ACGA—from wage caps, abysmal living conditions, the control of workers' internal mobility, their union-busting tactics, use of law enforcement to quell dissent, and the ability to deport workers at will—all constituted a highly controlled set of "permissions and denials as mechanisms of control" that immobilized a workforce brought to the United States to enrich the Goodyear Tire & Rubber Company, the growers, and the state (Smith, 2013, 20). Also clearer is the extent to which the SWCC and Arizona's governing officials ensured that a law written to restrict immigration was conveniently reinterpreted for the development of Arizona and the West to unfold. It is also unambiguous that the launching of large-scale commercial production of cotton and its lasting value to Arizona's economy would have been, without the mobilization of thousands of Mexican workers, as Seiberling duly noted, "as dead as Julius Caesar."

When the crisis hit, the ACGA and the growers who left workers and their families without pay, abandoned, without shelter, and without a means to return to Mexico, had the option to respond differently. Despite the $28 million their recruitment system and low wages reportedly saved the association and its growers, and the millions that were made, especially by the SWCC during the boom, the ACGA abdicated its responsibility, breached their contracts with the federal government (while the federal government granted amnesty to law violators), and fueled a divide, between nations and between people that would, nonetheless, result in a interdependent, contested coexistence.

There is, indeed, a story here, one of immense ramifications, for behind the seemingly innocuous inscription of "legally imported aliens" is a story that demarcates twentieth-century Arizona's tumultuous beginnings. Little did the governing elite know that laws designed to serve the interests of the agricultural empire would also continue and fortify the presence and permanent settlement of people of Mexican descent, and that the trend would continue. The SWCC, which later became Goodyear Farms, built the company town of Litchfield Park, became the home for multiple generations of Mexican families who settled in the West Valley and worked and lived in the labor camps that were closed down in 1986. These families and their descendants are now among the 25 percent that comprise Arizona's Mexican population. This permanent settlement also leads us, then, to consider another aspect to the mobility to immobility thesis—that is, the mobility that follows the immobility, both literally and in terms of social stratification, for what current demographic data makes clear, is that the state investment to bring in legally imported aliens resulted in a gradual permanent settlement of the Salt River Valley, as it did elsewhere throughout the United States. People of Mexican descent took it upon themselves to search for Cíbola—the legendary city of gold—as Peterson (1974) so aptly framed it, and in doing so, claimed their social, economic, cultural, and political presence onto the Mexico-U.S. borderlands. The desires and interests of agribusiness to stimulate mobility of a population whose return to Mexico was legislated, in effect, created a circular migration, both authorized and unauthorized, between two physically conjoined nations, verifying that their respective futures would remain vastly interconnected.

NOTES

1. The dedication concludes, "The restoration of this historical property could not be completed without the help of the community and Goodyear Farms, directed by Mr. Jose M. Villela, Historian and Dr. Grace Burruel Farnam, Consultant." The Arizona Pioneers Cemetery Association is credited with organizing this tribute.
2. *Alien* is a U.S. legal term adopted from British common law. In 2015 Texas congressman Joaquin Castro introduced legislation, Correcting Hurtful and Alienating Names in Government Expression (CHANGE), to remove this term from federal law.
3. Although literature dating back to Clark (1908) and Dillingham (1911) refer to "Mexican" laborers, in actuality the population included, at different times and in varying degrees, Yaquis (Yoéme), Tohono O'odham, and others. See Hu-Dehart (2016), Glaser (1996).

4. In my work with the Litchfield Park Oral History subcommittee, I am indebted to Belen Soto Moreno, Sonja Hendrick, and Sara Homan for the teamwork and dedication to preserving the history of the Mexican community of Litchfield Park. Celeste Crouch generously contributed photos from the LPHS Collection. More recently Judy Cook, current archivist at Litchfield Park Historical Society, has also been invaluable to our efforts. My introduction to Arizona history was facilitated by the former archivist of the Chicano Research Collection (CRC) at Arizona State University, Chris Marin, to whom I am eternally grateful for jumpstarting my journey and sharing her expertise about Arizona history and the CRC. In the project's early phase, I produced, with the assistance of ASU student Edward Burleson (director), the video *Voices from the Camps of Litchfield Park*. Throughout the entirety of the project, from 2006 to 2012 (and to the present), the work of my former ASU students Elizabeth Martínez and Tino Martínez, as interviewers and videographers, enabled the project to flourish. The project was made possible by grants from the Arizona Humanities Council and matching grants from several private and public entities.
5. For recent work on the mobilization/immobilization construct, see Bhattacharya and Lucassen (2005), Mohapatra (2004), Montejano (1987), Smith (2013), and Standing (2008). It is beyond the scope of this chapter to undertake the discussion of "free" vs. "unfree" labor and its relationship to the particular form of feudal, semifeudal, or precapitalist and capitalist arrangements. See Plascencia (2016) for a summary of the contemporary presence of "unfree" labor in advance/present capitalism.
6. "The Story of Goodyear Farms," n.d., 1.
7. Garcilazo (1995, 14–66), Reisler (1976a, 3–5, 16–17, 96–97), Dimas (1999, 7), Guerin-Gonzales (1994, 29–31); for works about railroads in Arizona, see Sheridan (1995a, 114–23), Trimble (1989, 184–93).
8. The number of workers was in the thousands—for some of the larger lines, the Atchison, Topeka, and Santa Fe Railway hired 2,598; the Southern Pacific Railroad 2,714 out of a workforce of 12,592. See *U.S. Immigration Commission: Abstracts of Reports of the Immigration Commission* (1911, 683).
9. The other areas include Mexicali and Imperial Valley, the San Joaquin Valley in California, the Yaqui and Mayo River valleys in Sonora, the Rio Conchos in Chihuahua, and the Matamoros and Brownsville region. See Walsh (2001, 46).
10. "Cotton One of Essentials for Modern War, Secretary Daniels Tells Manufacturers," *The Official Bulletin* (1917, 8).
11. For discussions of cotton in relation to U.S. Civil War, and foreign intervention in Mexico, see Walsh (2001, 61–66).
12. For a thorough discussion of the causes of Mexican migration during this period, see Corwin and Cardoso (1978, 38–66). Narrators in the oral history accounts of our project verified their families' reasons for leaving Mexico during this period.

13. This first started in 1867 when John W. "Jack" Swilling, a former Confederate soldier and Missouri native, later deemed "the Father of Phoenix," founded the Swilling Irrigating and Canal Company. See also Marin (1987).
14. The Goodyear Tire & Rubber Company paid an average sale price of $27 per acre; see "Goodyear Cotton Plantation" (1917, 3).
15. For discussions on early Mexican settlement in Salt River Valley, see chapter 1; see also Marin (1987), Dean and Reynolds (2006, 13–67), and Solliday (1993, 1–82).
16. Montejano draws on George Frederickson's work, who argues that "race situations exist when so defined by public policy" (1987, 4).
17. Reisler (1976a) draws from state and federal government sources, including U.S. Immigration, the Department of Labor, and congressional hearings and reports to document what he considers the "early" phase of recruitment of Mexican labor to the United States; Peterson's (1975) master's thesis focuses on the specific events that transpired with respect to the rise and fall of the cotton industry's initial period; Pendleton's doctoral thesis (1950) is invaluable for outlining the crisis through newspaper and labor union publications and contextualizing it within the rise of irrigated agriculture in Arizona; Lucio's master's thesis focuses on the suburbanization processes that led to the development and presence of Mexican Americans in the company town of Litchfield Park established by the Goodyear Tire & Rubber Company; Hill's (2007) dissertation focuses on the imprint of cotton on Arizona's urban and architectural landscape; Walker's (2012) dissertation provides an overview of the relations between Mexicans and whites in the context of agriculture's development in the Salt River Valley.
18. While I will include only select segments of the events of the 1917–1921 time period, a closer reading of cited sources can bring further detail to bear on our understanding.
19. For a discussion of the Immigration Act of 1917 and the temporary admissions program that developed as a result of the reinterpretation of the ninth proviso, see Reisler (1976a, 24–48). For how it affected the beet industry and Mexican workforce, see Valdés (1991, 8–10); on the Northwest, see Gamboa (1990, 8–9). To understand its relationship to the Bracero Program, see Plascencia (2009) and chapter 3 in this volume.
20. "Goodyear's Cotton Project near Phoenix, Arizona," *The Green Earth* (1917, 10–11).
21. Litchfield (1954, 161). This plowing, according to local lore and other sources, began on December 25, 1916, (presumably, this was by design and meant to coincide with Christmas, thereby rendering the event a "blessed one") although other sources report plowing began on January 2, 1917.
22. Parker was hired for a period of three years at a salary of $5,000 per year. See "Agreement," Contract between Edward F. Parker and SWCC (October 14, 1916), LP Collection, MS MSS 17, Box 7, Folder 77.

23. Correspondence between Parker and Seiberling may be found in the Seiberling Collection archives (Southwest Cotton Company Folders) of the Ohio Historical Society, Columbus, Ohio.
24. Southwest Cotton Company, Letter (May 11, 1917), MSS 347, Box 36, "Nov. 1, 1916 to July, 1917," Seiberling Collection, Ohio Historical Society, Columbus, Ohio.
25. Southwest Cotton Company, Letter (May 19, 1917), MSS 347, Box 36, "Nov. 1, 1916 to July, 1917," Seiberling Collection, Ohio Historical Society, Columbus, Ohio.
26. "Cotton one of Essential. . . ." (1917, 107).
27. On March 2, 1921, the U.S. Department of Labor officially terminated the waiver under the ninth proviso; however, Plascencia (2016) argues the recruitment of workers from Mexico continued until fiscal year 1922–23, under extensions granted for "certain especially meritorious cases."
28. Southwestern growers, accompanied by mining and railroad interests, relentlessly challenged the restrictions, bolstered as they were by Herbert Hoover who, in his post as head of the U.S. Food Administration, was able to successfully weaken or extend some of the restrictions to benefit the former. See Reisler (1976a, 32–34).
29. "Cotton Pickers Coming From Mexico," *Arizona Republican*, September 5, 1917. Litchfield Park and Goodyear Farms, Goodyear Collection, Box 119, Folder 2, Arizona State University.
30. For a discussion of the Immigration Act of 1917's impact on Arizona, based on archival sources from Mexico and the United States, see Peterson (1974, 1975); for the law's impact on the Southwest, see Reisler (1976a, 24–48); see also Brown and Cassmore (1939, 63–66), Weisiger (1995, 40–44), Meeks (2007, 78–80, 109–113), and Pendleton (1950, 105–59).
31. Plascencia (2016, 9) similarly argues this point; I am indebted to our ongoing conversations over the material and data to reach this conclusion.
32. Benton-Cohen notes how even single white men were paid a family wage, in contrast to Mexican family men and nonwhite family men who were not (2009, 90); see chapter 4 of this anthology for a discussion of dual wage.
33. In her study of women, including Mexican women, in cotton production in Texas, Ruth Allen reported similar practices, whether under tenant farmer arrangements or as paid laborers. "She does not collect her own money; she does not know how much is paid for her services; she seldom knows how much cotton she picks a day or how many acres she chops. The wage paid is a family wage, and the family is distinctly patriarchal in its organization" (Allen 1931, 233–34); for the entire chapter on Mexican women, see 209–39.
34. In light of the preference for family unit, the assessment of the ACGA and government reports on wages paid for poundage harvested needs to be carefully interpreted. ACGA reports amount paid for one hundred pounds of cotton should not be interpreted as

representing the amount paid to a single worker. It is possible that "high" wages reported are the wages paid to a household. When Congressman Carl T. Hayden noted in 1920 that Mexicans harvesting cotton in Arizona plantations were paid a "fair wage" (U.S. House of Representatives 1920, 265–66), he may have been misled by what ACGA reported to him.

35. For a more thorough discussion of the "labor shortage" constructions, see chapter 3 in this volume.
36. For a fuller discussion of this incident, see Walker (2012, 193–200).
37. See Campbell, "The IWW in Arizona: True Copy of the Notes of Honorable Thomas E. Campbell written between '34 and '39," CM Small Manuscripts, Hayden Arizona Collection CM MSM-141, Arizona Historical Society, 6–7; also cited in Walker (2012, 196).
38. "Some Cotton Patch," *Arizona* 7 (1917): 14.
39. Southwest Cotton Company, Letter (July 9, 1917), MSS 347, Box 42, "July 1, 1917 to Dec. 30, 1917," Seiberling Collection, Ohio Historical Society, Columbus, Ohio.
40. President's Annual Report, 1917, Seiberling Collection, Ohio Historical Society, Columbus, Ohio.
41. The case of AFL organizer R. M. Sánchez, more than any other, illustrates the collusion of local law enforcement with federal-level officials, as *Department of Justice officials* (my emphasis) were behind the arrest of Sánchez, whom they claimed was a deserter from U.S. Army. He was held "without a warrant, without charges, and without bond" and not released from jail until the end of the harvesting season (Peterson 1975, 57–59).
42. For sources pertaining to the development of conservatism in Arizona, see Larkin (2008) and La Bau (2010).
43. Southwest Cotton Company, Letter (January 7, 1921), MSS 347, Box 42, "Jan, 1921 to July 30, 1921," Seiberling Collection, Ohio Historical Society, Columbus, Ohio.
44. Campbell Papers, M61, Letter & Report, February 5, 1921. Servicio Consular Mexicano (Mexican consulate), Arizona State Library, Archives and Public Records.
45. Cited in Larkin (2008, 92); "Deportation of Pickers Underway," *Arizona Republican*, January 22, 1921.
46. Peterson (1975) notes that workers displaced from the copper industry were also among those seeking return passages to Mexico (79).
47. Goodyear Tire & Rubber Company Collection, "Chronology of Litchfield Park, Arizona and Goodyear Farms 1908–1947," by Clyde E. Schetter, Litchfield Park and Goodyear Farms, 16A, Folder 6, Arizona State University.

3

"GET US OUR PRIVILEGE OF BRINGING IN MEXICAN LABOR"

★

Recruitment and Desire for Mexican Labor in Arizona, 1917–2016

LUIS F. B. PLASCENCIA

INTRODUCTION

ON APRIL 20, 2016, Senator Jeff Flake (R-AZ) introduced the Willing Workers and Willing Employers Act of 2016 (S. 2827). The proposed bill expands the number of temporary migrant contract workers (also referred to in public discourse as bracero, indentured, guest, bonded, bound, temporary, or unfree workers) recruited to work in the United States through the creation of a new H-2C visa. Flake's bill increases the number of nonagricultural work visas beyond the total already authorized under the existing H-2B nonagricultural work visa. Although not noted in Flake's press release (Flake 2016), the premise of the bill is that there is a shortage of U.S.-workers for year-round nonagricultural work (e.g., house construction, home health care, landscaping, hotel maintenance, care of livestock). The press release also omits that the majority of contract workers authorized by the bill will originate in Mexico. Flake's proposal represents the most recent iteration of what Arizona leaders have argued since the start of World War I—that agricultural and nonagricultural employers face a perilous existence if the federal government does not aid employers in the recruitment of Mexican workers.[1]

For nearly a century, employers in Arizona sustained a labor-shortage argument for which the only evidence provided is the assertion of employers themselves. Federal regulatory agencies, as well as most members of Congress accepted employer attestations as factual and without need of verification. The labor shortage argument is salient to producing an elastic supply of labor that is tractable, can be coerced to work at lower wages, accepts poor and dangerous working conditions, meets high productivity standards, and allows employers to achieve desired profit margins. Lobbyists representing employer interests have convinced Democrat and Republican members of Congress that imminent specters of labor shortages confront employers. Additionally, commodity associations and corporations (e.g., the American Hotel and Lodging Association, the Arizona Cotton Growers Association, Facebook, Google, The Trump Organization, The Walt Disney Company) argue that looming dangers confront them if they are not allowed to recruit contract labor to meet alleged labor shortages.

This chapter examines the discourse and actions articulated by Arizona leaders from 1917 to 2016 regarding the specter of alleged labor shortages and why employers must have the federal government's aid in preventing catastrophic economic impacts. The foregrounding of the close to century-long discourse allows us to grasp the persistence of contract-labor regimes, and the adverse effects on contract workers as well as U.S. workers.[2] It also highlights the paradoxical process involving the aggressive recruitment of Mexican workers, and coexistence of cyclical periods of anti-Mexican fervor aimed at banishing workers whose mobility was encouraged. I argue that the unbroken continuity in the recruitment of Mexicano labor for close to a century is the product of state privileging of employers (i.e., capital), the persistent reluctance of the state to monitor or punish corporate violations of migration and labor regulations, and the state policy of lower-cost food that ensures agribusiness profits.[3] These, however, are accompanied by an increasing level of law enforcement actions against Mexican *obreros* (workers) who are blamed for taking jobs away from U.S. workers and for being a drain on society. Additionally, I suggest that contract-labor programs are sine qua non in the production of elastic labor supplies; that the construct of labor shortage is salient to this process; and that profit, coercion, and unfree workers are an intrinsic triad to the contemporary U.S. free-market economy.

The overall contract-labor logic and process represents a web of coercion and profit that rely on unproven assertions of labor shortages, which must be met by indentured workers whose wages are maintained at low levels for sustained periods of time.[4] The low wages and poor working conditions produce a self-reinforcing circular argument for more unfree workers because U.S. workers are not interested in working for the prevailing wages and working conditions offered to bonded workers, thus creating a "labor shortage" that must be met by additional indentured workers.[5] It is also a logic that depends on biopolitical arguments about inherent biological or social elements that make U.S. white workers unable or unwilling to carry out required work, and simultaneously characterizes African-descent, Chinese, Filipinos, Jamaicans, Japanese, Mexicans, Puerto Ricans, and other nonwhite communities as best suited for difficult and low-paid work.[6] Such biopolitical arguments can be thought of as part of what Anibal Quijano labels the "coloniality of power" (2000).[7] Stated more succinctly, contract-labor programs are structured by power relations that rely on racialized distinctions.

The core data for this chapter are congressional hearings, proposed and enacted bills, and federal reports that address the need for indentured workers from 1920 to 2016.[8] This chapter is divided into four parts. The first section summarizes the context and demand for unfree workers in the period between 1917 and 1926, and the actions taken by the federal government to meet employers' demands. The second section discusses the contract-labor discourse and actions taken between 1942 and 1951, and the third section examines the presentation of the arguments and federal actions from 1952 to 2016. The fourth section of the essay presents statistical data related to the unbroken recruitment of Mexican migrant contract labor between 1942 and 2016. In the final section I summarize the importance of understanding the unbroken recruitment of indentured workers and the impact of bonded labor programs on U.S. and contracted workers.

A NOTE ON TERMINOLOGY

The chapter uses the terms *contract labor*, *indentured workers*, and *unfree workers* interchangeably. The first term is a broad label for temporary worker visas (e.g., H-2A, H-2B, H-1B, J-1, L-1), which allow a non-U.S. national to enter and work for a single employer for a specified period of time, and under specified conditions, though these are commonly not adhered to on the part of employers. Employment-based visas—the contract—bind a worker to a single employer. The worker cannot leave the employer for another employer who may offer a higher wage or better working conditions. If a worker asserts a choice to leave the assigned employer, they become subject to deportation.[9] The employer, however, can terminate the contract without any reason or advance notice to the worker; the worker is then expected to leave the United States, and if they do not leave, they become subject to deportation. Moreover, under the lower-wage visas (i.e., H-2A and H-2B), the worker is excluded from gaining credit on the basis of time or work performed that would allow the person to gain permanent residence, or later citizenship, and they are excluded from most benefits that accrue to U.S. workers.[10] The state-sanctioned policy to refuse such credit fosters the circular migration of contract workers and ensures the permanency of their temporariness.

Within the political economy literature on labor, the term *indentured* refers to a labor relationship generally involving a state-sanctioned bonding arrangement that formally binds a worker to a particular employer, such as the nonimmigrant visas noted earlier.[11] During the contractual period the laborer is expected to work only for the assigned employer, to remain with the employer for the contracted period, and to accept employer-imposed conditions, including maltreatment. Henry P. Anderson summarized this situation in noting, "I have never talked with a bracero who had the slightest choice of what employer he was to work for, what crop he was to work in, or what wages and working conditions he would work under" (1958, 4). The use of the concept of indentured labor in this chapter is not wholly novel. In 1964 Dr. Ernesto Galarza noted the following related to World War II contract workers: "Is this indentured alien—an almost perfect model of the economic man, an 'input factor'; stripped of the political and social attributes that liberal democracy likes to ascribe to all human beings ideally—is this *bracero* the prototype of the production man of the future?" (1964, 16). Although Galarza does not explicitly discuss indenturedness, his detailed published descriptions of the labor relationship experienced by contract workers provide ample portrayal of the process.

The labor relationship relies on various degrees of state-sanctioned coercion to ensure that the worker adheres to the contract, even if there is discriminatory treatment of workers, employer violations of the contract, or even physical violence against the worker. In general, workers who abandon the employer, even for good cause, are punished in various ways such as blacklisting (i.e., excluded from future contracting by employers in the same area or industry) and, ultimately, deportation.[12] All of the current contract-labor visas in the United States, including those labeled high skilled (e.g., H-1B) involve such coercion and make the individual subject to deportation if they abandon the state-assigned employer.[13]

Unfree labor refers to a broad category of work conditions involving varying degrees of coercion that force an individual to labor for a private or government interest (e.g., chattel slavery, peonage, coolie, debt peonage, serfdom, forced-labor camps, prison labor), and wherein the worker is indentured to a particular employer.[14] A central factor is the absence of the ability of a person to freely commodify their labor in choosing whom they shall sell their labor power to, and to negotiate the wage at which they agree to sell their labor. Free workers are theoretically free to leave an employer at any time and seek work elsewhere for an employer who pays a higher wage or offers better working conditions.[15] As described earlier, temporary worker visas in the United States represent state-sanctioned contract-labor arrangements that indenture a worker to a single employer, and the worker does not possess the freedom to select who the laborer will sell their labor to—thus, they are unfree workers.

The reader will also note that the chapter does not use the term *bracero* or *guest worker* unless a source cited deploys them.[16] Based on the commonly noted translation of the former as a person performing work with their arms, the term is dehumanizing in its labeling of human laborers by a body part, and thus it is avoided. Moreover, it was never the label used in the formal agreements between Mexico and the United States.[17] The term *guest worker* is a euphemism.[18] Indentured workers may be labeled *guest*, but are not treated as one would expect to treat a guest.[19] The term *guest worker* in reference to Mexican workers was first used in congressional documents in the early 1980s.[20] I interpret the use of *guest worker* as a strategy to disavow the exploitative history of the World War II contract-labor regime and thus frame arguments about indentured labor through seemingly neutral terminology.

WORLD WAR I ERA: 1917–1926

As insightfully discussed by Cuádraz in chapter 2, World War I set the foundation for the contemporary discourse and policies regarding the recruitment of non-U.S. nationals from Mexico to meet the employer-attested labor shortages caused by the United States' participation in the war (April 6, 1917–November 11, 1918). Key reasons cited at the time were: (1) the impact of military conscription, (2) the lure of higher-paid urban jobs related to war production, and (3) the higher demand for war-related commodities such as copper, cotton, and food and fiber needed to aid European allies and for the U.S. military. Agricultural producers, railroad corporations, coal mining enterprises, and the U.S. Army were permitted to recruit Bahamian, Canadian, and Mexican labor to meet alleged labor shortages.[21] A peculiar interpretation of a provision in the Immigration Act of 1917 fostered the mobilization of a substantial number of indentured migrant workers to aid U.S. employers from 1917 to 1923.[22] Secretary of Labor William B. Wilson was persuaded by agricultural employers and others to believe that the Immigration Act's ninth proviso granted him the authority to waive the restrictions in the law.[23] The Arizona Cotton Growers Association (ACGA), as discussed in chapter 2, played an important role in promoting the use of the ninth proviso to recruit Mexican labor for cotton harvesting in the Salt River Valley during and after World War I.

The Immigration Act of 1917 was enacted on February 5, 1917, over President Wilson's veto, and represented a notable victory for organized labor that sought to limit increased competition from European workers, and for nativist/eugenicist groups that expressed much concern with the migration of Eastern and Southern Europeans. Such migrants were considered poor quality material in the manufacture of so-called real Americans, as well as polluters of a white nation. According to nativists/eugenicists, allowing their entry would lead to the end of the United States as a nation of and for whites.[24]

The Immigration Act of 1917 contained several important changes to the nation's migration statutes. The three most important provisions were the literacy requirement, the increase of the head tax to $8, and incorporation of exclusions imposed under the 1885 Foran Act (also known as the Alien Contract Labor Act). These provisions represented the first major actions that limited the relatively free movement of individuals from Mexico to the United States.

The ninth proviso is a vague sentence suggesting that the commissioner general of immigration (within the U.S. Department of Labor) could allow entry to individuals whom the act intended to exclude.[25] Moreover, the Foran Act made it illegal for all U.S. employers to facilitate the recruitment of foreign workers for jobs in the United States and provided substantial penalties for violations of the law. Employers, however, implemented artful strategies to bypass the act's exclusions, and illegally recruited "alien" labor.[26] Along the Mexico-U.S. border, some migration officials contributed to the violation of the law by assuming that the Foran Act did not apply to the southern boundary and observing local custom that granted special privileges to prominent agricultural employers.[27] In the Imperial and Yuma Valleys, for example, workers indicating they were entering to work in lettuce, cantaloupes, or cotton were allowed entry during the harvest periods without the requirements in law (Hernández 2010, 72).

Secretary of Labor William B. Wilson issued orders on May 23, 1917, indicating that he was taking action under the ninth proviso to waive the head tax, literacy, and contract-labor restrictions, and "to admit aliens from Mexico to U.S. to provide against farm-labor shortages" in Arizona, California, New Mexico, and Texas (U.S. Department of Labor 1917, 4). This marked the beginning of the World War I contract-labor arrangement. Although the ninth proviso was originally applied to Mexican migrants employed in Arizona and other Southwest agribusiness interests, it was subsequently amended to include Bahamians for agricultural work and construction, Canadians for agricultural work (principally logging), and Mexican workers for nonagricultural work: railway maintenance, lignite coal mining, and for the building of barracks for the U.S. Army in Arizona, California, New Mexico, and Texas.[28]

The total number of workers admitted under the ninth proviso arrangement is uncertain (Plascencia 2016). According to the U.S. Department of Labor, a total of 72,862 contracted workers were admitted (most of these were of Mexican origin), but it is not clear if the 10,000 Mexican workers contracted to work in railroads, and those authorized for the U.S. Army and coal mining (totals not reported), are included in the reported total. In contrast to the World War II indentured-worker scheme, the World War I effort allowed families to enter to meet alleged labor shortages. As noted by Cuádraz, the ACGA encouraged the migration of families. The general practice adopted by boundary officials was to grant a work permit to the adult head of household, though individuals over the age of sixteen were photographed, fingerprinted, and given an identification card. Children under the age of sixteen were not photographed, fingerprinted, or issued an ID card. During the period, children may not have been classified as workers or formally hired by cotton growers, but nonetheless labored in cotton harvesting alongside family members. Consequently, the total number of Mexican and non-Mexican workers authorized under the indentured-worker arrangement remains undetermined.

Information regarding the geographic distribution and economic classification of employers who contracted indentured workers is also limited. The inconsistent reporting by the Bureau of Immigration in its annual reports further complicates this. In some years limited data were reported; while in subsequent years additional data was presented, but this was not repeated in succeeding annual reports. The 1919 commissioner general of immigration's annual report, however, is particularly notable. In that report the commissioner reported that of the 20,643 Mexican indentured workers admitted in fiscal years (FY) 1918 and 1919, 10,491 were assigned to agricultural enterprises, 9,998 were authorized for railway maintenance, 89 to the army, and 65 to coal mines (U.S. Commissioner General of Immigration 1919, 13). Moreover, of the total number admitted in FY 1917 and 1918—29,563—9,036 had returned to Mexico, 240 had died, 20,278 were still in the United States, 14,016 were still with the original employer, and 6,252 "having left the service of those employers" (ibid., 13). Individuals in the last category were also referred to as *deserters*—meaning that about 21 percent of the contracted workers chose to accept the risk of being subject to deportation but secured the status of free workers. The Bureau of Immigration concluded that deserters were still in the United States but did not know the whereabouts of the 6,252 runaway workers. In contradiction to assertions that legal migration channels eliminate the presence of so-called illegal migrants, the World War I experiment shows the opposite effect: contract-labor programs stimulated the unauthorized presence of laborers and family members.

The 1919 annual report is also unique in reporting the geographic distribution of the contracted workers. Mexican workers were assigned to employers in twenty states; these encompassed the Midwest, Southeast, Northwest, and Southwest. The four principal destinations, and primary users, were employers in Texas (8,636), Arizona (6,803), California (6,382), and Idaho (1,549).[29] Within the two months of FY 1917, only two states received indentured workers: Arizona (243 for cotton) and Colorado (228 for sugar beets).[30] The Arizona Cotton Growers Association, Representative Carl T. Hayden, and other Arizona leaders fostered the recruitment of indentured workers for Arizona during and in the post–World War I era.[31]

TEMPORARY ADMISSION OF ILLITERATE MEXICAN LABORERS: 1920

Over five days in January and February 1920, the House Committee on Immigration and Naturalization held a hearing titled *Temporary Admission of Illiterate Mexican Laborers*. The 1920 hearing is the first held by Congress that focuses exclusively on Mexican migration to the United States. Its focal point was whether Congress should authorize a one-year extension of the "wartime emergency" adopted by Secretary of Labor William B. Wilson in May 1917.

The committee's concern centered on the question of whether the earlier waivers authorized by the Secretary of Labor should continue and be applied to "illiterate Mexican laborers" for an additional year. In other words, whether the Immigration Act of 1917's literacy, head tax, and contract-labor restrictions should be set aside because of the alleged postwar labor shortages being experienced in Arizona, Texas, and other states. Congressman Albert Johnson (R-WA), chair of the committee, and other committee members favored more restrictive migration policies and benignly opposed witnesses pleading for an open border and the need for an additional year of the 1917 waivers.

Although individuals representing Arizona were outnumbered by those testifying on behalf of cotton interests in Texas, Arizona representatives made their position clear: Congress should enact the pending resolution (H.J. Res. 271) and allow "illiterate Mexicans" to enter and work in Arizona as was done during World War I. Congressman Carl T. Hayden (D-AZ) made the following key points in his testimony: (1) the introduction of the Egyptian long-staple cotton in the Salt River Valley and other areas in the state required additional labor; (2) according to cotton growers, "unless they can secure seasonal labor from Mexico the production of long-staple cotton must be greatly reduced"; (3) "to meet an extraordinary situation, that certain Mexican agricultural laborer . . . be permitted to temporarily enter the United States [and] that when they have completed their year's work . . . they shall return to their own country"; and (4) "the Mexican agreed that if he attempted to engage in any other class of labor outside of agriculture . . . he would be returned to Mexico" (U.S. House Committee on Immigration and Naturalization 1920, 262–75).

When Congressman John C. Box (D-TX) who, like Johnson, favored greater restrictions on migration, asked Hayden about reported desertions from assigned employers by Mexican workers in Arizona during the war, Hayden indicated that he did not know of any such instances (ACGA representatives acknowledged that it did happen). And when Congressman Benjamin F. Welty (D-OH) asked whether tying a worker to a single employer violated an individual's liberty, Hayden responded that "aliens" have no right to do anything else than what the person was contracted to do. Welty went a step further and asked a more poignant question: "Why should capital place a chain around his neck and lead him around and when they are through with him kick him out again?" He also raised the issue of *peonage/indentured labor* prohibited by the Thirteenth Amendment (ibid., 265–66; emphasis mine). Hayden explicitly defended the ACGA and its treatment of indentured Mexican workers and indicated that there is no slavery in Arizona, and that the Mexican worker was paid a fair wage, though did not indicate actual wages paid or how the fair wages compared with wages in other cotton-producing areas. Hayden also did not address the issue of whether mandating a worker to work for one and only one employer—that is, creating an unfree, indentured worker—was a violation of the Thirteenth Amendment.

Like other witnesses representing cotton, Hayden offered a racialized perspective (an expression of coloniality of power) on why Mexican nationals and Indians were employed in hand-harvesting cotton. According to Hayden, "The white people do not usually want to do it, while the Mexicans from the other side of the border, and the Indians, who are employed to some extent *are glad to do it* . . . it is a question of *inclination* to do that kind of work" (ibid., 272; emphasis mine). He further noted the preference in Arizona for Mexican cotton workers: "As a practical proposition, the necessary temporary labor can come from but one source and that is Mexico" (ibid., 275). Witnesses representing cotton interests in Texas expressed much more racialized coloniality of power statements about biological, climatic, and cultural reasons why Mexicans are the preferred cotton pickers, and why whites are not suited for such work. What was not raised by committee members was whether higher wages would attract white or Mexican American workers, and what constituted a fair wage in Arizona.

Several important observations are found in the seventeen letters submitted to Hayden by Arizona leaders, and placed in the record of the hearing. Governor Thomas E. Campbell submitted a short letter emphasizing the "labor shortages here" and the need for "Mexican labor" (ibid., 276). The president of the Phoenix Chamber of Commerce asserted, "Without Mexican labor the Salt River Valley would be unable to keep up the production so insistently urged by the Federal Government" (ibid., 276). A. J. Garnett Holmes from Yuma forwarded a terse and informative telegram: "For sure get us our privilege of bringing in Mexican labor to handle our cotton, used only in agriculture. Conditions of industry at stake" (ibid., 276). Holmes, like cotton representatives in Texas, asserted that they were entitled to recruit Mexican labor, as was done in the past prior to World War I, and during that war. Thus, from their perspective they were not asking for something new, but rather were pleading with Congress to simply allow them to carry out what they were used to doing: freely recruiting Mexican workers without hindrances from government, even if done illegally in violation of the Foran Act. Although not labeled as such at the time, they were de facto pleading for an open border in the transnational labor market.

Two additional witnesses representing Arizona testified at the hearing: David Keane, and W. H. Knox. Keane resided in New York but attended the hearing on behalf of the Salt River Valley Cotton Company. In his testimony, Keane voiced several notable observations. One, he repeatedly labeled cotton farms as "cotton plantations" and reiterated the central importance of Mexican labor in the plantations. Second, Keane communicated the dependency of Arizona cotton plantations on Mexican labor, and the strong preference for Mexican workers over all other groups. Keane noted:

> Now, there is nothing we can get to take the place of the Mexican labor that will save us from great losses if not entire bankruptcy on these cotton plantations. And unless you give us this relief, it will cause not only the loss of the large investments that I represent . . . but it will also cause great loss to the United States Government, and also cause great loss to the State of Arizona. (ibid., 44)

Later in his testimony, Keane summarized his message to the committee: "Give us labor and do not put any restrictions of any kind on that labor" (ibid., 46). Representatives from Texas also expressed the argument for an employer-organized recruitment of Mexican labor, without federal interference—that is, an unobstructed practice of recruiting labor in Mexico and along the Mexico-U.S. boundary area; a de facto open-border labor market.

W. H. Knox, representing the Arizona Cotton Growers Association, reiterated most of the aforementioned arguments: there are drastic labor shortages in Arizona, particularly in cotton production; the ACGA had the "privilege of importing Mexicans" under the ninth proviso; and white people are recruited in Arizona and beyond, but they tend to abandon the work as soon as they start working. He did not address if the wages paid to cotton harvesters and conditions of work influenced the lack of interest on the part of white people and Mexican Americans to seek employment in the Salt River Valley's plantations.

In the end, H.J. Res. 271 was not approved by Congress. Secretary of Labor Wilson, however, authorized the continuation of the postwar "wartime emergency" recruitment of Mexican labor to meet the alleged labor shortages in agriculture in Arizona and other states. The ninth proviso was in effect from 1917 to 1923, despite the end of World War I on November 11, 1918. As noted later, the ninth proviso did not expire in 1923, but was applied at various times until 1952; it was the statute used in 1942 and early 1943 to admit the initial cohort of Mexican indentured labor referred to as braceros.

SHOULD IMMIGRATION QUOTAS APPLY TO MEXICO?: 1921-1924

The Senate Committee on Immigration held a series of hearings in January 1921. The seven-hundred-plus-page hearing report (*Emergency Immigration Legislation*) focused on a bill (H.R. 14461) that proposed to continue the aim of the Immigration Act of 1917: to restrict the number of migrants entering the United States. At the center of the debate was the question of whether the proposed quota should apply to Mexico. Interests opposing the inclusion of Mexico under the proposed quota won the debate. The 1921 and 1924 Immigration Quota Acts excluded Canada, Mexico, and Cuba from the numeric caps placed on all other nations. Employer interests in Arizona and other states could carry out business as usual regarding the recruitment of Mexican migrants without the hindrance of a government-imposed numerical cap.

Similar to the 1920 hearing, Texas was well represented at the 1921 hearing, and all agribusiness interests expressed their strong opposition to impeding Mexican migration to the United States W. H. Knox testified on behalf of the ACGA. He reiterated: "the industry is dependent entirely upon Mexican labor for its common or hand work," and provided the following figures for Mexicans recruited during the calendar years by the ACGA: 2,500 (1917), 3,500 (1918), about 10,000 (1919), and about 20,000 (1920) (U.S. Senate Committee on Immigration 1921, 87–88). This means that approximately 36,000 contracts were issued to Mexican workers for work in Arizona's cotton plantations for the period 1917–1920.[32] What Knox did not tell the committee was that families were encouraged, and allowed by federal officials, to migrate to Arizona's cotton plantations; thus, the estimated 36,000 contracts reported is not the actual total of Mexican individuals who hand-harvested cotton in the ACGA plantations. This reality also makes it difficult to calculate actual worker earnings when families harvest cotton. Employers tend to only record the payment to the head of household of a cotton-harvesting household. Consequently, state and federal statistics on wages earned in Arizona cotton plantations during the period overestimate what was actually earned by individual workers. Hayden's reference to "fair wages" in 1920 may also have been based on what the ACGA and other cotton growers reported as payment to households, not on actual payments to individuals who picked cotton.

SEASONAL AGRICULTURAL LABORERS FROM MEXICO: 1926

The House Committee on Immigration and Naturalization held a hearing in January and February 1926, which was titled *Seasonal Agricultural Laborers from Mexico*. Representatives from the ACGA, the Arizona State Farm Bureau Federation (also representing Pima County cotton producers, the Salt River Valley Water Users Association, and the Phoenix Chamber of Commerce), and the Nogales Chamber of Commerce testified at the hearing. Close to eight years after the end of World War I, the same wartime arguments were repeated. The one new dimension to the discourse was the statement that Arizona cotton growers were "empire builders" who, with the aid of the federal government regarding water (though the federal assistance in obtaining Mexican workers is omitted), built a successful cotton empire in Arizona. The sweat and labor of Mexicano workers made the empire possible, but their contribution is not acknowledged.

C. S. Brown, representing the Arizona State Farm Bureau Federation (and other interests), summarized what Arizona cotton plantations wanted: "We are satisfied with the kind of labor that we used to get when we could get that labor in sufficient amount" (U.S. House Committee on Immigration and Naturalization 1926, 32–33). What C. S. Brown did not communicate to the committee, and committee members failed to ask, was if owners of the cotton plantations—the empire builders—were aware that from 1885 to the time of the hearing, U.S. law (i.e., the Foran Act) prohibited all employers from recruiting foreign workers for jobs in the United States, with the exception of workers exempted under the ninth proviso in the 1917–1923 period.[33] Consequently, the admitted practice of recruiting Mexican labor in Mexico in the first decades of the 1900s was, in effect, an admission that employers in Arizona violated U.S. law, but were granted a special amnesty by federal law enforcement entities. The rule of law was made flexible for employers desiring Mexicano workers. What this suggests is that cotton plantations in Arizona were able to build an empire based on an elastic supply of Mexican agricultural workers. It was a profitable empire that depended on low wages paid to Mexican workers, a portion of whom were recruited in violation of U.S. law, and with a de facto exemption from punishment for violations of U.S. law. The Bureau of Immigration and the Department of Labor implemented the ninth proviso indentured-labor program with the assumption that employers would, without question, abide with all of the conditions imposed under the rules issued by Secretary Wilson. The Department of Labor ultimately relinquished its regulatory authority over agribusiness employers and thus fostered grower impunity to manage, pay, and house contracted workers as they saw fit without government interference; this allowed empire builders to generate substantial profits.[34] The free market was given state-sanctioned freedom to pursue greater profits.

WORLD WAR II AND POSTWAR PERIOD: 1942–1951

The broad outline of the World War II contract-labor arrangements between Mexico and the United States involving over five million contracts, generally referred to as the Bracero Program, is fairly well-known among historians and scholars of the Mexico-U.S. borderlands.[35] Scholarly discussions of the agricultural component for the 1942–1964 time period can be found in introductory texts in multiple disciplines. This is in addition to the significant volume of books, doctoral dissertations, master's theses, journal articles, and policy-oriented reports on the labor arrangements.[36] Despite the significant scholarly production on the Bracero Program, Henry P. Anderson's observation made over fifty years ago remains true today: "no full study of it has ever been published" (1963). The reason for this is that of the thirty states that received unfree labor, most of the research has focused on a single state: California. While the attention on California is understandable due to its position as the single largest recruiter of contracted Mexican labor in the 1942–1968 period,[37] the result is that we know relatively little about the operation of the labor arrangements in the twenty-nine other states, and of the nonagricultural contracts such as the specific experience of workers in the over thirty railroad corporations that employed Mexican contract workers.[38]

The conventional historiography of the 1942–1968 contract-labor effort begins with the assumption of a war-based emergency "labor shortage."[39] Similar to the arguments deployed at the start of World War I, agribusiness interests, principally in the Southwest, pressured the United States to formulate an agreement with Mexico to allow the admission of Mexican migrant agricultural contract workers to meet the alleged labor shortage. Formally, the original agreement suggested a fair position for contract workers. In actuality, however, growers were able to contravene the contracts they had signed with the federal government and implemented various degrees of exploitation that facilitated the accumulation of profits. Many of the multiple employer violations in the World War I labor arrangements were similar to those that surfaced during the 1942–1968 contract-labor arrangement.[40] I will return to examples of employer violations and exploitation of workers below after summarizing the overall organization of contract labor begun in 1942.

Although the conventional historiography of contract-labor arrangements during World War II privileges the Mexico-U.S. arrangement, the reality of the period is more complex.[41] Yes, Mexican agricultural workers were the single largest group of workers contracted to meet alleged labor shortages in the Southwest and beyond; however, they were not the only group of nonnationals admitted by the United States. Shortly after the Mexico-U.S. executive agreement was signed, the United States signed agreements with British colonies in the Caribbean (e.g., Jamaica, Bahamas), and others such as Newfoundland and Spain (for Basque sheepherders) to allow workers from these areas to come to the aid of U.S. employers. Additionally, arrangements were made with Canada, as a *verbal agreement*, to allow Canadian woodsmen to work principally in Maine; and after the war, Japanese were admitted to aid agribusiness. In short, World War II allowed the U.S. integration of not only natural resources from the Americas (e.g., marijuana hemp rope from Sinaloa, Mexico; rubber from Brazil), but also to integrate labor from the Western Hemisphere, as well as from Asia.[42]

In exact parallel to the contract-labor regime initiated in 1917, the original political strategy was to recruit Mexican labor for agribusiness interest in the United States (particularly cotton and sugar beets). Similarly, it was shortly thereafter expanded for railroads. And again, like its predecessor, it was originally promoted as a wartime emergency, but continued considerable beyond the actual end of the war (August 1945), as well as the Korean War (June 1950–July 1953). The World War II Farm Labor Supply initiative covered the period from 1942 to 1968 and involved over five million worker contracts.[43] In addition, approximately 135,000 workers were admitted for thirty railroad corporations. Indentured workers were allocated to employers in thirty states. And as discussed shortly, more workers were recruited after the end of World War II than during the war, despite the rationale that the war produced a wartime labor-shortage emergency.

Government sources primarily report the total number of agricultural worker contracts for the respective fiscal year and do not consistently report the state distribution of the contracts. Yet, these sources and testimony in congressional hearings make clear that California agribusiness was the single largest user of contract workers. Arizona was initially an important destination, particularly in cotton harvesting, but with the increasing mechanization of cotton harvesting after the war, and the decrease in the demand for and profit from cotton, Mexican contract workers became less important for cotton production. However, the expansion of winter vegetables and citrus in the Yuma Valley reinforced arguments about labor shortages and the need for Mexican labor.[44]

1950–1951: PRESIDENT TRUMAN'S COMMISSION ON MIGRATORY LABOR

On June 30, 1950, President Truman issued Executive Order No. 10129. The executive order created the President's Commission on Migratory Labor.[45] The commission was charged with examining the conditions of migratory agricultural workers ("alien and domestic"), whether there was a continued need for "foreign workers," and the problem of "illegal migration." The commission held a total of twelve hearings in the summer and fall of 1950. Individuals representing wide interests were invited to participate and submit written testimony. One of the hearings was held in Phoenix, on August 7 and 8.

Carson Morrow, chief border patrol inspector (Tucson sector), noted four key points in his testimony: (1) that although contract workers were being admitted as temporary workers, many became permanent workers; (2) that there was no labor shortage—"Insofar as Arizona is concerned, there is little or no doubt that sufficient farm labor will be available without the importation of foreign labor for harvesting the present crops if the standard price is maintained . . . I believe there will be a surplus" (Morrow 1950, 3); (3) that the substantial difference in the wages paid to "wet workers" and "domestic laborers," sixty cents and one dollar, respectively, made undocumented migrants the grower-preferred workers for hand-harvesting cotton and cantaloupe; and (4) that orders from higher-level officials within the Border Patrol limited his law enforcement activities. According to Morrow, "but for the past few years and especially last year instructions have come down to the field from higher authority instructing us to stop apprehending Mexican aliens employed on farms during harvest seasons," with the result that a larger number of such workers had entered Arizona to work in agriculture (ibid., 4). The long-standing practice of granting amnesty to agribusiness is not generally acknowledged—it remains in place to the present.

The Immigration and Naturalization Service (INS) officer in charge in the Phoenix office, O. W. Manney, also testified. In his testimony Manney also argued against a labor shortage. He acknowledged, "Possibly the importation of these Mexican nationals was necessary during the period of the active war. However, it has become more and more apparent to me during the past several years at least that they were no longer necessary in this area. I am absolutely convinced that none has been necessary during the past year" (Manney 1950, 1–2). Manney also reiterated the permanency of temporary workers: "Although the entire program [Bracero Program] has stressed the intention that these workers would be admitted only during emergencies and for temporary periods only, in this area they have been maintained on a permanent basis, some of them from more than seven years" (ibid., 2), and that local growers tended to hire contract workers rather than "local workers" (ibid., 3). As part of his testimony Manney submitted a page with data on the number of workers contracted at the end of 1949 and beginning of 1950: 4,936. The page shows that the Arizona Cotton Growers Association represented the single largest employer of contracted workers. It accounted for a total of 4,162 contracted workers (or 84 percent of the total).

Organized labor was also present and submitted their written testimony. The joint statement by the Congress of Industrial Organizations (CIO) and the Arizona State Federation of Labor (AFL) asserts that there is no labor shortage, and that there are in fact a large number of individuals qualified and willing to "do common labor," and that it is the low wages paid to contract workers that unfairly disadvantages U.S. workers (CIO-AFL 1950, 1). They also expressed their criticism of the ACGA and their demand for contract workers. According to their statement:

> It is to the advantage of certain groups like the Cotton Growers Association to get federal permission to get alien labor that is not guaranteed the rights of our Constitution into their employ and, thereby, setting up a paternalism that borders on *involuntary servitude and slavery*. (ibid., 2; emphasis mine)

Additionally, three individuals representing agribusiness also testified at the hearing—George Pickering (Yuma Producers Cooperative Association), O. W. Rugg (chairman of the Labor Procurement Committee, ACGA), and E. S. McSweeney (executive secretary of the ACGA). Pickering made it clear that Arizona agribusiness faces labor shortages. For Pickering, the labor shortage is driven by two key factors: (1) the fact that crops such as lettuce, carrots, and cantaloupes are "highly perishable"; and (2) the absence of migrant domestic workers. As noted by Pickering:

> In view of the fact that it appears definite that fewer migrant domestic workers come into our area, we believe that we will have a continuing need for imported workers and naturally in this area, they should be Mexican workers, as our Country adjoins Mexico. (Pickering 1950, 2)

He also urged the commission to recommend a "simplification of the contract" (i.e., the processing period be reduced), and that recruitment be "continued at the border" [as took place during the World War I program] (ibid., 2). On the question of why Mexicans are the preferred labor force (other than proximity to Mexico), Pickering offers a racialized view that domestic workers (presumably white workers) are not attracted to agricultural work because the "extreme heat" in the area; however, it is implied that Mexican workers, due to biology, seem to be suited to work in the "extreme heat" (ibid., 1). Pickering concludes his statement by asserting that in the absence of available domestic workers, "we must have a Program which will allow us to use Mexican agricultural workers when they are needed" (ibid., 2). Pickering appears to be arguing for the need for an elastic supply of Mexican labor that will appear when needed and can be banished to Mexico when not needed. As insightfully argued by Burawoy (1976), the expectation that workers return home is a strategy that capitalist agriculture deploys to eliminate any economic or social responsibility for unemployed workers—the externalization of social reproduction costs.

O. W. Rugg reiterated similar concerns to those of Pickering; however, he added that one reason for labor shortages in cotton is that in the post–World War II period there was a significant expansion of cotton acreage. Moreover, although he does not specify the years, Rugg notes that in recent times the high number of "wetbacks" in Texas aided Arizona. Their depression of wages in Texas allowed the U.S. Employment Service to recruit among the impacted Mexican American workers. In concluding his statement, Rugg observed: "We know from past experience we are going to suffer an acute labor shortage in the [future] harvest of our crop [cotton]" (Rugg 1950, 7). Rugg's statement foregrounds an intrinsic dynamic in the discourse—it was asserted months ahead that a labor shortage would irrefutably emerge before the actual start of the harvest, and federal agencies would approve the recruitment of contract labor to be present at the start of the harvest. In other words, the existence of a labor shortage was a priori certified as factual before the start of the actual harvest, and no verification was needed.

E. S. Sweeney acknowledged that the ACGA was the largest user of migrant contract labor. He also praised the availability of Mexican contract labor to meet labor shortages, but was quite critical of the Mexico-U.S. agreement and the requirements imposed on farmers. Sweeney pointed out:

> They [the recruited workers] were of real value in helping us overcome the serious labor shortage early in October and were life savers on several of the out of the way ranches where the growers have always had great difficulty obtaining domestic crews. (Sweeney 1950, 5)

President Truman's commission heard many of the same concerns in the eleven other hearings and submitted their report to the president on March 26, 1951. The commission recommended three policy actions related to U.S. agricultural workers, the recruitment of foreign contract labor, and a solution to address the issue of illegal immigration. On the first issue, they recommended that protections not granted to domestic agricultural workers under the 1930s New Deal labor protections (e.g., minimum wage, unemployment insurance, workers' compensation) be extended to agricultural workers. On the issue of illegal immigration the commission adopted the recommendation that "Legislation is needed to make it unlawful to employ aliens who have entered the United States illegally" (President's Commission on Migratory Labor 1951, iii)—in other words, that Congress should enact an employer sanctions law to prohibit the employment of undocumented migrants. More specifically, the commission recommended the removal of contracted workers from growers employing both contracted and undocumented migrants, fines and imprisonment for employers found in violation of the law, and the prohibition on the shipment in interstate commerce of any product on which undocumented migrant labor was used. Congress did not adopt an employer sanctions provision until its enactment by President Reagan in 1986—thirty-five years after the commission's report. Congress provided a de facto thirty-five-year amnesty for employers hiring individuals whose presence was not authorized and who were subject to deportation.[46]

With specific reference to the recruitment of Mexican contract labor, the commission recommended the following: "No special measure should be adopted to increase the number of alien contract laborers beyond the number admitted in 1950" (ibid., iii). Ultimately, President Truman failed to enact the recommendations of his commission, and the Bracero Program continued based on unsubstantiated assertions by agribusiness that they faced labor shortages. Since 1965, nonagricultural interests adopted the H-2 visa option made available under the McCarran-Walter Act (1952) to argue for the need of indentured workers in nonagricultural occupations.

EXPLOITATION OF WORKERS: WORLD WAR II CONTRACT LABOR

Prior to turning attention to the contemporary period, it is useful to summarize the exploitation of contracted workers during World War II and the postwar era, and the impacts on U.S. workers. The relevance of this is that it draws attention to parallels found in contemporary guest-worker arrangements. Although there is a substantial literature describing multiple forms of abuse and exploitation of Mexican contract labor and the negative effects on the wages, employment, and working conditions of U.S. workers, here I present the succinct statement submitted by Ernesto Galarza to a House committee hearing related to the extension of the Mexican farm labor program in 1960.[47] According to Galarza:

> For nearly a decade our union [National Agricultural Workers Union, AFL-CIO] has appeared before this committee in pleading on behalf of the farmworkers who have suffered the effects of the Mexican contract labor program under Public Law 1978 [1951]. We have submitted facts, provable facts, as evidence that this program had become a major *weapon of exploitation* of domestic and foreign workers alike. (U.S. House Subcommittee on Equipment, Supplies, and Manpower 1960, 237–38; emphasis mine)

He then proceeds to list the following examples of the intrinsic problems with the existing "*indentured labor*" (ibid., 238; emphasis mine) program: The Department of Labor "has admitted": (1) "in some places Mexican national were sent to camps unfit for human use"; (2) "it has failed to secure compliance from growers' associations"; (3) "Mexican nationals dominate many crops formerly served by thousands of domestic workers"; (4) "that it cannot determine a prevailing wage—the keystone of its system—in crops dominated by Mexican nationals"; (5) "the use of Mexican nationals has had an adverse effect through the years on working conditions in the fields"; and (6) "that the hiring of Mexican nationals has frozen wages and in many instances depressed them below former levels" (ibid., 238). Additionally, Galarza notes the presence of collusion between public officials and agricultural employers, graft and bribery, "falsification of payroll and other records," structural barriers for U.S. workers wishing to file complaints regarding program violations, and corporate farmers' ability to raise funds to fight unions "realized from the exploitation of Mexican nationals" (ibid., 237–38).[48]

By the 1950s the criticisms and opposition to the Bracero Program and its extension included not only organized labor—it also encompassed faith leaders, civil rights groups, and others. Critics were also found within the Department of Labor (DOL). Lee G. Williams, for example, was an official within the DOL who supervised the employment of migrant contract laborers between 1959 and 1964—he referred to the program as "legalized slavery" (Majka and Majka 1982, 136). Williams's conclusion rested on the observation that contracted workers were indentured to a single employer, did not possess the liberties and freedoms of free workers, and, thus, approximated enslavement.[49]

CONTEMPORARY PERIOD: 1952–2016

The conventional historiography of the Bracero Program tends to cite the year 1964, rather than 1968, as marking the end of the program, and often overlooks the importance of the 1952 H-2 visa in understanding the combined legacy of World War II contract labor and the H-2 visa in forming present-day indentured-labor programs. This section seeks to expand our understanding of contemporary contract-labor programs by foregrounding policy actions since 1952. After summarizing the importance of the H-2 visa, the section examines the testimony of Arizona leaders at the 1958 congressional hearing related to the extension of P. L. 78—the law that guided the contracting of labor from 1951 to 1968.

THE 1952 SAFETY NET: H-2 VISA

At several points during the implementation of the Bracero Program (1942–1968), in response to rising criticism regarding the extensive exploitation of workers within the program and violations of terms in the signed contracts with the federal government, some members of Congress considered ending the contract-labor arrangement with Mexico. The writing on the wall was clear: the program would come to an end in the near future. While Congress was in the midst of formulating a "comprehensive immigration reform," the McCarran-Walter Act of 1952 (Public Law 82–414, 66 Stat. 163), Congress adopted a provision in the law that appeared to be a "tiny provision" with little consequence.[50] It approved the passage of a new visa: the H-2 temporary worker visa. The H-2 visa was adopted in the context of debates in the post–World War II period regarding the impact of World War II and the Korean War on U.S. agricultural production. At the time of its passage the provision seemed to be a marginal and unnecessary visa. The "tiny provision" created a visa allowing the entry of temporary workers in agricultural and nonagricultural occupations where there was a need for such workers. Not surprisingly, the H-2 visa was imagined as a visa to allow the admission of Mexican workers to perform agricultural contract labor in the United States. The H-2 visa overlapped for sixteen years (1952–1968) with the Bracero Program.

President Harry S. Truman enacted Public Law 414 with a "tiny provision": 101(15)(H)(ii) (commonly labeled H-2). The provision specifies that:

> An alien having residence in a foreign country which he has no intention of abandoning . . . (ii) who is coming temporarily to the United States to perform other temporary services or labor, if unemployed persons capable of performing such services or labor cannot be found in this country. (66 Stat. 163, 168)

The H-2 visa had minimal use between 1952 and 1964. With the formal termination of the larger-scale recruitment portion of Mexican labor at the end of 1964, however, subsequently the provision took on a robust life. Starting in 1965 the United States allowed and increasing number of Mexican contract workers; most of these were assigned to agricultural employers in Arizona and other states. It should be observed that in place of a wartime emergency condition, the H-2 provision makes the inability of finding unemployed U.S. workers the central criteria justifying the recruitment of non-U.S. nationals as temporary contract workers. This also granted the Department of Labor the responsibility of determining what actions would be accepted as bona fide efforts on the part of employers in recruiting U.S. workers. What is or is not a bona fide employer effort remains a contentious issue up to the present. Employers assert they make every possible effort to locate U.S. workers, and critics point out that employers carry out perfunctory recruitment and ingenious actions to discourage U.S. workers from applying. After presenting the views of Arizona leaders in 1958 we will return to the importance of the H-2 visa starting in 1965.

1958: PROBLEMS IN THE SOUTHWEST AND MEXICAN LABOR

Although in the 1950s and early 1960s Senate and House of Representatives committees held several hearings, principally in California and Washington, D.C., regarding the extension of World War II bonded labor program, the Arizona Cotton Growers Association and other Arizona interests were generally absent from these.[51] However, the U.S. House Committee on Agriculture's Subcommittee on Equipment, Supplies, and Manpower held three hearings in February and March 1958. The first two hearings were held in California; the third was held in Phoenix.

E. P. Theiss testified that the AFL-CIO opposed proposed bills to make the P. L. 78 permanent, though conceded that the program could be extended for two-year periods. He also testified that the implementation of the program under P. L. 78 "makes it very plain that no domestic worker is to be denied employment [but in actuality] makes it practically impossible for a domestic worker to find out where these opportunities are" (U.S. House Subcommittee on Equipment, Supplies, and Manpower 1958, 191). Theiss also stressed labor's opposition to how the "prevailing [wage] rate" was established and observed that the common practice among growers was to use the starting wage rate for the previous season as the starting "prevailing rate" for the upcoming season (ibid., 194), and so, in effect, reduced the real wage earned by contract workers. U.S. workers were understandably not interested in the jobs offered under the prevailing wage rates and working conditions.

James A. Rork, director of the Employment Security Commission of Arizona, testified regarding the implementation of the contract-labor arrangement. Overall, he presented a positive picture of the program, and the importance of "the nationals" (i.e., Mexican nationals) in meeting the state needs for "stoop labor" and reiterated the "shortage of enough labor" (ibid., 196–98). When questioned about housing conditions and inspections carried out, Rork acknowledged that there is a "little problem" due to the lack of staff in the section related to compliance (ibid., 200). This suggests that Arizona agencies involved in the implementation of contract labor did not make enforcement compliance a high priority. Moreover, Rork points out, "There is a greater reliance upon the word of the farmer" (ibid., 200). Galarza discusses in great detail that in California there was a de facto conspiracy between state agencies and grower associations; thus there was no interest on the part of governmental agencies to interfere or find fault with the actions or assertions of agribusiness (1964). Agribusiness attestations of future expected labor shortages before the actual start of the harvest period and the wage fixing of prevailing wages became standard, and regulatory agencies did not question the logic or factual basis of attestations.[52]

Following Rork's testimony was that of E. S. McSweeney (executive secretary of the Arizona Cotton Growers Association). Not surprisingly, McSweeney expressed his support to make P. L. 78 permanent. According to McSweeney:

> We believe that, if the legislation is made permanent, it will overcome some of this constant quarreling and bickering about it. Most of our difficulty is not with the basic legislation of Public law 78, but arises through the administration or misunderstanding of the administration of the law (ibid., 201).

He also observed: "We think that in Arizona both the letter of the law and the intent of the law are carried out by the Employment Service 100 percent and that, as it is administered in Arizona, no domestic workers are displaced by Mexican nationals" (ibid., 201). McSweeney did not offer any evidence that displacement had not taken place, and committee members did not ask about the basis of his assertion.

William Larson (manager of the Vegetable Growers Association) also testified. In his brief testimony he indicated his support of the contract-labor program, that "the nationals" do not operate machinery, and that domestic and transient workers are given first priority in jobs (ibid., 204–5). He also expressed the view that P. L. 78 could be operated without an expiration date, since ultimately the program depended on the need for contract work; presumably the need would vary but would likely remain present and the Departments of Agriculture and Labor would support labor requests.

Two cotton growers testified at the hearing: Rudolph Johnson and Robert Schulke. Johnson and Schulke stated they use "Mexican national farm labor," particularly at the peak of cotton harvesting in December, January, and February (ibid., 205–6). With reference to housing, Johnson noted that existing housing is "sufficient," and that "the farmer shouldn't have to improve much more than what they are right at the present," and Schulke concurred (ibid., 206). Even though the two cotton growers did not explicitly state they support the extension of P. L. 78, their stated use of contract labor suggests that they would continue to rely on that labor. Committee members did not ask about the condition or status of housing.

Gail Pew of the Arizona Dairymen's League also presented testimony to the committee, but she focused on needed aid in the financing of dairy operations. Finally, H. S. (Casey) Abbott presented his statement to the committee, but at this hearing he focused on broader issues related to federal crop insurance assistance to farmers. Abbot did not mention his important role in shaping national farm labor policy. He served in the Department of Labor's National Farm Labor Advisory Committee—a small group that advised the Secretary of Labor regarding the implementation of P. L. 78.

The same year that the larger-scale portion of the Mexico-U.S. contract-labor program ended—1964—was also a presidential election year. Representing the Republican Party was Senator Barry M. Goldwater, the five-term senator for Arizona. His opponent was Vice President Lyndon B. Johnson (D-TX). In August 1964, the *New York Times* submitted a set of questions to Goldwater. One question asked was: "Do you have any comment on the Administration's bracero (seasonal Mexican farm labor importation) problem?" Goldwater's written response was:

> I certainly do. The citizens in this state [Arizona] in many instances are facing disaster because of Government meddling in a program that has worked well for years. Farmers can't get domestic labor to do the work. The only answer is to return to the bracero program and for the Government to keep its hands off a relationship existing between employer and employee [*sic*] that has been successful thus far. (*New York Times* 1964)

Putting aside the fact that the noted farm labor program was created by a joint agreement between the U.S. and Mexican governments, and that labor advocates would dispute whether the program was successful with reference to U.S. workers or the contracted workers, what is important here is that the Republican presidential candidate favored the continuation of the program. And that if he had won the election, he would have likely encouraged Congress to extend it beyond December 1964.

1965: THE POST-WORLD WAR II CONTRACT-LABOR DEBATE

One month after the official end of the World War II large-scale recruitment portion (i.e., December 1964), the Senate Committee on Agriculture and Forestry held a hearing: *Importation of Foreign Agricultural Workers* (1965). A paramount issue in the hearing was the H-2 provision in the McCarran-Walter Act (P. L. 414). Senator Allen J. Ellender (D-LA), committee chair, opened the hearing by reporting that the Secretary of Labor had issued rules for the implementation of the H-2 provision on December 19, 1964, and that the H-2 visa had great potential to address the so-called labor shortages in agriculture. The only Arizona-based representative testifying at the hearing was Senator Paul Jones Fannin (R-AZ). Fannin's one-page written statement highlights the grave labor shortages in Arizona, and the serious economic impact to Arizona agriculture if Congress fails to act and allow Mexican temporary contract workers to come to the aid of Arizona agribusiness.[53]

In addition, Fannin made two important points. The first focuses on his assessment of the Bracero Program, and the second on the potential of the H-2 provision. With reference to the former, Fannin asserts:

> For many years, particularly during the period I served as governor of Arizona, I had the opportunity to closely observe the bracero program in operation. I have some familiarity with how the program has successfully operated, what it accomplished, and why it is vital to the growers of Arizona. . . . Therefore I feel competent to express an opinion that the importation of Mexican workers is essential and should be continued. (U.S. Senate Committee on Agriculture and Forestry 1965, 40)

Other close observers arrived at opposite conclusions. In addition to the better-known work of Ernesto Galarza (cited earlier), a second close observer, though not cited as often as Galarza, is Henry P. Anderson. Anderson carried out field research over seven years in California and observed firsthand the relations between growers and workers, between federal officials and workers, the corruption among U.S. officials and growers, and interviewed a significant number of Mexican contracted workers. Based on his research and reflections on the Bracero Program, in 1958 Anderson concludes the following:

> I am convinced that the bracero program—indeed, foreign contract farm labor programs in general—indeed, contract labor per se as in whatever form or guise, will by its very nature wreak havoc upon the lives of the persons directly and indirectly involved and upon human rights which our Constitution still holds to be self-evident and inalienable. I am convinced that foreign labor programs must be extirpated root and branch, and that temporizing with then is as immoral as the programs themselves.[54]

For Anderson, the very structure of recruiting foreign workers for temporary work in the United States, not providing any permanent benefits for their contribution, excluding them from benefits provided to U.S. workers, and then forcing workers to work for a single employer under the threat of expulsion, makes bracero/guest-worker programs inherently coercive and exploitative.

On the question of P. L. 414, Fannin notes, "It is my understanding that a satisfactory Mexican labor program can be carried out under the provisions of the Immigration and Nationality Act of 1952 (Public Law 414) under workable regulations" (U.S. Senate Committee on Agriculture and Forestry 1965, 40). In other words, the H-2 visa could serve as a safety net for agricultural interests in Arizona who had previously depended on the unfree temporary indentured workers. The December 1964 regulations by the Department of Labor and the January 1965 hearing drew sufficient attention to a real alternative (i.e., the H-2 visa). At the start of calendar year 1965, migration and labor officials approved a significantly greater number of H-2 visas than they had in the previous decade—even though the "tiny provision" was enacted thirteen years earlier. The U.S. indentured-labor program in place between 1952 and 1968 under P. L. 78 was accompanied by a mechanism that could foster a surplus in the elastic supply of labor, the H-2 visa. The termination of the large-scale recruitment segment at the end of 1964, however, actuated the deployment of the provision in the 1952 Act to aid agribusiness meet alleged labor shortages.

1970S-2016 DEBATES

In the post–1965 period, the discourse of Arizona leaders regarding Mexican labor, as articulated in congressional hearings, is more difficult to discern. There are two key reasons for this. One, the hearings in the 1970s focus more on proposals by the Carter administration for "immigration reform," the initial activity of the Select Commission on Immigration and Refugee Policy, and partial attention to the work conditions of U.S. agricultural workers as a whole. And in the 1980s much of the attention of members of Congress shifted to the evolving dialogue regarding immigration reform plans and the eventual enactment of the Immigration Reform and Control Act (IRCA). President Reagan's enactment of the IRCA in November 1986 represented the culmination of a political debate begun in 1972 on how to best address undocumented migration, and what to do with the estimated 3.2 million persons subject to deportation residing in the United States, many of whom had been residents for substantial periods of time. In the early 1980s the primary policy debate focused on employer sanctions, an amnesty/legalization program, and an expansion of a guest-worker program. The third issue, however, was partially sidelined at the end in order to garner support for the Simpson-Mazzoli bill, which became IRCA.[55]

The reports by the Select Commission and the work of the U.S. Commission on Immigration chaired by former congresswoman Barbara Jordan attracted much attention in the 1990s. And between 2000 and 2012 Congress returned to examining guest-worker programs, primarily the H-2A program. From 1981 to 2016—encompassing eighteen sessions of Congress—the House of Representatives and the Senate held a combined total of thirty-five hearings on temporary contract-labor programs.[56] All thirty-five hearings included arguments about increasing the number of indentured workers through the expansion of the H-2A, H-2B, or H-1B visas, or creation of new visas (e.g., H-2C, W visa).

Two, the organization of congressional hearings changed in the post–1965 period. Instead of inviting multiple local representatives from affected states as in the past, the witnesses invited to participate were primarily individuals representing national employer and worker groups, staff from D.C.-based organizations, some academics, pro- and anti-migrant advocacy organizations, and representatives of federal agencies. Thus, members of Arizona's congressional delegation were largely absent from the thirty-five hearings.[57] Moreover, the list of witnesses in House and Senate hearings came to be constituted by usual suspects in hearings sponsored by both chambers, and reflected the political party holding the majority position in the respective chamber.

Within the 2000–2016 hearings held, Congressman Jeff Flake (R-AZ) is the only Arizona leader who testified.[58] In a House hearing in 2004, Flake provides a page-and-a-half statement. He asserted that there are labor shortages in Arizona in construction, hospitality industry, and agriculture, and asserted that this is not due to wage issues—though no factual data are presented to support the statement. Instead, Flake notes that the problem is that "native-born Americans" (i.e., presumably whites) are not available in "sufficient number . . . willing to take those jobs" (U.S. House Subcommittee on Immigration, Border Security, and Claims 2004, 4). Flake's assertion about wages not being a factor in attracting native-born Americans, as already pointed out earlier, is part of a long-standing argument by growers in Arizona and beyond. Agribusiness representatives had argued that alleged labor shortages were not linked to wages (i.e., that fair wages offered did not lead to U.S. worker interest in hand-harvesting crops). At more than one congressional hearing, growers in other states asserted that even high wages would not attract U.S. workers. However, no specifics are provided regarding what constitutes high wages, nor whether any agribusiness ever actually tested offering high wages to see if U.S. agricultural workers would be attracted to agricultural jobs offered. Similar to the attestation about labor shortages and that contract worker programs reduce or eliminate undocumented migration, the assertion that wages are not an issue in attracting U.S. workers is often repeated but no actual empirical evidence is provided to support the assertion, and U.S. Department of Labor officials and members of Congress have tended to uncritically accept the assertions by agribusiness.

What Representative (now Senator) Flake did not address is that if it is not wages, then what else could be impacting the lack of interest among U.S. workers in jobs in construction, hospitality, and agriculture. To simply say that "native-born Americans" are not available and wages are not a factor does not explain much. The "it is not wages" argument eschews the inseparable issues of working conditions, non-wage benefits, and wages. Workers in the free labor market judge jobs not simply on the basis of the salary offered—they also evaluate the working conditions demanded (e.g., whether it is indoors or outdoors, above-normal production demands, difficult and dangerous work tasks, etc.), and the job benefits offered by the employer (e.g., medical insurance, unemployment insurance, workers' compensation insurance, sick leave, vacation, etc.). Are employers in construction, the hospitality industry, and agriculture not able to attract native-born Americans because the norm in wages and working conditions offered is based on the lower wages, lack of benefits, high productivity, long hours, and difficult working conditions imposed on contract workers and undocumented workers? Thus, it can be argued that native-born Americans are not attracted to jobs in construction, hospitality, and agriculture because they know the wages and working conditions offered, and these are not viewed as providing a livable wage or attractive employment conditions.

Additionally, Flake's assertion does not take into account that employers have formulated multiple inventive practices aimed at excluding interested U.S. workers from applying or accepting job offers—specifying unwarranted times in the day to apply, needless tests of tasks that may not be part of the daily work tasks (e.g., demanding the applicant carry a heavy object several times around the perimeter of a building), drug testing, proof of extensive experience, etc. These practices, however, are not applied to indentured or undocumented workers. In this context, Flake may be correct in saying that it is not wages that create labor shortages, but leaves unstated if it is the combination of wages, working conditions, benefits, and recruitment processes in the three sectors that foster the so-called labor shortages. If this latter proposition is correct, then a logical solution to alleged labor shortages in the three sectors would be to ensure that employers in the affected sectors significantly improve the wages, working conditions, and benefits offered to make the jobs attractive to native-born Americans, as well as eliminate discriminatory application requirements applied only to U.S. workers. The substantial lower-wage cost extracted by employers from indentured and undocumented workers, and government support in sanctioning lower-wage/higher-profit contract workers reinforce the status quo.

At this time, there is no governmental or broad public incentive to change current practices and increase the employment of U.S. workers in construction, the hospitality industry, agriculture, or other sectors that rely on indentured contract and undocumented migrant workers. The formidable task of protecting and improving the wages and work conditions of contract workers has fallen on migrant advocacy organizations such as the California Rural Legal Assistance, Coalition of Immokalee

Workers, Colorado Legal Services, the Economic Policy Institute, Farmworker Justice, the National Guestworker Alliance, and the Southern Poverty Law Center.

CONGRESSIONAL PROPOSALS FOR CONTRACT WORKERS: 1989-2016

An important indicator of support for contract-labor programs is the legislative actions taken in the U.S. Senate and House of Representatives. A review of all proposed bills from 1989 (101st Session of Congress) to 2016 (114th Session) reveals that in eleven of the fourteen congressional sessions, a member filed a bill aimed at expanding the entry of indentured workers or filed a broader bill that included a provision related to an existing contract-labor visa. From 1995 (104th Session) to 2016 (114th Session), a total of 118 bills were sponsored that contained a provision to expand or modify an existing contract-labor visa.[59] I also include here proposals to improve an aspect of an existing program, as well as appropriation bills that included a contract-worker provision. No bill was filed to terminate or sunset an existing indentured labor visa.

Members of Arizona's congressional delegation participated in sponsoring several indentured-labor bills. Arizona senators and representatives sponsored or cosponsored 24 of the 118 bills filed between 1995 and 2016. Table 3.1 summarizes the contract-labor bills filed between 1995 and 2016 that were supported by Arizona senators and representatives.

Table 3.1 foregrounds that members of Arizona's congressional delegation supported the continuation or expansion of contract-labor visas in almost all sessions of Congress from the 104th to the 114th. The table also highlights that although the majority of 24 proposed bills were sponsored or cosponsored by Republican legislators, Democrats were also visible supporters. Republicans sponsored or cosponsored 78 of the 118 total bills (66.1 percent), and Democrats sponsored or cosponsored 40 of the total (33.9 percent). All 118 bills considered between 1995 and 2016 uncritically accepted the premise that an agricultural or nonagricultural sector faced a labor shortage, and that U.S. workers were not available or interested in jobs in the respective sector. And in the particular case of the H-2A and H-2B contract-labor visas, that Congress should authorize the entry of Mexican workers for employers allegedly facing the specter of a labor shortage.

ARIZONA LEGISLATURE AND THE "TEMPORARY WORKER PROGRAM" (2008)

The story of Arizona's SB 1482 in 2008 is instructive because it highlights efforts at the state level to also foster the expansion of indentured workers. In 2007 the Republican-controlled Arizona legislature passed the Fair and Legal Employment Act (FLEA) and Governor Janet Napolitano (D-AZ) enacted HB 2779.[60] FLEA was the state's employer sanctions law. Its aim is to reduce the presence of Mexican undocumented migrant workers by punishing employers who employ them. The rationale was that there were too many such workers (hundreds of thousands), and that their presence negatively impacted U.S. citizens' employment opportunities. Thus, the elimination of the magnet of jobs in Arizona would allow U.S. workers the opportunity to quickly fill the vacated jobs, and the state's unemployment rate as well as its public assistance costs would drop significantly. FLEA went into effect on January 1, 2008.[61]

In the first week of February 2008, with bipartisan support of twenty senators, SB 1482 was introduced. The bill called for the creation of the Arizona Temporary Worker Program. SB 1482 sought to address the "labor shortages" in "agriculture and meat production industries, hotel and hospitality industries, contractors, homebuilders, subcontractors for roofing and landscaping, hospitals and nursing homes" (SB 1482). SB 1482 did not pass. The irony between FLEA and SB 1482 are relevant to understanding contradictions in how temporary migrant contract-worker programs can be formulated alongside enforcement efforts to remove persons without employment authorization. Arizona legislators saying that the expulsion of undocumented migrant workers will open up jobs for U.S. workers who need jobs but cannot find work, and then asserting that temporary workers must be brought in to fill the many vacancies that exist due to the unavailability of unemployed U.S. workers is contradictory. SB 1482 also serves to underscore how elected officials can summon an unsubstantiated notion of a labor shortage and then propose a solution to the alleged fact. It can be surmised that the start of the Great Recession in December 2007 impacted the interest of elected county attorneys in prosecuting employers violating the employer sanctions law and legislative support for recruiting foreign workers as the state's unemployment rate began its ascent in 2008 from 4.6 percent in January to 11.1 percent in the same month in 2010.

2016 WILLING EMPLOYERS AND WILLING LEGISLATORS

As noted at the beginning of the chapter, Senator Flake's April 2016 Willing Workers and Willing Employers Act (WWWEA, S. 2827) represents the most recent federal legislative effort by a member of the Arizona delegation to expand the number of indentured workers in Arizona and beyond. The sixty-four-page bill calls for the establishment of a ten-year pilot program to establish a new temporary contract-labor visa—H-2C visa (U.S. Senate S. 2827).[62] The visa would be for year-round nonagricultural work involving low-wage workers—what the bills euphemistically labels "workers with less than a bachelor's degree." Annually, a flexible total of 65,000 to 85,000 workers would be allowed admission. In actuality, the total in a given year would be greater

Table 3.1 Support for Indentured-Labor Programs by Arizona's Congressional Delegation, 1995-2016 (104th-114th Sessions of Congress)

U.S. Senator/Representative (Political Party)		Contract-Labor Legislation	Session of Congress
Jeff Flake (R)		H.R. 2899	108th
		H.R. 3142	108th
		H.R. 1645	110th
		H.R. 2414	111th
	Gang of Eight Member[1]	S. 744	113th
		S. 153	114th
	Sponsor	S. 2827	114th
Trent Franks (R)		H.R. 2954	110th
Gabrielle Gifford (D)		H.R. 1645	110th
Paul Gosar (R)		H.R. 2215	114th
Raul Grijalva (D)		H.R. 3142	108th
		H.R. 4262	108th
		H.R. 884	109th
		H.R. 371	110th
		H.R. 1645	110th
		H.R. 2414	111th
		H.R. 4321	111th
	Sponsor	H.R. 3163	113th
J. D. Hayworth (R)		H.R. 4738	106th
Ann Kirkpatrick (D)		H.R. 2215	114th
Jim Kolbe (R)		H.R. 4548	106th
	Sponsor	H.R. 4738	106th
	Sponsor	H.R. 2899	108th
		H.R. 3142	108th
John McCain (R)	Sponsor	S. 1461	108th
		S. 1645	108th
		S. 359	109th
		S. 2611	109th
		S. 2612	109th
		S. 340	110th
	Gang of Eight Member	S. 744	113th
		S. 153	114th

Table 3.1 *(continued)*

U.S. Senator/Representative (Political Party)	Contract-Labor Legislation	Session of Congress
Ed Pastor (D)	H.R. 3142	108th
	H.R. 4262	108th
	H.R. 1645	110th
	H.R. 2414	111th
	H.R. 4321	111th
	H.R. 3163	113th
Rick Renzi (R)	H.R. 371	110th
Matt Salmon (R)	H.R. 2202	104th
David Schweikert (R)	H.R. 5006	114th
John B. Shadegg (R)	H.R. 2202	104th

[1]The Gang of Eight refers to the eight members of the Senate who negotiated the 2013 Senate comprehensive immigration reform bill, S. 744: Michael Bennet (D-CO), Richard J. Durbin (D-IL), Jeff Flake (R-AZ), Lindsey Graham (R-SC), John McCain (R-AZ), Bob Menéndez (D-NJ), Marco Rubio (R-FL), and Chuck Schumer (D-NY). The roll call on the bill was 68–32.
Note: Congressional Sessions: 104th (1995–1996); 106th (1999–2000); 108th (2003–2004); 109th (2005–2006); 110th (2007–2008); 111th (2009–2010); 113th (2013–2014); 114th (2015–2016).
Source: Library of Congress, Congress.gov database, https://www.congress.gov/advanced-search/legislation.

because S. 2827 exempts contract renewals from the annual cap. Flake's bill incorporates the logic of the 1952 H-2 visa, and is repeated in the H-2A, H-2B, H-1B and other contract-labor visas: employers who are able to show they were unable to find U.S. workers, are then authorized to recruit temporary contract workers. The sixty-plus-years experience with those criteria shows the creativity of employers in finding efficacious ways to ensure they do not find or hire U.S. workers, which then leads to the employment of temporary workers. The presence of the latter allows employers to offer lower wages and demand higher levels of productivity that then reinforce the artificial situation wherein available U.S. workers may possess the appropriate skills and be interested in the available jobs but not in the wages and working conditions demanded. This then becomes proof that U.S. workers are not available and justifies the federal authorization of bonded workers to meet the contrived labor shortage.

The press release on the bill notes the need to fill a "gap" between "visa programs for seasonal workers and the H-1B visa" (Flake 2016) but avoids explicitly noting the presence of the H-2B visa—a visa already set aside for nonagricultural work. The current cap on the H-2B visa is 66,000. Flake's bill would, in effect, increase the number of temporary nonagricultural visas from the current cap of 66,000 to 131,000–151,000 or more indentured-worker visas per annum. This, however, is not noted in the press release. A second important contrast to the H-2B visa is that the visa allows a certification of up to one year and a maximum period of three years. Flake's H-2C provides for step-wise periods that starts with a three-year certification, and then can be renewed in consecutive periods up to the ninth year in the ten-year pilot period. The initial cohort of workers would, in effect, be allowed to hold an H-2C visa for nine to ten consecutive years; subsequent indentured workers would hold such a visa for shorter periods of time.

Flake's WWWEA incorporates five notable provisions. First, it places the administration of the H-2C visa in the Citizenship Immigration Services (CIS) unit within the Department of Homeland Security (DHS), not in the Department of Labor, where other temporary visas are regulated. The CIS, nor its predecessor the Immigration and Naturalization Service (INS), has the historical knowledge or expertise in the management of national labor programs. Its focus is the provision of migration benefits such as migration petitions, asylum determinations, granting of temporary protected status, and naturalization.[63] The rationale for selecting CIS is part of a series of efforts dating back to the 1940s, wherein employers shop for a federal agency deemed to be employer friendly.[64] Over the past seven years the Department of Labor (DOL) has sought to provide greater protection to U.S. and temporary workers. These have been met with significant opposition from employers and some members of Congress, including employer-initiated lawsuits aimed at preventing the implementation of DOL rules. Congressional opposition to DOL actions includes provisions in appropriations bills prohibiting the use of appropriated federal funds by the DOL to implement rules to improve the status of contract workers. Thus, it is not surprising that Flake's bill does not place the H-2C pilot under the DOL.

Second, Flake's bill provides no additional funding to CIS for the implementation and monitoring called for in the program. According to S. 2827 the DHS secretary will establish the application fee charged to employer petitioners. But since a single petition can be for multiple workers, this limits the actual fees collected by the agency. An important issue not addressed in the press release on the bill is the fact that CIS's budget is largely based on user fees. This means that for CIS to effectively implement the H-2C visa, it would need to relocate personnel from other agency activities such as reviewing petitions for permanent residency (i.e., green card) or naturalization. The immediate impact of this would be to add to the already large backlog of permanent residency petitions (and other migration benefits), and this in turn would likely increase the number of persons who enter the United States without authorization rather than wait twenty-one years that may be required for petitioners from Mexico to wait to formally enter the United States.[65]

Third, it allows a partial portability for the worker. A selected worker is allowed to leave the initial employer, but the new employer must be a precertified employer. On the surface, this appears to reduce the degree of indenturedness of contract workers; however, depending on the context, it may not significantly improve the position of workers. What comes to mind here, for example, is a resort or hotel in a tourist-oriented location. Yes, the worker could leave the Mar-a-Lago Resort in Palm Beach, Florida, but other resorts and hotels in the same area work closely with fellow hotel managers, and thus would check with the previous employer before hiring the worker, and possibly lead to a collective determination not to hire the worker. This, in effect, would be a form of blacklisting and would force the worker to return to the initial employer, return to the community of origin, or remain in the United States and become subject to deportation/removal after the forty-five days of allowed unemployment. Moreover, the common practice of collective price-fixing of wages by employers in a given area may mean that most or all employers pay the approximate same wage, thus reducing the incentive to seek work with another precertified employer.

Fourth, the WWWEA calls for a study of the program. It calls for a joint three-year study by the Bureau of the Census, Department of Energy, Health and Human Services, Department of Housing and Urban Development, Department of the Interior, Department of Labor, Department of Transportation, Department of the Treasury, and the attorney general to assess the program's impact. Absent from this list are the two principal investigative entities in Congress with research expertise: Congressional Research Service (CRS) and General Accountability Office (GAO).[66] It then lists multiple factors that should be examined. The provision appears to reflect a non-researcher's list of elements that ultimately will lead to a study that says little about whether it should be continued. A salient problem in the design is that it does not call for a baseline analysis of the sectors and locations involved, thus there is little that can be said about the actual impact of the H-2C visa after its implementation.[67] If one does not have a solid empirical understanding of a particular county or Standard Metropolitan Area (SMA) prior to the introduction of the H-2C visa, then it is implausible to have confidence in a report claiming to have assessed the impact of the visa after it is implemented. It is important to also note that Senator Flake's bill does not allocate any funds for the required study. This suggests that the study will need to rely on existing data collection systems, but current federal and state databases do not compile many of the data items called for in the study. Consequently, the joint study would be carried out and presented to Congress, but its actual merit in examining the impact of the H-2C would be of limited value.

Lastly, Flake's WWWEA contains little regarding the enforcement of wage and hour standards, workplace safety and working conditions, copresence of violation of WWWEA provisions and employment of undocumented migrant workers, violations of E-Verify, etc. Moreover, the lack of experience on the part of CIS personnel in the enforcement of U.S. labor and workplace safety laws suggest that there is little interest in the actual enforcement of WWWEA provisions. In summary, like past indentured-labor programs, Flake's bill can be characterized as another effort to expand the number of unfree workers in general, but more specifically it continues the intention to increase the number of indentured Mexican workers for employers in Arizona and across the nation. The discussion so far has focused on the discourse and policy actions taken, however, to better grasp the actual human dimension of contract-labor policies, one has to also examine the historical volume of indentured workers recruited to work in the United States. The section that follows turns attention to the volume of workers involved.[68]

MEXICAN WORKERS CONTRACTED TO WORK IN THE UNITED STATES: 1942–2014

One way to gauge the contemporary level of Mexican contracted workers is to contrast this with the total number of bonded workers during World War II and the peak levels in the postwar period. Table 3.2 presents such a comparison. The table reminds us that although World War II and alleged labor shortages created by the war were the primary justifications for authorizing contract workers, the actual number contracted after the war was significantly greater. The single-year peaks in the number of Mexican contracted workers in 1957 and in 1959 is more than double the total contracted during the four-year period of the war.

As shown in table 3.2, the total of Mexican contracts during World War II, when it was argued there was an emergency labor shortage, represents 40 percent of the total contracts authorized in 2016. The Mexican total for 2016 is only 28,129 short of

Table 3.2 Comparison of Mexican and Total Temporary Contracts (H-2A and H-2B), 1942-1945, 1957, 1959, and 2016

Period	Mexican Contracts	Total Contracts
1942–1945	167,925	227,668
1957	450,875	483,569
1959	448,293	493,467
2016	422,746	467,509

Source: Immigration and Naturalization Service, *Yearbook of Immigration Statistics*, 2001, 2002; Office of Immigration Statistics, Department of Homeland Security, *Yearbook of Immigration Statistics*, 2003–2016.

the total Mexican contracts in the peak year of 1957; in other words, the 2016 total represents 94 percent of the historical peak.

While the H-2A (agricultural) and H-2B (nonagricultural) indentured-labor visas are the visas most commonly discussed in debates about Mexican contract workers, these represent a fraction of the total employment-based nonimmigrant visas approved to meet alleged labor shortages. Table 3.3 presents the number of such visas from 2000 to 2016. From 2006 to 2010, an annual total of more than one million visas were approved presumably because U.S. workers were not available, including for jobs requiring a bachelors or higher degree and paying over $50,000 annually. Over two million indentured contract workers per year were allowed entry to meet employer-asserted labor shortages in FY 2011, 2012, 2014, 2015, and 2016. Over the seventeen-year period from 2000 to 2016, over twenty-five million contract workers were recruited to meet alleged labor shortages in nonagricultural and agricultural occupations.

It is worth observing that even during the Great Recession (December 2007–June 2009), with national annual unemployment rates ranging from 4.6 percent (2006) to 9.5 percent (2010), and a peak of 10.0 percent in October 2009, corporations such as Facebook, Apple, Microsoft, The Trump Organization, as well as the hospitality industry, agribusiness, seafood processing, meat processing, and employers in other sectors convinced members of Congress and federal officials that migrant contract workers were needed because they could not locate available U.S. workers.[69] Members of Congress, the State Department, and the Department of Labor officials ultimately did not associate the labor market reality caused by the Great Recession with attestations from employers about the ominous labor shortages said to exist.

An important dimension concealed in table 3.3 is that the annual data reported are not cumulative and thus do not index the actual number of contract workers present in each fiscal year. Additionally, with some of the contract-labor visas, such as the H-1B visa, the particular visa is valid for three to ten years, the applicant is granted an H-1B visa and spouse and children are granted an H-4 visa, and the applicant and family members may apply for permanent residency. And under a 2015 executive action issued by President Obama, some H-4 spouses are granted employment authorization. Table 3.3 does not include H-4 visa holders. However, the Trump administration plans to end the employment authorization of the over seventy thousand H-4 holders.

As part of the broader demand for contract workers, for over three-quarters of a century (1942–2018), the United States has recruited Mexican contract workers to meet the unremitting desire of employers in Arizona and other states for an elastic supply of labor that can absorb the risks and social costs of contract workers in agricultural and nonagricultural industries.[70] It is a labor supply that is under greater employer control because of two principal features. First, it is a labor force that is

Table 3.3 Employment-Related Contract Visas Granted, 2000–2016

Fiscal Year	Total Visas
2000	851,877
2001	947,825
2002	889,462
2003	863,808
2004	914,167
2005	817,755
2006	1,006,884
2007	1,115,394
2008	1,206,215
2009	1,028,003
2010	1,853,948
2011	2,280,209
2012	2,030,323
2013	1,970,393
2014	2,249,607
2015	2,500,133
2016	2,628,981

Source: Immigration and Naturalization Service, *Yearbook of Immigration Statistics*, 2001, 2002; Office of Immigration Statistics, Department of Homeland Security, *Yearbook of Immigration Statistics*, 2003–2016. *Note*: The table includes all nationalities and the following employment-based visas: H-1A, H-1B, H-1B1, H-1C, H-2A, H-2B, H-3, L-1, NAFTA-TN, and O-1. The total would be about eight hundred thousand greater if it included the J-1 (students and exchange visitors) visas as well as the spouses and children of the primary visa holder, some of whom are granted employment authorization.

indentured to a single employer and does not possess the freedom to seek employment that offers a higher wage or better working conditions. Second, the worker is subject to deportation if the employer is dissatisfied with the worker (including workers who ask for minor improvements to working conditions), or the worker abandons the assigned employer. Employers understand the unequal power relationship and can use the threat of contract cancellation and calling *la migra* to ensure worker compliance with production demands, working conditions, and wages. Paradoxically, it is unfree workers who are essential to the free-market creed that contract-labor employers, chambers of commerce, members of Congress, and presidents commonly laud as the essential foundation of the U.S. economy. Employers demand limited or no interference from the federal government in order for the free market to work, but do not want free-market principles to apply to the labor market. It also should not be lost that the state plays a central role in the organization of the contract-labor regimes and sanctioning of the coercion in the regime. The threat of deportation is an essential element that employers draw upon for indentured-labor programs to work. As noted earlier, this is the problem that employers noted regarding hiring Mexican Americans, Puerto Ricans, and other U.S. nationals: the threat of deportation is not a serviceable weapon.

Figure 3.1 summarizes the unbroken recruitment of Mexican contract workers from 1942 to 2016. For the past seven decades employers articulated the same argument, irrespective of high or low unemployment rates, or economic recessions: they depend and demand a supply of Mexican contract workers to meet the immediate and looming wraith of labor shortages, and failure to be granted this privilege will result in dire economic consequences. Members of Congress, presidents, and U.S. federal agencies supported supplying needed workers to meet the unsubstantiated assertion of labor shortages.[71]

A commonly asserted argument deployed in favor of indentured-migrant programs is that guest workers eliminate or reduce unauthorized migrant flows. The argument is that an indentured program provides a legal channel for workers to seek

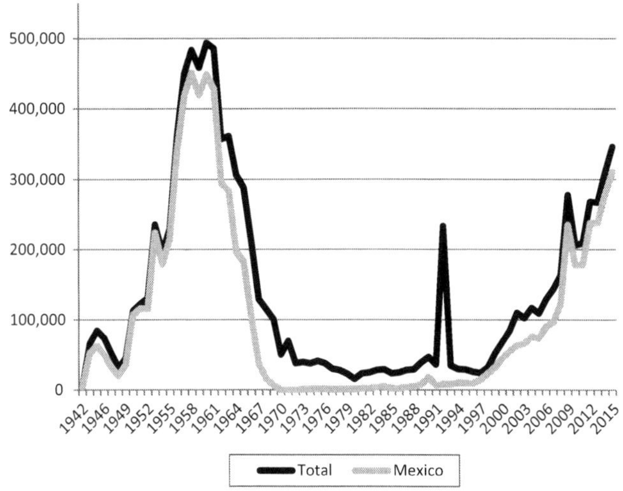

FIGURE 3.1 Total and Mexican Share of Contracted Labor, 1942–2016. *Note*: The data in the figure includes Bracero Program (1942–1968), H-2 visas (1952–1986), and H-2A and H-2B visas (1987–2016), and excludes the three years for which no data was reported (1980, 1981, and 1982), and the one year where only the total was reported by the INS. *Source*: Immigration and Naturalization Services, *Statistical Yearbook of the Immigration and Naturalization Service*, various years; and Office of Immigration Statistics, *Yearbook of Immigration Statistics*, various years; and data for 1997 was derived from State Department reports because INS did not report the data.

jobs in the United States, thus eliminating a large proportion of the illegal migrant channel. This, however, has never been the case for Mexican migrant contract-worker programs. In actuality, the opposite has been the case: contract-labor programs stimulate migration outside the programs.[72] President Trump's imagined border wall, as he noted on several occasions, has a "door." The unstated assumption of the door—the legal channel—is that the combination of the wall and the door will eliminate the presence of migrants subject to deportation. Such simplistic ideas ignore the fact that approximately half of the population subject to deportation were formally allowed entry through one of the many available doors.[73]

Figure 3.2 highlights the close association over the past twenty-three years between the reported increase in contract workers from Mexico to meet alleged labor shortages, and the parallel though larger growth in the number of migrants deported to Mexico. Even in the dramatic jump in contract workers from 2007 (123,054) to 2008 (234,507), the number of Mexicans deported/removed did not drop below the number of contracts approved. Deportations increased 18.3 percent from 2007 (208,996) to 2008 (247,263).[74] However, FY 2014 data reveal an anomalous pattern: the number of deportations was lower than the number of H-2A and H-2B visas granted to Mexican nationals. This pattern is most likely due to the fact that in the post–Great Recession period (2009–2014), there was a net drop in total Mexican migration to the United States.[75] And in light of the primary focus of Border Patrol and Immigration and Customs Enforcement on detecting and arresting Mexican migrants (Plascencia

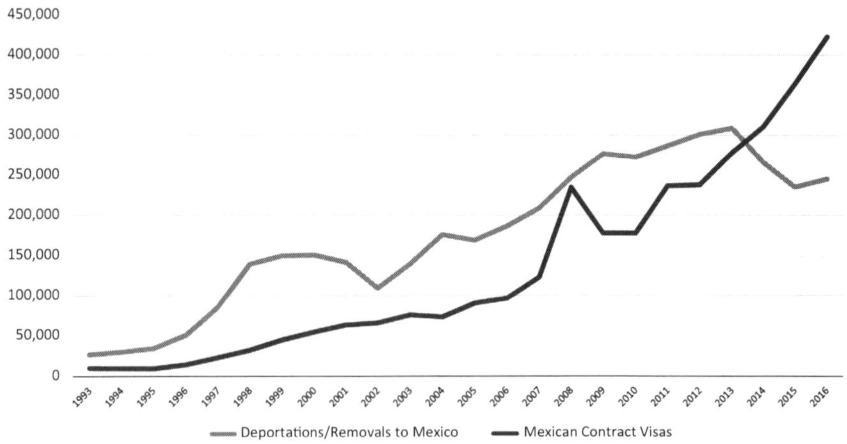

FIGURE 3.2 Deportations to Mexico and Mexican Contract Workers, 1993–2016. Contract worker data includes only H-2A and H-2B visas. *Source*: Immigration and Naturalization Services, *Statistical Yearbook of the Immigration and Naturalization Service*, various years; Office of Immigration Statistics, *Yearbook of Immigration Statistics*, various years.

2017), it is predictable that a drop in Mexican migration will result in a corresponding decrease on deportations of Mexicans subject to removal. There was, however, a small increase of 4.3 percent in the number of removals between 2015 and 2016; though the increase in contract visas for the same period was much greater (16.1 percent).[76]

In summary, the alleged argument that a guest-worker program somehow decreases undocumented migration is one that deserves greater critical review than has been allocated to it. Unsubstantiated attestations by employers and politicians that such a relationship exists, though sounding logical on the surface, should not be accepted simply because they sound probable.

DISCUSSION

The aforementioned discussion highlights the articulation by Arizona leaders of requests for assistance from the federal government to meet alleged labor shortages. Historically, the plea for assistance has focused on agriculture, though as noted by Congressman Flake in 2004 and 2016, there are also alleged shortages in nonagricultural sectors such as construction, hospitality, and care of livestock occupations. Over the period covering World War I, World War II, and the Korean War, Arizona leaders cemented the idea that wartime emergencies required federal government assistance in order for the state to meet its patriotic duty to provide food and raw materials needed to win wars. In all of these wars, the asserted wartime labor shortage outlived the actual end of the respective war by several years or decades. Carey McWilliams labels this often-voiced discourse of agribusiness for federal assistance to win wars and ensure national security, without any mention of the expected high profits to be gained, as "profit patriotism" (McWilliams 1940, 169). As illustrated in figure 3.1, from 1942 to 2016, employers successfully convinced policy makers that without the help of the federal government, Arizona and the rest of the nation faced a specter of disaster.

In defending the appropriations act enacted in December 2015 (H.R. 2029) with its provision to expand the number of unfree workers, Speaker Paul D. Ryan (R-WI) told media that U.S. companies will shut down without additional indentured workers: "The point is these businesses [seafood, tourism] would have to shut down without this and that's what we didn't want to see happen. We did not want to see businesses, who are seasonal, shut down because they couldn't get the labor" (Breitbart.com 2015a; Ryan 2015). Senator Barbara A. Mikulski (D-MD) also strongly supported the availability of indentured H-2B crab pickers as vital to Maryland's seafood sector.[77]

The long-standing discourse about needed indentured workers is linked with the view that there is only one potential source to meet the alleged labor shortage in agriculture and nonagricultural sectors: indentured labor from Mexico. As noted in the discussion of Senator Flake's S. 2827 bill, neither his press release nor the text of his bill actually states that the de facto labor reserve is Mexico. Agribusiness employers assert the collective rights of their quasi unions—labeled associations—but strongly oppose the possibility of workers possessing parallel collective power. Through crop associations dating back to 1917, growers have been able to fix prices related to wages, and establish norms of production.[78] The lack of interest on the part of the Department of Justice to investigate such price fixing as violations per se or violations of rule of reason under the Sherman Antitrust Act (1890) allows employers to pursue this form of labor control and anti-free-market practices. Moreover, individual migrant contract workers do not have a say to negotiate the prevailing wages that are determined between the Department of Labor and the employers requesting contract workers. Workers wishing to work to support their households have the choice to take it or leave it.[79] The Department of Labor has never implemented a process that includes the input of workers under the contract-labor arrangements during World War I, World War II, or since then.

Although Arizona and national leaders commonly assert that the expansion of contract-worker programs—as forms of legal migration—will solve the illegal migration problem, this is far from reality. In the case of the World War II program, the entire history of the contract-labor program was accompanied by a parallel stream of unauthorized migrants who, for various reasons, such as lack of funds to cover the application fees, or inability to pay the requested bribes by Mexican and U.S. officials, autonomously decided to make the migration. Border Patrol apprehensions for most years increased in tandem with increases in the number of contracted workers. Neither the Bracero Program nor the H-2, H-2A, H-2B visas—from 1952 to the present—undermines the accompanying undocumented migration. As shown in figure 3.2, for almost the entire twenty-three-year period covering 1993 to 2016, the undocumented migrant flow, as represented by apprehensions, and the number of contract workers increased in parallel.

This preference for Mexican workers openly articulated in the first half of the twentieth century is grounded on the racialization of Mexicans as embodying specific biological and cultural factors that allows them to carry out arduous tasks—such as harvesting cotton—in the hot climate found in the lower elevations in Arizona, or in the Yuma Valley. In contrast, it is argued that white workers will not seek the jobs held by Mexican contract workers. Over time, this expression of coloniality of power has been naturalized as the primary solution to address alleged labor shortages. In the case of cotton production in the Salt River Valley, experiments were carried out to recruit Jamaican and Puerto Rican workers. Both experiments failed, and in both workers walked off the plantations shortly after starting work. In the case of Puerto Ricans, the fact that they were not deportable removed an important labor-control practice. It also meant that neither employers nor local police could force Puerto Rican or Mexican American workers to work for only one employer; their status as free worker U.S. citizens meant they could vote with their feet and select a different employer. Mexican nationals, on the other hand, were susceptible to threats of deportation and as such became the preferred worker for employers in Arizona.

The assertion that a labor shortage exists requires that we ask two critical questions: What is the wage offered? What are the working conditions (including benefits offered)? The sociologist J. Craig Jenkins argues that labor shortages in agriculture are actually not common, and that allegations of labor shortages are more about establishing social and labor control (Jenkins 1978, 1985). It is a social control regarding wages and terms of employment, and one that relies on the deportability of foreign workers. As stated by multiple agribusiness representatives, the problem with U.S. nationals, including Puerto Ricans and Mexican Americans, is that they cannot be deported, and correspondingly cannot be threatened with deportation to ensure compliance.

The deployment of the construct of labor shortage in agricultural and nonagricultural enterprises is part of a larger dynamic. E. S. Morgan provides an important insight on what labor shortage means for some growers at a House of Representatives hearing in 1942.

> However, there remains the great problem of farm labor seen in light of employment standards and custom, as well as utilization. Our Questionnaire asked: Is it a real shortage? Is it a real shortage merely of surplus labor (which obviously works to the benefit of the employer in any field of activity)? Is it a shortage which might be overcome if better wages and more security on the job were offered? Significant was the number of responses (the majority) to the effect that the shortage was one of surplus labor. (U.S. House Select Committee Investigating National Defense Migration 1942, 12047)

Morgan's observation highlights that at least in agriculture, a shortage is not simply that a required worker per acre or worker per tree or bush number is not present, but rather that other production calculations come into play, including customary practices to ensure a rapid harvest and ability to enter the market as quickly as possible and obtain a higher price for the respective commodity. And these appear to rely on the presence of an available surplus beyond the actual number of needed workers.

We, the coeditors, argue that the broader dynamic is one that aims to create an elastic supply of labor that is tractable, and can be coerced to work for a lower wage, and higher levels of productivity. In the specific case of agricultural work in Arizona, this encompasses two major components. First, the recruited worker is mandated to work for a single employer. This means that the worker is made into an unfree worker. The individual does not have the commonly accepted liberty in a free-market economy to search for a job among available employers and negotiate the highest wage possible, and to leave that job for another that may be less arduous, have better working conditions, or pays more. Most of us take this liberty for granted. As a contracted worker, the individual has to remain with the assigned employer, even if the worker is exploited and abused (including physical violence) by the assigned employer or a supervisor at the job site. Second, the state-sanctioned coercion, involving the Mexican and U.S. governments, forces a laborer to work only for an assigned employer. This means that the worker must not create any problems, make any demands, or criticize the work or supervisors. Individuals that make demands, even if they are minor work-related issues such as portable toilets or access to water, are subject to immediate cancellation of the temporary-work contract. Moreover, since the validity of the temporary-contract visa requires that the person maintain their assigned employment, the employer can notify migration officials that the person no longer works for them. This makes the person subject to deportation.

The organization of contemporary contract or indentured labor relies on such coercion. This process aids the strategy of securing an elastic supply of labor that can be expanded or contracted as needed. An individual's well-being and human and civil rights, as protected by the Constitution and international human rights conventions, are marginal or irrelevant to the process. What is more central is the importance of sustained capital accumulation for owners and investors. Federal regulations and contract terms since the World War I ninth proviso contract-labor arrangement have been largely ignored by agribusiness and nonagricultural employers and remain a low priority for federal agencies charged with protecting the rights of workers related to wages, housing, and working conditions. The recent success of the Southern Poverty Law Center, and other migrant advocate groups, regarding lawsuits on behalf of H-2A, H-1B, and H-2B workers have made it clear that Department of Labor regulators pay minimal attention to the conditions that contract workers confront.[80] Almost all of the lawsuits brought against employers were initiated by migrant advocacy groups.[81]

An important dimension in the promotion of indentured-labor programs, though one that would require significant additional space to cover and so it is not addressed here, is that they can be considered forms of labor trafficking. The Mexican and U.S. governments are involved in the trafficking of labor. Based on the United Nations' protocols and conventions related to labor—no. 29 (1930), no. 105 (1957), and no. 203 (2014)—situations involving forms of compulsory labor ("performed involuntarily and under coercion") is considered "forced labor." And trafficking is defined as:

> The recruitment, transportation, transfer, harbouring or receipt of persons, by means of the threat or use of force or other forms of coercion, of abduction, of fraud, of deception,

of the abuse of power or of a position of vulnerability or of the giving or receiving of payments or benefits to achieve the consent of a person having control over another person, for the purpose of exploitation. (International Labour Organization 2016)[82]

The 2014 protocol makes it clear that forced labor and trafficking is not limited to the commercial sexual exploitation of women and children (the form of trafficking that generates the most attention by governments and human rights advocates), "but forced labour is also prevalent in sectors such as agriculture, fishing, domestic work, construction, manufacturing and mining" (International Labour Organization 2016)—forms of trafficking that generate limited attention.

Contract-labor arrangements, such as those managed through the H-2A, H-2B, H-1B, and other similar visas, involve the coercion and unequal treatment of workers within the United States. Contract workers do not possess the free-market right to negotiate the wages or working conditions, and their failure to abide by all employer-imposed conditions, even if in violation of the contract or federal and state wage and hour, housing, and occupational safety and health rules, can result in employer and state punishment: blacklisting and deportation. The multiple reports on the exploitation and abuse of contract workers by agricultural, livestock, and nonagricultural employers highlight the forms of coercion and abuse of power that exists. Together, they indicate that contract-labor programs encompass elements of compulsion and coercion and thus can be characterized of labor trafficking.

What the aforementioned discussion highlights, is the presence of explicit and implicit calls by Arizona employers and leaders to assert the privilege of having "our Mexicans." The calls for "grant us our Mexicans" are founded on the dual assumption of an existing labor shortage and expressions of a racialized characterization of Mexican workers as the preferred source of labor. What is left out in such statements is the importance of securing a tractable lower-wage labor force, and the maximization of productivity and profits. The employment of U.S. workers at higher wage and improved working conditions would radically alter the expected net profits.

In the late 1880s key Mexican leaders called for the recruitment of Chinese workers from China to be brought to Mexico for arduous jobs. The government's argument was that Chinese workers could do the work that Mexican nationals did not want to do—dangerous and arduous work—and that Chinese possessed unique biological qualities that allowed them to work in difficult climates and environments (Delgado 2012, 13–15). And, similar to the case in Arizona, the fact that Chinese laborers were paid a lower wage and could be deported was omitted from discussion. In the same time period, and an example closer to Arizona, the Colorado River Land Company (owned by Harrison Gray Otis, publisher of the *Los Angeles Times*) acquired over eight hundred thousand acres in the Mexicali Valley, Baja California, south of the

Imperial Valley. The company used the land to grow cotton. However, almost all workers were Chinese. Otis and partners used the argument that Mexicans shunned cotton harvesting, and so turned to Chinese because they made "better" workers (Kerig 1988).

The fact that Mexican workers were harvesting cotton north in the nearby Imperial Valley and in Arizona did not alter the Colorado River Land Company's arguments. In short, sociopolitical and economic arguments about alleged labor shortages, preferred workers, and racialized characteristics of workers become foundational tropes that are relied upon by agricultural and nonagricultural interests to pressure government officials to aid in the recruitment of indentured labor. Unfortunately, state and federal officials come to readily accept the unsubstantiated claims of those interests. Senator Flake's April 2016 bill represents the most recent example of proposed legislation to expand the supply of indentured workers, principally from Mexico. Although Senator Flake and supporters of contract labor (guest workers) would disagree, their efforts to expand indentured-labor programs are ultimately proposals to foster labor trafficking. And as such, their arguments merit closer scrutiny and a wider debate about whether human trafficking schemes—such as guest-worker programs—should continue to exist in Arizona and other states.

NOTES

1. In October 2017, Representative Robert W. Goodlatte (R-VA) introduced the Agricultural Guestworkers Act (H.R. 4092). Goodlatte's H.R. 4092 creates an H-2C temporary contract-labor visa for a broad categorization of agricultural activities, including forestry, handling and packing of agricultural or horticultural commodities, aquaculture and processing of fish or shellfish, and "special procedures industry" (i.e., sheepherding, animal shearing, goat herding, range livestock, beekeeping and pollination, and custom combining and harvesting). Several of these are currently excluded from the H-2A agricultural contract-labor visa.
2. The label *U.S. workers* refers to U.S. nationals and nonnationals who are authorized to work in the United States.
3. The reference to the state and the privileging of capital interest should not be interpreted as suggesting a view of the state as a homogeneous, singular actor that acts only on behalf of capital elites. As Calavita has clearly discussed in the context of the World War II contract-labor programs, state bureaucracies can at times work in contradictory ways (1992); more recently, the efforts under Secretary of Labor Thomas Pérez highlight the interest of one organ of the state to actually improve the conditions of H-2A and H-2B workers. Employers quickly responded directly by contesting the new Department of Labor rules in federal court and indirectly by pressuring friendly representatives and

senators to insert restriction in appropriations to the DOL. The restrictions prohibit the DOL from using federal funds to implement rules promulgated.

4. David Montejano deploys the notion of "labor repression" as part of a "web of labor controls" in his insightful analysis of how commercial agriculture in South Texas developed a stable workforce through violence, worker immobilization, and other forms of coercion. Montejano defines labor repression as "the use of compulsion for organizing the recruitment, work activity, and compensation of wage labor" in commercial agriculture in South Texas (1987, 197). I suggest the concept of web of coercion and profit as an attempt to build on the work of Montejano and other scholars of Mexican labor in the United States (e.g., Acuña 2007; Alamillo 2006; G. González 1994; Guerin-Gonzales 1994; Heyman 1991; Huginnie 1991; Park 1961; Perales 2010; Reisler 1973, 1976a; Ruiz 1987; Stuesse 2016; Vargas 2005; Zamora 1993; Zavella 1987; Zlolniski 2006), and highlight a broader web involving the Mexican and U.S. governments, agricultural and nonagricultural employers, the fostering of circular migration as a permanent cycle, and the creation and sustainment of an unfree workforce as part of a strategy to achieve the twofold aim of controlling labor and maximizing profits. The aim of the process is to control both foreign migrant workers and U.S. workers.

5. Lee (2016) presents a similar observation regarding the "cycle" where alleged worker shortages create the necessity for contract workers, and this in turn creates more worker shortages. Lee's primary focus are the "cultural narratives" that label U.S. workers as lazy or superior for low-wage jobs, and make contract workers suited for the available jobs, and the U.S. regulatory structure that regulates the H-2A and H-2B contract worker. This essay places greater emphasis on the political and economic dimensions of contract-labor regimes, rather than assert that the discourse is cultural.

6. For classic discussions of the conceptualization of biopower and biopolitics, see Agamben (1998), Foucault (2008), Mbembe (2003). In short, biopower refers to the form of modern power wherein the state/regime of power seeks to control and make human beings productive and comes to regulate who shall live and who shall die. Biopolitics encompasses racialized views of humans that define inherent biological elements that make one group of individuals suited, for example, for "stoop labor" or unaffected by debilitating desert heat, and others suited for managing lower-wage workers performing stoop labor. The political philosophy and practices of eugenics that emerged in the early twentieth century is an example of a form of biopolitics. While not as popular as in the past, eugenics survives in contemporary forms such as the Pioneer Fund, and its support for white supremacist and antimigrant groups such as Federation for American Immigration Reform and Center for Immigration Studies. The Southern Poverty Law Center labels the Pioneer Fund as a hate group.

7. The concept of coloniality of power, as introduced by Anibal Quijano (2000) and elaborated upon by Walter Mignolo (2000) and Ramón Grosfoguel (2003), takes into

account the formation of global capitalist systems, as argued by Immanuel Wallerstein (i.e., the "modern world system"), but seeks to expand its analytical strength by centering the element of racialization. The coloniality of power operating in the contemporary world, it is argued, is sustained by two key factors: (1) the centrality of race and racialization and (2) the assumed hierarchy of whites over nonwhites. As suggested by the aforementioned scholars, the domination and exploitation of the Other in the Americas depends on the racialization of an Other (generally as a nonwhite), their position as "naturally" inferior to whites, and intrinsically possessing biological and cultural elements that correspond to their position within the social, occupational, and wage hierarchies in operation.

8. It should be acknowledged that the presentation of material related to the persistent demand for Mexican labor is not unique. The notable work of Ernesto Galarza (1956, 1964, 1977), Mark Reisler (1973, 1976a), and Robert Tomasek (1957, 1961), as well as others, provide evidence of that demand, particularly for employers in California and Texas. The uniqueness of the chapter is its focus on Arizona and its period of concern: a century. More recently, Julie Weise (2015) provides an important contribution to our knowledge regarding the recruitment of Mexican labor for cotton harvesting in the early 1900s by planters in the south.
9. Although in 1996 Congress replaced the label *deportation* with *removal*, the former term remains the more recognizable term by the general public. I use the term *deportation* for this reason.
10. For detailed discussions of discriminations against H-2A and H-2B workers, see Holley (2001) and Costa (2016), respectively.
11. The term *nonimmigrant* is the formal statutory label for persons authorized to visit or work for a designated period and with specific limitations. An immigrant, on the other hand, is a person authorized to enter and live permanently under certain conditions. The latter are persons who are issued what is commonly referred to as a *green card*, although the permanent residency card has not been green for decades.
12. Although this description may seem doubtful, when one factors in that the employer, particularly in agriculture, may be a grower's association, this means that in cases such as North Carolina, where the North Carolina Growers Association (NCGA) is the contracting entity for H-2A visa workers for multicommodity growers, then to be blacklisted by the NCGA means that the worker will find it almost impossible to work in that state.
13. In the history of the United States, there is a long history of indentured labor dating back to the colonial period, and with the abolishment of slavery after the ratification of the Thirteenth Amendment (1865), several Southern states enacted a variety of laws related to vagrancy, debt, and prison labor that coerced individuals to work for specific employers until a real or bogus obligation was defined as met. In 1867 Congress passed

the Peonage Abolition Act, which abolished "voluntary or involuntary service or labor" for liquidation of a debt. Despite the formal elimination of peonage, multiple cases of forced involuntary labor continue to exist in the twenty-first century.

14. A segment of the labor history literature labels the production of indentured/unfree workers as a process of deproletarianization. The concept refers to the transformation of a free wage worker into an unfree worker (see Brass 1994).
15. For more in-depth discussions of the unfree labor process, see Brass and van der Linden (1997), van der Linden and Rodríguez García (2016), and Plascencia (2016).
16. What I am foregrounding here is the established, though erroneous, definition of *bracero* as a Spanish-language term referring to a person who works with their arms, and that it originated as part of the World War II labor arrangements between Mexico and the United States. It is erroneous on two grounds. First, the term was invoked in the United States before World War II. Second, the term is found in nineteenth-century Spain in reference to landless agricultural workers. Lastly, the unfortunate attribution to arms represents a dehumanizing term equivalent to referring to farm and ranch workers as hands. Classifying persons as singular body parts is dehumanizing. Lastly, most humans use their arms and hands—including work involving a keyboards or surgery instruments—in carrying out their work; thus, not much is actually said when indexing someone who works with their arms.
17. The formal Mexico-U.S. agreements known as the Emergency Farm Labor Supply Program, also referred to by other labels such as the Farm Labor Program, and Farm Labor Transportation Program, did not use the term *bracero* in official governmental communications or signed documents. Moreover, in the initial phase of the program (1942–1943) when recruitment was carried out in Mexico City, workers were referred to as *aspirantes* (aspirants), not braceros. Although the term *bracero* predates 1942 by a substantial period of time, I have not yet been able to document when it began to be used to refer to Mexican migrant landless agricultural workers; though by the early 1950s it appears in several media sources. A book review of Luis Pérez's *El Coyote, The Rebel* (1947) in the same year of its publication represents the first time that the *New York Times* used the term *bracero* with reference to Mexican agricultural migrants (Bracker 1947). I, however, located a June 5, 1925, news article in *El Universal* titled "*Las quejas de los braceros explotados en N. Laredo encuentran cerrados los oidos del J. de Migración.*"
18. Professor Gilbert G. González also sees the term *guest worker* as a euphemism (2006, 80).
19. The title of the report by Farmworker Justice, *No Way to Treat a Guest* (2011) makes this point.
20. A May 1977 article in the *New York Times* appears to be the first time the term *guest worker* is used in reference to U.S. contract workers (Sterba 1977).
21. In addition, a substantial number of nationals from U.S. insular territories (Philippines, Puerto Rico, and Virgin Islands) were recruited to work in agricultural firms. This is in

addition to the recruitment of women and children to carry out "patriotic" work and do their part in winning the war.

22. See Plascencia (2016) for a more detailed discussion regarding government statistics on the actual number of workers authorized under the World War I contract-labor program.
23. Congressman John L. Burnett (D-AL), the sponsor of the enacted bill and chair of the House Committee on Immigration and Naturalization, corresponded with Secretary Wilson questioning his authority to take the actions taken. He also took the immediate step to file a bill in the House (H.R. 4852) to eliminate the ninth proviso. Burnett's bill did not proceed beyond the initial committee assignment; he eventually accepted Secretary Wilson's explanation and so let Wilson's actions stand.
24. In the late 1800s and early 1900s there was much anxiety about race suicide, racial hygiene, and the low fecundity of white women. Theodore Roosevelt and segments of the national elite were concerned that the combination of low white birthrates and growth of migration from Southern and Eastern Europe would destabilize the supremacy of Anglo Saxon and dominance of Caucasians in the United States (See Gardner 2005, 166–67; Jacobson 1998). The result of the 2016 presidential elections in the United States and ascendancy of alt-right and white supremacy sentiments share some parallels with the earlier anxieties. A 2016 congressional candidate in Tennessee garnered much media attention when he paid for a billboard with the phrase "Make America White Again" (Bever 2016).
25. "*Provided further* [9] That the Commissioner General of Immigration with the approval of the Secretary of Labor shall issue rules and prescribe conditions, including exaction of such bonds as may be necessary, to control and regulate the admission and return of otherwise inadmissible aliens applying for temporary admission" (39 Stat. 874, 878).
26. The plaque discussed in chapter 2 indexes what it seeks to disavow: it seeks to erase what it suggests likely happened.
27. For a summary of the Foran Act and some of the violations, see Plascencia (2013a).
28. A fuller discussion of the ninth proviso can be found in Plascencia (2016). See also Alanís Enciso (1999), Cardoso (1976, 1980), Howard Johnson (1988), Kiser (1973), Mohl (1987), Reisler (1976a; particularly chapter 2), Schwartz (1942), and Scruggs (1960, 1988).
29. The twenty states participating in the ninth proviso waiver were Arizona, Arkansas, California, Colorado, Idaho, Illinois, Kansas, Louisiana, Maryland, Missouri, Montana, Nevada, New Mexico, Ohio, Oklahoma, Oregon, Texas, Utah, West Virginia, and Wyoming (U.S. Commissioner General of Immigration 1919, 13).
30. It should be noted that prior to 1976, the U.S. fiscal year covered the period from July 1 to June 30. Congress revised the fiscal year to October 1 to September 30. Since Secretary Wilson authorized the bonded worker waiver in May 1917, and the fiscal year ended on June 30, this meant that workers were authorized in May and June 1917, thus FY 1917 statistics cover only these two months.

31. Democrat Carl T. Hayden is one of Arizona's most influential federal politicians. He represented Arizona in the House of Representatives and later in the Senate; his combined tenure covered fifty-six years. He held his seat in the House for eight terms and in the Senate for seven terms. Hayden played a central role in securing large-scale appropriations for irrigation (e.g., the Central Arizona Project), electrical power, and reclamation for the West, but particularly for projects in Arizona. He was a solid supporter of the ACGA, as evidenced in this testimony to maintain the ninth proviso indentured-worker program. His views on the essential need for Mexican workers in Arizona changed between World War I and the Great Depression, and then again during World War II. As noted in his testimony at the 1920 congressional hearing, he claimed that Arizona needed such workers during the World War I era, but by the time of the Great Depression he supported the banishment of Mexican workers from the state. By World War II, he supported the recruitment of such workers.
32. The figure of 36,000 contracts also draws attention to the problem with the official total of 72,862 contracts. The figure cited by Knox represents close to half (49.5 percent) of the reported total, yet in 1919 Texas contracted a higher number than Arizona, and California contracted about 500 fewer than Arizona. Thus, if Texas and California had similar proportions to Arizona for the period 1917–1920, then their sum would easily exceed the 72,682 total.
33. The 1885 law was in effect from 1885 to 1952, though was generally ignored by U.S. employers, and at times by migration officials at southwestern ports of entry. Migration officials and some Department of Labor officials (e.g., Victor Clark 1908) assumed that the law applied only to European migrants recruited to work in the United States. For a brief discussion of the Foran Act, see Plascencia (2013a).
34. This is not a new insight. In 1958 H. L. Mitchell presented testimony at a House hearing wherein he notes that the Department of Labor "abdicates responsibility to farm employer associations" by "failing to enforce the job rights of Americans" and those of contract workers (U.S. House Subcommittee on Equipment, Supplies, and Manpower, Committee on Agriculture 1958, 500, 499). More recently, the multiple reports on the abuses of contract workers (e.g., Southern Poverty Law Center 2013; Colorado Legal Services 2010; and Costa 2016) offer numerous examples of the abuse of contract workers over several years. Although the focus of these reports is not on the inaction of federal agencies, what they document is the product of federal and state agencies deciding not to interfere with private employers, and thus allowing the exploitation of indentured workers.
35. I should note that the segmentation of the World War II and post–World War II labor contracting into two periods (1942–1951, and 1952–2016) is intended to highlight the early phase (the actual period of war, 1942–1945, and the immediate aftermath) and the subsequent phase that has been in effect since 1952. Moreover, the use of the year 1951 remains an important dividing point. From 1942 to the first half of 1951, the

contract-labor arrangement was based on binational agreements and U.S. statutes allocating monies for the program and extensions beyond the initial period. In July 1951, President Truman reluctantly enacted Public Law 82–78. The statue formed the foundation of the Mexican Farm Labor Program until its formal demise in 1968.

36. The World War II Mexico-U.S. contract-labor regime has been the focus of several book-length discussions. Among the more notable works are Anderson (1963, 1976), Calavita (1992), Cohen (2011), Craig (1971), Driscoll (1996, 1999), Galarza (1956, 1964), Gamboa (1990), Gilbert G. González (2006), Jones (1945), Don Mitchell (2012), and Ness (2011). These are supplemented by a significant number of academic articles, advocacy reports, and government documents, as well as over twenty-five doctoral dissertations dating back to 1957. García y Griego's 1988 unpublished doctoral dissertation remains the most comprehensive discussion of the policy history of the binational arrangements. For those interested in the work of Mexican scholars, Professor's Durand policy-oriented report (2006) and his anthology (2007) covering the period 1945–1964 are notable works. Readers interested in the parallel Caribbean contract-labor arrangements should review the excellent work of Griffith (2006) and Hahamovitch (1997, 2013).

37. The reader will note that the chapter uses the years 1942–1968 for the World War II Bracero Program in contrast to the conventional historiography that uses the years 1942–1964. I argue that a closer reading of the regulations of the period indicate that exemptions were made for special cases up to 1968.

38. Barbara Driscoll's general analysis of the employment of Mexican contract workers in the railroad sector (1996, 1999) remains an important supplement to the common focus on agricultural contract workers. The more recent scholarship by Chantel R. Rodríguez (2013) on the politics of medical care of contracted workers by railroad corporations that employed them is an important contribution to the analysis of the power relations experienced by workers. More recently, the historian Erasmo Gamboa produced an important work on contracted labor during World War II in the West (2016).

39. Elsewhere I discuss in detail the multiple limitations in the conventional historiography of the World War II Bracero Program (see Plascencia 2016). In short, the historiography overlooks prior state actions that encouraged the contracting of Mexican workers dating back to 1909, concurrent efforts during the 1942–1968 period, and the legacy of what took place during that period, specifically the enactment of the H-2 temporary contract-worker visa in 1952 and legacy of this to the present.

40. See the following for discussion of a range of abuses experienced by Mexican contract workers during the 1942–1968 program: Anderson (1963, 1976), Calavita (1992), Galarza (1956, 1964), Gamboa (1990), Juan Ramón García (1980), García y Griego (1983, 1988), Gilbert González (2006), and Mitchell (2012).

41. The accepted historiography of the World War II Mexico-U.S. contract-labor program tends to ignore the importance of prior similar arrangement, particularly the World War I

contract-labor program; it overlooks the relevance of the 1952 H-2 visa and tends to overlook the unbroken continuity in recruiting Mexican indentured labor from 1942 to the present. As suggested by Plascencia (2016), the continuity of the recruitment from 1942 to the present suggests that scholars and policy analysts should not uncritically accept the notion that the World War II program ended in December 1964.

42. The most detailed discussion of the specific national groups recruited during the 1942–1947 period is Rasmussen (1951). Sinaloa has a long history of marijuana production; it is also the operating base of the Sinaloa drug-trafficking organization. The role of the United States in promoting marijuana production in the 1940s is one that is often overlooked in discussions of the war on drugs.

43. It should be noted that I use *contracts* rather than *workers*—the latter is a common error made by scholars and policy analysts. The same individual could have worked for the same or different employer in the same or different fiscal year. Each employment authorization represented a different contract, not a different individual. Secondly, in contrast to the World War I effort, the World War II arrangement included only male workers.

44. It is beyond the scope of this essay to discuss the unique dimension of the labor dynamic of the Yuma and Imperial Valleys. Nonetheless, brief mention should be made of the commuter labor arrangement that allows Mexican labor to enter and exit daily, weekly, or for the harvest season in the two valleys. Commuter labor that entered during World War II is not counted as part of the bracero statistics reported. For a brief summary of the 1927 Department of Labor General Order 86, see Plascencia (2016).

45. It consisted of a chair and four additional members appointed by the president. The members of the commission were Maurice T. Van Hecke (chair), Noble Clark, William M. Leiserson, Robert E. Lucey, and Peter H. Obergard. A useful account of agribusiness and congressional opposition to President Truman's effort to improve conditions for U.S. migrant agricultural workers, elimination or limitation of foreign contract labor, and efforts to institute sanctions against employers of undocumented workers can be found in Robinson (2007, 2010).

46. One aim of the 1952 McCarran-Walter Act was to punish individuals and firms harboring individuals present without formal authorization and impose stiff penalties for those charged with harboring. However, representatives from southwestern and southern agricultural interests inserted what is known as the Texas Proviso. The provision explicitly exempts employment from being classified as harboring. The intent was clear: employers could continue to employ undocumented migrants as they pleased without fearing state actions.

47. Much of the scholarly literature on the World War II indentured-labor program, particularly that focusing on the component involving Mexican workers, portrays the contract arrangements as largely negative in terms of the impact on contracted workers and U.S. workers, and commonly refers to the effort as exploitative. Some of the more commonly cited sources include Anderson (1958, 1963, 1976), Cohen (2011), Galarza

(1956, 1964), García y Griego (1988), García (1980), González (2006), Griffith (2006), Mitchell (2012), and Ness (2011). Additionally, multiple congressional hearings related to the extension of the World War II arrangement contain assertions by opponents of the program regarding the exploitation of workers. On the other hand, there are a small number of scholars who conclude that the Mexico-U.S. Bracero Program had a positive effect in Mexico (Kosack 2015).

48. Galarza presents a more detailed discussion of these and other problems not listed here in *Merchants of Labor* (1964). Anderson also examined the actual operation of the World War II arrangement and highlights these and similar problems in great detail (1958, 1963, 1976). See also González (2006).

49. The analogy between temporary migrant contract labor and enslavement has been made on numerous occasions by journalist and migrant advocates—Kevin Bales of Free the Slaves is one such individual. In addition, multiple popular publications have appeared over the past decade referring to H-2A sheepherders and H-2B workers working for contractor on U.S. forests, for example, as "near slavery," "new slavery," or "modern slavery." Although there is no denying that work and living conditions are quite extreme for such workers, it is misleading to equate chattel slavery and contract labor as equal employer-worker relations.

50. The phrase *tiny provision* is the phrase Speaker Paul Ryan (R-WI) used in referring to a contract-labor provision in the Consolidated Appropriations Act for 2016 (2015). The provision expands the number of H-2B workers by excluding returning workers from the annual cap.

51. California's extensive diversification in the production of fruits and vegetables, and the simultaneous increasing mechanization of cotton in Arizona reduced the past prominence of Arizona cotton interests and augmented the leading role of California grower interest in the demand for the continuation and expansion of indentured contract labor. By 1957, according to McSweeney, close to 50 percent of the cotton in Arizona was machine harvested (U.S. House Subcommittee on Equipment, Supplies and Manpower 1958, 2013).

52. Congressional hearings in the 1930s reveal that an important function of grower associations in California was to set the association-wide price to be paid to labor. This collective strategy largely insured that association members would not use a higher wage to lure workers from another member. Additionally, this provided growers with almost complete control over wages, and thus diluted the bargaining position of workers to demand a wage higher than the wage fixed by growers. Frank Palomares's testimony to the U.S. Senate in 1940 noted that the practice of growers coming together to fix the upcoming wage to be paid by the members of the San Joaquin Valley Growers Association dated back to at least the early 1930s (Senate Subcommittee of the Committee on Education and Labor 1940, 18717).

53. Republican Paul Jones Fannin was an influential state and federal politician. He served as governor from 1959 to 1965. When Senator Barry Goldwater declined to run for

reelection in order to run for president, Fannin pursued the vacated seat and was elected as Arizona's junior senator. Carl T. Hayden was the senior senator at the time. Fannin was thought of as a strong conservative and had parallel views to those of Goldwater. Both Goldwater and Fannin opposed the 1972 Equal Rights Amendment, and favored preserving the provision in the Taft-Harley Act that impeded the unionization of workers.

54. See Henry P. Anderson (1958, 14). The unpublished 1958 mimeograph was made available to the author by Mr. Anderson through Dr. Gilbert González. It is worth pointing out that the initial report on his research led to the quick termination of his promising academic career as a graduate student at the University of California, Berkeley. Agribusiness interests and their links to the university led to the destruction of most copies of his report by officials at the university. A summary of Anderson's tragedy is found in Anderson (1964) and González (2006, chapter 4).
55. By sideline, I am referring to the fact that rather than outright expand the H-2A visa, Congress created a provision to expand the number of agricultural workers if the commission found potential labor shortages, based on independent research. The research, sponsored by the Commission on Agricultural Workers, concluded that no national labor shortage had emerged due to the legalization/amnesty granted to agricultural workers.
56. The count of thirty-five hearings refers to hearings that focused on issues related to the H-2A, H-2B, and H-1B visas, the creation of new contract-labor visas (e.g., the H-2C visa), or a general need for a guest-worker program. The list includes the hearing related to S. 744 in April 2013. S. 744 was passed by the Senate, but not by the House of Representatives. It excludes hearings that are more general but may contain secondary comments about contract-labor programs.
57. By "largely absent," I am referring to the absence of a statement submitted in writing by a member of the respective committee or subcommittee, or absence of testimony presented in person at the hearing. This includes hearings wherein an Arizona senator or congressperson may have been a member of the sponsoring committee or subcommittee, but no statement from the Arizona representative is included in the report of the hearing.
58. Efforts by senators and representatives from Arizona that took place in private with federal officials and members of Congress on the issue of labor shortages and the need for guest workers are unknown.
59. The table created for the 118 bills is eight pages long. In order to focus on the relevant bills supported by Arizona's Congressional delegation, the list is not included.
60. FLEA was later renamed LAWA—Legal Arizona Workers Act.
61. It is important to note that since January 2008, a total of two employers have been identified as violating the state statute regarding the employment of persons without employment authorization. Though, in fact, the two could be reduced to one or zero. One of the employers was actually identified by the Immigration and Customs Enforcement (ICE) and turned over to the Maricopa County attorney's office. Local officials identified the second company, but in reality, the company was in the process of liquidating, thus it was

moot to bring charges against a nonexistent corporation. However, Maricopa County sheriff's office used the law to arrest workers at sites identified as employing unauthorized workers, but no charges were brought against the employers who employed the arrested workers. Employers violating the state law were in effect granted amnesty for their violation of the rule of law.

62. It should be observed that congressional actions implemented as temporary or provisional often become permanent or assume a significant longevity. The World War II temporary indentured-labor program was adopted as a wartime emergency, yet the actual program lasted for twenty-three years after the war ended in 1945.
63. CIS has a role in the processing of visa petitions, and the State Department has a role in ultimately determining the granting of a visa petition, but neither agency regulates the actions of employers regarding the employment of contract workers.
64. The initial management of the Migrant Farm Labor Supply Program with Mexico was under the Farm Security Administration (FSA) in the U.S. Department of Agriculture. Many growers saw the FSA as a communistic agency interested only on workers; thus they successfully pressured the state to place it under the War Food Administration (WFA). The latter was thought of as a grower-friendly federal agency. This scenario was later repeated regarding the Department of Labor and the Department of Agriculture, with the latter being the grower-friendly entity of choice.
65. According to the State Department, the granting of permanent residency (i.e., green card) to an unmarried child of a U.S. citizen from Mexico has a twenty-one-year wait time as of September 2016. This reality is part of what motivates some individuals to seek entry without formal authorization or overstay the time limitation in their visa.
66. The inclusion of agencies such as the Departments of Energy, Interior, Transportation, and the attorney general—all of which have no role in the regulation of contract-labor programs—is unclear. Were they inserted to make the interagency task and the production of a consensus on the design of the study more convoluted and unproductive?
67. This is the same problem encountered in the passage of the 1986 Immigration Reform and Control Act (IRCA), particularly the potential discriminatory impact of the employer-sanctions provision. The absence of a baseline meant that whatever employment discrimination was reported, it could not be causatively connected to the passage of the IRCA.
68. It should be noted that the data presented here is for the United States as a whole. The reason for this is that the historical state-level data has been inconsistently reported for the period under discussion.
69. The annual averages represent the average for three months in each calendar year: January, June, and December. The monthly data are from the Bureau of Labor Statistics, Department of Labor.
70. Migrant contract workers absorb production risks in a variety of ways. The imposed flexibility means that workers must absorb costs associated with events that confront

employers such as dramatic drops in commodity prices, climate-induced damages to agricultural fields, and others. Employers may cancel the contract after meeting the minimum work period set in the contract, may provide only a short number of hours of work in a given day, may convince Department of Labor officials that the wage rate may need to be lowered and, knowing that there is little federal oversight of the program, may choose not to meet conditions specified in the contract. All such cases result in workers having to absorb loss of wages, costs associated with the migration to the place of work, inability to pay debts incurred in relation to the temporary migration, costs related to surviving while waiting for the normal flow of work to restart, and accept the living and working conditions provided.

71. Local and state employment service agencies, and national U.S. Department of Labor officials, carry out a largely pro forma review. Tomasek's observation in 1961 remains applicable in the present. Tomasek notes that on paper there is a process that seeks to locate available workers, but "In reality, though, the estimates of the growers for Mexicans usually are approved automatically by the local offices without any critical check, sent to the state and regional offices where they are given little review and then passed on to the national office" (1961, 308). Local and state social and political pressures from large agribusiness interest are not likely to be questioned or challenged regarding their veracity. Anderson (1964) provides a substantial discussion of the process in the same period (late 1950s to early 1960s).

72. In the case of the World War II arrangement, the recruitment process in Mexico City with its long lines and poor administrative procedures at the very start of the program in 1942 prompted some to bypass the recruitment and autonomously decide to migrate and seek agricultural and other work in the United States outside the governmental apparatus. As the years passed and it became clear that U.S. employers were more than willing to hire undocumented migrants, which continues to the present despite the 1986 law that made it illegal to hire migrant without employment authorization, it is not a surprise that contract-worker programs operate in tandem with a flow of unauthorized workers.

73. The reference here is to persons who entered with a valid visa but either violated the terms of the respective visa or remained in the United States past the expiration date. In both cases, the visa violator becomes subject to deportation. But in the case of politically connected individuals, no action is taken to initiate removal—they are granted an informal amnesty.

74. It should be made clear that the argument here is not that there is a clear ratio between contract and deportation, though one could be calculated. The reason for this is that deportations are driven by multiple decisions made by Congress and the administration in office, as well as local decisions made by Border Patrol sector chiefs and individual officers. Political and budget decisions can lead to an increase or decrease in the number of apprehensions and deportations. The actual number deported is not driven exclusively

by the decrease or increase in number violating visa conditions or entering without authorization. Oddly enough, though not often commented by media, the Border Patrol has formulated a public-relations formula that allows it to take credit for a *decrease* in apprehension, as well as an *increase* in apprehensions. In both instances, it alleges that effective law enforcement is responsible for the noted pattern. Unfortunately, national and regional media tend to accept the agency's explanations as official calculations and do not question the problematic logic.

75. See Pew Research Center (2015).
76. Initial federal reports for deportations under the Trump administration have decreased, but the number of apprehensions has increased. Given the backlog in immigration courts, the actual number of deportations may continue to lag for the next two to three years.
77. Former senator Mikulski (D-MD) is a notable federal politician. She was the longest serving woman in congressional history: she served in the House of Representatives from 1977 to 1987, and has served in the Senate from 1987 to 2017. After serving five terms and thirty years in the Senate, she retired in 2017 at the end of the 114th Session of Congress. Although Mikulski is generally considered a pro-labor senator, on the question of the important seafood sector in Maryland, she endorses the use of indentured H-2B seafood workers, most of whom are Mexican women recruited by the industry.
78. According to Galarza, the Valley Fruit Growers Association of Fresno dates back to 1917 (1964, 37). One of the most influential commodity associations, the Associated Farmers of California, was created in 1934 (ibid., 37).
79. The economic necessity of Mexican workers and the ample reserve labor pool in Mexico, as well as salient interest of the Mexican State to maximize remittances, leads the Mexican government to minimize its role in the direct protection of nationals it has participated in encouraging their migration to Canada and the United States. It should be acknowledged that in some locations Mexican consuls have sought to more actively assist Mexican nationals; however, none of the court cases filed to protect H-2A or H-2B visa holders were initiated by consuls.
80. See the report by the Economic Policy Institute (Costa 2016), Southern Poverty Law Center (2013), and the Colorado Legal Services report (2010) for examples of the range in exploitation of workers on the part of employers.
81. It should be acknowledged that the Department of Labor has initiated efforts to collect back wages and eliminate exceptional forms of labor exploitation.
82. The Palermo Protocol defines exploitation as "shall include, at a minimum, the exploitation of the prostitution of others or other forms of sexual exploitation, forced labour or services, slavery or practices similar to slavery, servitude or the removal of organs" (United Nations 2000).

PHOTO ESSAY

★

Work crew digging an irrigation canal, ca. late 1800s. Courtesy of the Tempe History Museum.

Tempe adobe brick construction site, San Pablo Barrio, Arizona, ca. 1900. Courtesy of the Tempe History Museum.

Interior of Spain's blacksmith shop on 6th Street, Tempe, Arizona, ca. 1910. Courtesy of the Tempe History Museum.

Celaya grocery store at 6th Street and Mill Avenue, Tempe, Arizona, ca. 1918. Courtesy of the Tempe History Museum.

Peterson dairy farm workers, Arizona, 1912. Courtesy of the Arizona Historical Society.

Vaquera Adelina Ruelas working at ranch in Box Canyon, Arizona, 1920s. Courtesy of the Arizona Historical Society.

Miners Reyes G. Moroyoqui (top right) and Ramon G. Moroyoqui (bottom right), Chrysotil, Arizona, 1921. Courtesy of the Arizona Historical Society.

Miners depicted in *los mineros* for the PBS program *American Experience*. Photography by Manuel Martinez, donated to Hector Galan. Courtesy of the Los Mineros Collection, Chicano Research Collection, Arizona State University Libraries.

Mexican wood vendor, Tucson, 1930. Courtesy of the Tempe History Museum.

Arizona Ice and Cold Storage Company workers, Arizona, 1931. Courtesy of the Arizona Historical Society.

Railroad construction crew, Arizona Eastern Railroad, 1928. Courtesy of Arizona Eastern Railroad Photographs, Arizona Collection, Arizona State University Libraries.

Child workers, J. J. Farms broccoli fields, Maricopa County, Arizona, 1942. Courtesy of the National Archives and Records Administration.

Southern Pacific Railroad female workers during World War II, Arizona. Courtesy of the Arizona Historical Society.

Rig workers (n.d.). Courtesy of José Villela Photographs, Chicano Research Collection, Arizona State University Libraries.

Cotton workers, Southwest Cotton Company, Arizona (n.d.). Courtesy of the Litchfield Park Historical Society.

Young cotton picker, Maricopa County, Arizona (n.d.). Courtesy of the Litchfield Park Historical Society.

Ramón Soto, irrigation foreman, Goodyear Farms, Arizona (n.d.). Courtesy of the Litchfield Park Historical Society.

Lucía Salinas with an eighty-pound sack of cotton she picked, Chandler, Arizona, 1952. Courtesy of the Chandler History Museum.

Sheepshearer, Dobson Ranch, Chandler, Arizona, 1987. Courtesy of the Chandler History Museum.

Citrus workers. Courtesy of the Philip Decker Collection, Arizona Collection, Arizona State University Libraries.

Yardero Domingo M. Agüero, Phoenix, Arizona, 2015. Photo by Sarina E. Guerra and Derick Douglas Washington.

Yardero Raúl Anzures Rivera, Phoenix, Arizona, 2015. Photo by Sarina E. Guerra and Derick Douglas Washington.

Day laborers, 2015. Photo by Sarina E. Guerra and Derick Douglas Washington.

Construction workers Aldo Reyes and Cesar Ochoa, Glendale, Arizona, 2015. Photo by Sarina E. Guerra and Derick Douglas Washington.

Jesús Frutos, cook at Taco Mich, Glendale, Arizona, 2015. Photo by Sarina E. Guerra and Derick Douglas Washington.

Roofers in central Phoenix, 2015. Photo by Sarina E. Guerra and Derick Douglas Washington.

Roofers in Central Phoenix, 2015. Photo by Sarina E. Guerra and Derick Douglas Washington.

José Arellano, baker at La Purísima Bakery, Glendale, Arizona, 2015. Photo by Sarina E. Guerra and Derick Douglas Washington.

Monica González, baker at La Purísima Bakery, Glendale, Arizona, 2015. Photo by Sarina E. Guerra and Derick Douglas Washington.

Maríbel Martínez, shoe cobbler, Martínez Shoe & Boot Repair, Phoenix, Arizona, 2015. Photo by Sarina E. Guerra and Derick Douglas Washington.

Martín Martínez, cobbler and shoemaker, and owner of Martínez Shoe & Boot Repair, Phoenix, Arizona, 2015. Photo by Sarina E. Guerra and Derick Douglas Washington.

4

MEXICANO MINERS, DUAL WAGE, AND THE PURSUIT OF WAGE EQUALITY IN MIAMI, ARIZONA

★

CHRISTINE MARIN AND LUIS F. B. PLASCENCIA

IN THE HISTORIOGRAPHY OF MEXICANO LABOR in Arizona and the Southwest, one commonly finds reference to the presence of racialized wage hierarchies in agriculture, construction, lumbering, mining, smelting, railroads, and services. Such hierarchies are commonly referred to in the literature as *dual-wage hierarchies*. Although wage hierarchies involving multiple groups such as whites, African Americans, Chinese, Italians, Japanese, Eastern Europeans, Mexicans, and Native Americans do not fit a binary categorization, the scholarly discussion of the unequal wages between individuals defined as white/Anglo and Mexican has unfortunately reinforced the perception and scholarly discussion of wage hierarchies involving Mexicanos as "dual" structures.

The earliest description of unequal wage payment systems involving Mexican workers is Victor Clark's 1908 report for the U.S. Department of Labor. In his report, for example, Clark notes that the Southern Pacific Company in California paid the following wages: "Greeks, $1.60; Japanese, $1.45, and Mexicans, $1.25 a day" (1908, 479).[1] Clark also provides other examples showing wage inequities in coal mining and agriculture, as well as limited number of cases of parity between Anglos and Mexicans. Subsequent to Clark's report, numerous scholars have commented on the presence of wage inequalities confronted by Mexicano laborers in various areas and occupations in the Southwest. From classic works such as those of Manuel Gamio (1930 [1971]) and Carey McWilliams (1949 [1968]), to the later works by Chicano scholars such as Tomás Almaguer (1984; 1994), Albert Camarillo (1979), Mario García (1981), Andrés Jiménez Montoya (1977), Richard Griswold del Castillo (1980), Antonio Rios-Bustamante (1998), and Ricardo Romo (1983), all index the presence of lower wages paid to Mexican workers vis-à-vis those paid to Anglos/whites—though the presence of other groups altered the hierarchical position of wages paid to Mexicans. In Arizona's history Mexicanos confronted the same wage inequality. As noted earlier, although wage hierarchies were common across economic sectors, most historians examining Mexicano labor in Arizona have focused on the racialized wage hierarchies in copper mining.

This chapter offers an analysis of the formation of a wage hierarchy impacting Mexicano copper mine workers in Miami, Arizona, and the response of Mexican laborers who challenged racialized wage inequalities. In the historiography of the region and in local discourse, the wage hierarchy is known as a *dual-wage system*. Consequently, the discussion that follows uses wage hierarchy and dual wage interchangeably, though it recognizes that across copper mines in Arizona, wage hierarchies varied geographically, across time, and in the groups constituting the hierarchy. Although multiple historians and social scientists have noted the presence of dual-wage systems in Arizona's copper mines, limited attention has been given to how these wage inequalities represent an amalgamation and articulation of gender, class, and racialized factors.[2] In the context of copper mining in Miami, Arizona, we interpret the dual-wage phenomenon as a practice imposed among male workers; was, at its foundation, a racialized process that relied on a notion of white supremacy; and allowed mine owners/operators to foster class and racialized divisions among workers.

Three important social processes are reflected in the aforementioned text. One, it allowed mine owners/operators to maximize capital accumulation. The lower wages paid to Mexicans created a subsidy for mine owners/operators (including investors). Two, it fostered, reinforced, and protected a boundary of whiteness, and simultaneously elevated the socioeconomic position of male workers classified as white. Three, it stimulated a practice that marked Mexicans as a community that was expected to survive on a lower wage, and cemented the idea that the work performed by Mexicans—"Mexican work"—was defined as inherently lower-wage work. And, simultaneously, low-wage work was considered as indexing the work performed by Mexicanos. This general process was not limited to copper mining—it was extended to other occupations and remains in present-day Arizona. Moreover, the fact that Arizona is a low-wage state that has never made education a high priority means that Mexicano workers have to make ends meet on generally lower wages. Even in public universities, Mexican and/or Mexican American staff and faculty confront the legacy of racialized labor markets. Lastly, the positioning of Mexicanos as a lower-wage group with a marginal relationship to copper production also reinforced the idea that Mexicans were a lower-cost elastic supply of labor that could be contracted or expanded based on the national and global copper market. Proximity to Mexico as a location perceived as having a near-inexhaustible supply of low-wage workers facilitated the perception that Mexicanos were intrinsic to producing and maintaining an elastic supply of labor for copper production. Moreover, proximity also aided the idea that banishment could be easily accomplished.

Theoretically, the racialized wage hierarchy discussed here bolsters two sets of prior discussions of the segmentation/splitting of the labor market and the racialization of labor in global capitalist systems. The sociologist Edna Bonacich's classic 1970s essay on "ethnic antagonism" and the "split labor market" suggests that capitalist employers gain a degree of control of labor by creating a significant differential in wages, and that internal conflicts emerge between the higher-paid and lower-paid segment of workers (Bonacich 1972). Higher-paid workers seek to justify and maintain their privilege through their distancing from, and exclusion of, lower-paid workers. In the context of Arizona's copper mining, whiteness was the arbitrary marker that segmented the labor market. Consistent with this are the conceptual insights provided by Anibal Quijano and his argument about how contemporary capitalism may not operate as an explicit imperial project, but nonetheless encompasses what he labels a "coloniality of power" (Quijano 2000). The core dimension of the structure is the centrality of racialization and the assumption of white supremacy over nonwhites. Bonacich, Alimahomed, and Wilson (2008) make a parallel argument about the racialization of global labor. The experience of Mexicano copper mine workers in Arizona encompasses both the segmentation of workers and the racialization of labor.

LOCATING MIAMI AND COPPER MINING

Miami, Arizona, is located in Gila County, approximately ninety-miles east of Phoenix, and close to one hundred miles north of Tucson. The incorporated city is six miles from Globe, and their proximity to each other and shared history in the production of copper results in a hyphenated label for the area as Globe-Miami, or vice versa. Miami's population reflects the demographic profile of the composition of the mining workforce recruited to produce copper for the national and global market. From 1910 to 1920 Miami's population rose to almost 10,500, a substantial increase from the estimated 1,800 persons recorded in the 1910 Census (U.S. Bureau of the Census 1913). The decennial census of 2010 estimated the population as almost identical to that of 1910: 1,837 individuals.

Mexicans, Southern and Eastern European, including Serbians, Finns, and Italian migrants, as well as native/American/white workers, constituted the labor force for the mining operations in the Miami-Globe area. The Old Dominion Copper Company in Globe was considered one of the richest in the world but closed in 1931 and moved mining production to Miami. Within the regional discourse in copper mines in Arizona, the Miami-Globe mining area was labeled a "white man's" camps, in contrast to locations referred to as "Mexican" camps. Clifton-Morenci mines were considered to be "Mexican camps." This bifurcation, not surprisingly, is misleading. Neither label means that the entire copper mining workforce at a particular mine was white or Mexican, but rather that the majority of the workers were considered to be white or Mexican. Mexicans were present in both types of camps, not just Mexican camps. It is also worth noting that the use of quotes around "Mexican" is intended to index the fact that at some mines, workers considered Mexican were neither born in Mexico or of Mexican ancestry. Native Americans and Spaniards, for example, were, at times, considered to be Mexicans. In such cases, skin color and/or language were thought of as racial markers of Mexicaness. Moreover, the category of *white* was also not fixed. European migrants may not have been considered as white upon arrival in copper mining towns in Arizona, but over time became white, and could then claim the privileges associated with whiteness. In addition to not receiving a "Mexican wage," and being allowed to live in better housing and granted access to white spaces, this reinforced the perception that they naturally constituted a higher social class. The higher valuation of whiteness remains in present-day Arizona.

According to historian Benton-Cohen (2009, 81–82), local ordinances implemented by white town officials and mine owners reinforced the racialized separation of whites from Mexicans, Chinese, and others. In some locations, Chinese were allowed to work or carry out business activities during the day but were prohibited from living within the boundaries of a town. And during the 1860s, as discussed by the historian Spude, some local placer mines prohibited Mexicans from filing mining claims in the Walker-Weaver District (1975). The combination of wage hierarchies based on whiteness and local ordinances regarding residence and economic activities reinforced the racial hierarchy grounded on whiteness, and the lower status of Mexicanos. An important outcome of this process was the association of lower wages as "Mexican wages." In the mid-1900s, mines in the U.S. territory acquired under the Gadsden Purchase (also known as Venta de la Mesilla), white mine speculators used the term *peon wages* to refer to the low wages paid to Mexicanos, and relied on peonage, although formally outlawed in the state (Park 1961, 60–69), in mines, ranches, and farms. The effects of these processes are evident in the present wherein in the private and public sector, including public universities in Arizona, such as Arizona State University, lower wages for Mexicans and/or Mexican Americans is naturalized, but administrators strongly deny that such a structure exists. An emphasis on a generic "culture of inclusion" is not the same as a culture of equity.

The major copper-producing companies located in Miami were the Miami Copper Company, the International Smelter and Refining Company, and the Inspiration Consolidated Copper Company. After 1931, the Old Dominion Copper Company became the fourth major copper enterprise. Unlike Clifton-Morenci and Bisbee copper towns, which were singularly owned by the Phelps Dodge Copper Company, Miami was not a company-owned town. However, copper corporations enforced a policy of segregation, including the Miami Catholic Church—whites sat on one side; Mexicans on the other (Rios-Bustamante 1998, 175).

The wage hierarchy practices changed over time and by location, in accordance with the managerial decisions and capital accumulation aims. With respect to wages, each of the companies created a pay scale and description of work. The adopted wage structure paid Mexican workers less than white workers. One mechanism that justified a lower wage for Mexicans was an arbitrary division of labor: surface mining activities in contrast to underground activities. In the early 1900s, distinct from Bisbee, Mexican workers in Miami were relegated to underground work, which in this instance came with lower wages, in contrast to Bisbee, where only Anglos worked underground and were paid higher wages (Benton-Cohen 2009, 83, 85). Mexicans working underground in Miami rode several levels below the surface, at least two thousand or more feet, in a cage (elevator) to begin work. Underground work included the use of drills, explosives, crowbars, picks, and shovels to dig tunnels and build chutes so that the ore fell from a higher level to a lower level; laying cement, or timbered drifts, or passages, and digging of tunnels to the veins of copper and drive raises, or passages, upward for excavation; placing vertical timbers to support dirt walls and ceilings; and dropping ore down timbered chutes to lower levels in the mine and then onto ore cars.[3]

Mining activities drew speculators such as Cleve W. Van Dyke from Alexandria, Minnesota, to Arizona: first to Bisbee in 1906; then to Globe; and then to the area known as Miami Flats in 1908. By this time, copper mining activity at mines such as the Miami Copper Company, the Black Warrior, the Cordova, the Live Oak, and the Keystone already existed in Miami Flats. Workers lived in their tents or makeshift wooden shacks or in small cabins in areas near the mines. At least fifty men worked at the Live Oak mine, and approximately eighty more worked at the Black Warrior (Pry 1997, 20–21). The Miami Copper Company built company housing for administrators, mine officials, and engineers. The mine company often hired single Mexican nationals from Chihuahua and Sonora to mine its copper. Here we should note that after the passage of the 1885 Alien Contract Labor Law (also known as the Foran Act), mine operators recruiting labor in Mexico were doing so in violation of U.S. federal law. Federal law enforcement, however, was not a priority within the relevant federal agencies, and thus copper mines recruiting labor in Mexico in effect were granted a kind of amnesty that allowed corporations to ignore the rule of law.

In 1909 Mexican nationals helped in the construction of the mill and began the process of extracting copper ore from rocks, concentrating and smelting the ore, and preparing it for transportation (Sain 1944, 38; Miami Copper Company 1909, 6–9). Van Dyke recognized that the mine and the workers needed goods, services, housing, and merchandise to go about their daily lives. He bought the Miami Flats property from the Miami Land and Development Company for $25,000, homesteaded available land in Miami Flats, named his new town Miami, and established his own real estate company, the Miami Trust Company (later called the Miami Townsite Company) to manage and prepare lots for sale. Van Dyke laid out the town, plotted it, graded its streets, and placed advertisements in the Globe newspaper announcing the sale of his lots on October 11, 1909. Van Dyke learned that the Gila Valley, Globe, and Northern Railroad planned on completing a branch line to Miami, enabling mining companies to ship their ore outside of Miami for smelting and production and bring in passengers to settle and establish new businesses. The railroad company completed the line just eight days before he made the first of numerous lot sales in his new town site, Miami (Sain 1944, 50, 58–59). The mining companies in Miami maintained their own corporate control of their mines, its workers, and its productions of copper, leaving land speculators like Van Dyke ready and willing to profit from his capital investment.

In Arizona the dual wage practiced in copper mining dates back to the 1850s (Park 1961). Andrés Jiménez Montoya argues that Arizona's copper mining companies created and upheld a job and wage hierarchy based on ethnic lines: Anglo work and Anglo pay as opposed to Mexican work and Mexican pay (1977, 24). Joseph Park describes wage scale for the years 1860 to 1910 (1961). For example, in the year 1900, Anglo workers earned $3.25 per day; Mexicans earned $2.00 per day for the same work. In 1905 the wages for whites increased by five cents, while the Mexicans' wages remained the same.

CONCEPTUALIZING WAGE HIERARCHIES/DUAL-WAGE SYSTEMS

As noted earlier, multiple scholars have noted the presence of wage hierarchies in Arizona's copper mines; however, the specific factors that motivated owners/operators to impose differential pay for similar work remains to be examined across copper-producing areas in the state, potential differences between white and Mexican camps, and how wage-payment systems changed across time. Although scholarly discussions of the dual wage in Arizona tend to cite racial discrimination as the principal motivating factor, this explanation is too simplistic and narrow. While it sounds logical that operators sought to maximize capital accumulation and show positive returns to investors and thus imposed a lower wage on Mexicano workers, this is not likely the full explanation. On simply economic terms, greater capital accumulation would have been achieved if Mexican wages were paid to all workers—whites and nonwhites.

This would have without question generated significantly greater profits—but this was not the action taken. This suggests that while wage systems were racialized, it was not simply because of discriminatory ideologies among copper mine operators against Mexicans.

Secondly, while copper mines had to be in Arizona, copper companies' administrative headquarters did not. Even the global Phelps Dodge Corporation did not move its headquarters to Arizona until 1928. This suggests that decisions about wage payments were not necessarily made in Arizona. Yes, local managers had to manage the local workforce, but they did not make corporate decisions about the payroll component of corporate expenses. Decision-makers of family or publicly held corporations in the Midwest or on the East Coast made decisions regarding corporate expenses. Moreover, European and East Coast investors may have held racist perspectives, but their principal concern was the return on their capital investments, not what should be the operational wage hierarchy. They would not have inserted themselves in suggesting that Mexicans should earn Mexican wages, and non-Mexicans should receive substantially higher wages. Within a vision of maximum returns on capital, the lowest wages possible would have been paid to all workers.

The aforementioned does not mean that race is not relevant. But rather, it is to suggest that greater exploration needs to be allocated to examining the key nodes of where racialized wage decisions were made, and reasons given justifying the differential wages. It is possible that local operators convinced corporate decision-makers that wage hierarchies were ideal organizations of production to achieve greater capital accumulation. In other words, the company could reduce their labor costs by paying one group a fair wage and a second (and other) group a lower wage; the net effect being that it would reduce the overall labor expense and increase profits. The decision of who would be positioned in the lower-wage category was one that deployed race as a distinguishing marker. But who exactly held these notions within copper corporations is an issue that needs to be explored across copper mines—in both Mexican and white camps.

Once the wage hierarchy was implemented along a white—nonwhite axis this, in turn, racialized the social and political life of the mining community. The process fostered the constructs of whiteness, white supremacy, and white privilege. The exclusion of Mexicans from this white matrix meant that Mexicanos could be considered a lower status/class and relegated to an elastic supply of labor that would shrink or grow depending on the status of the global copper market. The creation of the white matrix not only privileged male workers perceived as white, it also can be considered a strategy to protect whiteness. In other words, the exclusion of Mexicans from the "white wage" was an element in creating a boundary of whiteness to be policed and protected.[4] The boundary of whiteness was not limited to copper production in Arizona;

it became central to how many white Arizonans would come to think of the state. Debates related to New Mexico and Arizona statehood, for example, highlighted an imagined vision of Arizona as a white state—where whites were the majority—and New Mexico as a territory dominated by Mexicans. White Arizona leaders and lobbyists for Arizona statehood sought to convince Congress that granting statehood to Arizona would represent the integration of "real Americans" who knew how to govern themselves and would contribute much to the United States. The presence of Diné, Pima, Maricopa, Tohono O'odham, Gila River, Apaches, and other Native American communities, as well as a substantial number of Mexicans, was downplayed as relevant to statehood. Unfortunately, the legacy of this sociopolitical erasure remains in the contemporary dynamics in the state, and in the historical narratives about the state.

It also should not be overlooked that wage hierarchies in Arizona were nuanced and varied. Philip J. Mellinger, for example, observes that the wage hierarchy was differentiated in some cases. Mellinger acknowledges that Italians (who later would be labeled white) earned less than Anglo-Irish, were excluded from so-called skilled tasks, and so may have earned wages closer to the "Mexican wage" (1995, 170). The historian Linda Gordon informs us that "copper companies delineated three formal wage groups: Mexican, Italian and Spaniard, and whites, but there was slippage between the nonwhite groups and some Italians earned the Mexican rate" (1999, 102). More recently, Eric Meeks goes a step further and suggests that discussions of the dual wage in copper production needs greater scholarly reflection.

> Still, even by the turn of the century, it would be inaccurate to characterize the racialized class structure in the mining towns as a binary system. . . . Wage stratification was not based simply on different skill levels but on race and nationality . . . Racial classification, rather than nationality, language, or degree of skill, structured the wage hierarchy. Moreover, this was a multitiered rather than a binary or dual-wage system. . . . Indigenous workers—a group almost whole ignored by most historians of Arizona labor—were often relegated to the lowest-paid manual jobs . . . below . . . ethnic Mexicans. (2007a, 28–29)

Meeks advances our understanding of the process but does not address the actual construction and deployment of racialized classification in mining towns. This is an historical issue that remains to be examined.

The aforementioned observations remind us that, while we should acknowledge local understanding and discourse that privilege the construct of dual wage, attention must be paid to local and regional manifestations of racialized wage hierarchies and the position of Mexicanos within these. This also suggests that important transformations took place regarding the production of wage hierarchies in copper mining.

MEXICANO AND MEXICAN AMERICAN CHALLENGES TO THE "MEXICAN WAGE"

Prior to 1920, Mexicanos and Mexican Americans expressed their clear dissatisfaction with the unequal wage systems in Miami mines. They were minor yet important players in the short-lived strikes of 1915 and 1917 at the Inspiration Consolidated Copper Company and at the Miami Copper Company. While neither strike was nationally significant, they are important for several reasons. One, the Mexicanos and Mexican Americans made some gains in their push for unionization, and the aspiration that collective bargaining would improve their economic well-being. Second, they expressed their desire to end the wage system that disadvantaged Mexicanos in Miami mines. Third, they took initial steps to challenge white privilege.

At the Inspiration Consolidated Copper Company, a group of Mexicano miners formed the Comité por Trabajadores en General (General Workers Committee) in 1914. The Comité initiated communication with the Miami Miners Union (MMU) and expressed their concerns about the dual-wage system practiced at Inspiration. The MMU formed an alliance earlier with the Western Federation of Miners (WFM), already gaining in membership among Anglos at Inspiration and at other mines nearby. Primarily a white craft union of workers, the WFM showed no interest or desire in including Mexicans. The exclusion of Mexicans from most labor unions, whether based on race or citizenship, reinforced the boundaries and privileges of whiteness. To their short- and long-term detriment, the short-sightedness of labor unions impeded the formation of a class- and worker-based opposition to corporate copper mines, and worker improvements based on collective bargaining for mine-wide improvement in wages and working conditions.

The Comité ignored the snub by the WFM and aimed to build worker solidarity among themselves. When World War I broke out in 1914, at least 65,000 tons of the copper used by the Allies in the war effort came from Miami mines. Inspiration Consolidated Copper Company produced 30,000 tons (Sain 1944, 78–79). At the same time, labor unrest instigated by the WFM began to develop and threatened to stop wartime copper production at Inspiration in the spring of 1915. When the company hired "scab" labor to replace existing workers, the Miami Miners Union, joined by the WFM, and led a strike in protest. The WFM used the strike to show the company the worker-based power of the union. Over 1,600 men walked off their jobs at the concentrator. Already unhappy because their daily wages had been reduced the previous year from $3.75 to $3.38, the union men walked out. The Mexicanos working underground at Inspiration sympathized with the MMU and supported the Anglos in their protest through their Comité. The Comité realized the MMU-WFM–led strike did nothing to resolve their labor issue of a dual-wage system, but supported them in a show of worker solidarity. The strike lasted twelve days. Inspiration offered the MMU-WFM a sliding wage scale tied to the market price of copper; at that time, this was thirteen cents a pound. Considering the heightened demand for copper in wartime, they agreed to that condition (Sain 1944, 134). Copper production continued without disruption.

Mexicans' wages were not factored in the negotiations between Inspiration and the MMU-WFM. Comité's members' readiness for unionization caught the attention of the Industrial Workers of the World (IWW). The IWW had some success in promoting a class-based understanding of the experience of workers confronting capitalism. Labor historian David Brundage asserts that the IWW welcomed Mexican and Mexican Americans into its ranks because its egalitarianism crossed racial/ethnic lines in their effort to achieve a class movement of workers (1994, 3–4). The IWW's emergence in the Miami area came on the heels of the MMU-WFM strike of 1915. By 1917 the IWW gained allegiance from Mexican miners in Miami and labor troubles loomed ahead in the Inspiration and the Miami Copper Company mines. This time, the matter of wage differentials was at the forefront. In June 1917 IWW members threatened a strike. Union organizers demanded a fifty-cent increase in wages for its Anglo surface and underground members. For surface workers, it meant an increase daily wage from $5.00 to $5.50. For the underground workers—meaning the white foremen and so-called skilled workers such as trammers and machinists—it meant an increase from $5.50 to $6.00. The IWW, however, gave no consideration for the wages of the Mexicans who worked underground (Sain 1944, 134–35, 137–38).

When mine managers refused to meet with IWW representatives, approximately one thousand of its members from the two mines honored the July 2 strike. Members of the MMU, who figured prominently in the 1915 strike at the Inspiration mine, disapproved of the strike and of the IWW and stayed on the job. Comité workers at Inspiration and the Mexicans at Miami Copper also did not support the strike. To replace the strikers, Inspiration recruited, in violation of federal law, over three hundred Mexican nationals from Chihuahua. When they arrived at the company's railway station, about two hundred white IWW members attempted to prevent them from getting off the train. Their attempt proved unsuccessful. Inspiration and Miami Copper managers snubbed the IWW, and copper production continued. The race-based unequal wage system remained in place. The companies brought in more Mexican nationals, paying them the same wage as the Mexicans and Mexican Americans already working there. At least seven weeks of negotiations between the IWW and mine managers over wages failed; the strike lost its momentum. The 1917 strike, however, brought about the biggest change in the ethnic composition of the workforce at Inspiration and the Miami Copper Company mines: Mexicanos, including Mexican Americans, now made up a majority of workers at the Miami copper mines (Sain 1944, 139).

In 1920 approximately twelve thousand people lived and worked for the mines or as workers providing services to the mines. Census enumerators noted their race and skin color in the 1920 Census: *w* for white, *b* for black, and *ch* for Chinese. Mexicans, Mexican Americans, and Anglos were classified as *w*, for white (U.S. Bureau of the Census 1922). For this reason, it is difficult to determine the number of Mexicans and Mexican Americans in Miami. Closer examination of the 1920 Census, however, reports Spanish surnames and Mexico as country of birth (ibid.).[5] In that decade, wages for copper miners in Miami were reported to have been "about $5.00 to $6.00 per day for Whites and under $4.00 per day for Mexicans" (Rios-Bustamante 1995, 44–45). From 1921 to 1930 the Miami Copper Company's copper mining and smelting enterprises expanded considerably; the Inspiration Consolidated Copper Company and the International Smelting Company were part of this growth. The gradual drop of the price of copper foretold of upcoming declines. In March 1929 the price of copper stood at twenty-four cents a pound. In April 1930 the price fell to fourteen cents, and then the price fell again by the autumn of 1930 to ten cents per pound (Sain 1944, 183). Copper production came to a halt. The mines shut down in 1932, and 70–80 percent of the workforce was reported as being Mexican and Mexican American. By 1938, as the Great Depression appeared to be ending, and the prospects of World War II expansionism became clearer, the mines reopened and hired workers again, including Mexican and Mexican American workers. The racialized wage hierarchies also returned. Within two years, economic recovery improved and global prices of copper rose again; the Miami mines were working twenty-four hours a day, seven days a week (ibid., 190).

According to the 1940 Census, at least 4,722 people lived in Miami, Arizona. Mexicans, Mexican Americans, Italians, Serbians, Spaniards, Swedish, Irish, English, Lithuanians, Greeks, and Germans were among the groups classified by census enumerators as *w* for white. The 1940 Census notes that Mexicans and Mexican Americans with Spanish surnames spoke Spanish. Many were born in the United States. Many were bilingual and able to read, write, and speak English and Spanish and were educated in U.S. public schools in Arizona. World War II revitalized Miami's economy from the dismal state of affairs in the 1930s and made new demands for copper to provide electricity for war industries, and to support domestic demand for copper.

Mexicano *mineros* again turned to challenging the unequal wages and sought to revive unionism efforts. They welcomed the presence of the International Union of Mine, Mill and Smelter Workers (IUMMSW) to help them end the dual wage system and employment discrimination so prevalent in the Miami mines. They formed Local 586 of the IUMMSW, and hoped their union might be able to negotiate wage equality for them. Their objective was to end the dual wage, end workplace discrimination, and to be afforded opportunities for socioeconomic mobility. In 1941 a rivalry occurred in the Miami mines between the American Federation of Labor (AFL), a craft union comprised of whites, and the IUMMSW, with a dominant membership of Mexican and Mexican American workers. Heated arguments arose during collective bargaining periods between the two unions over the classification of workers, the parity of wages, and the types of work performed by workers. Arnold Rojas recalled how the AFL did not allow Mexicans or Mexican Americans to perform work except that performed by "common laborers," or "laborers," or "helpers," or "assistants"—work activities deemed to represent "Mexican work":

> We *Mexicanos* were considered as unskilled workers who worked for less pay. We couldn't get jobs as shovel operators, truck drivers, bulldozer drivers, electricians or machine operators because gringos said we weren't white. We were dirty Mexicans. The gringos in the AFL did that type of work. And they got more pay. *Mexicanos* were hired as "laborers" or as "common laborers" or as "helpers"—like in laborer one or laborer two and it went up like that. We could never get out of being a laborer. We couldn't rise above that classification. . . . So, we talked to Orville Larson, our union rep about it to see if we could get the IUMMSW to help us, in our Local 586. We wanted equal pay, equal work, the same that the gringo was making for the same jobs we were working at. What we *Mexicanos* wanted was equality. And we believed that our IUMMSW could make us equal (Rojas Interview 1999).[6]

As the IUMMSW's regional representative, Orville Larson brought the miners' complaints about the dual wage and the discrimination they faced as Mexicans and Mexican Americans in the Miami mines to the attention of the Fair Employment Practice Committee (FEPC) in June 1942.[7] Before the IUMMSW became a bargaining agent for workers in the mining companies in 1941, workers' committees usually handled their own labor relations in the Miami mines (Marin 2000, 67). At that time, workers' committees comprised of four workers elected from various departments and representatives from IUMMSW, Local 586, met monthly and discussed labor management issues such as the dual-wage system, racial and ethnic discrimination in the workplace, and other wage issues of concern (Chansley 1963, 23). But the Mexicans and Mexican Americans of Local 586 grew weary and frustrated over their mining companies' unwillingness to resolve their concerns over the persistent practice of the unequal, racialized wage system in the workplace. "Talking about it was just that—talk, and nothing else," said Arnold Rojas.

> We were sick and tired of being kicked around by the gringos. And we were doing the same kind of work they were and getting paid less money. We thought that if we had our own LULAC (League of United Latin American Citizens) council, it might help

> us end the racism and discrimination going on at the mines. With our Local 586 and the IUMMSW, we could only go so far because the company wouldn't take us seriously enough. The gringo foremen tried to discourage us and threatened to fire us. We thought we could get the Phoenix LULAC to help publicize our issues and put more pressure on the companies to change things. You know, stir things up a bit, maybe get the *Mexicanos* in Phoenix to help us, get the politicians involved. Maybe the governor.[8]

According to Joe Sotelo, the idea of forming a LULAC council in January 1941, in Miami, came from the Mexican American and Mexican miners who patronized Frank Chávez's barber shop. The talk among the men and miners like him centered on their distaste for the hierarchical wage system and the mistreatment they encountered at the mines. Some of the men recalled the separate pay lines on paydays, the Mexican line and the white line, and separate shower and bath facilities—one section for Anglos and another section for the Mexicanos.[9]

The LULAC Council No. 111 was formed at the barber shop in Miami. The *mineros* decided to use their locally based civil rights organization and exploit their political activism to call attention to their concerns over the dual wage issue and the racism they encountered.[10] To do that, LULAC Council No. 111 invited their compatriots, the Phoenix LULAC Council No. 110, to join them in their efforts to end the discrimination they faced in the mines. The mineros believed that a rural-urban connection might make a difference in how outsiders might view racism and discrimination differently in their copper state both locally and nationally. They decided to share their working-class lives and their union's history with others who did not know about them and their struggle to end unequal wage systems. And LULAC would be their tool to demand equality. Miami Council No. 111 established ties to the LULAC Council No. 110 of Phoenix in August 1941, when Council No. 110 held the first LULAC convention in Phoenix. The Arizona LULAC convention drew Mexican American and Mexicano delegates from the urban metropolises of Phoenix, Tempe, and Mesa and from the copper mining communities of Globe, Miami, Superior, Morenci, and Clifton.[11] The convention marked the first time that Mexican Americans and Mexicans from the state's copper mining communities in rural areas and those from the urban-centered communities discussed mutual concerns about unionism and labor, the discrimination the miners experienced in the mines, the dual-wage system of work and pay, and political and civil rights issues.

The Phoenix LULAC Council No. 110 saw itself as a defender of social and political justice in battle against racialized discrimination and the mistreatment of Mexicans and Mexican Americans in the Phoenix area. Members cosponsored a series of patriotic and pro-American lectures in English and in Spanish at Friendly House, an Americanization center for Mexican immigrants established in 1921. Lectures stressed the importance of obtaining U.S. citizenship and state legislators from the Democratic Party—James "Jimmy" Carreón and Frank Robles, both from Tucson—provided information on the bills and laws under consideration in Arizona's legislature (Marin 2001, 2). The largest Mexican American organization in the United States, the Alianza Hispano-Americana (AHA), a *mutualista* (fraternal) benefit society, supported the work of the Phoenix LULAC Council No. 110 in 1941 by encouraging its members to continue with its work, although the AHA did not fund any of LULAC's activities, nor did it get involved in any political endeavors that LULAC No. 110 pursued. Founded in Tucson in 1894 by the Mexican American elite, and conservative and apolitical in nature, the AHA filed incorporation papers with the Arizona Corporation Commission in 1907. By then, the AHA became the leading Mexican American mutual-aid society and organization in the United States. It offered its members low-cost life insurance and social activities. The Alianza's lead historian, Kaye Briegel (1974), explains in her dissertation, "Alianza Hispano-Americana, 1894–1965: A Mexican American Fraternal Insurance Society," the uniqueness of the organization's death benefit program and why it attracted membership. While the AHA offered no sickness benefits for those whose illnesses prevented them from working, it offered opportunities of "collecting one's life insurance before one's death" in cases of total disabilities. This important feature made it easier for members to absorb the costs of funerals and burials in times of economic distress and difficulties (Briegel 1974, 14). This was an important benefit among the Mexicans of Clifton-Morenci and in Bisbee in the early 1900s as well, since injuries and deaths caused by mining accidents created considerable economic distress for surviving family members. The historians Mellinger and Gordon identified the AHA's Clifton Lodge No. 2 in the early 1900s as a "social group" and a "leading benevolent society," with Gordon noting that the "Alianza grew to 1,171 members in 22 chapters by 1907" in the Arizona Territory (Mellinger 1995, 45; Gordon 1999, 39). And Benton-Cohen (2009, 92) found that the AHA lodge in Bisbee participated in social events that celebrated Diez y seis de Septiembre (September 16: Mexico's call for independence). It is one of the most important Mexican holidays celebrated in southwestern states, as well as beyond. The two organizations, the League of United Latin American Citizens and the Alianza Hispano-Americana, offered opportunities for Mexicans and Mexican Americans to belong to collective efforts for social justice and well-being. But LULAC's political involvement in issues such as school segregation and racism aimed against Mexican Americans in Arizona, found another reason for their political activism and another fight for equality and justice for its members: the practice of the dual wage in the copper mining industry in Miami, Arizona, in 1941.

The year 1941 is an important year for mineros in Miami mines. It began with a group of Mexican and Mexican American miners organizing and forming the new

LULAC Council No. 111 in January and its collaboration with the LULAC Council No. 110 about the dual wage practiced in Miami mines. Orville Larson, IUMMSW's representative, stood ready and willing to help Mexicanos fight discrimination in the mines. The mineros were ready for change. On June 25, 1941, President Franklin Delano Roosevelt established the Fair Employment Practice Committee (FEPC) by Executive Order 8802, in effect from June 25, 1941, to May 27, 1943.[12] Government agencies were ordered to end discriminatory hiring practices, and examine practices related to unequal pay. This meant that the Inspiration Consolidated Copper Company, the Miami Copper Company, and the International Smelting Company, holding defense contracts in a wartime industry, had to comply with the president's order. The agency held public hearings in western states such as Arizona, California, Nevada, Oregon, and Washington, which provided opportunities for labor unions and employers to discuss and identify instances of discrimination and wage differentials in the workplace (Gritter 2012, 11). An FEPC office was established in El Paso, Texas, in July 1942, and Ernest Trimble, Daniel Donovan, and G. James Fleming began the task of investigating complaints of the exploitation of Mexicano miners in Arizona, including the Miami Copper Company, the Inspiration Consolidated Copper Company, and the International Smelter (Daniel 1999, 52–76, 151).

In his book *Chicano Workers and the Politics of Fairness: The FEPC in the Southwest, 1941–1945* Clete Daniel noted that an FEPC investigator, Barron Beshoar, traveled to Miami in August 1942 to investigate complaints about the dual-wage system and the discrimination against Mexicans and Mexican Americans at the Miami mines (Daniel 1991, 64–65). Orville Larson urged an investigation of the long-standing practices there via the IUMMSW. The FEPC began contact with Inspiration Consolidated Copper Company officials through their letter of August 20, 1942, requesting the company's wage policy and demographic information using questionnaires in order to determine the composition of the workforce (Gritter 2012, 52). Richard Newlin and Richard Hughes, superintendents at Inspiration and the Miami Copper Company, questioned the reason for FEPC's investigation, claiming there was no reason for it. Inspiration's attorney suggested that the IUMMSW used discrimination and the dual wage as wedges to strengthen their union, and to create trouble among the men when there was no trouble brewing (Daniel 1991, 64–65). Nevertheless, the FEPC investigator found that Mexican Americans and Mexicans at the Inspiration mine comprised "approximately 30 percent of the company's 1,500 employees [and] occupied a collective status distinctly inferior" to that of their white counterparts, and performed "the same or similar tasks at or near the bottom of the company's job hierarchy" (ibid., 63). He also found similar disparities among workers at the Miami Copper Company. When questioned about the differences, Newlin insisted that "merit" determined that Anglos had the better jobs than the Mexicans and Mexican Americans because they had "physical and mental shortcomings" and Anglos did not (ibid., 64). As for Hughes, he said that Miami Copper's top-level officials in the New York headquarters "dictated" the company's work assignments, classifications, and wage practices, and that he had no authority to change them (ibid., 65).

The questionnaires from the Inspiration Consolidated Copper Company were examined and data revealed that 1,556 persons worked at the mine. At least 1,429 of them spoke English, and Mexicans and Mexican Americans were among them; however, their exact number is unclear. "Of that total of 1,556 employees, 1,429 were designated as English-speaking Americans (some of whom were also of Mexican background), 120 as Spanish-speaking persons, 456 as persons of Mexican background, 2 as Negroes, and 5 as English-speaking aliens" (Gritter 2012, 52).[13] Ernest Trimble, a FEPC investigator, used that data, as well as the numerous complaints gathered from Mexicans and Mexican Americans about wage differentials and discrimination in the Miami mines, to begin his formal dialogue with Inspiration officials through his August 27, 1942, letter: "We are in possession of a number of complaints from some of your employees alleging that they have been discriminated against . . . The complaints alleged a wage differential as between Mexican wages and so-called Anglo wages for the same work, the Mexicans receiving the lower wage; also, they alleged a failure on the part of the company to up-grade Mexican workers, thus confirming them to certain low-paying jobs" (ibid., 52). Barron B. Beshoar, a FEPC field investigator, followed up on the letter and went to the Inspiration Consolidated Copper Company mine and interviewed numerous Anglo and Mexican and Mexican American workers. Interviewees acknowledged the dual-wage practice, that "Mexicans are paid at a lower scale than Anglos for the same or similar work and that there is a general failure to upgrade or promote qualified Mexican workers to the higher classifications and better jobs" (Daniel 1995, 63). Beshoar further found evidence that confirmed these opinions. For example, in the crushing plant, Mexican Americans and Mexicans outnumbered Anglo workers and worked in the lowest wage category, which was at the bottom of the wage scale. Additionally, Beshoar noted that Mexican and Mexican American workers were "excluded from skilled occupations and denied wage parity with Anglos performing the same job" (ibid., 63). Despite such findings, the FEPC did not have the authority or political will to force concessions or solutions to racialized wage inequalities at the Inspiration Consolidated Copper Company and the Miami Copper Company. Not surprisingly among capitalist corporations, the mining companies did not heed the FEPC recommendations. The Mexican American miners were not surprised at the outcome.

> We knew the company wasn't going to do anything about the discrimination. Hell, it's been going on for many years and why should they care about us? Once those

government guys left, we knew they weren't coming back. The company is more powerful than some damn government agency. (Rojas Interview 1999)

Arnold Rojas was correct. The FEPC failed them. Meanwhile, in August 1943 contract negotiations between the IUMMSW and the Miami Copper Company, the Inspiration Consolidated Copper Company, and the International Smelting and Refining Company broke down over the union's efforts to eliminate the dual wage and discriminatory rates for Mexican and Mexican American workers. IUMMSW representative Larson looked to the Non-Ferrous Metals Commission, a subagency of the War Labor Board, with jurisdiction within the copper industry, to look into the matter. His action gave new hope for resolutions, according to Rojas: "He [Larson] talked to us about the commission and said we needed to take our battle to Washington, D.C. We agreed. We were excited about it" (ibid.).

In the autumn of 1943, some members of LULAC No. 110 traveled to Miami from Phoenix and met with Arnold Rojas, members of Local 586, and Orville Larson. They carried with them a letter of support from LULAC No. 110 that spelled out their concerns regarding the civil rights of the Mexican American miners in Miami. Placida García Smith, president of LULAC No.110, asked Larson to present their letter to a representative of the Non-Ferrous Metals Commission.[14] This gesture of good will on the part of LULAC Council No. 110 did not go unnoticed by the mineros in Miami. "We appreciated their letter and for driving all the way up here because at that time, during the war, we were limited to three gallons of gas per week because of rationing," said Rojas (Interview 1999). It is not clear what, if any, impact the letter from LULAC Council No. 110 may have had when Orville Larson made contact with the Non-Ferrous Metals Commission, or if he actually sent the letter to the agency. Cordial and amicable relationships continued between LULAC Council No. 110 and LULAC Council No. 111 during the war years and continued in the postwar period. It is important to note, however, that LULAC Council No. 110 and LULAC Council No. 111 of Miami challenged the views of labor relations and mining companies' patterns of a dual-wage system of pay in the Miami copper mines.

In 1944 the Non-Ferrous Metals Commission began their investigation into complaints by the IUMMSW of employment discrimination in the Miami mines. The commission required the Inspiration Consolidated Copper Company, the Miami Copper Company, and the International Smelting and Refining Company to prepare and submit for analysis all employee statistical payroll data from January 1, 1941, to September 15, 1943. The commission wanted to review data that showed the dispersion of employees at the three companies by job classification, wage rates, education, and length of service (*War Labor Reports* 1944). The commission reviewed the data provided and learned that all three companies classified employees into two groups:

"Anglo-American" and "other" employees. The "other" employees' category included "Anglo-American females," "Latin American males," "Latin American females," and "Negro males" (*War Labor Reports* 1945, 592). The commission determined the following: the mining companies maintained lower wages for "common labor" jobs with classifications such as laborer, helper, mucker, millman, and skinner. The commission learned that Mexican and Mexican Americans and Negro males received lower wages per shift than those classified as white/Anglo. In addition, the commission determined that such wages ranged "below the minimum of sound and tested going rates for the [mining] industry and area and based [them] upon racial discrimination" (*War Labor Reports* 1944, 147).

The data analyzed by the commission revealed discrepancies. For example, in September 1943, the companies employed 3,068 men and 153 women, a total of 3,221 employees. At least 72 percent, or 2,320 employees, were categorized as "Anglo-American males." The remaining 28 percent, or 748 employees, were categorized as "other employees" (*War Labor Reports* 1944, 151). Included within the "other" employee category were 153 women hired during the war by the Miami Copper Company and the Inspiration Consolidated Copper Company. Data further showed that 141 "Anglo-American" females worked as chemists, assistant chemists, telephone operators, and clerks. Anglo American female chemists earned $7.45 per shift, Anglo female telephone operators earned $6.07 per shift, and Anglo American female clerks earned $6.36 per shift (ibid., 152–53, 158). The female laborers, comprised of Anglo women and Mexican American women, dug ditches, filled ore carts with waste materials, mixed and made concrete slabs, sawed wood and mixed oils for machinery, and cleaned tools and machines (Rojas Interview 1999). However, Anglo women in this "laborer" classification earned higher wages per shift than Mexican or Mexican American female laborers earned. The earnings of thirty-one Anglo female laborers ranged from $5.21 to $6.36 per shift (*War Labor Reports* 1944, 151–53, 147–59). Thirteen Mexican American or Mexican women hired as "laborers" earned only $5.21 per shift for the same work and for the same hours per shift (ibid., 153). Mexican American and Mexican male employees at the three mines worked within common labor job classifications such as laborer, helper, and mucker during the same period. These workers are also included within the "other" employee category. According to the commission's analysis, this group comprised a total of 647 minority employees. The earnings of 153 Mexican and Mexican American employees at the three mines ranged from $5.21 to $6.36 per shift (*War Labor Reports* 1944, 151; 153). By comparison, Anglo males earned wages from $6.51 to $6.94 per shift for the same type of work (*War Labor Reports* 1944, 153). Mining companies did not provide the reason for these wage differences for "laborer" or "common labor" classifications among Anglo males and Mexican and Mexican American male employees.

Upon completion of its study of the statistical payroll data, the Non-Ferrous Metals Commission concluded the following: (1) a consistent pattern of discriminatory wage rates for "other" employees (Anglo women and Mexican American or Mexican men and women) existed in the Miami mines, (2) mining companies classified male laborers as "Mexican" and as "white" laborers, (3) mining companies paid Mexicans and Mexican Americans wages based upon their race or ethnicity, and (4) wage rates for Mexican and Mexican American males remained well below wages paid Anglo males for the same type of work. As the result of their findings, the commission issued the following orders to the three Miami mining companies: "eliminate wage rates below $6.36 per shift because they are based on racial discrimination,"[15] and the companies and the union must review all labor contract provisions as to nondiscriminatory hiring, discharge, promotion, demotion, and lay off, if necessary, and revise such provisions to the end that they may clearly include provision for nondiscriminatory hiring (*War Labor Reports* 1945, 592).

The IUMMSW welcomed the commission's decisions and viewed their orders as a victory for democratic rights for working men and women and a "serious blow at the practice of discrimination against the great Spanish-speaking population of the Southwest."[16] Representatives for the three mining companies disagreed with the commission's findings, saying that the IUMMSW manipulated and exploited the matter of wage differentials to claim racial or ethnic discrimination at the workplace when it did not exist, and were going to challenge these claims in due time. Representatives claimed that the mining companies had "excellent" grievance procedures for any employee to follow and to discuss any concerns relating to one's job or classification, wage, or matters of discrimination, with or without the IUMMSW's permission. Representatives claimed matters could easily be resolved (*War Labor Reports* 1944, 761, 765).

The union and mining representatives remained at bitter odds and disagreement over the findings of the Non-Ferrous Metals Commission and the recommendations made to bring justice for the workers. Mine representatives issued an appeal to the National War Labor Board to review the data and study the issues and review the matter of wage differentials and the issue of discrimination against Mexican and Mexican Americans in the work place. On June 30, 1944, the National War Labor Board held a public hearing on the merits of the discrimination issue and the dual wage issue. The board agreed with the findings of the Non-Ferrous Metals Commission and recommended that "the parties should . . . resurvey the non-discrimination provisions of bargaining agreements for employees to determine whether they are adequate to guard against discriminatory hiring and promotion into [common laborers, or other] grades . . . which now exist in the company's wage structure."[17] Meanwhile, the demand for copper in the nation's war effort grew and the IUMMSW and company representative continued to debate the issues and complaints. The National War Labor Board, established by President Franklin D. Roosevelt in January 1942, ceased operating in December 1945. It is unclear if the succeeding federal agency, the National Labor Relations Board, considered the dispute between the IUMMSW, Local 586, and the mining representatives of the Miami mines. The dual-wage battle in the Miami mines continued. The IUMMSW continued to challenge the racialized wage system during contract negotiations. The debate carried over into the post–World War II era and into the mid-1960s.

The orders and recommendations and the concerns of the workers took a back seat in the larger political drama of World War II. The country was at war, fighting for democratic ideals and a sense of justice and freedom. This reduced some of the criticism against copper mining companies and the state. Mexican and Mexican Americans continued to work under a racialized wage system. The IUMMSW's limited resources, intra-union conflicts, and the limited political power and public support of Mexicanos limited their ability to eliminate the long-standing racialized wage system in the Miami copper mines.

CONCLUSION

The scholarly documentation of when the hierarchical/dual wage for Mexican workers in Arizona's mining industry ended remains to be written. Benton-Cohen notes that starting in 1944 there was a stronger push among unions in Bisbee to dismantle dual-wage practices (2009, 271), though it is not clear when they actually ended. In Miami the mining companies ignored the FEPC's findings and they disregarded the conditions to resolve the dual-wage issue.

Specific concrete evidence of when the dual wage may have ended in copper mines in Arizona remains wanting. In the specific case of Miami copper mines, however, we have at least some evidence of why we will likely never know in precise terms when the racialized wage system ended. John Smith, a retired employee of the International Smelting and Refining Company and the Inspiration Consolidated Copper Company, noted that in 1955, a mine manager told him that in the early 1940s workers for the Miami Copper Company "came in and took all the personnel records and threw them over the dump at the Pinto Valley mine and buried them because they didn't want the documents to show how they discriminated against the Mexicans in the 1920s and 1930s. There were two separate pay rates: one for Mexicans and one for Whites for the same job. It was institutionalized. They knowingly did that. And everyone knew that. They threw all those payroll records out and buried them."[18] If similar actions were repeated at other mines, accounts by historians that the dual wage ended in other mines in the 1940s or later periods should be more carefully reviewed. This suggests that more solid interpretations of when a particular wage hierarchy ended should be based on an actual review of payroll records for specific mines or smelters.

To avoid further litigation and investigation by the government and other agencies and pressures from the AFL-CIO and their local affiliates, copper corporations began to more carefully delineate a classification of wages, pay grade, and type of work. Although overt wage disparities in Miami mines may have been reduced by the 1960s, this should not be interpreted as automatically ending the long-standing unequal wage system. Yes, Mexicanos may have experienced an increase in wages, but this does not mean that wage parity was established between whites and Mexicanos performing the same work. It would not be surprising to find that unequal opportunities in promotion and work allocation may have continued beyond the 1960s. Under such a scenario, it may be the case that the racialized dual wage may in fact have persisted beyond the mid-1960s. Unless one is able to obtain detail payroll records for the postwar period from each of the copper mines and the smelter in Miami (as well as other mining areas), one cannot definitely assert that the dual-wage system came to an end in Bisbee, Miami, Clifton-Morenci, or other copper mining communities.

In this essay, we sought to examine the context and background to copper mining in Miami, and the long-standing presence of a racialized wage system. Within this, we (following the work of Mellinger, Gordon, and Meeks) have argued for the need to more closely examine the actual formation and transformation of hierarchical wage systems across multiple copper mining areas. The essay also provided a description of how Mexicanos in one mining area (Miami) repeatedly challenged the dual-wage system. Though admittedly, we could not provide a definitive date of when the racialized wage system actually ended in Miami copper mining. It is suggested that there was a change in the mid-1960s, but in the absence of access to detailed payroll records for the copper corporations in the postwar period, it remains an open question when white-Mexican parity was achieved—if at all. Scholars must keep in mind that improvements in wages and occupational opportunities may take place, but this is not the same as wage parity. To take a contemporary example, a public university may advertise itself as operating with a culture of inclusion and of making equal opportunity a priority, but yet may maintain a racialized dual wage between white and minority (i.e., African American, Asian Pacific Islander, Mexican, Native American), and unequal promotion and tenure for minority staff and faculty. This is in addition to great inequalities between males and females. A cursory review of administrators and faculty promoted in recent years may show the privileging of white males.

The case of Mexicano mineros foregrounds not only wage inequalities, but also how Mexican workers were perceived as part of an elastic supply of labor to meet general labor needs, as well as to defeat labor disruptions. Arizona mining companies ignored the 1885 Alien Contract Labor law (Foran Act) and illegally recruited workers from Mexico as a response to strikes. Although not discussed here, presumably once a strike ended and striking workers returned to work, workers recruited from Mexico would likely be expected to depart because they were no longer needed. In such a scenario, Mexicanos were intrinsically part of the elastic supply of labor that allowed mining corporations to achieve short-term profit goals, and reestablish control of workers.

NOTES

1. Although not noted by Clark, whites presumably were paid a higher wage.
2. The extent of wage hierarchies within work performed by Mexicanas remains to be examined across the Southwest and beyond.
3. Marin's maternal and paternal grandfathers worked underground as laborers for the Miami Copper Company and the Iron Cap mine in Miami.
4. The notion of a "boundaries of Whiteness" is drawn from the historian Kelly Lytle Hernández (2010, 42) and her argument about how the land border patrol's policing of Mexicans was a way to policing the boundaries of whiteness.
5. In the 1930 Census, Mexican was introduced as a racial category; though it was dropped in the 1940 and subsequent censuses.
6. Arnold Rojas was born in Miami, Arizona, on February 13, 1924, and educated in Miami public schools.
7. Orville Larson's local labor and political ties to Miami explain his warm relationship with Mexicans and Mexican Americans and their concerns for equality and the end of the dual wage. As a longtime Miami resident, Larson was employed at the Inspiration Consolidated Copper Company in the mid-1930s. At that time, he served as a justice of the peace in Miami. The town's residents elected him as a school trustee for Live Oak District No. 26, Miami Public Schools. In 1934 he joined the IUMMSW in Miami as a charter member. By 1937 Larson served as secretary-treasurer of the IUMMSW, Local 38, in Miami. See "Miners Organized," *The Labor Journal* (1937, 153).
8. Sotelo, Joe, Interview (2002); "Latin Americans Elect Officers," *Arizona Silver Belt* (1941). Interviewed by Christine Marin.
9. On page 12 of *Burro Alley* (2006), Joe Sotelo explained that he worked at the leaching plant at the Inspiration Consolidated Copper Company in Miami. He submerged copper sheets in acidic copper solutions heated to 105 degrees Fahrenheit and pulled them out. For that, he was paid $3.03 per day—"Mexican pay"—he said. The work was strenuous and dangerous.
10. The history of LULAC has received attention from scholars. See Márquez (1993), Gutiérrez (1995), García (1989), Orozco (1992).
11. *El Mensajero* (1941). "Actividades de LULAC," (Phoenix, Arizona), August 22.

12. The FEPC's history is organized into two periods and became known as two agencies: FEPC one, which became effective on June 25, 1941, to May 27, 1943. FEPC two was designated by Executive Order 9346 in 1943 and remained effective until 1946.
13. See also Gritter's note number 25, page 141: "There was some specificity for the Spanish-speaking persons; parenthetical information for Spanish-speaking persons was added, noting that 120 '(101 Mexican-born aliens, 19 Mexican-born naturalized U.S. citizens all but approximately 10 speak and understand English),' and a proviso was also added noting that 336 persons of Mexican background were considered as Spanish-speaking Americans while 120 were classified as Spanish-speaking persons." In reviewing Gritter's explanation of this data, we found it ambiguous and problematic because definitions for the Spanish-speaking groups are not provided for the reader to be able to distinguish them. Did the Inspiration Consolidated Copper Company identify the groups?
14. Plácida García Smith, president, LULAC Council No. 110 Phoenix, Arizona, to Orville Larson, representative, International Union of Mine, Mill and Smelter Workers, Miami, Arizona, September 10, 1943. Copy of the letter in the personal collection of Arnold Rojas. Marin thanks Mr. Rojas for allowing her permission to read the copy of the letter and cite it in this essay.
15. *War Labor Reports*. (1945, 592), vol. 18. Anglo female laborers earned $6.36 per shift and Mexican and Mexican American female laborers earned $5.21 per shift. It is unclear if the wages of these women were considered in this recommendation. See *War Labor Reports* (1944, 153), vol. 14. "Table IV: The Number of 'Anglo American Males' and 'Other Employees' by Wage Rate, Classified as Laborers, September 23, 1943."
16. "Anti-Discrimination Case Won by IUMMSW," *Union* (Denver, CO), February 14, 1944.
17. *War Labor Reports*. (1945, 593). The National War Labor Board was reestablished by President Franklin D. Roosevelt on January 12, 1942. It served as an arbitration tribunal in labor-management disputes, thereby preventing work stoppages that might hinder the war effort. It administered wage control in national industries such as automobiles, shipping, railways, airlines, and mining. It ceased operating on December 31, 1945. See *National War Labor Board*, http://www.en.Wikipedia.org/Wiki/National_War_Labor-Board.
18. John Smith (a pseudonym) was interviewed by Christine Marin in Tempe in 1999.

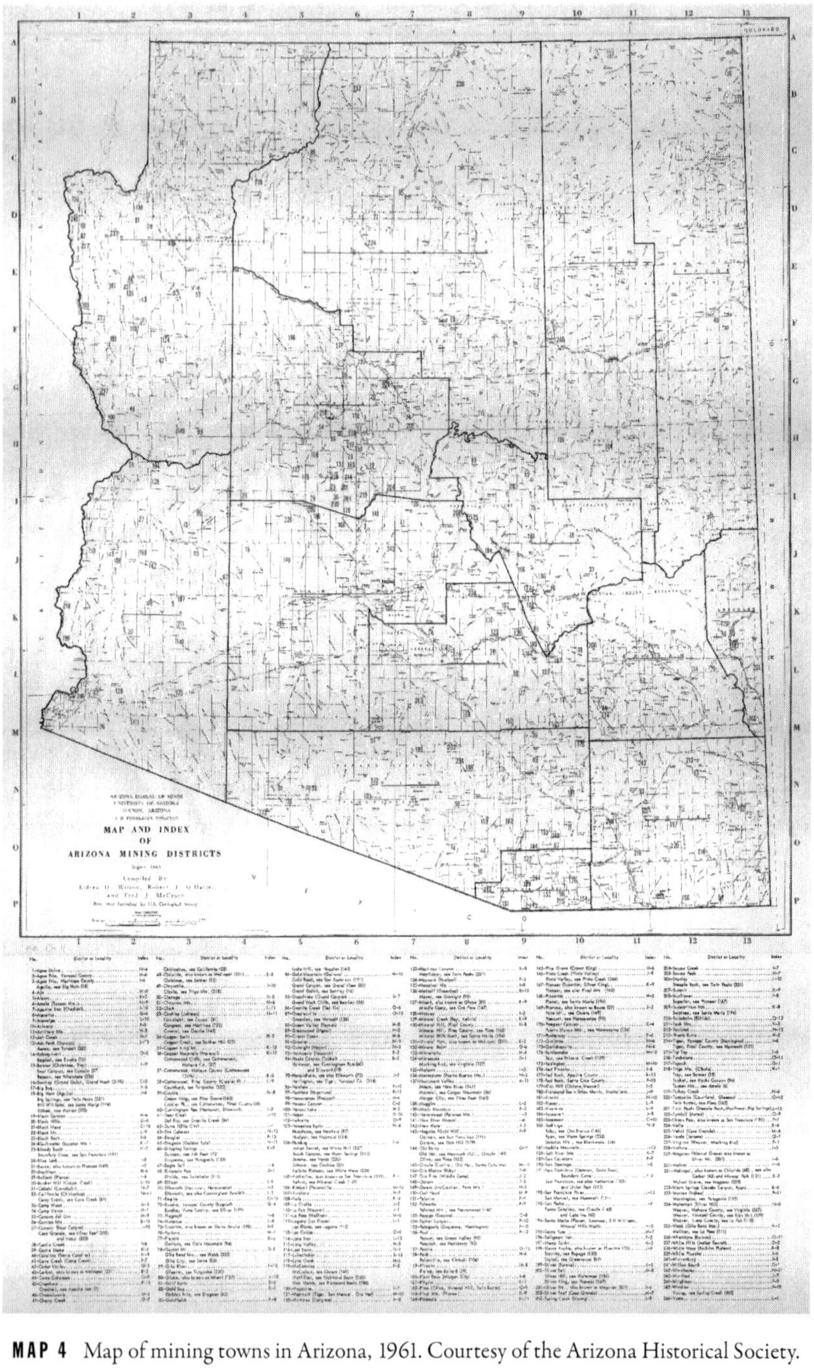

MAP 4 Map of mining towns in Arizona, 1961. Courtesy of the Arizona Historical Society.

5

MEXICAN AMERICAN WOMEN WORKERS IN MID-TWENTIETH-CENTURY PHOENIX

★

JEAN REYNOLDS

THIS CHAPTER FOCUSES ON LABOR EXPERIENCES of Mexican American women in Phoenix, Arizona, during the 1930s and 1940s. Using oral history, city directories, Spanish-language newspapers, and other archival sources, this study provides an overview of the kinds of work that women of the Mexican American generation performed. This generation represents U.S. citizens of Mexican descent who came of age during the 1930s to the 1950s. The following pages examine individual experiences, nuances of job status, and the variety of work women performed, particularly highlighting stories of five women interviewed in 1997 and 1998 who lived in Phoenix during the Great Depression and World War II.

Set in the context of central Arizona in the mid-1900s, these women not only experienced social disadvantages based on racial and gender barriers, but their lives were also impacted in various ways through other social identity structures, such as class within the Mexican American community, marital status, income level, their occupation, and the social status these jobs created. While this intersectionality created many limitations in the lives of these women and the overall Mexican American community, it also created unique economic experiences, opportunities for social mobility, and led women (often driven by a strong internal motivation) to play a significant part, and sometimes a leading role, in sustaining their families and community during this period. And, as in other communities during this period, Mexican American women through their labor contributed to Phoenix's overall economic growth in the mid-twentieth century.

HISTORICAL CONTEXT

Since the founding of Phoenix in 1867, Mexican Americans' labor and economic contributions proved vital in building and sustaining Arizona's state capitol and other communities throughout the Salt River Valley. The earliest Mexican settlers generally migrated from northern Sonora, Wickenburg, Yuma, Tucson, and other towns in southern Arizona (Rosales n.d., 3–8). In the late nineteenth century, work connected to town building, railroads, and agriculture attracted thousands to the area. Mexicans of all social classes composed half of Phoenix's population, becoming "property owners, teachers, dressmakers, grocers, laundresses, blacksmiths, harness-makers, bakers, butchers, saloon-keepers, jewelers . . . and as such, provided essential services to Anglo and Mexican members of the community" (Dimas 1991, 35).

By 1910 the role and status of Mexican Phoenicians had greatly diminished; a community which by now composed only 10 percent of the population (Luckingham 1994, 2). The power base shifted as promoters desiring to boost Phoenix as a good town for new residents focused on recruiting only European Americans. The economic ties that linked Mexican and non-Mexican settlers began to disintegrate as European Americans took advantage of new railroad lines bringing in mass-produced items from the eastern United States. Mixed marriages and interethnic business partnerships decreased, with growing discrimination forcing the Mexican community into a second-class status (Rosales n.d., 16). Many of the original neighborhoods where Mexican Phoenicians settled were deemed as undesirable areas by the majority population. After 1910 the city became more racially divided as European Americans who had the means moved northward into more valuable property and homes. Blacks and those of Mexican and Asian descent generally remained in the city's southern sections (Dean and Reynolds 2006, 25–26).

During the 1930s census figures counted nearly 7,300 residents of Mexican descent, about 15 percent of the total population in the city limits (Luckingham 1994, 39). The thriving community included a mix of socioeconomic classes, churches, small businesses, and cultural aspects, such as organizations, newspapers, Spanish-language radio programs, and more. The Mexican American community was comprised of a number of barrios in present-day south-central Phoenix, most of which were rural in nature, dotted with small homes, gardens, and irrigation ditches next to open fields. Outside of the barrios, Mexican families resided in unincorporated agricultural areas (Dean and Reynolds 2006, 27–37). A 1938 report by Phoenix's Mexican Consul found that 3,500 Mexican agricultural workers lived around the city in growers' camps, cheap auto courts, or "squatters' camps" located near canals and dirt roads (Urtuzuastegui 1972, 6). During the 1930s these workers often competed for work with Okie and African American migrants, contending with unclean drinking water, poor nourishment, diseases, and exposure to the desert elements (Carey McWilliams Collection 1243, Box 12, Folder: Migratory Labor).

AGRICULTURAL, DOMESTIC, AND SERVICE WORK

Agricultural work played a part in many women's migration stories to Phoenix. Mary López García was born in 1915 in Albuquerque, New Mexico. The López family traveled to Colorado fields in response to heavy recruitment by sugar beet farmers during the 1920s. Mary remembers that while there her uncle suggested a move to a warmer climate; shortly after the family arrived at the outskirts of Phoenix in 1927, where they lived in farmworker camps and later moved into the city into the Cuatro Milpas neighborhood (López García 1997).

Mary recalled young women who had arrived in the area in the 1920s from mining towns. Falling copper prices closed or dramatically slowed Arizona's mines and many displaced families headed to the Salt River Valley seeking work. They also hoped for better opportunities and education for their children (López García 1997). One example is Esther Ramírez Díaz. Born in 1923, Esther and her family migrated to Phoenix from Christmas, Arizona. The family of nine moved to Phoenix in 1929, after the bank in Miami, Arizona, closed, hoping to withdraw money from the associated bank in Phoenix. After they were able to secure some of their savings, the family moved around the Salt River Valley looking for work. They traveled to Buckeye and picked cotton, then moved closer to Phoenix and bought a ranch. By the late 1930s they settled in the city (Ramírez Díaz 1997).

Many families arrived from Mexico as part of the continuous flow of people between borders. Ernestina (Tina) Ruiz Saldate recalled that her grandmother, mother, and aunt joined a *renganche* (a group of people recruited to work in the United States) from Cananea, Sonora, in 1923, which aimed to bring workers to Scottsdale, Arizona, most likely for farm work. The women traveled from Sonora to Arizona without male family members, although they enlisted the help of a young man to pose as their head of household in order to avoid being questioned by immigration inspectors. In addition, Dolores escaped the required exam that would have revealed her pregnancy with Tina, without a husband. Tina recalls that such a discovery would have resulted in Dolores being denied entrance into the country on moral grounds, and potentially because she could become a public charge. The family followed agricultural work to Laveen and Aguila, and eventually settled in Phoenix in 1932 (Ramírez Díaz 1997).

Women such as Mary, Esther, and Tina arrived with their families during the Great Depression and its period of recovery. Phoenix felt the economic effects of the Great Depression, but not to the degree that other large, urban cities around the country experienced. The historian Bradford Luckingham noted that "For 80 percent of the work force with regular jobs in 1931 to 1933, life continued in a subdued 1920's fashion. By 1934 the worst was over and economic activity, by and large, had returned to the 1929 level" (1989, 102). While this assessment may have applied to European Americans, who were in the majority of the population, it was not completely accurate for Mexican Americans. Some Mexican Americans did live frugally and retained stability and jobs during the Depression. Others faced poverty—by 1933, in fact, 59 percent of Mexicans in Phoenix were without steady employment (Roberts 1973, 354).

During the difficult times of the Depression, wives and daughters worked to supplement the family income. Widowed or single mothers labored as well in order to support themselves and their families. Some young women, living with parents who maintained financial stability during the 1930s, worked because they enjoyed the opportunities that came with their own paycheck.

Jobs within the Valley's primary industry, agriculture, were always an option. One of the most important agricultural industries, cotton, required a great deal of hand labor. One source estimated that between 1912 and 1958, the Salt River Valley grew nearly half of all Pima cotton produced in the United States (McGowan 1961, 102). Workers also planted, weeded, and harvested in melon and vegetable fields, citrus and date groves, and worked with dairy and beef cattle (Tetreau 1939, 297–318). The Arizona Cotton Growers Association (ACGA), and later the Farm Labor Service, heavily recruited workers through radio, newspapers, placards, and word of mouth, often creating an elastic supply of migrant workers who competed with each other and resident workers for jobs (Pendleton 1950, 239–46).

During the 1930s, women and men struggled to survive in Arizona's agricultural wage structure. For example, when cotton growers lowered the rate of pay in 1937, many Mexican workers flooded into the city for the relief programs offered by social service organizations. This resulted in a labor shortage, which the farmers blamed on the relief system, claiming that these laborers wanted welfare relief rather than work. In response, Governor R. C. Stanford ordered the welfare board to implement a "no work, no eat" policy, and mandated that "the names of all pickers refusing harvest work be stricken from the relief rolls." While it is unknown how they documented the names of pickers, this incident reveals the power held Phoenix area growers (Kotlanger 1983, 443).

Toiling five to six days a week in the fields, farmworkers usually earned $1.50 to $2.50 a day (Urtuzuastegui 1972, 3, 7). Entire families participated in this labor, especially in the cotton fields, where one family could possibly earn four to five dollars a day (Tetreau 1939, 312). Francisca de la Huerta, a resident farmworker, remembered laboring and living on the ranches in and around Phoenix. During the early 1930s, she recalled that men made 25 cents a day more than women. Her family did not save enough money to buy their own land and home until 1942, when they established a small dairy farm in Glendale (Celaya 1977, 8–9).

Mary López García recalled that one of her first experiences working in the fields was picking olives. She says, "I helped a little but I didn't like it. I was afraid to get up on the ladder. I just picked them up off the ground." Mary didn't like working in the fields and would stay home to care for her younger family members while her father and brother and sisters went to work: "It's so dirty. It was in the mud . . . when they irrigated everything was nothing but mud. It was hard work—the fields are very hard work, chopping and piling the vegetables. . . . I never went to field work here (as a steady job)—no way!" Seeking better working conditions and higher wages than what the fields could offer, many women looked to the city for employment (López García 1997).

Women interviewed for this study defined the status of their jobs by social standing and pay. Generally, these women viewed agricultural work as the lowest, a step up being domestic work and, above that, working in the laundries. Mary's niece, Annie García Redondo, reflected that it "was a big step to go from housekeeping to work at the Phoenix Laundry . . . because that was a job in a company, you weren't working for one person, you were working for a boss" (García Redondo 1997; López García 1997; Ramírez Díaz 1997; Ruiz Saldate 1997).

Moving out of the service sector meant entering clerical, professional, or sales jobs. Again, mobility occurred at this level as well. Within retail stores, the jobs with higher pay and more status included up-front jobs, like sales or layaway clerks. The lower-paid and lower-status jobs entailed marking and working in the shipping room. The highest-paid and highest-status jobs, according to Annie, were stenographers or typists for businesses. Further up the scale were the women who owned or managed small businesses in the formal economy (García Redondo 1997).

A survey of the 1931, 1935, and 1939 Phoenix city directories provides a glimpse of the kinds of work Spanish-surnamed women found in Phoenix. The directories listed a few women who owned or operated small businesses, such as grocery stores or small cafés as part of, or near, their residences. For example, Modesta (Molly) Ruiz owned the Spanish Town Café, which her daughter Margarita helped operate (Phoenix City Directory 1931, 1935, 1939). Another Phoenician, Elvira Durán, and her husband, José, owned and operated Durán Rooms and Durán's Quick Lunch, a two-story boardinghouse and café on 7th Street and Jefferson. This business developed out of an earlier restaurant operated by Elvira's mother, Petra Quihuis (Durán 1989).

Women also secured retail jobs. For each of the years surveyed, women listed in directories as clerks numbered the greatest, working at S. H. Kress & Co.; J. C. Penney Co.; Sears, Roebuck and Co.; and Korrick's Dry Goods Co. A few women were listed as saleswomen, mainly for the Jewish family-owned Boston department store. High school student Esther Ramírez Díaz worked here in 1939 as a transfer girl. Her job was to take the merchandise ticket, after the saleswoman made a sale, to the cash register with the customer's money, then to return the change and receipt to the customer. She remembers that she was favored over the other Mexican American girls who worked there. She speculates it may have been because of her fair complexion and blue eyes, or due to her outgoing personality. She gave her earnings to her mother, who gave her an allowance. By the early 1940s she earned $26 a week (Ramírez Díaz 1997).

WHITE-COLLAR WORK

A few women secured white-collar jobs, such as nurses, teachers, bookkeepers, secretaries, and stenographers. In 1936 *El Mensajero* reported that Concepción Pérez obtained a job as a stenographer in Attorney General Sullivan's office through recommendations by "various Democratic Clubs and influential people of La Raza in politics," while Lydia Aguirre held a clerical position with the State Motor Vehicle Division, where she earned $125 monthly (*El Mensajero* October 17, 1936, June 13, 1936). In the 1939 directory, three women from the Valenzuela family worked as nurses at local hospitals (Phoenix City Directory 1939).

For each year of city directories surveyed, the number of Spanish-surnamed women listed in service jobs outnumbered white-collar positions. According to the report of the 1930 census for employment of all women living in Phoenix, 57 percent worked in white-collar positions, while 37 percent were in service occupations. Comparing these two trends reveals that Mexican women most likely filled the ranks of service workers to a larger extent than Anglo women, keeping in mind that Mexicans comprised only 15 percent of the city's population (U.S. Bureau of the Census 1931–1933). This analysis reflects the larger pattern that historian Vicki Ruiz describes for Mexican women in the Southwest. She found that in 1930, 15.4 percent of women worked in white-collar occupations, while 25.3 percent worked in blue-collar positions, and 38.4 percent in service jobs. As in other southwestern cities, the largest percentage of Phoenix women in service jobs worked in laundries and domestic service, traditional female occupations that were not heavily impacted by the local economic downturn (Ruiz 1988, 118).

SERVICE INDUSTRY WORK

Phoenix's tourist industry remained relatively steady in spite of the Depression, which brought business into hotels and restaurants. This in turn provided clients for commercial laundries (Kotlanger 1983, 240). Mexican American women were the key to this business, and most were employed by Phoenix Laundry, Maricopa Laundry, Arizona Laundry, and the Bell Laundry. Mary López García worked at Phoenix Laundry in the late 1930s and early 1940s, after she married her husband, Archibaldo García. Men generally sorted and washed dirty clothing in another section of the laundry. Mary remembers that the women usually worked the mangles—machines that steam dried and ironed the clothing and linen. "Some of the women would feed the clothing and linen into the mangle, while others would fold as it came out. Others would count the stacks. . . . It was very hard. You had to be real fast. . . . We'd feed for an hour, then fold for an hour, and then we'd turn around." Mary earned thirty-five cents an hour at the Phoenix Laundry (López García 1997).

Also in large percentages in the 1931, 1935, and 1939 directories were women working as maids. Some women worked as live-in maids. Others did day work in homes or public institutions, such as hospitals. Mexican American women filled the ranks of workers cleaning hotels, auto courts, and many other types of businesses (Phoenix City Directory 1931, 1935, 1939). Many of these were teenaged girls. Mary López García left school in 1929 as the Depression hit, at the age of fourteen. "I wanted to keep going but couldn't because my father didn't have any work. There was no WPA then, when the Depression started, there was nothing, no work, nothing (for men)." Mary turned to the Friendly House in her search for employment (López García 1997).

THE ROLE OF AMERICANIZATION PROGRAMS AND WOMEN'S WORK

An outgrowth of the national Americanization movement to assimilate immigrants in the early 1900s, the Friendly House opened in 1922 as a two-room community house under the Phoenix Americanization Committee. Unlike earlier settlement houses in the United States, this organization did not focus on social reform or religious proselytization, but rather on providing classes in English, citizenship, hygiene, and homemaking to Mexican residents (Titcomb 1984, 7–17, 38–41). While the Americanization movement was designed to teach Mexican women how to behave and act like middle-class white households, it ultimately failed in this attempt because Mexican households often lacked the resources to "act" middle class. In the 1930s, Plácida García Smith directed the settlement house, and she focused on more realistic goals impacting the community. Originally from Colorado and well-educated, Plácida implemented federal relief programs, domestic training classes to provide avenues of employment to women, and established the first Mexican American Boy Scout Troop, the Mexican Orchestra, and the Mexican Dance Project. In partnership with the Friendly House, she organized the Southside Improvement Club to increase services in local parks, as well as helping to set up a prenatal and well-baby clinic in cooperation with the U.S. Public Health Department (Autobiographical Resume: Plácida Elvira García Smith; *Arizona Republic* July 24, 1981).

Although just shy of the minimum age of fifteen to gain work through the Friendly House, Mary took advantage of Plácida's domestic training program. As in many

Americanization programs targeting young Mexican women, these classes taught them how to set tables, how to serve coffee and meals, and how to present themselves to their employers. They also received two "house dresses to wear during work hours" (*El Mensajero* August 8, 1936). Mary remembers that women were sent to other kinds of jobs besides domestic work "if they had the education" (López García 1997). Phoenix native Minnie Rangel Martínez recalled, "I don't remember there being ads in the paper to hire anyone at that time . . . it was just by word of mouth that you found a job, or through the Friendly House" (Rangel Martínez 1998). Women earned between $4 and $7 weekly, with the agency providing 2,500 temporary and 320 permanent placements per year throughout the 1930s (Titcomb 1984, 44–45).

Mary vividly recalls her first maid's job with a European American woman. After Mary cleaned the house, the woman offered her some lunch: "She made cabbage cooked with spareribs. That was the first time I ever had that kind of food. It was good because we didn't have much food at home." Mary eventually settled into a job working five days a week for Myrtle Pruitt, the wife of a doctor, who lived in the prominent Encanto-Palmcroft neighborhood. She enjoyed working for Myrtle, and earned $3 a week, sometimes $3–$5 extra when she stayed to help with a party. She held the job for four years, until her employer could no longer afford her services (López García 1997).

While young Mexican American women played a key part in the management of wealthy Phoenicians' homes, they didn't always play a subservient role. One example is a story told by Ruth Carrillo Villa, who worked for Dr. Charles Palmer, but didn't see eye to eye with his wife.

> Mrs. Palmer was real bossy and very dirty. She told me once to dry the dishes with one of the babies' diapers. I had never heard of such a thing. I didn't think it was to[o] sanitary. I worked very hard but finally I got tired of Mrs. Palmer and her ways. By then I was very good at what I did and I had several other clients, including Mr. Allison of Allison Steel and the attorney Allen Perry. I went on strike. I told her I did too much work for what she paid and if she wanted me back she would have to pay me twenty-five cents an hour. Well, that was never heard of before. But Mrs. Palmer finally gave in and asked me to come back. She had been paying me $2.50 a week for seven days. This was the first time any domestic worker had gotten paid on an hourly wage. When the rest of the workers, mostly my friends, heard, they also began to charge by the hour. I started setting my own hours and worked for several families, dividing my time equally among them. (Villa 1988, 15–16)

Women also worked as waitresses, cooks, or in other capacities in Phoenix's Mexican, Anglo, and Chinese-owned restaurants and cafés. In 1936 Tina Ruiz Saldate quit school at the age of sixteen in order to help support her family. She worked as a dishwasher and a waitress at the New York Café, owned by Santos Vargas. A lady who brought clothes to her grandmother to wash told Tina about a better-paying waitressing job at the Sing Hi Café, and soon the teen secured a night job there. Tina says of the 1930s, "It was hard to start with, since we were raised without a father and then it was a depression. It was real hard. It got a little better when I started working" (Ruiz Saldate 1997).

Others found jobs through government agencies set up during the Depression. For example, from 1931 to 1932, fifty-five Phoenix Mexican American women found work through the Unemployment Relief Bureau, while 571 men secured jobs. Of the total women who received work in Phoenix at this time, 82 percent were white, 12 percent were Mexican, and 6 percent African American (Report of the Governor's Unemployment Relief Bureau, G. P. W. Hunt Papers 1932). The National Youth Administration offered work for young women, such as the 1938 Work Project 471 in Phoenix, which employed nine Mexican American girls in repairing and readying books and magazines for distribution to rural areas of Apache and Navajo counties (Records of the National Youth Administration 1941–1943).

Mexican Americans, as in times past and as they would in the future, labored in home industries, taking in laundry, selling food, sewing, or renting to boarders (Anderson 1996, 105; González 1990, 40–41). Margarita Miramón advertised in *El Mensajero* from 1936 to 1938, offering her services of hemstitching and making artificial flowers. Several women listed in the directories identified as tamale or tortilla makers in their homes. Tina's grandmother, Juana, worked as a *lavandera* in her home. Single Mexican women had been working as laundresses in the Southwest since the late 1800s. Tina recalled that Juana began in the late 1920s by working for a woman named Petra, "who used to do a lot of hand-washing and ironing for people in hotels and barbershops . . . she had her own little business in her house." Juana took on some of Petra's business when Petra became sick. Tina remembers Juana washing female hotel employees' dresses and underclothing. Most of the customers were European American (Ruiz Saldate 1997).

TURNING THE TIDE: WORLD WAR II AND CHICANA LABOR

As the United States' entry into World War II finally pulled the country out of the lingering effects of the Depression, Phoenix residents felt the tide turn. In his study on Phoenix in the early 1940s, the historian Michael Duckett found that "almost every kind of business or economic concern was on the rise in Phoenix," with the city, for example, placing third in the nation for the largest per-capita sales (1977, 11).

The population increased as soldiers and defense-plant workers entered Phoenix after the establishment of air fields and flight-training schools around the Valley, as well as defense plants, such as Goodyear Aircraft, the Aluminum Company of America, and AiResearch. The rise of wartime manufacturing companies heralded the manufacturing boom of the 1950s, and a decrease in an agricultural-dominated economy (Preisler 1992, 63–64).

In 1940 Phoenix's Mexican population was 9,740 and in 1950 it had risen to 16,000. While Phoenix's overall population nearly doubled by 1950, the Mexican population still held at 15 percent of the total population, as during the 1930s (Luckingham 1994, 45–46). Although a minority population, their patriotism was no less evident than Phoenix's European American community. A month after the attack on Pearl Harbor, *El Mensajero* stated: "The Spanish Americans and citizens of Mexico were an element of great energy and aid in the last war with Germany, and now we should show that we are of the same disposition, ready to sacrifice all that we possess, and even the precious blood of our sons, to the end that the nation reaches a decisive victory" (*El Mensajero*, January 16, 1942). Thousands of Phoenix women's sons, brothers, and other male relatives enlisted or were drafted into the armed forces (Marin 1981, 7).

Mexican American women also became part of the more than 350,000 women who served in the military. They could join organizations such as the Women's Army Auxiliary Corp (WAC), the Navy's Women Accepted for Volunteer Emergency Service (WAVES), the Coast Guard Spars, the Army Nurse Corps, the U.S. Marine Corps Women's Reserve, or the Women's Air Force Service Pilots (WASP) (Honey 1984, 34–35). The Office of War Information encouraged women to join, emphasizing their equally important role in the war effort. In February 1943 *El Sol* announced openings for registration into WAVES or SPARS. Young women read newspaper advertisements such as, "If you want the thrill that comes from doing a man size job in this war . . . join the WAVES," and "It's a woman's war too!" (*El Sol* February 18, 1943, April 4, 1944).

These service organizations required women to be between the ages of twenty and thirty-six, married or single, and childfree. They were required to have finished two years of high school or commercial school. The women in these two organizations could earn up to $126 per month. In addition, they obtained free uniforms, medical and dental care, and allowances to help relatives financially stabilize (*El Sol* May 5, 1944). *El Mensajero* encouraged women to sign up at the Phoenix WAVES recruiting office, stating, "First, she will be performing an essential job; second, and much more important, she will make it possible for a man, who occupies those positions, to be placed at disposal to carry out his duty overseas where his training and ability is needed in order to overthrow the Japanese and Nazis" (*El Mensajero* February 10, 1944).

The first Phoenix Mexican American woman reported to enlist in the WAVES was Angela Cruz García, in 1944. The middle-class daughter of a jeweler and watchmaker and a graduate of Phoenix Union High School, she was to be trained in naval dispatch and other clerical jobs. She traveled to Hunter College in New York for basic training. *El Sol* noted that her training would be similar to men's but with no onboard training (*El Sol* January 21, 1944). Those from working-class backgrounds may have wanted to join, but economic obligations kept them at home. Annie García Redondo recalled, "I wanted to join the Navy—the WAVES—because I heard that they taught them to use the phone as operators . . . I wanted to learn that and more office stuff than I knew because I wanted to advance myself to earn a better wage . . . but I couldn't afford to leave my parents by themselves. I had to stay" (García Redondo 1997).

Both *El Sol* and *El Mensajero* discussed Dorita Domínguez López, another young woman who joined the WAVES. *El Mensajero* reported that she obtained one of the highest aptitude scores in the entrance test for the WAVES. Before applying, she worked at a Phoenix telegraph business. She wanted to take advantage of the training offered in the WAVES in the field of communication, "one of the 250 service jobs every woman could be assigned, inspired by love of their country and its future well-being." While stationed in Stillwater, Oklahoma, Dorita taught English to Mexican marines (*El Mensajero* February 10, 1944; *El Sol* June 30, 1944). Spanish-language newspapers reported that the WACS also recruited Mexican American women for their Spanish-speaking ability, offering them positions in cryptology, interpretation, and communications (Marin 1981, 8).

Women endured the loss of the presence of their loved ones in military service and gave of their time to support the war effort on the home front. Community social and political organizations, such as the new Phoenix LULAC council established in 1940 by community leader María García, encouraged support of the war. They organized various activities such as dances, dinners, and lectures to show support of Latin American soldiers stationed near Phoenix. People also donated money for purchasing items for soldiers, participated in war-bond drives, collected scrap materials for recycling, and over five thousand Mexican Americans responded to worker shortages by joining Victory Labor Volunteer groups to pick the Valley's cotton crop of 1942 (*El Mensajero* April 4, 1941; *El Sol* March 10, 1942; *El Mensajero* August 8, 1941; Marin 1981, 2–6; *El Sol* September 10, 1943).

As the male labor force dwindled on the home front, the government and mass media encouraged women across the country to enter blue-collar industries. By 1943 one-third of all workers in the United States were women, and they composed over 50 percent of those employed in munitions or aircraft industries around the country (Chafe 1972, 137). Patriotism, better pay, and a chance to gain new skills and freedom from strict homes attracted "Rosita the Riveters" into this new workforce (Santillán

1989, 124–25). Although unmarried women were initially recruited, by 1943 married female workers outnumbered their single counterparts (Gluck 1987, 13). The changes in Phoenix during the war mirrored the national scene.

Three of the largest industries in the Phoenix area were defense factories established in 1942. These included the Aluminum Company of America (ALCOA), Goodyear Aircraft, and AiResearch. Located between 35th and 43rd Avenues south of Van Buren, the ALCOA plant produced aluminum for military use. The Goodyear plant, built near Litchfield Park on the Southwest Cotton Ranch, constructed parts and fuselages for navy bombers, as well as blimps for antisubmarine patrols. The AiResearch plant, located south of the Sky Harbor Airport, built aircraft systems related to cooling, heat transfer, cabin-pressure control, and other operations. These industries and new airfields, such as Luke Field and Williams Field, employed residents from around the Valley, the state, and from other cities across the country (Duckett 1977, 13–14; Alderman 1959, 26; *Working Together at AiResearch* 1944).

Women in these Phoenix industries worked as riveters, drillers, mechanics, clerks, and typists. Julie Campbell found that 40 percent of the employees at Goodyear Aircraft were women (Campbell 1980, 9). The percentage of Mexican American women who worked there is unknown. A 1942 report from Verda Barnes regarding the activities of the National Youth Administration in Arizona noted, "The personnel man at Goodyear stated that they will not accept negroes or dark skinned Mexicans. This makes our problem quite difficult since a fairly large number of our NYA girls and boys fall into these categories" (Records of the National Youth Administration, Records of the Service Products Section 1942, RG 119, Box 1). In addition, a 1942 *El Mensajero* article also mentioned that although aircraft plant jobs in the Valley were increasing, "very few Mexicans present themselves for these jobs" (Dimas 1991, 111). On the other hand, Esperanza Montoya Padilla recounts how she moved from Globe during the war and worked at the Goodyear plant as a riveter. She resided in Alzona Park, a temporary community for defense-plant workers. As part of the married female workforce, Esperanza worked the night shift at the factory, came home and cared for her four children and home, and even washed laundry for the Italian families who lived in the community (Martín 1992, 115).

Local Mexican American women worked in other defense-related jobs. Glendale native Guadalupe Verdugo Huerta became an aircraft mechanic. She recalls that in eleventh grade she dropped out of high school in Prescott and went to work. As a young mother, in 1942 she attended a riveting class after seeing it advertised in the newspaper. She remembers, "I thought there was a good chance to get a good paying job." After receiving her certificate, Guadalupe put her young daughter into her mother's care and traveled to Phoenix to live with her aunt and work at Luke Field. She joined the swing shift from 3:00 p.m. until 1:00 a.m. "The job that I had was assembling planes, putting on the wings on the bodies of the planes. We'd hang on the wings and the tails . . . we also used to put in the cable. . . . I was very thin and they always wanted to put me in the cramped place to put in the cable. . . . They found that I could put on those governors [a speed regulator device in the engine] . . . because my hands were real small and thin."

Guadalupe noted that men were paid more than women for the same kind of work: "I didn't like it very well because we worked just as hard and did as much as they did . . . but we were glad to work the way we did because we thought we were doing something for our country" (Verdugo Huerta 1998). Men's wages remained higher than women's during the war due to the war industries' discriminatory pay scales and organized labor's protection of men from women's occupational competition (Gluck 1987, 14).

Major changes in the labor force also impacted employment opportunities within the city. Minnie Rangel Martínez recalled that in Phoenix there was a "need for workers in places where they probably wouldn't have been hired before. If they needed somebody to work and there was a Mexicana there, of course they would take her." Just as lower-paying jobs opened to African American women as European American women moved into better paying industrial jobs, so did Mexican American women step into positions once reserved only for European American women. Annie García Redondo remarked, "When the war was on, things changed. Because they didn't have that many people, they had to hire some of the Mexicans—the women—at Woolworth's and Newberry's and Korrick's . . . then all the other places started hiring Mexicans" (Rangel Martínez 1998; García Redondo 1997).

Although encouraged by patriotic advertising and the lure of good pay, Mexican American women still worked mainly out of necessity. Annie remembers that when young men entered the military, families who depended on their sons' income experienced financial hardship. As during the Depression, Phoenix women's wages replaced the income traditionally brought home by male family members. Annie says, "A lot of families were forced to give up a lot of things they were doing at the time, but in the mean time they were proud to have their family—their son, their daughter, their husband—in the service . . . it made them [women] work harder to survive. Maybe they found talents that they never thought they had." Minnie Rangel Martínez had stopped working after her marriage in the late 1930s. Once her husband, Ray, joined the service, she moved in with her parents. Although she received an allotment of eighty dollars a month, the money wasn't enough to cover her finances. As a result, she reentered the workforce as an assistant to a Phoenix optometrist (García Redondo 1997; Rangel Martínez 1998).

A comparison of Phoenix city directories from the 1930s and the 1940s provides glimpse into the changes in women's occupation over these two decades. Although city directories often undercount Mexican Americans, they provide a good resource for capturing a sense of women's occupational experiences. These directories reveal that women advanced in numbers in the white-collar occupations during the 1940s, especially in the areas of nursing, clerical occupations, and sales (see table 5.1). This reflects the shift for Mexican American women throughout the Southwest: In 1930 15.4 percent held white-collar positions, while in 1950 the percentage rose to 32.4 percent (Ruiz 1998, 153).

CHICANAS AND ENTREPRENEURSHIP

With the economic boom during the 1940s, female proprietors opened more small restaurants or successfully continued to operate their establishments begun in the 1930s. Another kind of woman-owned business on the rise was the various beauty shops catering to Mexican clientele. María Amaya owned the María Beauty Shop at Third Street between Washington and Jefferson. One of her creative newspaper advertisements in 1941 proclaimed, "We can create hairstyles as elegant and exquisite as those of Patricia Morrison, star of 'Rangers of Fortune', the movie to be shown in the Ramona Theater the 11th through the 13th of this month" (*El Sol* August 18, 1942, February 18, 1944, August 18, 1944; *El Mensajero* March 7, 1941, October 24, 1941).

NURSING, RETAIL, AND CLERICAL WORK

Mexican American women also moved into nursing in greater numbers, thanks in part to St. Monica's Hospital, established in the midst of the Mexican American and African American community. St. Monica's began its nursing school in 1944, the first west of the Mississippi to be integrated. Of the first class's thirty-seven students, about half were American Indian, black, Mexican American, or Asian (Lambesis 1976, 595). The number of Spanish-surnamed women listed as practicing or student nurses in the Phoenix city directories increased from six in 1941 to fourteen by 1949. Only a few Mexican American women became teachers. Phoenix native Rebecca Muñoz began teaching in 1940 at the Webster School, having just graduated with her master's in education from Arizona State Teacher's College. The Arizona Educational Directory for 1929–30 and 1939–40 revealed that less than 1 percent of teachers in Arizona had Spanish surnames. The directory showed that this percentage reached 1.5 percent in 1949–50, a very minuscule increase (Flores 1951, 75–76).

Mexican American women began to increase in the ranks of clerical workers in Phoenix. For Arizona, the percentage of Mexican American women in clerical/sales positions grew from 14.8 percent in 1930 to 28.4 percent in 1950 (Blackwelder 1997, 130). Just as African American women secured positions in the federal government

Table 5.1 Phoenix Spanish-Surnamed Women's White-Collar and Service Occupations, 1931-1949

	Phoenix City Directory Years					
Occupational Category	1931	1935	1939	1941	1946	1949
	White Collar					
Professional/Technical						
Nurse (including student nurse)	3	4	7	6	9	14
Teacher	3	3	0	0	3	2
Music/Artist	0	0	0	0	2	2
Social Worker	0	0	0	1	1	0
Managerial/Proprietor						
Restaurant	0	4	4	6	4	7
Grocery	2	3	7	6	4	7
Beauty Shop	1	1	0	2	1	1
Clerical/Sales						
Secretary	0	0	1	4	8	9
Saleswoman/Girl	1	5	1	1	27	24
Retail Clerk	7	8	14	21	34	25
Non-Retail Clerk	3	7	1	2	19	13
Clerk (unidentified)	6	0	0	0	16	12
Stenographer	3	3	5	8	15	28
Typist	0	2	0	0	3	5
Bookkeeper	0	2	0	2	7	5
Cashier	1	1	3	3	1	9
Telephone Operator	0	0	0	0	3	1
Total	30	43	39	62	140	150
	Service					
Laundry Worker	29	24	32	31	66	51
Maid	11	16	6	10	60	3
Waitress	8	4	11	21	24	31
Restaurant Worker	4	3	7	0	34	6
Cook	0	0	0	6	8	12
Barmaid	0	0	1	0	0	0
Medical Attendant/Helper	0	1	2	3	4	17
Day-Care Helper	0	0	0	3	0	4
Usher/Theater Worker	0	1	0	0	4	3
Janitress	2	0	1	1	5	4
Home Food Preparation	0	0	2	2	0	0
Total	55	49	62	77	205	131

Source: Phoenix Directory, 1931–1949.

Note: Very few agricultural and blue-collar occupations were listed in directories, so these categories were not included. The numbers in the above chart generally represent Spanish-surnamed women listed as heads of household or as women without a spouse.

during the 1940s, Mexican American women entered clerical jobs in local government. For example, in 1941, María Espinoza, Paz Fernández, and Felice Crowder worked in the Arizona senate, perhaps in secretarial positions. In a fairly unique instance, Margarita López secured a position in 1944 as a stenographer in the office of Congressional Representative Richard Harliss. After graduating from Phoenix Union High School and enrolling in the Gregg College, she began working for Harliss. She later moved to Washington D.C., and worked for him there. *El Sol* commented proudly, "We are honored that a truly distinguished and fine young woman is in a position of representation and responsibility that gives pride to the raza" (*El Sol* August 25, 1942, February 4, 1944; *El Mensajero* March 7, 1941, July 12, 1944).

Another area that increased during the 1940s was in retail sales positions. Raymond Flores found that "Salesgirls, although hired in numbers proportionate to the population, were usually to be found in the 'bargain basement' counters of the Phoenix department and novelty stores. . . . Much of the trade coming into Phoenix from the outlying agricultural areas was from the Mexican American group, which sought out these bargain counters and thereby made Spanish-speaking clerks a practical asset to the store" (1951, 44).

Skin color often played a part in what kinds of retail jobs Mexican American women could obtain. Annie García Redondo worked at Sears in the shipping and receiving room as a bookkeeper in 1941, at the age of seventeen. "They wouldn't accept me to work in the front, on the floor, because my skin was dark and I looked like a Mexican. It was only light-skinned people who could work in the front. So I had to work in shipping and receiving behind the door." She recalled that the maintenance man told her that she would develop better skills than the saleswomen because she was learning to use her mind. "To me at that time it wasn't that important. I wanted to be in the front. . . . It was the prestige of the thing, you know. The people would see you there and say 'Oh she's selling.' You know what I mean? In the back the only people you contacted were the people that worked there. You wanted to be in the front where people you knew would see you working." Although she had obtained a white-collar position, she desired the status that came with working in the sales department (Ruiz 1993, 111; García Redondo 1997).

Annie remained at Sears until she graduated from high school in 1943. It didn't take long for her to find a new retail job on 2nd Street and Washington at the Boston Store. She remarked, "In that store everybody was somebody. There was no restrictions for color . . . if you knew the job, you got the job. I went and applied over there, because I had a lot of friends working there and they said they liked it because everybody was friendly. If a Mexican came in and they didn't know how to speak English, they had somebody there that was qualified to talk to them in Spanish." With her increased wages, she purchased consumer goods that reflected aspirations for a more middle-class lifestyle. She proudly recalls, "I was the only girl that had a record player when I lived on 12th Street . . . I had a record player, I had the records, I had a dresser, I had a bed, I had a couch, and we had a stove, and we had a telephone—and I paid for all of that with my wages." Later, she transferred to the layaway department, and worked there until 1950, when she married her husband Armando. Annie has many fond memories of the Boston Store: "It was quite an experience and I always appreciated the Diamonds [the family], they considered everybody that worked for them as part of their family . . . You learned to get together with people of different ethnic groups, you know" (García Redondo 1997).

Another experience in Phoenix's Boston Store reveals how women of Mexican descent began to assert themselves and demand better pay or improved work environment. In January 1943, Esperanza García, a clerk and a member of the Retail Clerks Union Local 99, lost her job at the Boston Store after being employed there for ten years. The union investigated and concluded that she lost her job as a result of her union membership. They also noted that other clerks had been fired and blacklisted from other stores for being union members. According to the union, 50 percent of the store employees had signed union cards, but store management discouraged employees from signing through intimidation. Female union members picketed in front of the store, while the union advertised in *El Sol*: "The Retail Clerk Union asks for the help of all union sympathizers and members of the working-class to not patronize the Boston Store, while we are obligated to maintain our group of union sentinels exhibiting signs which denounce the Boston Store's attitude." The union emphasized that the firing demonstrated how Mexican American employees were treated unfairly, especially since the store catered to the Mexican population.

Through *El Sol*, the union argued that the Mexican American employees' desire to have a union should be respected since they brought in customers, and that store management should appreciate "that speaking two languages is a merit in the job." The union asserted that it would ensure that Spanish-speaking clerks did not earn less than other clerks, as well as enforcing the legislated forty-hour workweeks. With the ratification of the Fair Labor Standards Act only five years before, unions used this protective legislation as part of their arsenal in the fight for workers' rights. In May 1943 the union praised the female members who continued to picket, remarking that they represented "each and every one of the men and women workers in the state of Arizona," while the Boston Store represented Wall Street, which had "only one goal, to give the workers only what is sufficient to subsist and to pay $1.00 weekly in credits." Although union advertisements continued to urge a boycott of the Boston Store through October 1943, the newspaper did not mention the success or failure of the boycott, or the outcome of the organizing efforts (*El Sol* January 21, 1943, January 28, 1943, February 11, 1943, April 2, 1943, May 21, 1943).

The percentage of Mexican American women in service jobs in Arizona dropped from 55 percent in 1930 to 37.7 percent in 1950, perhaps reflecting the numbers of women who stopped working after the war, or the shift of more women entering white-collar positions (Ruiz 1998, 118). The 1949 Phoenix City Directory reveals that a larger number of women worked in white-collar occupations than in service jobs, mirroring the general trend for women of Mexican descent in the Southwest. Although more Mexican American women moved into higher-status jobs, they also continued to fill the ranks of workers in the service industries, which grew along with the 1940s economy (Phoenix City Directory 1949–1950). With this came an increase of union activity in these sectors. Raymond Flores found that most of the cooks and waitresses in Mexican food restaurants were women of Mexican descent, and that they composed 26 percent of the total membership in the organized hotel and restaurant employees' union. They were paid $4 to $11 per day (1951, 45).

Unions also attracted Mexican women in the laundry industry during the 1940s. The American Federation of Labor organized 150 employees of McKean's Laundry in 1943, and they went on strike after union workers lost their jobs and were replaced by nonunion workers. The strikers demanded their jobs back and forty cents per hour as minimum wage, ten cents above the national minimum wage for that year. Interestingly, a few weeks later *El Sol* published an advertisement in which McKean's requested Mexican women to work in all departments of the laundry, from 5:00 a.m. until 4:30 p.m., perhaps in an effort to recruit scabs (Peterson 1981, 77; *El Sol* April 16, 1943, May 5, 1943).

After working at the Phoenix Laundry for several years in the early 1940s, Mary López García quit and began working at American Linen, where she made fifty-five cents an hour, twenty cents more than her previous job. Mary recalls that at American Linen, men earned more than women. European Americans usually held management positions, with the exception of the head of the mangle unit, who was a Mexican American woman named Lupe. She notes that European American, black, and Mexican women worked the pressers. At American Linen, Mary joined the Laundry Workers Union: "We got the union in there and that helped us a little more. I used to get twenty-seven dollars and ninety or eighty cents a week. Sometimes if I worked overtime, I got thirty or thirty-two dollars a week. This helped get a little more money" (López García 1997). Increased union activity in clerical and service occupations in Phoenix reflects the general trend of increasing participation of women in organized labor movements during the 1940s. Nationally, between 1939 and 1943, women's membership in unions grew from eight hundred thousand to three million (Blackwelder 1997, 131).

Along with other sections of the local economy, the Valley's agricultural business grew during World War II. For example, by 1950 Arizona produced 5 percent of the nation's cotton, and ranked seventh among the cotton-raising states (Rork and Sutter 1951, 1). That same year, the percentage of Mexican American women working in Arizona's fields decreased from 7.6 percent in 1930 to 6.4 percent (Barrera 1979, 135). The drop in agricultural occupations for women came as a result of increasing mechanization, reduction of child labor, and increasing opportunities in manufacturing, clerical, and sales work (Anderson 1996, 112–13). The emergence of the Bracero Program in 1942–1943 brought more male workers into the Salt River Valley and reduced the number of jobs available to women. Women who did continue to labor as farmworkers often received less pay than their male coworkers. The 1949 survey of Arizona agricultural workers revealed that the weekly average earnings for "Latin American" domestic farmworkers equaled $39.30 for males and $30.45 for females, while braceros earned $30.95 per week. All were performing the same labor (Rork and Sutter 1951, 27).

After 1945 many industries laid off female employees as product demands decreased or men returned to claim their prior positions. Many Mexican American women ceased working after the war once they married or their husbands returned. The notion that a woman's place was in the home remained strong, and some women preferred to maintain that role. While acknowledging the importance of their roles as wives and mothers, Annie, Esther, and Minnie all returned to the workforce in the postwar years in order to support their families. Working just as they had during the 1930s to supplement the family income, these three women enjoyed the independence of their jobs (Gluck 1987, 269; García Redondo 1997; Ramírez Díaz 1997; Rangel Martínez 1998).

Those who continued in the local workforce often reentered traditional female white-collar and service occupations (Gluck 1987, 262). The Phoenix City Directory reveal that in 1949 the numbers of Mexican American women listed in white-collar positions (173), particularly clerical and sales, remained high, and did not fall back to the numbers listed in those occupations (63) in 1941 (Phoenix City Directory 1941, 1950). In 1950 future education administrator Raymond Flores interviewed Friendly House director Plácida García Smith, who provided an upbeat report on the status of female employment: "When I first arrived in Phoenix [1931] the Mexican American girls were hardly seen in any of the establishments around town. Now one sees them working in offices as secretaries, stenographers, beauticians, waitresses and sales clerks. Some of the girls have gone into the nursing profession and others are developing an interest in newspaper work" (Flores 1951, 44).

Reflecting back on the changes brought about by World War II, Annie García Redondo stated: "It was the beginning of the end of a little bit of the discrimination. World War II gave the Hispanic women and men a chance to better themselves. I know there was a lot of discrimination ... even in the service there was discrimination.

But it gave you a chance to survive. You had a chance to go and look for a different kind of job, if you wanted it. It gave women a chance to get into the movement of the war—like working in one of the factories, making plane parts, which was good-paying work at the time. The boys that went into the service got to have a college education through the G.I. Bill" (García Redondo 1997).

CONCLUSION

As in other Mexican American communities and other time periods, gendered expectations, racial restrictions, and economic crises and disparity all shaped women's lives. Like their male counterparts, women of Mexican descent experienced the dynamics of being a member of a group viewed as an elastic labor supply—particularly those women working in agriculture and the service industries. They found employment when European American employers needed them, and were pushed out during economic downturns or when seen as challenging through union activity their designated "place" in the labor hierarchy. Many of the stories told in this chapter show how these women were "used as needed" during the Great Depression and World War II. With changes during World War II, some women moved into a different economic world by owning a small business, attending nursing school, securing a job as a secretary, or moving into other types of white-collar jobs. Regardless of their work experience, these women actively bettered the lives of themselves and their families.

The women who shared their life experiences through oral history also reveal the complexity of intersectionality, while each woman faced broader racial and gender discrimination felt by most in the Mexican American community, each was uniquely impacted by other social categories. Marital status, occupation level and associated income, the ability of other family members to earn income, their age and physical appearance, and their internal motivations to better their lives are elements that took them along different paths. For example, both Esther Ramírez Díaz and Annie García Redondo commented on how a lighter or darker complexion impacted their social status in a white-collar position, even though wartime prosperity and the need for women in the work place opened up more opportunities (especially for younger women) to increase their income and improve their own social status as defined by their community. Women's wages often replaced men's wages in the survival of the family: Mary López García remembered how she left school at the age of fourteen in 1929 to find work in the service industry, which hadn't been as impacted by the Great Depression, because her father lost his job and struggled to find employment. Her niece, Annie, desired to join the WAVES during World War II and pursue the opportunities of new job skills that newspaper and radio advertising promised, but she declined when faced with the reality of the importance of her current income to support her parents and family.

These women negotiated the maze of intersecting social advantages and disadvantages to provide for and sustain their families, to create a thriving Latino community, which has only since grown, and they contributed along with all others to Phoenix's mid-twentieth-century economic growth. Whether the 1870s, the 1930s, or the present day, these women stand as a critical part of the fabric of Phoenix's history, a legacy for future generations.

6

THE MORENCI MINERS WOMEN'S AUXILIARY DURING THE GREAT ARIZONA COPPER STRIKE, 1983–1986

ANNA OCHOA O'LEARY

ON THE MORNING OF AUGUST 19, 1983, sleepy residents of the sister cities of Clifton and Morenci in southeastern Arizona awoke to a strange pulsation: a miles-long convoy of armored tanks, vehicles, and Huey helicopters, fully equipped with armed soldiers and SWAT teams, making its way up the mountain road to its new front line: the gates of the company facilities. The drama unleashed by Arizona governor Bruce Babbitt to quash the Phelps Dodge copper strike at the Morenci mine was impressive even when the century-long struggle by workers to achieve better working conditions in Arizona's copper industry is considered. It is within this broader historical context that we can examine the changing role of women in the Morenci Miners Women's Auxiliary.

This chapter examines the role of the Morenci Miners Women's Auxiliary (MMWA) in mobilizing resources that helped sustain one of the longest strikes in the history of the state, and how in doing so, fostered a gendered form of community empowerment.[1] The chapter also reflects upon, assembles, and integrates into this history a firsthand account of the events. Certain dilemmas are inherent in this exercise. Writing about these events over thirty-four years later is challenging enough without writing about a personally tumultuous time for many, risking reopening many wounds. The strike virtually ripped families apart, mine included, having one brother on strike and another a strikebreaker. The scars left by the emotional wounds still haunt many today.

The strike was also economically catastrophic. It is unpleasant to remember, yet I harbor some pride in doing so that I, too, like many striking families, suffered the indignity of being caught without enough money to buy a gallon of milk, and to suspect that it would only be a matter of time before economic necessity would uproot us from the life we knew to face uncertainties elsewhere. I am certain that among many striking families were children who could not understand their parents' decision to participate in the strike, denying them stability and security. The strain on marriages, while mostly invisible, would on occasion come to light. In *Holding the Line*, Barbara Kingsolver documented some of the strain as women, inspired by the strike, became more bold and defiant.[2] My marriage to one of the informal leaders of the strike, Dr. Jorge O'Leary, was certainly no exception.[3] However, with a growing awareness of one's subjectivity, and with time, came a heightened sense of purpose. More recently, the analytical skills that came with earning a doctorate, and working my way up through the academic hierarchy at Arizona's flagship research university to achieve a role of leadership and privilege as head of the Department of Mexican American Studies offers a lens through which I examine the articulation between strife and agency of working-class women.

Because of the relevant invisibility of accounts of women who have historically organized as auxiliary members, when the MMWA burst into the limelight in 1983, it seemed new to many, myself included. Indeed, I was oblivious to the role of the MMWA in labor history. Ladies' auxiliaries, or women's auxiliaries, have long been known to be an important part of labor organizing (Sangster 2000). Primarily made up of the wives, sisters, and mothers of usually male workers—auxiliaries have been primarily responsible for supporting workers on strike, such as by preparing food and feeding workers during picketing. For example, in Canada in the 1940s, the Ladies' Auxiliary of the International Union Mine Mill and Smelter Workers helped feed hundreds of striking miners (Steedman 2000). Auxiliaries have also organized activities that have supported a striker's family. These activities have included organizing clothing drives and fundraising to help meet families' unexpected costs, such as medical emergencies.

Consistent with the traditional form and function of other auxiliaries, the MMWA had for generations activated only when husbands, brothers, fathers and sons went on strike. What was relatively new in the copper strike of 1983–1986 was the idea that women could (and did) move beyond the domestic sphere of duties to contribute to political mobilization both at local and national levels. Women of the MMWA were invited to give talks in other parts of the country, were interviewed by reporters from national news outlets, and responded to requests to attend marches and rallies of supporters in states where these took place. This resulted in unprecedented national visibility which, arguably, brought greater pressure upon union leadership to support the strikers. In this way, they helped shape the course of events.

As the MMWA's work became more politicized, it also attracted the attention of scholars. Feminist scholars Aulette and Mills (1988) observed women challenging male-centered norms as they worked to bring media attention to the strike even if they themselves were ignored. Aulette and Mills (1988), and to some extent Rosenblum (1995a), capture the role that this organization had in reframing, channeling, and operationalizing ideas and, ultimately, serving to reconceptualize the political arena that was (and to large extent continues to be) staunchly male centered, patriarchal, and exclusionary of women. Barbara Kingsolver's writing career was launched with *Holding the Line* (1986), which focused on the changes in women's lives that resulted from the strike. Ultimately, the auxiliary's waning efforts would parallel the weakening and eventual demise of the unions. However, the ultimate transformation of the MMWA would emerge as emblematic of the changes occurring elsewhere, as economic restructuring introduced instability in other parts of the world.

A BRIEF BACKGROUND TO THE GREAT ARIZONA COPPER STRIKE

Arizona's history is inextricably linked to copper mining, and mining is inextricably linked to the state's geography and the geology of copper-ore deposits. There is no shortage of scholarship on this history. Early period mining was done on an individual basis, usually by prospectors who searched for surface mineral outcroppings, where they could be assured a high return for a low investment of time and money and little technology. In these early cases, the mine worker was likely to also be the mine owner (Navin 1978). As bonanza–type vein deposits became depleted, mining became more capital and labor intensive. Together with the lack of technology to make extraction of copper deposits more efficient, the self-financing of mining operations by individuals became less profitable over time.

The Industrial Revolution stands out as a turning point in terms of the scale of production in the copper mining industry (Cleland 1952; Sheridan 2012). The growing demand for copper followed the expansion of telegraph communication and, later, the electrical power needs of American industries and households. In turn, these would drive the technological innovations that would make the extraction of copper from low-grade ore possible and profitable. New ways of organizing production for greater efficiency also paved the way for how copper-producing companies would consolidate their power in the modern era (Navin 1978). Wealthy European and East Coast investors began to buy out the small claims of individual prospectors. It is in this way that Arizona copper mining companies, such as the Phelps Dodge Corporation, came to control the natural resources needed for production (land, timber, and water) and, ultimately, amass great power and wealth (Byrkit 1982). By the 1920s six companies were producing 56 percent of all the copper being produced in Arizona (Sheridan 2012).

To be sure, the geographic isolation of most mining operations provided both disadvantages and advantages. The sister cities of Clifton and Morenci are geographically isolated in the rugged mountainous area of eastern Arizona, about 115 miles northeast from the nearest metropolitan city, Tucson, Arizona. With the lack of a diversified economic base that large population centers provide, the livelihood of families in these two small towns were largely dependent on the mine, as they continue to be today. Moreover, the skills acquired in mining production are not those that are easily transferred to other economic sectors (Bulmer 1975). With greater consolidation and vertical integration, companies such as Phelps Dodge were able to exert greater control of its workers.

Arizona's copper companies maintained their control of operations in several ways. They exerted power over labor *directly*, using intimidation, threats, and physical force and violence against workers to exploit them as much as possible (Byrkit 1982). A famous example from history comes from the 1917 Bisbee Deportation, where Phelps Dodge, with the help of local law enforcement agents, rounded up presumed strikers and strike organizers and "deported" them to a remote location near Columbus, New Mexico (Byrkit 1982). However, copper companies in Arizona also exerted their power *indirectly*, such as by influencing politicians and lawmakers to pass laws that were favorable to the industry. Such laws allowed companies to exploit natural resources and undermine competitors and unions (Heyman 1995).

Consequently, Arizona's history is also pockmarked by acts of resistance by workers against mining companies, which many times resulted in turbulent labor strikes (Mellinger 1995). In addition, while not all the striking miners were Mexican, Mexican laborers made up the largest percentage of the workforce (Benton-Cohen 2003). Several of these disputes are historically notable. In 1903 Mexican miners instigated a strike in Clifton over wage discrepancy (also referred to as the *dual-wage system* discussed in greater detail in chapter 4) in the first significant strike in the Southwest (Mellinger 1995). Benton-Cohen (2003) notes that this strike was primarily organized by Mexican workers. In 1906 a strike in the Mexican town of Cananea was primarily directed at the American-owned Green Copper Company. The strike deserves mention because although it was on Mexican territory, the workers were both American and Mexican, and it was quelled by the use of armed Arizona Rangers, who entered Mexico in support of an American mining operation.

During World War I, a series of strikes were organized in mining towns across Arizona (Clifton, Morenci, Ray, Globe, Miami, Jerome, and Bisbee), targeting the most wealthy and powerful companies in Arizona, including Phelps Dodge. During this time, workers had been drawn ideologically and politically to the Industrial Workers of the World (IWW; also known as the Wobblies). A mine strike in Jerome organized by the IWW in May 1917 ended with strikers and union organizers, accused of being foreigners and subversives, being rounded up by armed agents of the mine owners and shipped by railroad cattle cars to Kingman, after being threatened with death if they returned to Jerome. Similar events took place in Bisbee, Arizona, in 1917 (Benton-Cohen 2003). During this rash of strikes across Arizona, copper companies were riding the wave of patriotism of the time and were able to violently suppress strikes with impunity. American labor leader Frank Little was lynched during this time. Violations of basic workers' rights were so egregious that President Woodrow Wilson ordered an investigation of Arizona's copper companies.

Consistent with this history, Chicago attorney Jonathan Rosenblum's analysis of the 1983 copper strike demonstrates its national implications (Rosenblum 1995).[4] In 1983 Phelps Dodge became a case study for defeating "union power buildup" (Rosenblum 1995a, 44). Ten years before the strike, Wharton School professor Herbert Northrup had developed a playbook, *Operating during Strikes* (Perry, Kramer, and Schneider 1982), containing strategies, which, if followed, were predicted to undermine strike actions. These included the contracting of tour buses to transport scabs to worksites en masse, reimbursing strikebreakers for any extra costs associated with strike activity, threatening strikers with the loss of their jobs with outside replacements, permanently replacing striking workers with nonunion workers, and cutting off medical benefits to strikers. All of these strategies were implemented in the 1983 strike. Scabs were bussed in from outside of Clifton and Morenci. Medical benefits were cut off. Letters were sent to strikers, threatening them that they would lose their jobs if they did not return to work at once. An open letter to John Bolles, manager of Phelps Dodge operations in Morenci, published in the *Copper Era* in July 1983, was written by an infuriated striker, Paul M. López, who accused Bolles and the company of "scare tactics" and intimidation to get strikers to cross the picket line. Following the Wharton playbook, the cost to implement the tactics was irrelevant. Rosenblum reports that the company lost $100 million in operations and claimed another $100 million in write-offs in 1984. Stockholders lost $220 million, or $92,000 per striker, demonstrating that Phelps Dodge's refusal to settle with the thirteen striking unions went beyond efforts to save on the cost of wages. Even so, nothing was left to chance. Phelps Dodge also had the support of the state. Undercover agents with the Arizona State Criminal Intelligence Systems Agency (ACISA) infiltrated every union in the Clifton and Morenci mining district early in the strike, bugging nearly one out of every two meetings and monitoring the rest with informers (Rosenblum 1995a). The history of Arizona's copper mining industry is in this way a story of the collective efforts of workers, equipped only with time-tested ideologies and cultural practices designed to fulfill obligations to each other, resisted against all odds.

THE END OF COLLECTIVE BARGAINING AND THE 1983 STRIKE

To preempt the high cost of labor management conflicts, the major copper companies in Arizona and their labor unions historically relied on collective bargaining. Collective bargaining was a long-established practice in which every three years the big five Arizona copper mining companies negotiated with all of Arizona's unions at the same time (Rosenblum 1995). As part of the collective bargaining practice, every three years since 1968 there had been short (six- to eight-week) strikes, which offered a measurement of economic stability (Heyman 1995; Rosenblum 1995b). In fact, mining families often planned vacations around these work stoppages.

However, a series of events would contribute to the demise of collective bargaining. The demand for copper significantly declined with the end of the Vietnam War. Mining had also become highly vulnerable to world market prices and competition.[5] The World Bank increased its loans to copper-producing Third World nations whose lower production costs were possible with lower wages and lax environmental laws, and copper from these nations flooded the market (Rosenblum 1995b). In 1980 the price of copper fell from a high of $1.27 per pound to $0.83 per pound. Phelps Dodge began to reduce some of its mining operations to cut operating costs. In April 1982, with the price of copper falling to $0.69 per pound, Phelps Dodge suspended all mining, milling, and smelting operations, and laid off most of its workers. In October 1982, more than half of the workforce was recalled and limited production resumed (Briggs 2016), while many waited to return to work.[6]

In 1980 President Ronald Reagan sought economic relief for the nation through neoliberal policies. The worldwide recession had brought some of the highest unemployment rates in the nation's history (United States Misery Index 2017), and a surplus of workers. Reagan's policies centered on reducing governmental regulations as a cost-saving strategy for industries to stimulate hiring. In 1981 Reagan's also took a hardline stance against the air-traffic controllers union, the Professional Air Traffic Controllers Organization (PATCO) resulting in its decertification (McCartin 2006). This signaled to U.S. industries that the climate was ripe for ridding themselves of costly regulations and worker protections negotiated by unions over the years. A major casualty of these economic and political shifts was the loss of good-paying blue-collar jobs, which had been made largely possible through years of hard-fought negotiations by unions.

However, what remained imperceptible to the casual observer was that Phelps Dodge, with its extremely conservative views, had shown early signs of breaking from this collective bargaining pattern. Phelps Dodge had been openly critical of the largest of the Arizona copper companies, Kennecott, for its more liberal stance in bargaining with the unions (Heyman 1995, Rosenblum 1995b). During their negotiations in the spring of 1983, Kennecott took its usual lead in negotiating a contract with its workers. The other companies—Magma, Inspiration, and ASARCO—pressured to enter into similar agreements with their workers out of fear of losing money, fell in line. However, Phelps Dodge, emboldened by one of the "harshest cost-benefit calculus possible," held out (Rosenblum 1995a, 70). Not only did it refuse to agree to the basic terms as the other companies, it asked for additional concessions from its unions and an end to all side agreements dating back to the 1950s.

What followed was a strike by now-isolated thirteen union locals at the Morenci mine, and union workers in Ajo.[7] Events climaxed on August 8, 1983, after Phelps Dodge reopened the mine with replacement scab labor, and thousands of strikers in Morenci blocked the gates to the mine.[8] Reportedly to avert violence, Governor Babbitt traveled to Clifton and Morenci to force parties to the table to negotiate. A ten-day cooling-off period was agreed upon, during which time Phelps Dodge was to suspend operations. The workers were encouraged, and it was not until the morning of August 19 that they realized that they had been betrayed. The ten-day period had been used to organize the military intervention by way of 350 National Guard troops and 425 Arizona Department of Public Safety (DPS) troopers (Briggs 2016), who made their way up the hill in a convoy on that day. They set up camp outside the company gate while a team of 160 SWAT sharpshooters were also positioned in the hills outside the gates. Supporting this intervention was a restraining order signed by Judge John L. Claborne, which made it impossible for strikers to set up a picket line at the company gate.

Six months later, union negotiators again sat across company officials to offer concessions only to find that Phelps Dodge had increased its demands (Rosenblum 1995a). By this time, it was clear that it was more than a patterned agreement process that the company wanted to end. The strike's conclusion in 1986 bore this out: It marked the defeat of thirteen union locals made up of over 2,400 workers (Rosenblum 1995a). Rosenblum (1995a) documents that at the peak of the labor dispute, about 4,250 residents, about half of whom were of Mexican descent, inhabited the incorporated town of Clifton. Another 2,300 lived four miles north in Phelps Dodge-owned housing. The end of the labor dispute also brought about the near collapse of the communities that surrounded the most profitable copper-producing company in the nation, with $110 million in profits in 1980, and the end of an era (Kristof 1985).

THE SOCIAL CONTEXT OF THE CLIFTON AND MORENCI MINING COMMUNITIES

The social context of Arizona mining communities in general, and in Clifton and Morenci in particular, relied on the historical geopolitical and economic forces that gave rise to mining operations and company towns throughout the Southwest. The U.S.-Mexico borderlands region has historically been a region of dynamic American capitalist transformation in which the transnational nature of Mexican labor has figured prominently (Heyman 1995; Acuña 2007; Sheridan 2012). A catalyst for this transformation has been the copper mining industry, which over time and space integrated thousands of Mexican workers into the U.S. economy (Acuña 2007). Allen (1966) notes that although workers from many ethnic backgrounds came to work in the various mining industries that dotted the Southwest, the development of the Morenci mine was largely made possible with the attraction of mostly Mexican laborers, and for most of this history, they were subject to the racial segregation that has been common in mining communities for generations (Allen 1966).

Mining settlements are typically geographically isolated and difficult to access (Allen 1966; Bulmer 1975). Mining companies need to lure laborers to where mining operations are located. For this purpose, mining companies often erected company towns, complete with essential schools, housing, hospitals, stores, and the electric and water utility infrastructure. Company towns also provided spaces for local businesses to operate, and recreational venues for workers (movie theaters, bowling alleys, and baseball fields). Together with the isolated-ness of mining operation, a pattern of power relations is built into company towns, allowing companies to exert control over labor and the civic function of communities (Heyman 1995, 156–57). Companies thus assured themselves a near-dependent, quasi-permanent supply of workers—an "isolated mass"—singly committed to mining (Bulmer 1975, 69). Bulmer (1975, 85) describes a company town as that which "the company is a party to all the principal economic transactions carried on within it." Allen (1966, 4) describes a company town as:

> Any community which has been built wholly to support the operations of a single company, in which all homes, buildings, and other real estate property are owned by that company, having been acquired or erected specifically for the benefit of its employees and in which the company provides most public services.

Although Allen goes on to describe variations in the aforementioned definition among the two hundred communities he studied, Morenci, Arizona, conformed to the classic definition. However, it is also noted that very often, developing alongside company towns were other settlements, which complemented and served mining operations. Clifton, located just under two miles in the valley below Morenci, (4.03 miles by car), fits this description. In such settlements, mining companies may own property, but most is privately owned by residents and businesses, affecting the degree of control that a company may have there. Service utilities in these settlements also tend to be publicly owned, and therefore not under the control of the mining company, making it more difficult for a company to coerce workers. Thus, although residents and business owners in such communities may also economically depend on the mining operations for their livelihoods—sharing similar concerns as their company-town counterparts—they are less controlled by the company than those living in the company town.

A research article by Graham (1980) contrasts the conditions in two neighboring Arizona mining communities that I suspect were Clifton and Morenci. Although the two communities in her study are referred to by two pseudonyms, the descriptions of each are uncannily similar to those that I was personally familiar with, having lived in both Clifton and Morenci. In Graham's study, one community, Townsite, is an "administered community" in which residents have no decision-making power. During the time of the strike, I lived in Plantsite, a section of the company town of Morenci. Such communities are characterized by Graham as having a single purpose. Residents here lack participation in policy-making, communities are hierarchically ordered based on occupation, and are in direct control by employers—in essence, a "company town." The other community in Graham's study, Red Butte, is an incorporated town administered by an elected town council. I grew up in such a town, Clifton, which is located at the base of a large butte (Mares Bluff) and a large red granite mountain.

Graham examined the organizational structures in each of the two Arizona mining communities and considered how each impacted individuals' decisions and behaviors (Graham 1980). She notes that one of the dangers of living in an administered occupational community such as a company town (Townsite) is that important human qualities such as personal freedom, autonomy, and responsiveness to the needs of others are destroyed. These human qualities are replaced by loyalty to the primary purpose of the administered community (in this case, mining), and there is a corresponding emphasis on occupationally centered career goals. Paralleling this definition is the concept of "occupational community" (Bulmer 1975). Bulmer also analyzes the structure of mining communities and how its structure influences behaviors in these communities. Bulmer (1975, 69) argues that companies use a community's isolation to their advantage by controlling workers' upward mobility, and by molding workers' interests. Central to this endeavor is shaping workers' identity as one that is *different and separate* from the rest of society. This separateness, the "conscious apartment from the wider society," fosters loyalty to the company (ibid., 86). Thus, a careful orchestration of workers' chief life interests promotes the "internal solidarity" needed to consolidate the loyalty of the "isolated mass" to the operation. Depending on the mining settlement and the degree of local autonomy, the isolated mass in this way can be disarticulated from "the whole" of society—the communal social relationships rooted in families and other types of companionships that counteract an identity premised on occupation (ibid., 87–88):

> Social ties of work, leisure, family neighborhood and friendship overlap to form close-knit and interlocking locally based collectivities of actors. The solidarity of the community is strengthened not only by these features . . . but by a shared history of living and working in one place over a long period of time.

These different models of behavior based on community structure studied by Graham and Bulmer were brought to life in the 1983 strike in Morenci (the company town) and Clifton (the incorporated town). Both were, to some degree, occupational communities; but structured in different ways. Both were to different degrees economically dependent on Phelps Dodge, but in one (Morenci), its control by the company was near absolute. The company nearly assured itself of the isolated mass needed to hedge against strikes. However, in the other community (Clifton), not so much. In Clifton, work and nonwork spheres of interaction overlapped, allowing "the whole" to counteract any sense of disarticulation that characterized the "isolated mass" of the company town. This dynamic helps account for the enormous resources that the company expended and convened (through the state) to break the unions. The dynamic also accounts for the subsequent long-held bitterness and the longevity of the 1983–86 labor-management conflict.

After my husband, Dr. Jorge O'Leary, a company physician working at the Morenci Hospital was fired from the company for his very visible and vocal support of the strikers, our family was evicted from the company-owned home in Morenci (in the section of town known as Plantsite).[9] We moved to nearby Clifton, where striking workers rallied to our support and used their skills and time to renovate an abandoned feed store for what became the People's Clinic, where Dr. O'Leary was able to medically serve the communities of Clifton and Morenci. The clinic, located near the public roadway leading to Morenci, became the center for picketing and other strike activity. On private property and surrounded by other local businesses that were for the most part supportive of the strikers' causes, the People's Clinic became a symbol of community solidarity and cohesion. It also became strategically important when the legal injunction against the unions limited striker activity on the same roadway once it entered company-owned property near the entrance to the mine, where the traditional picket line had been.

The patterns of mutual aid and commitment to community solidarity and welfare—important for framing strike activity—had implications for women in general and for Mexican-origin women in particular, which should be examined critically. Bulmer (1975) points out that in mining communities, the marital roles of husband and wife are typically sharply segregated with those of women centered on the home and reproductive activities. A 1985 interview shows that these sharply defined gender roles were true in Morenci (Izakowitz 1985). True to this form, the overwhelming majority of workers in the Morenci mine were men. Over time, the rise of union wages, the result of generations of labor union collective bargaining with their employers, had realized numerous benefits for the workforce and their families. Miners enjoyed living wages, cost of living increases, antidiscrimination and job-safety regulations, medical, disability, accidental death insurance, and retirement pensions. These, in addition to the low rents paid for company-owned houses, resolved many economic concerns. Women were not forced into the labor force to make ends meet.

Even if women chose to work, opportunities to do so were few. Indeed, the Clifton and Morenci mining communities have offered little in terms of formal educational or career opportunities.[10] The nearest community college, Eastern Arizona College, is available in Thatcher Arizona, fifty-five miles away. With mining as the single most important industry within a fifty-mile radius, an entry-level job with "the company" as we all called it, would easily fulfill a family's material needs. Decades of union negotiations had secured this material well-being, allowing working-class men and women to achieve suburban-like middle-class lives and security for their families as wage workers and without having attended college.

In this light, I see now that any goals that women might have had that competed with domestic roles were easily subsumed by the political economy of the community. And, although few would argue that many indeed possessed some degree of independence and freedom within their spheres of domestic activities, the importance of women's roles was essentially associated with reproductive activities rather than productive ones since relatively few women were employed outside the home.

This not to say that any idea of straying away from the traditional expectations for women growing up in the Morenci mining community did not exist. These may have been only poorly documented. A rare glimpse of the dilemma that surely consumed many women is articulated in the following passage from "Blossom in the Wind," written by Elena Díaz Bjorkquist, who grew up in Morenci (Bjorkquist 1996, 137). The protagonist's contemplation in this short story captures a moment in the reality of a high school senior finding herself trapped at a critical juncture in her life, where her visions of her future after graduation appear before her.

> "Her life would be like her mother's and her grandmother's—married to a miner, having babies, living in Morenci the rest of her life. That wasn't what she wanted."

Ironically, the same gendered expectations that had prescribed my various roles of daughter, wife, then mother, prompted my involvement in the 1983 labor strike against the Phelps Dodge Corporation, our community's single, most important employer. When Jorge O'Leary was fired for his support of the strikers, it was the women of the MMWA that came to my door to express regret and solidarity. It was then that the alternative to acquiescing to company dictates and absolute control became clear.

Castillo's essay on the Watsonville Women's Strike (Castillo 2014) points out that labor activism and stirring debates among women raises their consciousness by opening their eyes to how economic, racial, and gender inequalities permeate the lives of the working classes. My own community disintegrated before my very eyes as families moved to larger cities such as Tucson and Phoenix in search of work, not unlike thousands of communities facing global economic recession during the 1980s. It would be much later that I would find out that during this decade, more and more women, in dire need and destitute, unprepared and untrained, were economically pressured into the labor market as secondary wage earners (Gilbert 1994). Back home, few employment opportunities had been available for women. Some had worked as cashiers, clerks, or cooks before the 1980s when many businesses closed, reducing such jobs to almost nothing. The better, more stable jobs were somehow and understandably associated with having training, skills, or experience, including better English skills. Women who worked in higher-level administrative jobs or as secretaries or teachers were usually Anglo. They often were the wives of company officials or, in any event, had come from somewhere else with the certification or the knowledge that it took to work in those jobs. The comparative productive and reproductive roles of women in this way is shaped by their relationships to labor and the economy, and the structural constraints within which they operate.

THE MORENCI MINERS WOMEN'S AUXILIARY

Soon after the strike began, the MMWA began organizing and attending union meetings. At the start, there were reportedly over a hundred women who called themselves members of this organization. Meetings were in the evening and weekly, in the metal trades union hall, one of the buildings used by the unions on Chase Creek in Clifton. Chase Creek is the name given to a narrow street running somewhat parallel to a creek bed by the same name. The creek is normally dry except during periods of heavy rain, at which time it runs with several feet deep of water, draining into the nearby San Francisco River that runs through the town.

It is a great historical loss that records of these meetings have been lost. The meetings were used to update each other on strike developments, union discussions, and to plan events. For the most part, the women were wives of strikers. However, there were other members who joined to support the strikers and to support the women and their efforts. The first of the MMWA's presidents, Fina Roman, was not a striker's wife, but rather an articulate supporter of the strike and long-time Clifton resident. The ages of the women ranged from mid- to late twenties to mid- to late forties. About half were of Mexican heritage, reflecting the general demographic makeup of Clifton and Morenci's population in general. U.S. census records for Greenlee County, where the Morenci mine is located, indicate that Latino/Hispanics made up around 47 percent of the total population in 1980, three years before the start of the strike (U.S. Bureau of the Census 2015).

Aulette and Mills (1988) note that the MMWA operated similarly to other auxiliaries in similar circumstances, but point out that such activities remain relatively invisible. They argue that in spite of a wide range of activities undertaken by the MMWA during the Arizona copper strike of 1986–1986, the organization was virtually ignored by the media. Table 6.1 lists a range of activities, many of which were activities that took place alongside men, such as picketing (figures 6.1, 6.2), organizing solidarity events and marches, and speaking at rallies. Others were more gender specific, such as organizing clothing drives. In their examination of women's auxiliaries elsewhere, Aulette and Mills note the role auxiliaries played in a 1964 strike by the Teamsters union, a 1937 autoworkers strike in Flint, a Colorado coal strike in 1913, Harlan County strikes in West Virginia in the 1970s, and the 1950–1952 strike by zinc miners, which was later made famous in the film *Salt of the Earth*. Sangster (2000) concurs that there has been scant scholarly attention to the work of auxiliaries, which obscures them in the historical record.

Sangster (2000) blames the invisibility of women in labor union conflicts on how working-class activities are conceptualized as being segregated and gendered. The separation of the male-centered productive sphere from the female-centered reproductive sphere has also been reaffirmed by the scholarly focus on mostly formal institutional dynamics of labor-management relations. In this way, the roles of informal social institutions and the women who took part in them remain neglected (Sangster 2000). This changed to some extent after the 1970s, when the feminist movement brought into focus women's roles in working-class history. Over time, critical feminist scholarship has worked to conceptually integrate gendered spheres of interaction and, to lesser degree, their intersection with other societal categories such as race and ethnicity (Sangster 2000).

During the strike, I joined the Morenci Miners Women's Auxiliary (MMWA). The strike began on the morning of July 1, 1983. I was unaware of its existence until the day that my husband, Jorge O'Leary, one of several company physicians working for the Phelps Dodge Hospital was fired for his support of the striking workers. That afternoon, on October 8, 1983, in an act of solidarity, members of the MMWA knocked on the door of our company-owned home and greeted me with gifts of food. Overcome by the urge to reciprocate, I joined their efforts and learned about the all-important role that this organization had played for generations. In this way, I was also privileged to witness and to form part of its evolution.

Table 6.1 Selected Events and Activities in the Work of the MMWA

"Holding the Line"	Several days after the workers at Morenci went on strike, a court order limiting the number of union picketers was issued. Because the women were nonunion members, they began to picket at the Phelps Dodge gates.
Strike Anniversary, July 1, 1984, Labor Rally	The MMWA was primarily responsible for organizing a march and rally to commemorate the one-year anniversary of the strike. Although the march started peacefully, down Route 66, carrying banners, a few strikers broke off to heckle scabs leaving the mine. This set off a chain of events resulting in police officers ordering the crowd to disperse; about twenty demonstrators were arrested.
5 de Mayo Fiesta	MMWA organized a 5 de Mayo Fiesta on Chase Creek (in Clifton). The festivities included booths, food sales, dance groups, guest speakers, and a dance. Proceeds would be used by the MMWA to help high school students defray the costs associated with graduation.
Speakers Bureau	Speakers from the MMWA were featured in the "Support the Arizona Copper Strikers Labor Solidarity Tour" in 1984. By then, the one-year strike anniversary had come and gone. Dolores Huerta, famed leader of the United Farm Workers, was also featured as a speaker. Speakers are at the Chicago Coalition Labor Union Women (CLUW) convention.
Social Solidarity	Saturday, May 3, 1995. Opening of the Ice Cream Palace for Clifton residents, funded by a grant from the Ms. Foundation in New York.
Potluck for the Solidarity Committee of the Capital District	On March 20, 1985, MMWA hosted a potluck to show their appreciation to a couple from Albany, New York, who traveled with supplies and clothing for the families of strikers, in behalf of the Solidarity Committee of the Capital District. The MMWA subsequently organized the distribution of the clothing.
Community Education Event	*Copper Era* news item, November 6, 1985: MMWA listened to a report about investigation into an asbestos dump at a Phelps Dodge property south of Clifton. The members also listened to a county health officer about proper food handling, which was part of the MMWA's efforts to self-educate about proper food handling for weekly food sales and catering.

(*continued*)

Table 6.1 *(continued)*

Community Education Event	The MMWA hosted a report to the membership about an asbestos dump site near the Phelps Dodge property in Clifton. The talk was supplemented with photos and was part of efforts by Greenpeace, G.A.S.P. (Group Against Smelter Pollution) and the Citizens for the Right to Know.
Clothing Exchanges	The MMWA would use some of the monthly meetings to exchange children's clothing.
Community Education Event	The MMWA showed a film to its members and the wider community titled *El Salvador—Revolution or Death*.

Months had passed since the August 19 military-type intervention had occurred, in what in hindsight was the de facto end of the strike. As time wore on, the MMWA stepped up their fund-raising efforts, and increased pressure on union member husbands to reach out to national union leaders to get them to show their support of the strike. However, as months came and went, union efforts appeared to stagnate, and the MMWA began to break with tradition by becoming more outspoken, more critical, and more politically active. The reasons for this evolution that invited, pushed, and drove the women out of the domestic sphere are intertwined and complex, but can be summed up by three. The first reason is a practical one. Fearing that union locals were not doing enough to call attention to the strike and that the cause was being relegated to oblivion, the MMWA endeavored to rouse support for the strikers by organizing and speaking out at public rallies and marches. Much of this public speaking was harshly critical of the union locals, which raised tensions between the women and union leaders. Many of us were invited to participate in speaking tours in different parts of the country, and there was little hesitation to use these venues to solicit both moral and financial support for striking families (Aulette and Mills 1988; Kingsolver 1989). However, for these activities, the MMWA was increasingly challenged and criticized by both the union leadership and husbands. Eventually, and due to our defying union leaders' demand that we stop organizing unsanctioned union demonstrations, the MMWA was banned from attending union meetings.

These indignations fueled a second reason that contributed to the MMWA's break with tradition. MMWA members were often accused by union leaders, family members, and husbands of stepping outside the traditional boundaries of a support organization and the corresponding activities that had for generations helped define it (traditional activities such as feeding workers stationed at the picket lines and seeing to the needs of families). Differences in viewpoints thus became more pronounced. True

FIGURE 6.1 Women on the picket line. Photo by Mari Schaefer, 1983. Courtesy of Ricky Wiley, *Arizona Daily Star*.

to the account by Aulette and Mills (1988), MMWA meetings became forums for articulating feminist perspectives. As more and more nonunion "outsiders" answered our calls to support the copper strikers, we became increasingly aware of competing ideologies and emboldened to questioning the authoritative structures of which women were part, albeit unequally so.

The third reason is that we became increasingly aware of our evolving subjectivity and our place in history. Some of the most lasting impressions came from our hosting activists and labor organizers that came from cities as far away as New York and Detroit. These meetings reaffirmed solidarity with strikers, but also became forums for information exchange. These were also opportunities to talk to others about labor history and other social justice issues. For example, a coalition of Tucson supporters organized a visit to Clifton, and they brought the film *Salt of the Earth* to show at a public forum. Although set in the 1950s, the film was nevertheless eye-opening and relevant. It demonstrated the struggle for gender equality and its competition with other social justice struggles such as for fair pay and worker safety—struggles that can only be achieved through awareness and collective action. Women of the MMWA could easily identify themselves with the women of *Salt of the Earth*: the criticisms they endured while suffering the material hardships resulting from a strike against a powerful company and who (like Phelps Dodge) relied on support from local law enforcement to protect its interests.

FIGURE 6.2 Women on the picket line. Photo by David Schreiber, 1984. Courtesy of Ricky Wiley, *Arizona Daily Star*.

A personal account illustrates this evolving consciousness. Meetings almost always involved the preparation of food, coffee, or other refreshments to offer guests—tasks most often relegated to women. At one of these, my traditional role was brought into focus. I noticed that some women from out of town were not eating like everyone else, so I asked them if anything was wrong. They hesitated before answering, looking at each other as if unsure of how to best express their thoughts without offending their host, but eventually they shared with me that as feminists and on principle, they could not legitimize my subservient domestic role by accepting my offer to serve them. Thus, it was through these meetings and the interactions with others that I grew keenly aware of the evolution that we embodied: the history of Arizona and labor's uneasy relationship with the state's copper barons and women's historically ancillary "place" during labor disputes. It was apparent that our role in the strike was laden with contradictions: the unions were to fight for the workers but in unifying workers, women as nonunion workers were excluded. National union leaders were calling to their memberships to rally in support of the copper strikers, yet the strike was being abandoned.

While we, as members of the MMWA, sorted out these contradictions, we relied on our instincts and resorted to what we knew best and what we thought was the right thing to do: organizing, networking and, increasingly, speaking out. This externalized our "breaking out" of traditional expectations. As already mentioned, our networking enabled us to reach far outside our small community, to state and national audiences, where we continued to denounce injustice. This included being barred from union meetings, state-imposed restrictions on our picketing, and the governor's betrayal. We proceeded to defy union leadership "orders" by organizing large nonunion-sanctioned public rallies to bring the world's attention to our labor struggle.[11] The people we were able to bring together and the places where we were invited to speak necessitated a global perspective. One of these events was advertised as a struggle of "Third World women"—a new concept for me at the time. In this way, the women of the MMWA traveled far and wide on the invitation of organizations that supported our work. The connection between our struggle and the struggle of others in other parts of the nation and world became clearer. As part of my role in the MMWA, I was invited to speak at the Coalition of Labor Union Women in Chicago and invited to apply to attend the UN Decade of Women Conference in Nairobi, Kenya. The application was accepted, and I qualified for a Ford Foundation scholarship for NGO leaders to attend this conference. Later, I was to write about this experience.

> My experiences at Forum '85 will be ones from which I will draw upon for the rest of my life. The conference was an intense concentration of cumulative cultural forces drawn together in a relatively short time period, that strained at the seams of intellect—a whirlwind of new and old ideas that left one drained and often disorientated at the end of each day, creating a series of "highs" that propelled into full force changes that ignite global politics today. . . . The Conference called on the international community to enforce the laws already enacted. . . . to enable women to take advantage of opportunities for education and training and to "recognize that women and children tend to be the hardest hit by poverty, drought, apartheid, armed conflict, family violence and the marginalization caused by refugee, migrant, or ethnic minority status." Many issues which concern women, and my particular role as a member of the Morenci Miners Women's Auxiliary were addressed at the conference: such as the value of women' economic contribution to national wealth. . . . For me, the conference opened new doors of valuable networking with people concerned with issues that concern me. The most important thing we can do now is to strengthen independent nongovernmental organizations. If we fail to do so, any women's organizations become nothing but a social club, glittery on the outside, but void of principle and purpose. (O'Leary 1985)

My scholarship to attend the world conference in itself validated the MMWA's work, and if any connection was to be made, if any lesson was to be learned, it was that small-town activism was part and parcel of a greater ocean of economic forces much larger than we.

CONCLUSION

In the end, the union struggle was defeated. In 1986 a vote was put to the permanent replacement workers, the strikebreakers, and scabs that had filled the jobs that had belonged to the strikers. Not surprisingly, after three years of hostilities, the replacement workers voted against forming a union. Thus ended the MMWA's work and, to large degree, the community work that had generated immense solidarity. Workers recruited by Phelps Dodge to replace the strikers also replaced the face of familiarity and loyalty to local community.[12] They spent their paychecks elsewhere, and local businesses were shuttered. The county's population decline is remarkable (table 6.2). The county lost 3,474 residents between 1982, before the strike began, and 1987, when the unions were decertified and the strike officially ended.

The largest percentage decrease was among Latinos. McConnell (2013, 5) shows that in Greenlee County the percent decline among Latinos between 1980 and 2000 was 32 percent, compared to an 18 percent drop among non-Latino whites in the county. At a time when in all other counties the percentage of Latinos as part of the total population was on the rise, only Greenlee County suffered a loss in population between 1980 and 2000.

By examining the MMWA's work, the ideological currents that gave meaning and shape to our efforts again become visible, and the memories and lessons learned assume new significance. Without a doubt, the strike caught workers and their families off-guard. Union leaders were unaware of the Wharton School playbook (Rosenblum

Table 6.2 Population Trend for Greenlee County, 1960–1990

Year	Population Count	
1960	11,509	
1970	10,330	
1980	11,406	
1981	11,478	
1982	11,747	
1983	10,694	The strike begins in July 1983
1984	10,204	
1985	9,052	
1986	8,407	
1987	8,273	
1988	8,105	
1989	7,839	
1990	8,008	

1995a) and, as such, there was no way to prepare for the company's litany of methods to break up the unions, and the betrayal by the state.

In reflecting on these events, I regret having little knowledge of any history that might have provided some understanding of what we were experiencing. It was not a history we as students were exposed to. As children growing up, we were not exposed to anything we might recognize as multicultural or culturally relevant education that might have highlighted the contributions of Mexican labor. This was also the pre-internet age. Today, information can be easily searched on a smartphone or laptop. Even so, Clifton and Morenci became a magnet for labor activists from across the nation and allies shared information and perspectives the old way: through personal connection, conversation, and discussion, and through the literature or other media they brought with them. This interaction was essential to planning our next steps. The knowledge acquired by our speaking engagements in cities across the United States was also quickly shared and put to use. Through these activities, our isolated world became connected to that of others and, with this experience, we learned of what others were thinking—and what they knew or didn't know about us. In the process, we learned about ourselves.

Meeting celebrities who were sympathetic to the cause—Bruce Springsteen, Ed Asner, César Chávez, and Jessie Jackson—was also reaffirming, and inspired us to continue our fight against the Phelps Dodge Corporation.[13] Traveling to Chicago to attend the Chicago Coalition Labor Union Women (CLUW) convention, speaking to several hundred other women, and hearing their thunderous applause in support of the strike opened my eyes to this other world. My participation at the NGO conference at the UN Decade of Women Conference in Nairobi, Kenya, over the objections and anxieties of my family about my traveling internationally for the first time alone for nearly three weeks was life-changing and reaffirmed my self-confidence to meet future challenges. An invitation to speak to a class of Women in Development at the Department of Anthropology at the University of Arizona opened doors to people, mentors, and possibilities, and to an advanced degree that I could not have before imagined.

The connection between action and knowledge—and missing knowledge—continued to stoke my curiosity as did the need for social justice. Perhaps because of this curiosity and need, I became determined to continue my education after we left Clifton—after the thirteen unions were decertified and the strike came to an end. I returned to the University of Arizona to pursue a masters' degree then, later, encouraged by mentors and advisors, entered a PhD program in anthropology. The research projects for my master's and doctorate demonstrated that I still had many unanswered questions that had emerged from the strike experience. My master's research addressed concepts of family, culture, and the divisiveness experienced in my community during the labor strife. My doctoral thesis examined if and how Mexican-origin households invested in the education of their female members. I continue to research issues of gender and reproduction and social injustice, especially that which impacts Mexican immigrant women.

Undoubtedly, the strike provided difficult lessons and many unanswered questions and it is difficult to gauge the impact it had on other MMWA members before we all scattered to different places after the strike ended. To be sure, many women experienced heightened political awareness and autonomy as they journeyed to distant cities—many for the first time, and without husbands. After the strike ended, some women stayed in Clifton and Morenci if their husbands had retired or had been rehired by the company. For those who left, many say that it was one of the better decisions of their lives. The truth about living in isolation and in service to a company, such as Phelps Dodge, had been laid bare. There was no future there other than to produce copper. However, for women who undertook and stepped into roles that they never imagined they would, as labor activists, organizers, and as speakers, they were transformed as they themselves transformed the political spheres in one of Arizona's more formidable and consequential labor struggles.

NOTES

1. Involved in this strike were other auxiliaries as well: the Safford Women's Auxiliary, and the Ajo Women's Auxiliary.
2. In Kingsolver's interviews, women mention some of the difficulties that come with defying gendered norms and expectations. For example, in the chapter titled "Women's Work," an interview with Alicia documents a marital confrontation arising from her strike activities.
3. See, for example, the 1985 *Arizona Daily Star* article (Izakowitz 1985), "Anna O'Leary: 'We've got to battle not only the company and the DPS, we've got to battle the husbands.'"
4. In the aftermath of the strike, Phelps Dodge's more nefarious tactics, its permanent replacement actions, became the subject of Congress' proposed Workplace Fairness Act. The proposal was defeated by conservatives, resulting in Senator Edward Kennedy's characterization of the Phelps Dodge strategy as shameful and a low point in American labor-management relations. The permanent replacement doctrine has subsequently restricted union action in later strikes: an American Airlines flight attendant strike in 1993, and strikes by major league baseball players and auto workers in 1994 (Rosenblum 1995a). The conservative pundit and author Ann Coulter, whose father was a Phelps Dodge vice president and attorney during the strike, referred to the outcome of the strike as "the largest union decertification ever" (Coulter 2008).
5. American companies were also unable to compete with copper-exporting companies whose lower prices and production levels were possible with currency devaluations in

their countries or the nationalization of mines, such as in Chile, the Democratic Republic of the Congo (formerly Zaire), and Zambia (Edelstein 1988).

6. Through personal communication (July 12, 2017), University of Arizona professor James Greenberg shared with me that during that time he had conversed with a psychologist working for Phelps Dodge to strategize how to take advantage of the reserve of workers weakened by lay-offs and exhausted savings in advance of contract renegotiations. Although also communicated in Heyman (1985), this information assumes new meaning as it could conceivably be among the tactics found in the Wharton School's *Operating during Strikes*.
7. Of the thirteen locals on strike, the Steelworkers Union was the largest. Other locals included Machinists, Boilermakers, the International Brotherhood of Electrical Workers (IBEW), Pipefitters Union, and the United Brotherhood of Carpenters.
8. Although the strike's focal point was Clifton-Morenci, parallel demonstrations were held in other Phelps Dodge-owned mines and operations in Ajo, Bisbee, and Douglas.
9. Consistent with the Wharton School strategy, medical benefits were denied to striking workers. Dr. O'Leary defied company orders and provided medical services at no cost to strikers, for which he was fired by Phelps Dodge. The denial of medical benefits to striking workers was later ruled to be illegal by the National Labor Relation Board.
10. Clifton is an incorporated town in Arizona. The Phelps Dodge mining camp of Morenci is located four miles north of Clifton. Both these communities experienced a drastic decline in population after the copper miners' strike in 1983, which lasted three years. In 1980 Clifton's population was 4,245, and Morenci's population was 2,736; in 1990 Clifton's was 2,840 and Morenci's was 1,799 (U.S. Bureau of the Census 1993).
11. Aulette and Mills (1988) note these tensions and disagreements about strategies and goals are an anomaly, as most auxiliaries have historically worked harmoniously with unions.
12. Phelps Dodge took out full-page ads in newspapers across the country, offering new hires the same deal the unions had turned down if they would come to Morenci to work (Briggs 2016).
13. Through his "Born in the USA" tour, Bruce Springsteen donated $10,000 to the strikers' cause, which was used to move the People's Clinic out of the small feed store into a double-wide mobile home.

7

CONSTRUCTING ARIZONA

★

The Lives and Labor of Mexicans in the Valley of the Sun

CRISTINA GALLARDO-SANIDAD

DESPERATELY NEEDED YET CONSISTENTLY UNDERVALUED, Mexican workers labor in Americans' private homes, in the backs of restaurants, in factories, and in the unforgiving Arizona heat to create the foundation on which Arizona builds its economy and its residents build their lives.[1] Arguably, these contributions continue largely unacknowledged. In this chapter, I bring their stories to the forefront for study as I explore Mexicans' contributions in the context of Arizona's twenty-first-century residential construction industry, Arizona's sixth C.

In the late twentieth and early twenty-first century, Arizona was a site of a boom economy fueled largely by residential housing construction, making it a fertile place for settlement. Mexican migrants were among those who settled in Arizona. With stricter border enforcement in the early to mid-1990s in neighboring states, undocumented Mexican migrants were funneled into and stayed in Arizona; at the same time, as cross-border travel was more regulated, families that were established in the state and had traveled between countries also chose to settle in Arizona (Parrado and Kandel 2008). Meanwhile, Arizona also welcomed migrants from Canada and northern U.S. states to the Sunbelt—retirees choosing Arizona for its weather and low taxes, and big-city dwellers seeking the Southwest's low-density communities after the 2001 terrorist attack (Vest 2004, 2006b). Between 1993 and 2003, Arizona's population had grown 37.3 percent, outpacing every other state except Nevada (Poole et al. 2005). Between 2000 and 2006, Latinos accounted for 48.9 percent of Arizona's total population increase, a rate 39 percent higher than the national average (Pew Hispanic Research Center 2008, 6).

Although statistics specifically regarding Arizona's undocumented and foreign-born Mexican populations are not readily available, statistics on Arizona's foreign-born Latinos shed some light on their reality. In 2006 Mexicans represented a disproportionate 88.7 percent of the 1.8 million Arizona Latinos and 91.3 percent of Arizona's 603,000 foreign-born Latinos (ibid., 3, 7). A 2005 survey showed that Mexicans are the most likely of all foreign-born immigrants in the United States to be undocumented (Passel 2006, 5–6). Given the high concentration of foreign-born Mexicans in Arizona, it is no surprise that in 2006 Arizona had double the national average of undocumented Latino migrants in its workforce (11 percent of the total workforce) (Pew Hispanic Research Center 2008, 8).[2] Arizona Latinos tend to also have more recently arrived as migrants to the United States and to have lower levels of English-language fluency and formal education. In fact, 70 percent had a high school diploma or less in 2006 (ibid., 20). Along with institutionalized discrimination and fewer opportunities for mobility, among other things, these factors result in a higher concentration of Arizona Mexicans working in blue-collar industries and occupations.

As an integral part of the nation's and the state's bedrock, Latinos contribute to a legacy of foundational work in agriculture, mining, ranching, large and small business development, the arts, and entertainment (Arizona Latino Research Enterprise 2009). Of the state's 2.9 million person workforce, Latinos compose 27.6 percent (800,000) and account for at least one-fifth of employment in each of the following: farming, fishing, and forestry (64.2 percent); building and grounds cleaning and maintenance (49.7 percent); construction trades (43.3 percent); production (26.4 percent); and food preparation and serving (25.7 percent) (Pew Hispanic Research Center 2008, 8).

In this chapter, I focus on the recent contributions Mexicans have made to the state's economic growth as residential construction workers and the context in which they work, specifically in a business-friendly state with low union density, under-resourced and insufficiently staffed government enforcement agencies, and strong anti-immigrant sentiments. Through the stories of five workers, I highlight their recruitment and integration into the Arizona residential construction market from the 1980s through 2008, when their labor yielded significant profits for their employers. I then highlight how, at the onset of the 2008 economic crisis, business owners forced these same workers to absorb many of the risks and costs of the crisis in violation of numerous employment laws and by breaching contracts. To survive, workers assumed the flexibility imposed in order to work and earn some compensation.

This chapter is divided into six sections. First, I present an overview of Arizona's economy and the health of the construction industry between 2000 and 2008, highlighting the fluctuating housing demand that Mexican labor met. Section two explores how Mexican workers became over-represented within the construction industry and employers' efforts to informalize the market which, coupled with low union density and lack of government enforcement, has corroded industry standards. In section three, I focus on structural and microlevel employer strategies to steal wages and Arizona's enforcement efforts, and in section four, I look at the shifting perception of Mexican workers amidst the recession and at a time of increasing anti-immigrant sentiments. Section five is dedicated to an explanation of my data collection and an introduction to the study participants. The last section is devoted to the stories and work experiences of five Mexican construction workers, the wage theft schemes to which they were subjected, and their survival of the recession and political rejection.

ARIZONA'S ECONOMY AND THE CONSTRUCTION INDUSTRY, 2000–2008

Since 1987, Arizona's economy has largely shifted away from agriculture and mining to expand in industries like retail, manufacturing, transportation, public utility, services, and trade that cater to and facilitate the continued increase of its growing population (Hogan 2014). Between 1987 and 2008, Arizona's population exploded, nearly doubling from 3.4 million to 6.6 million at an average growth rate triple that of the growth rate nationwide (ibid., 3). Strong economic growth was inevitable given the large population influx, which created a demand for infrastructure construction, home building, home remodeling, and manufactured housing as well as construction workers. The population growth was supported by strong growth in manufacturing and exports, which led to higher spending and lower interest rates (ibid.).

Highly profitable, construction and real estate became the foundation for Arizona's economy like in other Sunbelt states, resulting in low industrial diversity. Overreliance upon construction and real estate is dangerous given their highly cyclical and volatile nature; also, they add low- to average-paying jobs and depend heavily upon migration, business growth, and the cost and availability of financing (ibid., 16). Timothy Hogan describes a construction and real-estate-reliant economy as "resembl[ing] the driver of a car that either has his/her foot pushing the accelerator to the floor or is stomping on the brake pedal [*sic*] with both feet. It usually ranks first or second in job or income growth during its booms, but it is down near the bottom of the rankings during its busts" (ibid.).

The impact of the 2001 recession on Arizona was small when compared to the nation. Though the recession was felt in the manufacturing, commercial construction, and business service sectors as well as the tourism and airline industry after September 11, 2001, residential construction and home sales did not drop off (ibid., 20).

The home-building momentum was sustained by out-of-state investors who, after the stock market collapsed at the beginning of the decade, withdrew their stocks, pouring money into housing in the Sunbelt region. In fact, total employment grew 1 percent compared to the national average of .1 percent, and only four of twenty sectors saw job loss (Hogan 2014). In 2001 construction accounted for 7.3 percent of Arizona's employment, compared to the national level of 5.1 percent, and 5.9 percent of the GDP compared to 4.7 percent nationwide (Economy.com 2002, 7).

Arizona's real estate mega boom lasted from 2002 through 2007. Stimulus money through the Federal Reserve monetary program coupled with low interest rates flooded the market with liquidity. Between 3,000 and 8,500 new single-family housing units were authorized for construction each month of June through October every year between 2001 and 2008 in the state (Vest 2000, 2002, 2003, 2004, 2005, 2006a, 2006b, 2007, 2008). Arizona was the fifth fastest-growing state at 27.1 percent compared to the national average of 14.2 percent. This population growth kept single- and multi-family home building near record levels and construction payrolls grew as construction trades employment increased at two times greater than the population growth rate of the past decade, accounting for 9 percent of statewide employment in 2003 (Poole et al. 2005, 5). In 2004 nearly one in eleven Arizona jobs were found in this billion-dollar industry, and 84 percent were in Phoenix and Tucson (Poole et al. 2005).

In 2006 the Arizona Department of Economic Security released its new population projections. Rather than assume the boom would be short-lived, it projected growth remaining at boom levels over the next couple decades through the 2010s and 2020s. In fact, its estimate for population change was 47 percent too high between 2000 and 2010, and the actual population growth in the 2000s was 15 percent less than in the 1990s (Rex 2013, 3). Eager to join in on the profitable boom and hoping the population would continue growing to sustain high home-building levels, construction companies continued hiring. At the same time, in 2006, the U.S. economy and real estate began losing steam and home building fell to pre-2001 levels. As a result, Arizona's recession started in September 2007, three months ahead of the rest of the country. As interest rates rose, homeowners were not able to pay their mortgages; delinquencies and foreclosures increased and the subprime loan industry collapsed in 2007.

Among the fastest to grow, Arizona was among the fastest to drop, and it fell hard. The national average for job loss was 3.4 percent between 2007 and 2009, and Arizona outpaced the nation in job loss at 7.1 percent (Hoffman and Rex 2011, 13). Fifty percent of job loss was in the construction industry, followed by a 20 percent loss in manufacturing jobs (Arizona Department of Economic Security 2012, 8). Arizona's economic structure was not designed to improve prosperity and productivity for average people as would be evidenced by solid measures such as per capita personal income or earnings per employee (Hoffman and Rex 2011, 12). Aggregate statistics were strong but masked distribution issues like wage inequality. In fact, between 1970 and 2003, Arizona ranked forty-six out of fifty for real per capita personal income growth at 1.8 percent per year despite the fact that the state was ranked second in the nation for real aggregate personal income (Hogan 2014, 5). In the years following the 2006 peak, workers saw a decline in real wages and were faced with high debt burdens; homeowners and prospective buyers saw higher credit restrictions and reductions in mortgage lending; unemployment rates rose to a fourteen-year high of 6.5 percent; and economists warned of the lowest readings of consumer confidence since the early 1990s. A 2009 University of Arizona study showed home building dropped to its lowest level since 1945, new housing unit construction declined by nearly two-thirds from its peak, and building permits fell 56 percent since 2005 (Vest 2009).

In the 1990s and through 2007, Arizona grew and prospered in large part because of Mexican labor in construction. Viewing Mexicans as an elastic supply of labor, capitalist investors, the state, and construction employers recruited them, demanding access to Mexican workers' bodies, control over their wages and working conditions, mobility, and high productivity in order to maximize capital accumulation and create optimal conditions for the housing boom. In 2008 and through the bust, Mexicans softened Arizona's fall. When the housing bubble burst, the same actors demanded that Mexican workers either disappear completely or live in the shadows, absorbing the cost of the risks capitalists took, unable to draw from the system they had paid into and helped build. Forced to scrape together what they needed to survive without state assistance, Mexicans waited out the recession until their labor was needed again. Even whilst unseen during the recession, the general public and state actors blamed the presence of Mexican workers for the state of the economy. It is at this juncture, in 2008, that I interviewed the workers whose labor experiences in Arizona's construction industry are told and analyzed in this chapter.

DEFECTS IN ARIZONA'S CONSTRUCTION INDUSTRY

Nationwide, the construction industry has been under the investigation of the U.S. Department of Labor (DOL) since 2009 for prevalent wage, hour, and health and safety violations, warranting a multiyear enforcement initiative focused on the industry (U.S. Department of Labor 2014). Current and past priorities, as outlined in the DOL's strategic plans, have focused on "vulnerable workers": those who are "at risk of exploitation at work, such as workers who are reluctant to complain when they are subject to violations for fear of retaliation," and those employed in high-risk and fissured industries, such as agriculture, janitorial, construction, and hotel/motel industries (U.S. Department of Labor 2010b, 18).[3] In all areas of compliance, the construction industry needs great improvement. The construction industry accounted for 8 percent of the Wage and Hour Division's (Wage and Hour) investigations between 1998 and 2008, although approximately 5 percent of people were employed in construction (Weil 2010, 8).

Before discussing conditions in the construction industry, let us look first at why Mexican and foreign-born workers are overrepresented within it. As described in this anthology's prologue and chapter 1, Mexicans have constituted an elastic supply of labor—ever accessible, flexible in terms of the conditions in and wages for which they work, and highly productive—making them the preferred workforce in Arizona's construction industry for decades. For example, Balderrama and Rodríguez (1995) document that government officials, tasked with locating Mexicans in Southern California amid the Mexican repatriation of the 1930s, found many of them on construction sites.

What has changed is that greater numbers of foreign-born Mexicans are found in both commercial and residential construction and in a wider variety of trades due to an exodus of domestic workers from the industry for reasons that will be outlined here. First, Parrado and Kandel's (2008) research shows that as education levels rise among the general population and, consequently, new employment opportunities become available, domestic workers are not choosing to labor in the construction industry, where work is largely unstable and seasonal and where job quality, wages, and benefits have declined over the years. Such decline is an intended consequence of a decades-long orchestration by the state and employers to meet the surging demand for cheap labor with workers known to and recruited because they accept the low wages and poor working conditions inherent to flexible labor regimes. The increasing incorporation of Hispanic workers into the industry in both traditional and metropolitan magnet areas has kept labor standards low, pushing out domestic workers (ibid.). This trend is further facilitated by the shift away from union to nonunion work in Arizona, effectively translating to fewer benefits, lower pay, and less oversight of labor practices (Stepick et al. 1994; Northrup 1990).

Second, industry pay in Arizona is below average. The Arizona Department of Commerce reported that in 2003, Arizona's wages were 84 percent of the national average (Poole et al. 2005). Carpentry, the largest employing occupation, falls into the median wage range, with entry-level pay around $9.50 per hour or $19,748 annually, and a median wage of $31,641 annually. The second largest occupation—laborers—falls within the lower wage range, averaging a median wage of $21,002 annually. Wages for helpers are especially low—approximately 72–77 percent below the national average wage (ibid). Worse still, Latinos' hourly wage rates are lower than their non-Latino counterparts in the western United States by ninety-three cents an hour and increase at slower rates per year of work experience (Goodrum 2004); in fact, despite average wage growth for U.S.-born workers, for foreign-born Latinos, the median wage has actually declined.

Third, the stigma, danger, risk, and discomfort involved in manual, outdoor labor also makes construction work less appealing (Poole et al. 2005). Exposing workers to greater occupational safety risks than most other workers—the 2002 DOL's Bureau of Labor Statistics data shows that the rate of work-related injuries for construction workers was one-third higher than the mean rate for all private industries. Because companies cannot outsource construction work nor pay the labor costs of an increasingly more educated domestic population, they utilize flexible labor regimes, which favor vulnerable workers, for both cost savings and profit maximization (Ong 1991; Parrado and Kandel 2008), and damage the integrity and health of the industry.

Though nonunion workers generally have no job security and little bargaining power, scholars (Bernhardt et al. 2008; Bernhardt et al. 2009) generally acknowledge and refer to *vulnerable workers* as women, foreign-born migrants, undocumented migrants, and those with lower levels of education, English fluency, and job tenure. Structural disadvantages and fear drive these workers to endure low pay and substandard working conditions and make claims-making more difficult when their rights are violated (De Castro et al. 2006; Sanidad 2011; Bernhardt et al. 2009; Foo 1994; Gammage 2008). Consequently, the business practices of the companies for which they work go unreported and unchecked, allowing employers to minimize industry standards and ignore the laws. Emboldened by anti-immigrant sentiments, companies need not fear oversight or sanctions, given low union density nationwide, the lack of political will to regulate business or interfere with the interests of business owners, and the exhaustion of government resources for enforcement efforts. The DOL is overextended and underfunded, relying on 50 percent fewer investigators than it did when it was created in 1941, despite a 900 percent increase in the size of the U.S. workforce (Bobo 2009, 121). Specifically, in 1941 there were 1,769 Wage and Hour investigators who covered 360,000 employers nationwide; in 2007 just 750 Wage and Hour investigators were responsible for keeping 7 million employers in compliance (ibid.). Given this reality, independent investigations are rare unless part of a targeted initiative, leaving those workers who do not file a claim unprotected.

The workers' stories shared herein exemplify Avirgan, Bivens, and Gammage's (2005) structuralist explanation for the growth and existence of unregulated work; "unregulated work is generated by capitalist strategies to keep labor costs low" (Bernhardt et al. 2008, 4). Structuralist theories account for the different players in society and how each contributes to the deregulation of work. In describing the gloves-off economy—"a set of employer strategies and practices that either evade or outright violate the core laws and standards that govern job quality in the U.S."—and the fall of work regulation, Annette Bernhardt and collaborators (ibid., 2, 12–14) explore how labor cost reduction progressed along four axes:

> Business has become less inclined toward self-regulation, government regulation of business has increasingly gone unenforced, the decline in unions has limited civil society regulation of business, and government has reduced the social safety net and adopted policies that expand the group of vulnerable workers.

This work focuses on the shift away from "self-regulation" of business and the government's complicity in the degradation of labor standards. It is worth mentioning here the role of unions and public benefits in this context. First, without equivalent spending cuts, Arizona slashed taxes, including significant business tax cuts in 2005 and across-the-board tax reductions in 2007 and 2008 (Hoffman and Rex 2008, 4). With less tax revenue the state has less purchasing power to fund schools, construction, and a public safety net (Hansen 2014). Rather than rely on public funds, the poor are "encouraged" to work, often in low-wage jobs. Consequently and by design, Arizona businesses have easy access to low-wage workers, which when coupled with the low business tax and business-friendly laws, attracts more businesses to the state (U.S. Department of Labor 2010a).

Unions are another "player" in the deregulation of work; their lack of strength and membership in Arizona has rendered the workforce's power to regulate employer business practices near nonexistent. Unions play a significant role in negotiating and improving wages, hours, and working conditions above the minimum standards set by the legislature, enforcing state and federal laws, and lobbying for and organizing around worker protections.

Due to a Republican-controlled legislature, unions have been weak in Arizona since the passage of the right-to-work law in 1946.[4] According to the Bureau of Labor Statistics, between 2004 and 2010, a range of 6.3 percent to 8.8 percent of workers were represented by unions in Arizona (2013). Largely excluded from those numbers are workers found in the informal market, in residential construction, and undocumented workers generally. Without unions to represent them, workers are left to rely upon the state and each employer to regulate and enforce the laws, leaving many vulnerable and without power to challenge their employer's business practices.

In the context of this business-friendly, low-union-density state, I study two players in the deregulation of work and specifically the wage-theft phenomenon: construction contractors and the state labor enforcement agency. A pioneer of wage-theft research, Kim Bobo (2009, 7) defines it as the deprivation of legally mandated wages to workers through employment law violations. She and others have focused on the employee's experience with wage theft. My work includes the stories of contractors (one legitimate independent contractor and two misclassified contractors) because their relationship to the business owners who steal from them, in terms of power, is as distant as the employees' whose stories are told here. The contractors similarly had little power or leverage to enforce their rights (either under the law or as provided by contract) through the court system, leaving them in a similarly vulnerable and powerless position in relation to those procuring their work. To augment and extend the applicability of wage theft to include contractors, I borrow from academics (Lambert 2008; Ong 1991; Sassen-Koob 1988, 1989; Zlolniski 2006) who explore how migrants and other vulnerable workers sustain flexible labor regimes that allow procurers of labor, such as a homeowners, business owners, or other persons that contract work from another person, to control work without the risk or liability.

Aihwa Ong (1991) characterizes such flexible labor regimes as those that deregulate work and work relationships, creating systems that operate outside of traditional models and maximize profits. In her research, Susan Lambert (2008, 1203) observed employers benefiting from flexible labor regimes by "readily adjust[ing] the number of employees and their work hours" to accommodate the ebbs and flows of the market and company needs. Ong's and Lambert's work reinforce and validate my study participants' experiences and analysis of their own work life experiences. Positioned as an elastic supply of labor, they must be willing to work whenever called upon without the promise of stable work or pay, regardless of their relation to power as a contractor or employee. Like my study participants, Mexican workers assume risk, liability, and instability to meet the needs of the person or entity willing to provide them with work and, as the need for them and their labor retracts, they are marginalized and let go, expected to disappear.

The line between the formal and informal economy is blurred and fluid as similar illegal and legal strategies for cost reduction and flexible labor strategies are found in both. Saskia Sassen-Koob (1989, 71) describes the informal economy as distinct from the formal in that it is the space where exploitative employers escape the state's watchful eye thereby able to reduce labor and production costs and sell licit goods and services "outside the regulatory apparatus covering zoning, tax, health and safety, minimum wage laws, and other types of standards" (Sassen-Koob 1988, 288; see also Fernández-Kelly 1984). My study participants' work experiences, however, highlight that employers within the formal economy similarly escape regulation and utilize comparable cost-reducing strategies that result in worker exploitation. In contrast, Christian Zlolniski's (2006) work shows how the two economies are married. He highlights how the informal economy, which he describes as "those income-generating activities that escape the control of the state and local government authorities," is an integral part of the larger economy (Zlolniski 2006, 73). Low-wage workers within the formal economy must rely upon their survival strategies and also upon the existence of an informal economy where they earn supplemental wages and access lower-cost goods and services produced within the informal economy for their own consumption (ibid., 75). Because employers in the formal economy externalize the social costs of reproduction and provide little by way of wages and benefits to its low-skilled workers, the informal economy necessarily must coexist with the formal economy. From a low-wage workers' perspective, there is little difference between their treatment and pay; in the informal economy they have little or no enforceable rights, and in the formal economy their rights are not enforced.

Misclassification of workers is a structural effort to more permanently move workers outside the scope of government regulation. It occurs when an employer erroneously treats or classifies an employee as an independent contractor for tax, benefit, and pay purposes. In mimicking a contractor-subcontractor relationship, the employers escape requirements for paying minimum and overtime wages and toward social security taxes and providing workers' compensation, safety training, and equipment, along with other legally mandated guarantees and protections.[5] In addition to not receiving guaranteed protections, these misclassified contractors must assume the costs of their own safety, wages, benefits, and materials in order to work, without having power or control over their pay, work conditions, schedules, or how the job is executed.

Another similarity between work experiences in the formal and informal economies is the expectation that workers will assume costs of social reproduction. Externalizing business costs onto workers is a popular strategy for businesses to reduce their own expenses, relying upon workers' flexibility, powerlessness, and an inability to change the conditions of their labor.

As Michael Burawoy (1976) has found, rather than rely upon compensation from their employers to maintain a household and provide their families with medical care, food, education, and housing, workers must utilize survival strategies to earn additional income or cut personal expenses. Saskia Sassen-Koob (1988, 2) similarly found that employers depend upon and abuse immigrants' propensity to replicate survival strategies typical of their home countries to run their businesses. Both Burawoy's and Sassen-Koob's findings play out in the work experiences of my study participants who, when denied their wages, found side jobs or borrowed money from friends or family to make ends meet, or the ends did not meet and they simply did without staple food items, stable housing, or services like their telephone or car (For a larger discussion of the survival strategies of Mexican laborers in Arizona who have been subjected to wage theft and other abusive business practices, see Sanidad 2011).

The ease with which the exploitative labor systems are created and re-created can, in part, be explained by the lack of unions in the context of a Republican-controlled, business-friendly state; however, the analysis is not complete without understanding the laxity of the state in interfering with capital accumulation and how it contributes to the presence and prominence of abusive employer business practices.

The focus of my work is on residential construction because it represents between 55 to 65 percent of the construction awards in Arizona (Vest 2000, 2002, 2003). In part, residential construction is less regulated than commercial and industrial contracts because the latter have higher values and higher investments requiring increased regulation, oversight, and accountability. Another contributing factor is that single-family home remodeling and new construction require less technical skill, knowledge of information and communications technology, formal training, and experience (Martín and Whitlow 2012) and, because it is less regulated, draws an overrepresented number of Latinos and foreign-born workers. The demand for cheap housing is met by the maintenance of an exploitable workforce in the formal and informal markets.

An emerging trend reported in Arizona is the increasing prevalence of brazen, noncompliant contractors providing services within commercial and new residential construction, which traditionally are highly regulated (ABC15 News; Stone 2015). More contractors are slashing their overhead costs and prices by contracting work out to subcontractors who work without proper licensure, insurance, or bonds, and who do not pay the appropriate taxes or comply with applicable employment laws. This cost-reducing strategy gives legitimate businesses that comply with the laws an unfair disadvantage in the market, affecting work standards, the viability of compliant businesses, and public coffers.

Latino workers' assumption of labor production costs through participation in flexible labor regimes makes them "a buffer to economic downturns" (Haq 2010). A provocative example of how Mexicans serve as a buffer between the recession and the average American is that in Tucson where, by locals' estimates, undocumented workers comprise 50 percent of construction workers (Stauffer 2006), housing prices are held down by as much as $38,000 due to the lower wages paid to undocumented laborers (McCombs and Stauffer 2006a, 1; McCombs 2006; McCombs and Stauffer 2006b). One contractor conceded: "eliminating the illegal work force would mean higher pay for legal workers . . . [pushing] up home prices . . . [and driving] down profit margins" under 10 percent, which would force some contractors to leave the industry all together (Stauffer 2006). Quite literally, the cost of labor and social reproduction has been externalized and placed on the worker.

A well-known example of Latino participation in flexible labor regimes on a micro level is in the form of day labor. In May 2006 Jacob Fisher (2006) surveyed 105 day laborers in the Phoenix metropolitan area—91 percent were men, 80 percent were under 40 years old and had less than eight years of formal education, and 99 percent were not U.S. citizens. He found that 69 percent of them worked in construction, most specifically as construction laborers, painters, roofers, and drywall installers, and that

30.9 percent had been hired by contractors and subcontractors to work on construction sites (ibid., 101). Forty percent of those surveyed experienced wage theft and 43 percent were paid less than the amount for which they had agreed to work (ibid., 104). Valenzuela and collaborators (2006, i–ii) found similar exploitative practices against day laborers nationwide in their study of 2,600 day laborers; importantly, 43 percent of workers surveyed were hired by construction contractors and performed work as construction laborers, gardeners/landscapers, painters, roofers, and drywall installers. Perhaps not surprisingly, almost half of day laborers had been denied their wages for work completed during the two months prior to the survey (ibid., 14).

The structural disadvantages and the costs assumed by low-wage Mexican workers directly correlate with the disproportionate burden they shoulder through unpaid wages, higher workloads, lower workplace standards and safety measures, discrimination, and the accompanying emotional, familial, and physical health issues (Sanidad 2011). Arguably, this burden is not accidental. The reliance on Mexican workers and their labor without regard to their social, financial, emotional, familial, and physical well-being is nothing short of a biopolitical statement of the value of their lives. In studying California farm laborers and South African immigrant mine workers, Burawoy (1976) concludes that the reproduction of our labor system and "our" profits rely upon the powerlessness and the limitations of vulnerable workers to influence the systems that oppress them. This analysis similarly applies to the context of Arizona's residential construction industry.

WAGE THEFT IN ARIZONA CONSTRUCTION AND GOVERNMENT COMPLICITY

Although some employers are confused about their obligations under the law and which laws apply to them, wage theft is largely intentional, executed either by "directly putting in place systems and approaches for stealing wages or by indirectly failing to install systems to prevent wage theft" (Bobo 2009, 23). The law is violated in many ways. Some employers pay less than the applicable minimum wage or engage in business practices that bring workers' wages under the minimum wage, such as paying nonexempt workers a set salary for all hours worked, taking illegal deductions from their paychecks, paying by the day or by the job, failing to pay tips or commission, denying time-and-a-half pay for overtime hours, or not paying them for all hours worked (such as during lunch periods or for pre- and post-shift work). Other employers pay workers with checks that bounce or do not pay them at all.

Fissuring is another pervasive structural strategy for stealing from workers through which a company's services are externalized to vendors, subcontractors, and franchises for a fee to minimize costs. Effectively, the strategy confuses who is ultimately responsible for the legal obligations to workers, such as paying them the minimum wage. Fissuring within the residential construction industry resulted in 72.2 percent noncompliance with paying all hours worked (off-the-clock violations), 70.5 percent noncompliance with overtime regulations, and 12.7 percent noncompliance with minimum wage requirements in 2009 (Bernhardt 2009; Weil 2011).

As an intentional economic decision and strategy, wage theft does not just occur during bad economic times, though its consequences and workers' resistance against it are more pronounced during recessions. Contractors wanting to reduce costs and increase profits do not cut from fixed expenses like rent, electricity, and material, because—as opposed to labor—if they do not pay in full, they lose the service or product. Labor costs are viewed as flexible and negotiable as business owners have continued to rely upon workers who will work for less compensation and are less likely to challenge unfair business practices.

The Labor Department of the Industrial Commission of Arizona (the Department) was established in 1925 as the workers' compensation system, and expanded in the 1970s to include enforcement of occupational safety and health, youth employment laws, and state wage laws, among other things. The Department enforces state wage payment laws by investigating workers' claims that allege minimum-wage violations or nonpayment of wages under $2,500 in unpaid vacation, commissions, tips, mileage, and unauthorized deductions.[6] The Department has jurisdiction over Arizona employers which, according to the U.S. Census, numbered 97,758 in 2003 and 102,200 by 2010. Between 2005 and 2010, the Department investigated an average of 2,896 wage-theft claims with the highest number, 3,295, being investigated in 2008 as construction work was slowing and less profitable (Arizona Industrial Commission 2007, 2008, 2009, 2010, 2011, 2012, 2013, 2014).

Karen Axsom, then-interim director of the Department, shared that the largest percentage of claims arise from the construction industry and in the form of unpaid last paychecks (Axsom 2012). She further commented that by 2012, with little construction underway, wage claims were the lowest they had been in years. During the recession, larger numbers of unpaid wage claims were the result of business closures and fewer employers were paying the claimants after a determination was made in the claimants' favor. Frequently, employers explained to her: "Yes, I owe these people, but I'm a subcontractor and the contractor owes me. I'll pay them as soon as I can." Anecdotal evidence reveals that the majority of claimants are Spanish speakers and, in Axsom's opinion, fewer claims are received than would be representative of the wage-theft problem because of fear of retaliation (ibid.).

In the midst of the recession and in the context of increasingly fewer workers receiving their wages, minimum-wage complaints have remained shockingly low in the state. In 2007 only twenty-one minimum-wage claims were filed, five of which were resolved. In 2010, 2011, and 2012, an average of 27.5 complaints were filed, and as many as fifteen were resolved (Arizona Industrial Commission 2010, 2011, 2012). The years 2008 and 2009 saw the highest numbers of complaints filed—at fifty-eight and eighty-three, respectively—commensurate with the lowest home-building rates and highest construction job loss. I posit that the increase in claims can be explained by either an increase in wage theft or, faced with job loss and already experiencing nonpayment of wages, fewer workers feared retaliation.

The low numbers of minimum-wage complaints are alarming principally because they elucidate how infrequently the state enforces its wage-payment laws both because workers are not reporting wage theft and independent audits are not conducted. To put the enforcement in perspective to the size of the problem, I compare Phoenix, the sixth largest city in the nation, to the three largest U.S. cities—Chicago, Los Angeles, and New York City—where researchers found that 26 percent of workers were paid less than the minimum wage and 60 percent of those workers were underpaid by more than one dollar per hour (Bernhardt et al. 2009, 2).

The state fails to provide adequate protections for workers against wage theft. The low number of complaints can, in part, be explained by the fact that only the wage claim form (for nonpayment under $2,500) can be found online or at the Labor Department office, but the minimum-wage claim form is not available publicly. Further, the department is underfunded and understaffed. From 2006 through 2011, the department expended only $750,000 annually compared to its counterpart in Connecticut, a state responsible for enforcement over a comparable number of employees and workplaces, which expended approximately $3 million annually and had thirty investigators (Meyer and Greenleaf 2011, 44–61, 74). What is more, at the time of the interview, the department had only twelve full-time employees (ibid., 73), fewer than three of whom were bilingual investigators in its Phoenix office, which serves over two million people in northern Arizona (Axsom 2012). The lack of resources also hinders the department from engaging in meaningful outreach efforts to employers, churches, and employee and advocacy organizations (Meyer and Greenleaf 2011, 155) and updating its antiquated and corrupted computer system, which could facilitate employer tracking and compliance efforts (Axsom 2012).

Perhaps what is most alarming is how the department defines a successful investigation. Article 10 of the Arizona Administrative Code sets forth statutory time frames in which the wage-claim investigation must be processed. A successful investigation is that which meets the statutory deadline; therefore, the department is quick to close claims to meet its numbers. According to data provided in response to a record request, between July 2008 and June 2012, 103 claims were closed due to employer bankruptcy, 153 claims were closed for having "no employer," 332 claims could not be resolved as there were disputed facts, and 152 were closed because the worker was allegedly an independent contractor. The department has no further role in a claim after it has been closed, and the worker is left to find an attorney and sue in court. Success is not measured in a meaningful way, like the dollar amount of back pay collected or the number of repeat offenders whose business practices were corrected.

Given the stated expectations of and goal for the Labor Department, it is easy to see how the state re-creates oppressive labor systems as Burawoy suggests. Given the department is understaffed and under-resourced, has no authority to enforce its determinations, and that the statutory focus is on procedural timelines rather than meaningful outcomes or quality of investigations, it is clear the agency is not equipped or meant to prevent, deter, or meaningfully correct wage-theft abuse.[7]

SHIFTING PERCEPTIONS OF MEXICAN WORKERS: THE IMPACT OF POLITICS ON WORK STANDARDS

During the first half of the decade, the demand for the construction of homes, commercial buildings, roads, universities, schools, highways, and other facilities created a high demand for Mexican workers who were key to the economic growth. While in heavy demand, Mexican migrant labor participation was welcomed yet their civic, social, and political participation was rejected and their rights largely unprotected. As the economy declined, Mexican migrant workers were blamed for "stealing jobs" and utilizing public benefits at the same time that employers (who create financial instability for families by failing to comply with even minimum legal standards) and the health of their business remain a top priority for the state.

The blame for the economic downfall was not solely directed at undocumented Mexican migrants, explains local civil rights attorney Daniel Ortega.

> The hostility has spilled over to citizens in the form of racial profiling, which is occurring at all levels, whether it involves getting services or public benefits, finding a job or in areas of law enforcement. The color of your skin and how you look now make [Latinos] suspect. People are afraid of their government. Employers are afraid to offer jobs. We are not only suspect, but we have to be afraid of being suspected [of violating the law], even if we've done nothing wrong. (Arizona Latino Research Enterprise 2009)

The hostility, the wave of anti-immigrant laws in the early 1990s and 2000s, and the loss of jobs in construction and tourism industries have resulted in some migration to nearby states (González 2012; Huffington Post 2012). Yet, those who stay remain subjected to systemic violence within the construction industry and social spaces placing undue and disproportionate burden on Mexicans and their families as Mexicans physically bear the weight of the state's growth on their backs and financially bear the costs of recession. What is worse, their employers face no consequences for widespread abuse and maltreatment of Mexican workers and are not deterred from repeating their offenses.

The concept of Mexicans "belonging" is still rejected and questioned by white America, which partly explains the total disregard for workers' well-being, health, and stability, as evidenced by the workers' stories of treatment as second-class citizens without rights. It is at the nexus of Arizona's recession and the acrimonious political climate that I examine the labor experiences of those Mexican construction workers who stayed in Arizona.

METHODOLOGY AND INTRODUCTION TO ARIZONA'S WORKERS

My interest in the labor experiences of Mexican workers developed through exposure to workers' rights issues at the Arizona Worker Rights Center (WRC), a Phoenix affiliate of the Interfaith Worker Justice network (Téllez et al. 2011, 145). The center was opened in 2008 in response to the harsh anti-immigrant climate, in acknowledgment of Arizona's inadequate enforcement of workers' rights and minimum legal standards, and in the interest of developing workers' leadership and knowledge base. Due to structural obstacles to accessing recourse, such as low English proficiency, low literacy rates, and nativism, the center has primarily served low-wage earning Mexican migrants, providing case management, labor rights trainings, and opportunities for political conscientization and leadership development (García 2014; Téllez et al. 2011). Study participants sought out services in 2008 and 2009, and I worked as their advocate to document labor rights violations and support them in resolving their wage-theft cases.

Data was collected between March and November 2010 as part of a larger project that explored the labor experiences of fourteen low-wage Mexican workers in various Phoenix industries who were being affected by the passage and implementation of Arizona's SB 1070 (Sanidad 2011).[8] In this chapter, I analyze interviews of five construction workers from the initial study to more narrowly explore the work experiences of Mexican contractors and employees within the increasingly deregulated construction industry. A distinction is necessarily made between contractors and employees because they have different rights, protections, and recourse, which are governed by distinct laws, namely employment law and contract law. A distinction is also made between documented and undocumented migrants and citizens, not because their status affects their rights under applicable employment laws, but because status affects their vulnerability and willingness to challenge abuses and seek recourse when their rights are violated.

The lives and experiences of five Mexican, male construction workers provide profound insight into Arizona's residential construction industry and how county, state, and federal politics, the economy, and anti-immigrant sentiments shape those experiences at the local level. (Though instructive, I do not assert that these participants and their experiences are representative of all Mexicans or all construction workers in Arizona.) Regardless of their distinct professional backgrounds, training, and goals, all were welcomed into the construction industry as causal labor, contractors, and employees because of their willingness to work hard and be flexible with their payments, hours, and working conditions. To show the diversity among them and the circumstances that shape each of their stories, I introduce them briefly here.[9]

Juan migrated from Mexico in 2002 with two friends from his hometown with whom he continues to live in Phoenix. Through his friends' connections, they quickly found construction work and housing, which was facilitated by his ability to speak and understand about 50 percent of English. With an equivalent of a junior high education, Juan had worked in various industries in Mexico, but in the United States, he became an adept, highly trained, and in-demand flooring installer. Attuned to the political climate, Juan was informed of his civil and workplace rights from listening to Spanish-language radio programs, participating in activities at nonprofit, community-based organizations, and watching the news.

Originally from Chihuahua, Mexico, Diego is an industrial engineer who had obtained a university degree and licensure in Mexico and was working in the maquiladora industry. When the maquiladora closed, he worked various other jobs to earn an income, including as a cowboy and a painter. He and his family traveled to Phoenix on tourist visas in 1999 and settled near his brother. Using their visas, they were able to secure Arizona driver's licenses. In Phoenix he was employed and trained by a plumber who fraudulently assigned him an Individual Taxpayer Identification Number (ITIN), a nine-digit IRS-generated tax-processing number.[10] His visa had expired by the time he decided to open his own company; however, with his driver's license and ITIN, he obtained a valid contractor's license, and in 2005 he started his own plumbing business. He lives with his wife, also a small-business owner, and their three children in a home they recently purchased.

Jorge, a fifty-three-year-old Mexican American, was born in Laredo, Texas, and lived in Michigan for thirty years before moving to Phoenix with his second wife. He proudly put his kids through college, and now lives alone in a mobile home in Phoenix. Although Jorge himself did not graduate from high school, he has earned certification in auto mechanics and heavy-equipment operating and has work experience as an electrician, plumber, and block and paver installer. Several years ago he started his own stone-paver installation company, though he does not have a contractor's license. He initially went to the WRC to translate for an undocumented friend whose wages were stolen and returned when he was not paid in full for a paver job he completed.

Trained as an agricultural engineer in Mexico, Marco immigrated, without authorization, to the United States seven years ago with his wife, after his brother told him he could earn more money as a construction worker in the United States. Now with two U.S.-born children who have dual citizenship, his family is of mixed immigration status. Both he and his wife support their growing family—he with the temporary work he finds in drywall installation, remodeling, framing, or concrete—his wife with consistent part-time work in a fast-food restaurant. Marco claims he can speak and understand about 10 percent of English and admits initially he only understood technical English terms for plant biology, diseases, and care due to his university training. His English has not improved much, as he has worked solely with other Spanish speakers.

A migrant from Leon, Guanajuato, Mexico, Alfonso traveled to the United States in 1989, shortly after the 1986 Immigration Reform and Control Act was passed, which granted amnesty to migrants between the years 1987 and 1988. He has "followed the work," laboring in both agriculture and residential construction and living in five states: North Carolina, Kentucky, Arizona, California, and Wyoming. He considered moving to a sixth state after SB 1070 passed. Alfonso attended elementary school in Mexico and says he understands about 35 percent of English. He is the sole provider for his wife, an undocumented migrant, and their six U.S.-born children, supporting them with his earnings from construction and remodeling work.

THE GLOVES-OFF ECONOMY, FLEXIBLE LABOR, AND COST EXTERNALIZATION

None of the five workers initially entered into construction work as a career. Rather, they responded to the labor needs of the Phoenix market, enticed onto job sites and into private homes to labor at a time when construction work was stable and they were welcomed. Each of them secured constant work for decent pay through word of mouth, and few questions were asked regarding experience or work authorization. Reflecting on his early experiences finding work in the industry, Marco reasoned:

> Before, since there was a high demand for construction, the construction companies needed labor . . . [and they] opted for convenience. It is convenient for [the contractors]

> to not verify the legal status of workers [because they] employ Latino people who you can pay less and who will sacrifice more to work.

Through various workplace experiences, the five workers learned that employment verification and licensing requirements were not the only requirements contractors ignored. Companies were also lax on paying minimum wage and overtime, making payments on the designated payday, providing workers' compensation after workplace accidents, and adhering to health and safety regulations. Contract law was similarly ignored as written and oral agreements between contractors were not respected nor enforced.

> In the beginning . . . I worked comfortably with my boss. . . . Then suddenly he started falling behind. . . . When there wasn't enough money, he did not pay us. But when there was he would pay us everything he owed us. So that is how we went along, but we began to see that he would not finish one job or the other and the amount he owed us began increasing.

For much of his employment, Alfonso had been paid on time and in full. His employer, Mr. Reynolds, was the sole business owner of a remodeling company that worked without licensing, bonds, or permits in the informal economy. He secured jobs through word of mouth. For years they had worked together, Alfonso becoming like a son to Mr. Reynolds. So, when Mr. Reynolds told Alfonso that the homeowners were not paying him, preventing Mr. Reynolds from paying him, Alfonso continued working, understanding he would have to be flexible and "accommodating" with pay dates and pay amounts. Throughout his employment, Mr. Reynolds had Alfonso purchase tools, wood, or other supplies needed for projects, and reimbursed him; although if Alfonso needed safety equipment or water, he was to purchase his own. Alfonso eventually approached the homeowners directly to notify them that he had not been paid his wages or reimbursements as the contractor was waiting for their payments. Alarmed that Mr. Reynolds had pocketed their large payments without compensating Alfonso, the homeowners began working with Alfonso directly to finish the job and paid him directly.

"We were enduring our job for the money he owed us . . . the amount kept increasing until he was the one that left. We did not see him anymore." Alfonso attempted to track down Mr. Reynolds, calling and visiting his home to collect his wages with no success. On one occasion, when Alfonso did locate Mr. Reynolds, he denied owing Alfonso a dime.

The only one to work completely outside of all regulatory systems, Alfonso witnessed the ease with which his employer stopped paying him and disappeared. Left to regulate himself with no oversight, his employer simply chose not to comply with state or local laws, including those regulating the employee-employer relationship. His experiences of nonpayment and the expectation of flexibility as to pay dates and amounts are not dissimilar to those of Jorge, the misclassified contractor, or to the employees, leaving us to question the real difference between the "informal" and "formal" economies from the workers' perspective.

Jorge's experience as a misclassified contractor was perhaps most similar to Alfonso's in that he absorbed and became responsible for the costs of doing business. The business model of Creative Atmospheres, for which Jorge worked, was informalized by shifting from employing landscapers to contracting out all its jobs.

Jorge recounts that when he applied for employment with Creative Atmospheres, he learned that the company required applicants to become contractors. Each was required to take on additional work like a contractor—such as assembling and paying a crew of workers and filing for a trade name with the secretary of state; however, he would have no control over which jobs to accept or bidding prices like a contractor would. Proper licensure, insurance, or bonds were not required by Creative Atmospheres in order to work. Realizing that the business was "training all the crews to be subcontractors, so that [the company] wouldn't have all the responsibility or anything fall back on them," Jorge knew he was taking a risk, but work was slow and there were few options. The company transferred a large financial burden onto him. Jorge lost money when the cost of the projects exceeded the contract price. He fronted the costs for material, tools, and travel expenses out of his own pay, and he was on the hook for compliance with employment laws when he was not able to pay his crew members in full and on time.

Unlike a legitimately classified contractor, Jorge had no control over his project budgets, which forced him to work cheaply to stay within his budget, a trend that lowers wage standards and working conditions across the industry.

> The big companies and the general contractors knew how the economy was and that they could get just about anybody to do the work for cheap, next to nothing. Not only ourselves who aren't illegal, but the ones that are illegal are even cheaper because they have to eat too. All these general contractors were taking advantage of the situation. It makes it harder for us that are from here to even compete. I mean, $2.50 a square foot will give me enough to pay four workers plus myself and have a little bit of extra money . . . But, when somebody is bidding 70 cents to $1.25 [per square foot], I can't compete with those prices and everybody is doing it.

By being underpaid and assuming costs such as safety equipment, tools, and material, Alfonso and Jorge were forced to assume their own costs of social reproduction. With these businesses "freed" from their obligations to workers, compliant contractors—who pay taxes, licensing fees, insurance costs, and a fair wage—have a distinct market disadvantage which puts them out of business.

Regulated, licensed construction companies fall in and out of compliance, expecting flexibility from workers, as a way to maintain their businesses. Study participants shared a wide variety of experiences that constitute violations of law, including: denial of workers' compensation benefits, denial of water and safety equipment, racial discrimination, wage payments tendered from closed or insufficiently funded accounts, nonpayment of overtime pay, and nonpayment of minimum wage (most often experienced as incomplete or no payment for work performed). Of all these issues, the participants agree that the most significantly damaging were the pay-related issues.

As a pretext for not compensating them, Juan's, Alfonso's, and Marco's bosses attributed the nonpayment of wages to the failure of the labor procurers to pay. Irrespective of that fact, the employer has an obligation to pay his workers on time and in full; however, workers were especially accommodating of their employers, accepting lack of payment or late payments when they believed their employer was struggling financially. As the economic boom ended and businesses were less economically viable and stable, the nonpayment of wages and other law violations became more egregious and blatant.

Juan worked for two years as an hourly employee for a locally owned and licensed tile- and stone-installation company. One payday, Juan's boss told him that the homeowners of the house where Juan had been installing flooring had not yet paid him, so he, in turn, could not pay Juan. Encouraging Juan to finish the job, the employer promised that once the job was done, they would all get paid. Juan worked for five weeks without pay, at the end of which his employer owed him and his coworkers $3,600 each. After finishing the job, Juan confronted the homeowners about their failure to pay the company owner, complaining he and his coworkers had yet to be paid by the employer; he was dismayed to see copies of their voided checks, proving they had been paying the employer all along.

Marco's story highlights the extreme expectations for "labor flexibility." Understanding the company's hardship and feeling grateful for the work they received in the past, Marco and his nineteen coworkers were flexible with payment amounts and pay dates. The concrete company for which they worked lined up construction jobs, spending the money it received upfront to cover expenses on other projects, and when the time came to do the work they had postponed, there was no money for material or labor. Between March and October 2007 Marco was only paid $100 to $300 per week, though he was earning $500 per week. The employer gave each worker enough to survive and to keep coming back to work, each hoping for full payment at some point.

> If we had been receiving on average $500 per week, they were giving us half or a little less than half, 40 percent of our wages, to keep us more or less content, because they were saying there was no money and that they still had not received the pay from the project. . . . In the end, I calculated my hours, and they owed me $4,000 in wages. For the others, it varied. Two of my co-workers are owed almost $10,000 for that time. To the others, it was some $2,000, $4,000, $3,000.

When Marco and his coworkers sought assistance from the WRC in 2008 they were each owed between $2,000 and $10,000. Without his full wages, Marco was unable to sustain the simple life he had created with his wife and two children. His marriage and family life were quickly affected by the financial problems as the family absorbed the employer's costs by minimizing their own, only having enough for the most essential items. His physical and emotional health also deteriorated.

It is noteworthy that Juan and Marco never received overtime pay despite their entitlement to it, though this was never mentioned in their interviews. Ignoring ongoing violations for the opportunity to work was a trend across interviews, and speaks further to workers' flexibility in accepting substandard conditions and pay to be able to work and earn an income. Marco admitted he has come to expect lower pay for the same work that a documented migrant or citizen performs: "An immigrant perceives that you don't have the same rights as a citizen. So, as long as they pay me less, but always pay me, I do the work gladly."

Wage-theft research generally does not include the stories and experiences of contractors who, by definition, are the business owners in control of their own pay, schedules, and safety. Diego's story is included here because his immigration status, which affects how he is perceived and treated as well as his willingness to challenge others' power at the risk of exposing himself, equates him more with an employee in terms of his distance from power and control.

Diego's licensed and bonded plumbing business suffered at the onset of the recession, taking a hit when several of his clients breached their contracts by refusing to pay him for work performed and services rendered. One client had contracted him to install plumbing units in a shop being renovated into a hookah lounge. On-site, he met the contractors, at least one of whom was also undocumented, who were hired to complete the framing, drywall, and electricity. They had all negotiated verbal contracts with the owner. For eight units' worth of labor, materials, and fixtures, Diego typically charged $7,200, though he lowered his bid to $6,500 when the storeowner complained the price was too high. Because Diego had not requested any payment upfront which, like reducing contract bids, was becoming an expected accommodation in the industry during the recession, he began the job using material and revenue from other projects to start the work. As negotiated, once Diego completed half the project, he asked for the first payment. The owner told Diego he would receive his check by the following week, but weeks came and went before he received his first payment, which he later learned was written from a closed bank account and bounced. The owner hid from him and avoided his calls. Eventually, Diego located and confronted the owner, who begged him to finish the work and even bought him the supplies he would need to finish. Diego left the work 95 percent finished, never having received payment for his labor or reimbursement for supplies he had used. The framer, drywall installer, and electrician stopped working as well.

Jorge's story highlights another nonpayment scheme utilized by contractors against each other. When Jorge received his projects from Creative Atmospheres, he signed a contract that outlined the duties and responsibilities of each party as well as the project details. On one such job, after signing the contract, Jorge went to the private residence where he had agreed to build a brick wall fence and patio and discovered the measurements the company gave him were off by one hundred linear feet, adding an additional labor and material expense to the project. He contacted the company, which approved the extra work but refused to put the changes—including the increased project cost—in writing, even though the contract explicitly stated that any changes would need to be memorialized in the contract. The company assured him not to worry and that "it [would] be taken care of." After the pavers were laid, the homeowners decided they did not like the color they had initially approved and asked Jorge to remove and reinstall new material twice. In the end, despite the additional material costs and linear footage, Jorge was only paid the amount initially negotiated in the contract and is owed an additional $3,400. This scheme had a significant impact on Jorge because, as the subcontractor, he was responsible for paying his crew's wages out of pocket, despite not having been fully paid by Creative Atmospheres.

Through the experiences of these five construction workers, it is clear that regardless of the formality of the market in which they work or their position within the market, Arizona's construction workforce is highly vulnerable. While illegal business practices are used against construction workers of all ethnicities, skill levels, and backgrounds, we cannot ignore the ways in which race and immigration status affect their experiences. In the next section, I describe how the recession and local politics shape Mexicans' workplace experiences.

BREAKING THE BEDROCK: THE IMPACT OF THE RECESSION AND POLITICS ON MEXICAN LABORERS

The recession had a tremendous impact on both the work experiences and survival strategies of study participants. Because workers are not fully or properly paid and they produce more work for the same pay, the company is less impacted by the recession. Workers themselves cannot externalize or pass down the costs of business and social reproduction that they absorb from their employers. In fact, the five workers indicated that, normally, when in need of additional financial resources, they secure side jobs or offer their services on small projects for friends or acquaintances. However, during the recession, side work was not easily found and that which was found was done cheaply, because competition was fierce and fewer people were willing to spend money to have work done. In effect, workers do twice the work to earn the same amount. Workers typically also relied on savings or borrowed money from friends or family; however, these funds were also less available during the recession. Without access to other work and with few options, especially in the case of the undocumented migrants, workers felt stuck in their jobs. They stayed despite poor working conditions and substandard (and illegal) pay.

The impact of wage theft was devastating to study participants' financial and emotional health. Impeded from paying bills and daily expenses (such as for a phone, car insurance, gas, rent/mortgage, or medical services), sending money to family in Mexico, or saving money, workers experienced extreme amounts of stress and instability that manifested in illness, lack of sleep, emotional exhaustion, and strained family relations. I elaborate and expand upon these measurable effects in other work (Sanidad 2011; Téllez et al. 2011, 151).

The effect of both the recession and the normalized and institutionalized discrimination against Mexican workers in the form of wage differentials, fewer benefits, and greater workloads worsened with the political climate, which facilitated an implicit and explicit culture of violence in the workplace. Both Diego, a contractor, and Marco, an employee, experienced verbal threats, including the threat to call the sheriff should they pursue their wages further. In their experiences, employers utilize the harsh anti-immigrant political climate to maintain the existing power relations, keeping laborers, including contractors, in a vulnerable state.

> After a while, I realized [the contractor] was [giving us orders] without the intention of paying us. He told us he was a friend of Arpaio. He probably felt backed by the anti-immigrant sentiment or the anti-immigrant situation here in Arizona. One sees that we are Mexicans with a high probability of being undocumented. Maybe this was making him think that he could do what he wanted with us. After all, we are wetbacks. —Diego

> We didn't receive our wages. We received the opposite. We received discrimination. The owner, the manager was threatening that he was going to report us to immigration, to the sheriff, in order to intimidate us. Some of my co-workers, yes, he scared them and they preferred not to push the matter and leave it in peace. The majority was like that. [They] were uneasy about finding solutions to this problem. —Marco

In the face of harsh intimidation tactics, a recession, and institutional barriers, pursuing recourse was difficult for all workers. Filing with the Department was not an option as each was owed more than the $2,500 maximum claim amount. Similar to the migrant workers, Jorge claimed that before he sought assistance from the WRC he was unaware of which government agencies or other entities enforce employment laws or the steps to initiate the claims-making process. He also claimed he lacked the confidence to properly file the complaint on his own. Juan added a number of other reasons why recourse seemed out of reach, speaking to the perceived barriers his coworkers put forth.

> They say it's the time [investment] more than anything. Many say that you are going to have to waste time going to court, even taking time away from the job you currently have . . . and then the majority say that they need the money, so they choose to work. . . . Also, they are scared to go to court because there, in court, they ask for an ID. Then, there's the fact that when they call upon you in court, they call you in English.

Alfonso and Diego focused on the explicit barrier that documentation status and being a migrant presents. Alfonso claimed:

> It is like [the employer] takes advantage of the fact that one does not have papers, because if I had papers, if I had a license, I could talk more and I would go to court . . . In my country, I am free to talk more comfortably. You *have* to pay me in *my* country, or we are going to figure out how to resolve this. Give me *something*! But here, you cannot do any of that.

Other obstacles cited by both the migrants and U.S.-born worker include low literacy rates, confusion about the U.S. regulatory system, the costs associated with the court and hiring an attorney, and the long duration of court and government processes.

Both immediately following and as a consequence of the wage theft each experienced, the five participants expressed feeling paranoia and a lack of trust toward employers. Wage theft and the lack of consideration, justice, and fairness made them realize that their employers must not view them as fathers, sons, community members, or as humans. Commodified, they are their work. This realization was keenly expressed in the interviews with employees who loyally made sacrifices to support the growth and success of the employer's construction business. Relational dynamics and perceptions of workers had an unexpected but important impact on work experiences.

While the perceptions of Mexican laborers were not the focus of the interviews, the dynamics between Mexican migrant and citizen workers and between Mexican laborers and their employers were salient; for the purposes of this chapter, these relationships are particularly insightful for their implications on Mexicans' sense of belonging in Phoenix and of being equals with their peers and employer. One salient example is that of Alfonso, who was effectively fired upon completing a project for his employer of over three years; when he sought out his employer to ask for his unpaid wages, the boss simply hid from him.

> He loved me like a son, because we were together all the time. I have never failed him. And suddenly it changed. I really felt dismal. I didn't want to bring him problems because he had been very good to me, but I did not see him anymore. For two months he hid from me. . . . They would tell me he was not home, and I would call his phone and he never answered.

Paranoid about working for another employer again, Marco commented that

> [Employers] see you with the need to work, and they simply don't pay. They deny it; they hide. It affects you. One feels repressed or worthless. One feels less valuable. Problems occur, because they spurn you.

Each worker who participated in this study had experienced wage theft on at least two occasions before being interviewed and, to varying degrees, views wage theft as systemic abuse, the price you pay for being a Mexican construction worker.

Another noteworthy dynamic between Mexican workers was articulated by Jorge, who expressed a clear resentment toward Mexican migrants, whom he claimed underbid on jobs, "cut corners" to make more money and, amidst a recession, sent their financial resources to Mexico. While acknowledging the additional barriers migrant workers experience in challenging abuse of power and asserting their rights, Jorge commented many workers just leave the state or the country, preferring to "cut their losses" rather than "deal with it." Mexican migrants, he claimed, are just here to make their money, to invest in their homes and families in Mexico, and leave—an opinion arguably shared by fellow Americans who see migrants as passers through as opposed to sustaining community members. Jorge also expressed frustration with the treatment he experienced from big companies who take advantage of him, realizing that their greed, not migrant coworkers, was at fault.

These perceptions of migrants and of Mexican workers are fueled by anti-immigrant and antiworker rhetoric in the media. The resulting political climate impacts worker organization and workers' willingness to challenge and confront illegal business practices for fear of retaliation. Before the passage of SB 1070, for the opportunity to work, they withstood and accepted the costs associated with ongoing violations until it became more costly to keep their work than to quit. Generally, they came to the

WRC once they no longer worked for the employer or were owed several paychecks. Even then, they chose the least confrontational methods of recuperating unpaid wages. Discussed later in this chapter, these methods tend to also be the least effective in terms of drawing attention to the issue, correcting an illegal business practice, and recuperating all back wages and damages owed. After the passage of SB 1070, workers, many afraid to leave their homes, did not attend the WRC's events or trainings, much less file claims against abusive employers (Téllez et al. 2011).

Workers selected the most cost-effective and least aggressive or rewarding methods of recourse. Juan and Marco chose to file insurance claims through the Registrar of Contractors against the contractors' bond because their employers were not solvent and the bond was the only known pocket of money left. An investigation of the claims resulted in the revocation of the contractors' license and the collection of a small percentage of the amount owed. Their coworkers, who expressed fear of and little interest in pursuing back wages, received none of the wages owed them. Juan's employer continues working without a license. Marco's employer opened a new business entity without any investigation performed by government agencies in regards to complaints, debts, or penalties assessed against his former entities; his debts did not transfer from one company to another, and he continues to use the same business strategies.

Similarly, Alfonso saw that his employer suffered no negative consequence for his failure to pay wages; his employer simply skipped town for another job opportunity. Though Alfonso secured a default judgment in civil court in 2009—one year after performing the work—the judgment lien for $10,080 has yet to be paid, and Alfonso has had to absorb the court-related costs. When Diego organized a protest with a small group of supporters to shame his boss into paying him, he found the business closed with no trace of the former owner. Unlikely to locate the owner and find him solvent, no attorney would take his case, and no other options were pursued. In the same vein, Jorge became overwhelmed by the complexity of justice court documents and the thought of defending himself, and he struggled to raise the $85 to initiate the lawsuit. Pushing it out of mind, he let it go.

Both in terms of justice and employer compliance, these cases are clear examples of the harm that is done when recourse is not accessible and abusive employers are left unchallenged due to lack of unionization, government enforcement, access to courts, and failure of employers to self-regulate. In these five cases, not a single worker was even fully compensated for the work they had already done, much less were they made whole by receiving damages. Notably, none of the noncompliant businesses were brought into full compliance with the law or faced penalties, fines, the possibility of being blacklisted from future contracts, or any other deterrent for future noncompliance. Without strict measures of accountability and effective, accessible recourse through which to seek justice, workers and their families assume the burden of unpaid wages, and their employers continue utilizing profit-driven illegal business practices.

With the 2016 closure of the WRC due to lack of funding, the prospect of creating a more informed workforce, recuperating vulnerable workers' wages, challenging employer and industry-wide abusive business practices by bringing more businesses into compliance, and changing the culture around work and the perception of Mexican workers is dismal, as no other local organizations have stepped up to continue this work, and it is not in employers' self-interest nor the government's purview to do so. As the construction industry recovers in Arizona, large numbers of Mexican workers will be recruited and reincorporated again into the industry despite the fact we have yet to deal with the decades-long deregulation of their work or the consequences that their exploitation has on the stability in and perception of Mexican workers and their families or on public coffers, crumbling labor standards, undercut and legitimate businesses, and other community stakeholders.

CONCLUSIONS AND RECOMMENDATIONS

This chapter is as much a celebration of the work and contributions of Mexican laborers in Phoenix as it is about the systems that continue to fail them. Our state's legislature has produced anti-immigrant, antiworker, and anti-union laws that put vulnerable workers at a distinct disadvantage in the workplace and when accessing recourse. Federal and state governmental bodies that are intended to enforce laws equally for workers are woefully inadequate in terms of resources, staff, and judicial and prosecutorial power. Prejudicial laws and broken enforcement systems fail to serve Mexican and other vulnerable workers, leaving them largely unprotected. Caught between the government's ongoing orchestration of their recruitment and banishment, Mexican workers participate in their permitted roles within flexible labor regimes. Ironically, while laying the foundation for growth and ensured progress of the United States and its citizens, Mexican workers must fight to exercise the full expression of their citizenship, calling into question whether their "belonging" has ever been accepted.

To belong is to suggest privilege or, at least, equity with others who belong. Scholars (Coutin 2000; Gordon 2005) suggest that key elements of equal citizenship are formal legal status, rights, and belonging, and that the rights and responsibilities of citizenship are as much political and social as legal. Were Mexicans and all others granted the practice of equal rights and status under the law and served well by our systems and institutions, the economy would be enriched by tenets of fair play, diversity, skill, knowledge, increased investments in family and community life, and untapped human potential. The value of equity for community and state vitality and resilience cannot be underrated.

Progress for lower- and middle-class working people begins with ensuring equality among all. Specifically, all workers must have the same rights, those rights must be equally and fairly enforced, and all workers must have equal access to claims making processes when rights are violated. Surely, no one thing in isolation—good intentions, structural changes, ideological shifts, or new framing in public discourse—will address the fractures in our labor and economic systems. For structural reform to take root, public discourse and ideology must also shift to reflect the value of equal rights and liberties for all those who build our state through their labor.

Numerous scholars, independent research institutes, and government entities (Bernhardt et al. 2007; Bernhardt et al. 2008; Bernhardt et al. 2009; Bobo 2009; Foo 1994; General Accounting Office 2002; Sanidad 2011; Smith, Avendaño, and Ortega 2009; United Nations Human Rights 2010; Zatz 2008) offer valid structural recommendations to address weak employment laws and protections, ineffective law enforcement, and lack of access to state and federal government agencies, many of which address the concerns raised in this study. This chapter calls our attention to the immediate need to act on their suggestions given President Trump's administration, which promises the weakening of labor unions, deregulation of labor and employment, the slashing of public safety nets for low-wage workers, and the further emboldening of employers to abuse vulnerable workers. The consequences of Republican-controlled, pro-business, and anti-union leadership in Arizona will be seen played out on a national scale with the institutionalization of flexible labor regimes as a springboard for business growth and the continued dependence upon an elastic supply of labor.

NOTES

1. *Mexican* refers to people of Mexican descent. *Latino* is used only when statistics from my data sources referenced Latinos, Hispanics, or people with origins in Latin America.
2. In an effort to be sensitive, rather than use *illegal* to describe migrants, pro-migrant activists utilize the term *undocumented migrant* when referring to those without legal documents to live or work in the country. I recognize the inadequacy of the latter term as well in that it continues to focus on the legality of the person as opposed to how government and laws shape migration and define migrants' status (see Plascencia 2009). Despite its inadequacy, I use *undocumented migrant* in this chapter to describe those who have yet to be granted authorization to work and live in the United States
3. Fissured industries are "those sectors that increasingly rely on a wide variety of organizational methods that have redefined employment relationships: subcontracting; third-party management; franchising; independent contracting; and other contractual forms

that alter who is the employer of record or make the worker-employer relationship tenuous and less transparent" (U.S. Department of Labor 2010b, 30).

4. *Right-to-work* means that no individual can be compelled to join a union nor can he or she be denied employment for membership or nonmembership in a union, which is a dues-sustained organization. Where workers have won a union at a job site, it must represent all bargaining unit employees and not just its dues-paying members, taxing its limited resources.
5. While the workers' stories suggest that misclassification is a willful and manipulative economic strategy to exploit workers, that is not always the case (Bobo 2009, 23). A growing body of case law shows the complexity of worker classification (e.g., *Juárez et al. v. CC Services, Inc.* 434 F.Supp.2d 755 [D. Ariz., 2006]).
6. The maximum wage claim amount was raised to $5,000 in 2012 (AZ Rev. Stat. Sec. 23–356). Since that time, the number of wage claims filed increased approximately 12 percent from 2,570 in fiscal year 2011–12 to 2,896 and 2,882 in fiscal years 2013–14 and 2014–15, respectively (Arizona Industrial Commission 2011, 2012, 2013, 2014, 2015).
7. Based on a survey of 137 construction workers and interviews with representatives of construction firms in Austin, Torres and colleagues (2013) concluded that the industry is one with poor and dangerous working conditions, low wages and wage theft, limited benefits, and organized around racialized divisions of labor. Much of what is presented about Austin mirrors the situation described for the Phoenix area.
8. Passed in April 2010, Arizona's SB 1070 is an anti-immigrant law that legalized ongoing state-sponsored violence against Latinos by allowing police to verify lawful presence of suspicious persons and arrest potentially deportable persons without a warrant by charging immigrants with a state crime if they do not carry federal registration papers on their being or if they seek or accept work without authorization (Arizona State Legislature 2010).
9. Workers' names and the names of companies they worked for have been assigned pseudonyms in order to protect their anonymity.
10. Beginning in 1996 the IRS issued nine-digit numbers called ITINs to those unable to secure a social security number for the purpose of meeting their tax obligations.

EPILOGUE

WE BEGAN THIS BOOK WITH the assertion that Mexicans occupy a paradoxical position in Arizona's economy and politics, and that Arizona has been quite influential in the nation's public discourse and policies on migration and anti-Latina/o sentiment. The contributors to this volume capture the processes by which people of Mexican descent came to be positioned not only as an acutely needed and near inexhaustible workforce, but of equal importance, as an elastic labor supply that could be recruited to work at low wages when needed, pressured to achieve a high productivity, accept poor working conditions, and then driven out during cyclical crises in the economy. We argue that the making of an elastic supply of labor is central to federal, state, and local efforts to regulate and control the Mexican community, migrants and U.S.-born Mexican citizens as a whole, and that the concept of elastic supply of labor, as simplistic as it may appear, draws attention to an important process of labor control.

To understand the process of producing an elastic supply of labor, one must take into account how multiple factors foster and rationalize that production. Our conceptualization acknowledges and builds on the scholarship that discusses the creation of Mexicans as a surplus labor force also labeled industrial reserve army, reserve army of labor, or relative surplus population, but adds dimensions not commonly found in that literature. We suggest that the elastic supply of labor process is involved in not only creating an apparent surplus, but that it also involves the dissolution of that surplus—involving a passive or active banishment of workers—and then the recomposition of a surplus based on global commodity prices and capitalist speculation aimed at making short-term profits.

The elastic supply of labor process is also best understood as a racialized phenomenon, an aspect firmly addressed by Chicana/o labor historians and social scientists in their theorizations to center race as an organizing principle in the machinations of capitalist accumulation. Often based on racial/eugenicist assumptions about ability, culture, heat tolerance, and a parallel rationalization of white labor as being deficient, employers in agriculture, copper mines, railroads, construction, and services asserted a strong preference for Mexicano labor. They claim that American (i.e., white) workers are not available or that such workers will not do certain kinds of work. Often left out of this claim is the reality that U.S. workers will not, in fact, do certain kinds of work, at least not for the wages employers want to pay and the working conditions imposed. Thus, in order to guarantee a maximum profit rate, employers required the federal government's assistance to ensure a plentiful supply of Mexican workers. It is a process that led to the formation of Mexican labor as an elastic supply of labor that could be sought after to work when needed and banished when speculative bubbles collapsed. Although the pursuit of Mexican labor is evident prior to and in the first decade of the twentieth century, in our view the legitimation of these processes in light of the federal government's role and the institutionalized racialization of the elastic supply of labor insofar as Mexican workers is concerned was formalized in 1917, with the ninth proviso waivers of the Immigration Act of 1917.

The elastic supply of labor also possesses a gendered dimension, historically contingent, which at times depending on the industry relies on the family as the production unit. The positioning of women as both paid and unpaid laborers has, to varying degrees, augmented the overall vulnerability of women in the workforce. Women's role in reproduction, in home and the workforce, and the extent to which social reproduction costs are externalized to the worker's household, and secondly to Mexico, remain in need of further exploration. Although the U.S. state is a central actor in creating and supporting employers' aim to maximize profits, the Mexican state also plays a central role in facilitating the existence of the elastic supply of labor that makes the accumulation possible. The billions of dollars in annual remittances sent, by both men and women, to Mexico ensure Mexico's strong endorsement of the arrangement. In calendar year 2017, Mexico reached a record $28.8 billion in remittances from the United States.

One hundred years later, as they did in 1917, employers still allege to face labor shortages—they do not ask for "braceros," but instead allege they urgently need "guest workers." Meanwhile, nativists and Republican elected officials, with the support of some Democratic officials, bemoan and demean the presence of a Mexican community. Nativists of multiple stripes assert that Mexicans, particularly undocumented migrants, are the cause of a myriad of social and economic problems. According to these, Mexicans are a budget and tax drain, are the source of imagined crime waves, take jobs from Americans, harm the environment, and demographically harm the nation—a nation that is perceived to be for, and of, whites. Sustained empirical scholarship, in contrast, has shown the erroneous bases and conclusions of most such assertions. Instead, the scholarship has shown the net positive economic and social impacts that migrants, including those without formal authorization, have on communities and the broader society.

Recent court rulings lay bare the tenuous and paradoxical position of Arizona's Mexican-descent population and the extent to which an elastic supply of labor undergirds the perennial paradox. In the *Ortega Melendres et al. v. Joseph M. Arpaio, et al.* racial-profiling lawsuit, the ruling by federal Judge G. Murray Snow, and the later conviction of Sheriff Arpaio for criminal contempt of court, reveal that while a police action may be framed as one against persons not formally authorized to be present, in actuality, persons possessing Mexican appearance are also targeted. Both Native Americans and Mexican citizens were stopped by Maricopa County Sheriff's Office deputies for suspicion of being unauthorized Mexicans. It was thus no accident that the nativist perspective fostered by presidential candidate Donald J. Trump, and now by President Trump, resulted in his decision to pardon Arpaio, codifying once again that the civil rights of Latina/os holds less weight than those found guilty of violating their constitutional rights, and that the rule of law is, at best, arbitrarily applied. In this context, reports throughout the country begin to note the shortages of workers, especially in agriculture and construction, as the most recent bubble of capitalist speculation unfolds.

Yet another example of how efforts to control Mexican labor is simultaneously about regulating the Mexican community as a whole, may be found in the case of the elimination of the Mexican American Studies Program (MAS) in the Tucson Unified School District (TUSD). Seemingly, this case exists in the educational sphere and has little to do with Mexican labor or the making of its elasticity. But upon closer examination, it is important to note that the gauntlet to abolish the program was enacted shortly after the passage of Arizona's SB 1070. Without reiterating the entire sequence of events, in effect, outgoing Arizona superintendent of schools, Tom Horne, charged that the MAS was in violation of HB 2281, a statute signed by then-governor Jan Brewer in May 2010, maintaining that public and charter schools could not advocate ethnic solidarity, "promote the overthrow of the United States government," "promote resentment toward a race or class of people" or create programs "for pupils of a particular ethnic group." Were TUSD to refuse to abolish the program, TUSD's state funding would be reduced by 10 percent. Like the contention that illegal immigration posed a threat to national security, a parallel claim was made that the very existence of the Mexican American Studies Program and what was being taught in their curriculum posed a threat to national security. By 2012 TUSD responded to the charges of noncompliance and abolished the Mexican American Studies Program. In 2017 Judge Tashima, of the Ninth Circuit Court of Appeals but designated to hear the case for Arizona district court, ruled that "racial animus" was the motivation behind the closure and that it violated the students' First and Fourteenth Amendment rights. Under the auspices of educational reform, the message that Mexicans do not belong is strategically and politically catapulted into the American psyche and imaginary. The insidious objective is for Mexican-descent people to occupy the majority of the surplus army of labor, and its concomitant elasticity, in accordance with the cycles of capitalism. On the one hand, schooling may be understood as the portal through which a stratified, obedient, and disciplined workforce is produced for capital; on the other hand, schooling may also produce a foundation for critical thinking that can ultimately result in a critique of the larger society and a belief in one's individual and collective agency to change the conditions under which one lives. Indeed, the controversy animated a youthful activism parallel to the heyday of the Chicana/o movement. To raise the educational levels—to imbue students with a critical education—to produce college graduation rates in parity with their representation in the population, risks capital's access to a steady supply of an exploitable labor pool. Capital cannot risk that a true shortage of labor would materialize. Hence, the existence of a Mexican American Studies Program is indeed a threat, but not to national security, but rather to capitalists' unquenched, unfettered access to an elastic supply of labor, citizen and noncitizen, forced to work for low wages, adverse conditions, and imposed high levels of productivity.

It is to the credit of past Mexican groups and individuals that they have been able, in small and larger efforts, to challenge the hegemonic arc that has sought to control the physical and economic mobility of households. Hegemonies, as recently argued by Vélez-Ibáñez 2017, are never complete, but can have a deep impact on the communities they seek to discipline and control. Mexican communities have a long history of initiating and participating in labor strikes aimed at improving wages and working conditions since the early 1900s; challenging public school segregation since the early 1930s; organizing large-scale marches across the United States, such as those that took place in 2006 and 2007; and using the federal courts to challenge a host of anti-migrant and anti-Mexican initiatives such as the multiple laws enacted in Arizona between 1996 and 2010 (see following discussion).

The national and international attention allocated to the passage and enactment of Arizona's SB 1070 in 2010 drew much attention to efforts in the state to regulate the undesired presence of Mexicans. Media, politicians, advocacy groups, and some scholars reiterated the phrase that former Republican congressman J. D. Hayworth had noted about Arizona in 2006: Arizona was "ground zero" for the nation's migration problem. The phrase has been repeated often since 2010. Observers invoking the phrase often take SB 1070's enactment as the initial political stance against undocumented Mexican migrants. SB 1070's importance, however, is best understood in the context of the multiple actions taken by Arizona legislators, local law enforcement and electors since 1996. Table E.1 summarizes the ten statutes enacted and the one joint local-federal police action taken between 1996 and 2010.

Prior to SB 1070, the individual measures were adopted as specific solutions to alleged migration problems related to the presence of undesired Mexicans. SB 1070's enactment, however, evoked a broader policy: "attrition through enforcement." The singular aim of the established policy in Arizona is to make life so difficult for Mexican migrants that they will "self-deport." In other words, while the state cannot formally deport/remove migrants, it can, nonetheless, create conditions that will lead to the departure of a segment of unwanted persons.

Taken together, the eleven actions index an antimigrant, particularly anti-Mexican, political stance. While promoters and supporters of the measures would argue that they are not antimigrant or anti-Mexican actions, but are instead about the rule of law and public safety, the geographic, historical, and law enforcement context suggest something different. Measures dating back to the early years of statehood, the 1980s, and the post-1995 period (Plascencia 2013) strongly suggest that the aim of the measures is to limit and control the status and mobility of Mexicans.

The measures and law enforcement actions implemented under the various statutes, such as the 2007 Arizona employer sanctions law, HB 2779, were efforts that simultaneously achieved what on the surface appear as contradictory aims. On one hand, they can be characterized as exclusionary; and on the other as inclusionary. However, rather than understood as a contradictory binary, they should be conceptualized as simultaneous, reinforcing actions (Chauvin and Garcés-Mascareñas 2012; Plascencia 2012). This dual process of exclusion/inclusion is made evident in former sheriff Arpaio's implementation of the state's employer sanctions law. MCSO officers raided close to sixty businesses under the explicit rationale that they were enforcing the state's employer sanctions law. The raids led to the arrest of a sizeable number of workers at the workplace during normal business hours, but MCSO deputies did not file any charges against the employers who the raids made amply clear were employing persons without employment authorization. Workers were arrested, employers were granted amnesty. From this and other examples, we believe that the police actions implemented were ultimately not aimed at eliminating the presence of Mexican undocumented migrants but, more importantly, at securing their insecurity and flexibility. The police actions reinforced the position of undocumented migrant workers as a precarious low-wage workforce that could be coerced to accept difficult and hazardous working conditions, and could be pressured to achieve a higher than normal productivity. More broadly, this ensured that Mexican workers remain within

Table E.1 Arizona Statutory and Police Actions Aimed at Regulating Mexican Migration

Year	Policy Action	Description
1996	Restriction on Drivers' Licenses	Required proof of U.S. citizenship or authorized presence.
1997	Chandler Roundup Looking Mexican	Chandler Police Department and INS apprehension of individuals suspected of being present without formal authorization; U.S. citizens and permanent residents were detained.
2000	Proposition 203, English for Children	Limits English as a Second Language ESL instruction.
2004	Proposition 200, Protect Arizona Now	A multiprovision statute targeted at noncitizens; included provisions regarding voting, public benefits, mandates state employees to report persons suspected of being present without authorization, and others.
2005	Coyote Law Antismuggling	Aimed at reducing human smuggling; though used to charge undocumented individuals with self-smuggling.
2006	Proposition 100	Denies bail to undocumented persons.
2006	Proposition 300	Denies in-state tuition for students without a social security number.
2006	Proposition 103, English-Only	Asserts that Arizona's official language is English and mandates all official actions to be conducted in English.
2007	HB 2779, FLEA/LAWA, Employer Sanctions	Allows for the cancellation of licenses of businesses that employ persons without employment authorization.
2010	HB 2281	Prohibits ethnic studies programs.
2010	SB 1070/HB 2162	Establishes the statewide policy of attrition through enforcement; requires local law enforcement officials to verify migration status, and other provisions.

Source: Plascencia 2013, 106.

an elastic supply of labor—a supply that could be mobilized when needed, banished when conditions merited this, and then reconstituted in the next cycle of expansion in the economy.

The strong and persistent call for guest workers on the part of agribusiness, home health-care firms, livestock enterprises, hotel/tourism sector, and others, including The Trump Organization for H-2A workers in its Virginia vineyards and for H-2B workers at the Mar-a-Lago Resort, should also be understood as parallel efforts that rely on the production of an elastic supply of labor. The underlying unproven allegations that U.S. workers are not available become the foundation for seeking the support of the U.S. federal government in producing a sizeable workforce that can be coerced to accept lower wages, difficult working conditions, and forced to achieve high productivity. Workers incorporated in this process are not only part of an elastic supply of labor but are structurally positioned as ideal workers. A large number can be recruited; they are indentured to a specific employer, do not gain any credits toward petitioning for permanent residency or later citizenship, and the employer can dismiss them at any time with or without cause. At the point they are dismissed or chose to vote with their feet and walk away from the indentured-relationship, the "guest workers" are no longer guests—they are transformed into persons subject to deportation/removal.

President Trump's continued call to build the border wall and Attorney General Sessions's implementation of selected raids in "sanctuary" cities can be understood as largely symbolic efforts to appear to be addressing the Mexican migrant problem. This does not mean that they are not devastating for the individuals and families affected by such actions. All seven to ten million undocumented migrants of working age will not be deported/removed. They are essential to U.S. enterprises that generate substantial profits from the labor of those workers. Nonetheless, the threats of a border wall and workplace raids can be interpreted as political actions aimed to ensure that such workers remain fearful of apprehension, and thus are willing to work for lower wages, endure difficult working conditions, and accept demands for high productivity.

As already noted, the Mexican state has a central role in aiding the production of Mexican nationals as a dependable, elastic supply of labor that can aid U.S. employers to meet unproven alleged labor shortages. While Mexican consulate offices can and do play an important role in seeking to protect Mexican nationals in the United States, there is an inherent limit in their interest and/or ability to protect its nationals. There is no mechanism in place within the consulates to monitor all of the employer exploitations of contract or undocumented migrants in their respective cities or regions. In addition, their standing in state or federal court would be challenged by attorneys representing employers or employer associations, and there is very little interest in encouraging collective bargaining power for affected Mexican workers. Lastly, there appears to be a tacit understanding that if Mexican consulates momentously interfered with the flow of Mexicans north, this would impact the remittances conveyed to the Mexican economy.

Returning to the question of where we are and the implications of the Trump administration to the well-being of Mexican workers, the indicators suggest negative impacts and outcomes. Regulatory changes by the Environmental Protection Agency regarding agricultural pesticides will without question negatively impact many agricultural workers who in the recent past achieved some basic protections—the deregulation rhetoric will trump worker health. Deregulations under way at the Department of Labor affecting U.S. and contract workers, particularly H-2A and H-2B visa holders, will revert the modest improvements made under former Secretary of Labor Tom E. Pérez toward ensuring statutory protections.

All of the aforementioned, however, will depend on the dynamic confrontation in U.S. politics between nativist/nationalist and employer corporate/capital priorities. The former asserts the position that jobs belong to Americans (i.e., white, native citizens), and employers deploy the arguments initiated in 1917 that they face a severe labor shortage; that U.S. workers are not available or capable of doing the work performed by undocumented migrants or contract workers; and that if indentured workers are not made available, entire crops or industries will close operations, and consumers will face astronomical increases in the cost of food, etc. Under this scenario, there will either be a collusion or collision of interest. Nativists will either temporarily accept that employers do seem to be facing alleged labor shortages in selected sectors such as agriculture, and so go along with the interests of capital, or employers will partially acquiesce and concede that they can operate with a lower level of undocumented workers and contract workers, but will need the help of the federal government to guarantee that the necessary surplus of indentured workers will be made available to them so they can transition to a legal workforce.

The likely impact of the above confrontation is that U.S.-born Mexican-origin workers and Mexican migrants will not lose their position as part of a corporate-desired elastic supply of labor, but instead may be furthered cemented as part of that supply. This is particularly likely to happen if the federal governmental solution to the political confrontation is to agree to expand the elastic supply of contract workers. Mexicana/os formerly functioning as undocumented migrant labor will be transformed to indentured workers subject to greater employer control. In the present, ironically, undocumented Mexican workers possess the freedom to leave an employer for one that offers a higher wage and better working conditions; contract workers do not have this accepted freedom of workers. One important intervening factor is the extent to which the federal government or state governments with employer sanctions laws make the difficult political decision to implement the employer sanctions enacted in 1986 by President Reagan. The 1986 law prohibited all employers from hiring persons without employment authorization—it was an action that President Reagan envisioned as the "keystone" to the elimination of the magnet that fostered unauthorized migration. However, from President Reagan through President Obama, and now President Trump, the regime in office is not actually committed to fully enforce the law, despite much rhetoric about the United States being a nation of laws and the importance of the rule of law. On October 8, 2017, President Trump released his immigration policy priorities. The document promotes E-Verify, but nothing is said about ensuring employer compliance with the 1986 law. This oversight reinforces the view that the federal government will ensure an amnesty for prominent employers, particularly in agriculture, services, and construction who violate federal law. Large agribusiness interests in Arizona and California, for example, are accorded a kind of "too big to fail" policy that shields them from labor disruptions due to workplace raids during the harvest period.

Despite the aforesaid assessment, we remain optimistic about the future status of Mexicans in Arizona and the United States. Our optimism is grounded on the reality that many of the executive actions and administrative rules initiated under the Trump administration will be challenged in federal court. The Mexican American Legal Defense and Education Fund, the American Civil Liberties Union, the National Immigration Law Center, and other national entities, as well as some state attorneys general, have made clear their intention to support local and state challenges to negative political actions. In the case of Arizona, almost all of the ten antimigrant initiatives were challenged in court. Although local challenges were not successful in all cases, they nonetheless stymied the implementation of several of these e.g., Proposition 300, and in other cases successfully stopped the full implementation of measures enacted, e.g., the self-smuggling charges. Even in the case of Arizona's SB 1070, the Supreme Court rejected three of the four major provisions. Secondly, there is no doubt that Arizona, as well as the nation, is undergoing a demographic transition. The demographic projections are simply projections, but the reality remains that between 2030 and 2060 close to half of Arizona's population will be Latina/o, and those of Mexican descent will comprise the largest segment. Nationally, it is estimated that Latina/os will make up close to 30 percent. Such major demographic transition strongly suggests that the dynamics and politics within and outside of Arizona will be different. We hope it is one where the humanity and Constitutional and human rights of all persons are recognized, and that a strong economy will emerge that recognizes the importance of providing livable wages to all workers.

ACKNOWLEDGMENTS

WE ARE HUMBLY HONORED TO HAVE co-edited this anthology, which we believe, with its focus on Chicana/o/Mexicana/o labor history in Arizona, will fill a long-standing gap in Mexican Southwest history. We are proud to sit on the shoulders of previous scholars who have centered their scholarship on documenting the history of Mexicans in the United States. This collection of works would not have been possible without the research undertaken by our esteemed contributors, the late F. Arturo Rosales, Jaime Águila, Christine Marin, Jean Reynolds, Anna Ochoa O'Leary, and Cristina Gallardo-Sanidad. It is a long-known ethos in our community that we are stronger when we speak and act from a sense of collectivity; we trust this collection embodies these values and that our work will serve as a building block for future research.

We want to thank the Center for Cultural Studies and Inquiry at Arizona State University for their generous support of our project and the Arizona Historical Advisory Commission for recognizing our project (under a different book title) for the Arizona 2012 Centennial Legacy Project Designation.

We want to thank Pete Dimas for his parallel effort to foster a fuller understanding of the Mexicana/o community in Arizona through his multipart documentary, *Arizona's Mexican Heritage: An American Story* (2014). His project and this anthology represent similar visions. Carlos Vélez Ibáñez' scholarship and his interest in formulating a fuller picture of the Southwest North American Region also inspired us to present a slice of that broader regional social dynamic.

The collection of photographs was made possible by the assistance of a number of archivists, curators, and contributors. We want to thank Nancy Godoy, archivist at the Chicano Research Collection, and Robert Spindler, university archivist and head of archives and special collections at Hayden Library at Arizona State University Libraries; Josh Roffler, senior curator of collections at Tempe History Museum; Judy Cook, curator for the Litchfield Park Historical Society; Nate Meyers, curator of collections at the Chandler Museum; Rebecca Tabah at the Arizona Historical Society; and Anna Ochoa O'Leary, contributor to this volume, for obtaining photographs of women's activism during the Arizona Copper Strike (1983–1986) against the transnational Phelps Dodge Corporation. The Phelps Dodge Corporation, now part of Freeport-McMoRan, not surprisingly, won the battle against the largely Mexicano workforce, but did not erase the aspiration of workers and allies who continue to seek a better life in largely anti-union Arizona. We want to extend a special thank-you to Sarina Guerra and Derick Washington, newly minted graduates of New College at Arizona State University, for their contemporary photographs of workers in Arizona and the Goodyear Farms Historical Cemetery.

Luis: Meeting Gloria was an auspicious moment. My arrival in Arizona was welcomed by Gloria, even though we were both initially unaware of the multiplicity of common interests. Cotton, agricultural labor, the World War I ninth proviso contract labor program, and Chicana/o/Mexicana/o labor history were some of the topics that animated many discussions; they allowed us to think about conceptual and empirical questions related to how these had been examined by scholars. The more we talked about the ninth proviso, for example, the more we realized how its importance has been overlooked by labor and migration scholars, and made us independently seek a more solid understanding of its development and implementation. She reflected on its central role in the development of Goodyear cotton farms, and I on the importance of its implementation to the World War II contract labor arrangements.

I want to also acknowledge my appreciation and pleasure in collaborating with Gloria. Her insight and skill in conceptualizing the framing of issues and arguments greatly strengthened the anthology. Our collaboration aided my appreciation of the potential in collaborative ventures.

My familiarity with the scholarship on Mexicana/o labor in California and Texas, as well as other locations such as Chicago, led me early on in my stay in Arizona to recognize the clear absence of comparable research on Mexican labor in the Grand Canyon State. Our discussions about this stimulated our dialogue about how to partially address this academic lacuna in Southwest scholarship. This anthology represents a small step toward addressing that lacuna. We are cognizant that a long research agenda remains regarding the role of Mexicana/o labor in Arizona. The relatively small cadre of scholars at Arizona's three public universities with a major interest in Mexican labor limits our enthusiasm about the emergence of a robust effort to examine the many pending research topics.

I, and Lucy, also feel lucky to have been welcomed into Judith's and Gloria's home and accepted into their wide circle of family and friends. The multiple times we shared meals were highly pleasant and joyful. They were pleasant opportunities to not talk about the making of an "elastic supply of labor."

Lastly, I want to personally express my gratitude to Lucy, my friend and spouse, who instinctually tolerated my long hours at the computer, long telephone conversations with Gloria, and the multitude of other tasks involved in editing this anthology.

Gloria: My interest in Arizona's labor history came about in the context of my participation in an oral history research project of Mexican workers and families that worked and lived in the labor camps of the former cotton company town of Litchfield Park. My partnership with members of the Litchfield Park Historical Society led to my interests in Arizona's history and, more specifically, to the history of cotton, agriculture, and the history of Mexican people in Arizona. I am eternally grateful to former archivist of the Chicano Research Collection at Arizona State University, Christine Marin, for directing me to key works, collections, and sources on said topics when I first began this work in 2005–06. She enthusiastically opened the doors to this body of knowledge and continued to answer my queries throughout the course of this anthology, as did her successor, Nancy Godoy. I also hold a special appreciation to the Arizona Humanities Council for their invaluable support of our work in Litchfield Park and all the wonderful community-based research they support in a given year.

I feel especially fortunate to have collaborated on this anthology with my *colega* and friend, Luis Plascencia, whose intellectual expertise in the areas of migration, citizenship, and the law substantively influenced the framework for this anthology and the direction of my own analysis with respect to the history of cotton and Chicana/o labor history. The integrity of our working relationship, the *feminista* praxis with which we engaged each other, reinforces my faith in collaborative ventures. I could not ask for a more respectful, kind, patient, rigorous, and methodical coeditor than I found in Luis. Through him I was happy to enjoy the friendship of his wife, Lucy, who steadfastly supported our lengthy and odd working hours, and made our personal gatherings, with her adept Texas-style storytelling, far more enjoyable.

Last, but by no means least, I thank my life partner, Judith Levin, and family members, Jessica, Arielle, and grandson, Mason Caiazzo, for their enduring support during the writing of the book. They know all too well what my juggling of work and family meant for our daily lives. As always, I thank my parents, Miguel Cuevas Cuádraz and Nellie Holguín Cuádraz, both now deceased, whose commitment to family and striving for better lives continues in our immediate and extended families. My siblings—Olga, Michael, Elvira, Alicia, Darlene, Irene, and Leticia—all deserve a shout-out for understanding and supporting my path as a scholar. To all, and my family of friends, I extend my love and immense gratitude to everyone for their support.

In sum, we want to thank editor Kristen Buckles and the entire production and editorial team at the University of Arizona Press for their utmost dedication and work on this manuscript. We also want to thank the anonymous reviewers, whose thoughtful insights surely guided us in our revisions.

REFERENCES

Abbey, Sue Wilson. 1973. "The Ku Klux Klan in Arizona, 1921–1925." *Journal of Arizona History* 14 (Spring): 10–30.

ABC15 News. 2012. "Illegal Subcontractors Work Home Construction Sites." September 12. http://www.azcentral.com/video/1825311306001.

Acosta, Sal. No date. "Hispanics in Arizona: The History Continues." http://www.lib.az.us/convocations/images/pdf/acosta2.pdf.

———. 2010. "Crossing Borders, Erasing Boundaries: Interethnic Marriages in Tucson, 1854–1930." PhD diss., University of Arizona.

Acuña, Rodolfo. 1972. *Occupied America: The Chicano's Struggle Toward Liberation*. 1st ed. New York: Canfield Press.

———. 1988. *Occupied America: A History of Chicanos*. 3rd ed. New York: Harper & Row.

———. 1996. *Anything But Mexican: Chicanos in Contemporary Los Angeles*. New York: Verso.

———. 1998. *Sometimes There Is No Other Side: Chicanos and the Myth of Equality*. Notre Dame, IN: University of Notre Dame Press.

———. 2004. *Occupied America: A History of Chicanos*. 5th ed. New York: Pearson-Longman.

———. 2007. *Corridors of Migration: The Odyssey of Mexican Laborers, 1600–1933*. Tucson: University of Arizona Press.

Adams, David Wallace, and Crista DeLuzio. 2012. *On the Borders of Love and Power: Families and Kinship in the Intercultural American Southwest*. Berkeley: University of California Press.

Agamben, Giorgio 1998. *Homo Sacer: Sovereign Power and Bare Life*. Stanford, CA: Stanford University Press.

Agar, Michael H. 1996. *The Professional Stranger: An Informal Introduction to Ethnography*. 2nd ed. London: Academic Press.

Águila, Jaime. 2013. "Immigration and Politics: Arizona Then and Now." *Aztlán: A Journal of Chicano Studies* 38 (2): 131–49.

Akers, John H. 1997. "From Dale to Hollow? The Urban Transformation of Glendale, Arizona, 1940–1990." Master's thesis, Arizona State University.

Alamillo, José M. 2006. *Making Lemonade Out of Lemons: Mexican American Labor and Leisure in a California Town, 1880–1960*. Urbana: University of Illinois Press.

Alanís Enciso, Fernando Saúl. 1999. *El Primer Program Bracero y El Gobierno de México, 1917–1918*. San Luis Potosí: El Colegio de San Luis.

Alba, John R. 1988. "Heritage: Longstanding Leadership of Hispanics in Tucson Contrasts Sharply with Their Development in Phoenix." *Metro Phoenix Magazine*, 53–58.

Alderman, Royal. 1959. "Phoenix Big Six in Electronics . . . and What They Do." *Western Electronic News*.

Aleinikoff, T. Alexander, and Rubén G. Rumbaut. 1998. "Terms of Belonging: Are Models of Membership Self-Fulfilling Prophecies." *Georgetown Immigration Law Journal* 13 (1): 1–24.

Allen, Hugh. 1949. *The House of Good Year*. Cleveland, OH: Corday and Gross.

Allen, James B. 1966. *The Company Town in the American West*. Norman: University of Oklahoma Press.

Allen, Ruth. 1931. *The Labor of Women in the Production of Cotton*. Austin: Bureau of Research in the Social Sciences, University of Texas.

———. 1941. *Chapters in the History of Organized Labor*. Austin: University of Texas Press.

Almaguer, Tomás. 1984. "Racial Domination and Class Conflict in Capitalist Agriculture: The Oxnard Sugar Beet Workers' Strike of 1903." *Labor History* 25: 325–50.

———. 1994. *Racial Fault Lines: The Historical Origins of White Supremacy in California*. Berkeley: University of California Press.

Almaguer, Tomás, and Albert Camarillo. 1983. "Urban Chicano Workers in Historical Perspective: A Review of the Literature." In *The State of Chicano Research on Family, Labor, and Migration*, edited by Armando Valdez, Albert Camarillo, and Tomás Almaguer, 3–32. Stanford, CA: Stanford Center for Chicano Research.

Alonzo, Armando C. 1998. *Tejano Legacy: Rancheros and Settlers in South Texas, 1734–1900*. Albuquerque: University of New Mexico Press.

Alvarez, José Hernández. 1966. "A Demographic Profile of the Mexican Immigration to the United States, 1910–1950." *Journal of Inter-American Studies* July: 471–96.

Alvarez-Smith, Alma. 2008. "Perpetuating Poverty through Benevolent Rhetoric: Case Study of an Arizona Colonia." PhD diss., Arizona State University.

Anagnost, George T. 2010. "The 1910 Arizona Constitutional Convention: The Daily Proceedings and the Question of Original Intent as an Interpretive Guide." *Phoenix Law Review* 3: 43–61.

Anderson, Henry P. 1958. Social Justice and Foreign Contract Labor: A Statement of Opinion and Conscience. Unpublished mimeograph.

———. 1963. *Fields of Bondage: The Mexican Contract Labor System in Industrialized Agriculture.* Mimeograph.

———. 1964. *A Harvest of Loneliness: An Inquiry into a Social Problem.* Berkeley: Citizens for Farm Labor.

———. 1976. *The Bracero Program in California: With Particular Reference to Health Status, Attitudes, and Practices.* Berkeley: University of California School of Public Health.

Anderson, Karen. 1996. *Changing Woman: A History of Racial Ethnic Women in America.* Oxford: Oxford University Press.

Anderson, Mark C. 1998. "'What's to be Done with 'Em?' Images of Mexican Cultural Backwardness, Racial Limitations, and Moral Decrepitude in the United States, 1913–1915." *Mexican Studies/Estudios Mexicanos* 14 (1): 23–70.

Arau, Sergio. 2004. *Un Día sin Mexicanos/A Day Without a Mexican.* Santa Monica, CA: Xenon Pictures.

Ardizzone, Heidi. 1997. "Red Blooded Americans: Mulattoes and the Melting Pot in U.S. Racialist and National Discourse, 1890–1930." PhD diss., University of Michigan.

Arizona Academy. 1967a. *Tenth Arizona Town Hall: On Do Agricultural Problems Threaten Arizona's Total Economy?* Tucson: University of Arizona Press.

———. 1967b. *38th Arizona Town Hall: Arizona's Hispanic Perspective.* Tucson: University of Arizona Press.

Arizona Department of Economic Security. 2012. *Arizona Integrated Workforce Plan: 2012–2017.* Phoenix: Arizona Department of Economic Security. https://www.azdes.gov/uploadedFiles/Employment/Arizona-Integrated-Workforce-Plan-2012-2017.pdf.

Arizona Employment Security Commission. 1957. *Maricopa County Migratory Farm Labor Housing Study November 1–December 15.* Phoenix: Arizona State Employment Service.

Arizona Industrial Commission. 2007–2014. *ICA Annual Reports.* http://www.ica.state.az.us/ADOSH/ADOSH_Research_Statistics.aspx.

Arizona Latino Research Enterprise, Department of Transborder Chicana/o and Latina/o Studies, and ASU Office of Public Affairs. 2009. *State of Latino Arizona.* Tempe: Arizona State University.

Arrington, Leonard J. 1968. "Arizona in the Great Depression Years." *Arizona Review* 17: 11–19.

Associated General Contractors of America-Arizona Chapter. 2011. "Construction and Transportation's Influence on Arizona's Economy." http://www.azagc.org/wp-content/uploads/2011/01/booklet-january-17-2011.pdf.

Associated Press. 2005. "McCain Apologizes for Comments about Resort, Immigrant Workers." May 18, 2005.

———. 1999. "Weitz Co. to Pay Bonuses for Spanish Proficiency." March 10, 1999.

Auerbach, Jerald S. 1966. *Labor and Liberty: The La Follette Committee and the New Deal.* Indianapolis: Bobbs-Merrill.

August, Jack. 1979. "The Anti-Japanese Crusade in Arizona's Salt River Valley, 1934–35." *Arizona and the West* 21 (2): 113–36.

Augustine-Adams, Kif. 2011. "Marriage and Mestizaje, Chinese and Mexican: Constitutional Interpretation and Resistance in Sonora, 1921–1935." *Law and History Review* 29 (2): 419–64.

———. 2009. "Making Mexico: Legal Nationality, Chinese Race, and the 1930 Population Census." *Law and History Review* 27 (1): 113–44.

Aulette, J., and T. Mills. 1988. "Something Old, Something New: Auxiliary Work in the 1983–1986 Copper Strike." *Feminist Studies* 14 (2): 251–67.

Avalos, Manuel, Lisa Magaña, and Adrian D. Pantoja. 2010. "Battleground Voters in a Battleground State? Latinos in Arizona and the 2004 Presidential Election." In *Beyond the Barrio: Latinos in the 2004 Election*, edited by Rodolfo O. de la Garza, Louis DeSipio, and David L. Leal, 159–70. Notre Dame, IN: University of Notre Dame Press.

Avila, Joaquín G. 1997. "The Political Integration of Racial and Ethnic Minorities." Twelfth Annual Ernesto Galarza Commemorative Lecture. Stanford, CA: Stanford Center for Chicano Research, Stanford University.

Avirgan, Tony, L. Josh Bivens, and Sarah Gammage, eds. 2005. *Good Jobs, Bad Jobs, No Jobs: Labor Markets and Informal Work in Egypt, El Salvador, India, Russia, and South Africa.* Washington, D.C.: Global Policy Network/Economic Policy Institute.

Babu, Shankara. 2010. "Environmental Justice in Arizona: A Case Study." PhD diss., Arizona State University.

Baca-Ramírez, Reynaldo, and Dexter Edward Bryan. 1980. "The Undocumented Mexican Worker: A Social Problem?" *Journal of Ethnic Studies* 8 (1): 55–70.

Bach, Robert L. 1978. "Mexican Immigration and the American State." *International Migration Review* 12 (4): 536–58.

Bada, Xóchitl, Johathan Fox, and Andrew Steele. 2006. *Invisible No More: Mexican Migrant Civic Participation in the United States.* Washington, D.C.: Woodrow Wilson International Center for Scholars.

Badiou, Alain. 2004. *Infinite Thought: Truth and the Return of Philosophy*. Translated and Edited by Oliver Feltham and Justin Clemens. London: Continuum.

Bahti, Dolores Rivas. 2001. "*Aztlán* in Arizona: Civic Narrative and Ritual Pagentry in Mexican America." PhD diss., University of Arizona.

Bair, JoAnn W., and Richard L. Jensen. 1977. "Prosecution of the Mormons in Arizona Territory in the 1880s." *Arizona and the West* 19 (1): 25–46.

Bakhtin, M. M. (1981) 1998. *The Dialogic Imagination: Four Essays*. Edited by Michael Holquist, translated by Caryl Emerson and Michael Holquist. Reprint, Austin: University of Texas Press.

Balchin, W. G., and Norman Pye. 1954. "Recent Economic Trends in Arizona." *Geographical Journal* 120 (2): 156–72.

Balderrama, Francisco E., and Raymond Rodríguez. 1995. *Decade of Betrayal: Mexican Repatriation in the 1930s*. Albuquerque: University of New Mexico Press.

Bancroft, Hubert Howe. (1889) 1962. *History of Arizona and New Mexico, 1530–1888*. Reprint, Albuquerque: Horn and Wallace.

Bandzak, Ruth Anne. 1991. "Collective Bargaining in the Copper Industry: A Case Study of the Phelps Dodge Strike of 1983." PhD diss., University of Notre Dame.

Barnes, Elinor J. 1964. "Arizona's People Since 1910: County by County—Decade by Decade." *Arizona Business Review and Public Administration* 13 (January): 3–10.

Barrera, Mario. 1978. "Class Segmentation and the Political Economy of the Chicano, 1900–1930." In *New Directions in Chicano Scholarship*, edited by Ricardo Romo and Raymund Paredes, 167–81. La Jolla: Chicano Studies Monograph Series, University of California, San Diego.

———. 1979. *Race and Class in the Southwest: A Theory of Racial Inequality*. Notre Dame, IN: University of Notre Dame Press.

———. 1983. "Traditions of Research on the Chicano Worker." In *The State of Chicano Research on Family, Labor, and Migration*, edited by Armando Valdez, Albert Camarillo, and Tomás Almaguer, 51–74. Stanford, CA: Stanford Center for Chicano Research.

Bashi, Vilna. 2004. "Globalized Anti-Blackness: Transnationalizing Western Immigration Law, Policy, and Practice." *Ethnic and Racial Studies* 27 (4): 584–606.

Bassett, Jenna. 2011. "Restricted Citizenship: The Struggle for Native American Voting Rights in Arizona." Master's thesis, Arizona State University.

Bauböck, Rainer. 2001. "Cultural Citizenship, Minority Rights, and Self-Government." In *Citizenship Today: Global Perspectives and Practices*, edited by Thomas A. Aleinikoff and Douglas Klusmeyer, 319–348. Washington, D.C.: Carnegie Endowment for International Peace.

Bellah, Robert et al. 1985. *Habits of the Heart: Individualism and Commitment in American Life*. New York: Perennial Library.

Benmayor, Rina, and Rosa M. Torruellas. 1997. "Education, Cultural Rights, and Citizenship." In *Women Transforming Politics: An Alternative Reader*, edited by Kathy Jones, Juan Tronto, and Cathy Cohen, 187–204. New York: New York University Press.

Benmayor, Rina, Rosa M. Torruellas, and Ana L. Juarbe. 1992. *Responses to Poverty Among Puerto Rican Women: Identity, Community, and Cultural Citizenship*. New York: Centro de Estudios Puertorriqueños, Hunter College.

Benson, Peter. 2008. "El Campo: Facility and Structural Violence in Farm Labor Camps." *Cultural Anthropology* 23 (4): 589–629.

Benton-Cohen, Katherine. 2002. "What about Women in the White Man's Camp?: Gender, Nation, and the Redefinition of Race in Cochise County, Arizona, 1853–1941." PhD diss., University of Wisconsin.

———. 2003. "Docile Children and Dangerous Revolutionaries: The Racial Hierarchy of Manliness and the Bisbee Deportation." *Frontiers: A Journal of Women Studies* 24 (2–3): 30–50.

———. 2005. "Common Purposes, Worlds Apart: Mexican American, Mormon, and Midwestern Women Homesteaders in Cochise County, Arizona." *Western Historical Quarterly* 36 (4): 428–52.

———. 2009. *Borderline Americans: Racial Divisions and Labor War in the Arizona Borderlands*. Cambridge, MA: Harvard University Press.

———. 2011. "Other Immigrants: Mexicans and the Dillingham Commission of 1907–1911." *Journal of American Ethnic History* 30 (2): 33–57.

Bernhardt, Annette et al. 2008. *The Gloves-Off Economy: Workplace Standards at the Bottom of America's Labor Market*. Champaign, IL: Labor and Employment Relations Association.

———. 2009. *Broken Laws, Unprotected Workers*. Chicago: University of Illinois at Chicago, National Employment Labor Project, UCLA Institute for Research on Labor and Employment.

Bernhardt, Annette, Siobhán McGrath, and James DeFilippis. 2007. *Unregulated Work in the Global City: Employment and Labor Law Violations in New York City*. New York: Brennan Center for Justice.

Bever, Lindsey. 2016. "'Make America White Again': A Politician's Billboard Ignites Uproar." *Washington Post*, June 23, 2016.

Bhattacharya, Sabyasachi, and Jan Lucassen, eds. 2005. *Workers in the Informal Sector: Studies in Labour History*. India: Macmillan.

Bjorkquist, Elena Diaz. 1996. *Suffer Smoke*. Houston: Arte Público Press.

Blackwelder, Julia Kirk. 1997. *Now Hiring: The Feminization of Work in the United States, 1900–1995*. College Station: Texas A&M University Press.

Blaine, Patricia A. 2003. "José María Redondo: Yuma Pioneer and Entrepreneur 1830–1878." Master's thesis, Arizona State University.

Blanton, Carlos Kevin. 2014. *George I. Sánchez: The Long Fight for Mexican American Integration*. New Haven, CT: Yale University Press.

Bobo, Kim. 2009. *Wage Theft in America*. New York: New Press.

Bogardus, Emory S. 1934. *The Mexican in the United States*. Los Angeles: University of Southern California Press.

Bolinger, Sara L. 2009. "The New Desaparecidos: Effects of Missing Migrants on Families of Sending Communities in Southern Mexico." Master's thesis, University of Arizona.

Bonacich, Edna. 1972. "A Theory of Ethnic Antagonism: The Split Labor Market." *American Sociological Review* 37 (5): 547–59.

Bonacich, Edna, Sabrina Alimahomed, and Jake B. Wilson. 2008. "The Racialization of Global Labor." *American Behavioral Scientist* 20 (10): 1–14.

Bonilla, Frank, Edwin Meléndez, Rebecca Morales, and María de lo Angeles Torres, eds. 1998. *Borderless Borders: U.S. Latinos, Latin Americans, and the Paradox of Interdependence*. Philadelphia: Temple University Press.

Booth, Peter MacMillan. 1991. "Cactizonians: The Civilian Conservation Corps in Pima County, 1933–1942." *Journal of Arizona History* 32: 291–332.

Boswell, Terry E. 1984. "Race, Class and Markets: Ethnic Stratification and Labor Market Segmentation in the Metal Mining Industry, 1850–1880." PhD diss., University of Arizona.

Boswell, Terry, and Diane Mitsch Bush. 1984. "Labor Force Competition and Union Organizing in the Arizona Copper Industry: A Comment on Jiménez." *Review: A Journal of the Fernand Braudel Center* 8 (1): 133–51.

Boswell, Thomas. 1979. "The Growth and Distribution of Mexican Stock, 1920–1979." *Mississippi Geographer* 7 (1): 57–76.

Bracker, Milton. 1947. "*El Coyote, The Rebel* by Luis Pérez." *New York Times*, June 22, 1947.

Branstrom, Christian. 2010. "Forests for Cotton: Institutions and Organizations in Brazil's Mid-Twentieth-Century Cotton Boom." *Journal of Historical Geography* 36: 169–82.

Brass, Tom. 1994. "Some Observations on Unfree Labour, Capitalist Restructuring, and Deproletarianization." *International Review of Social History* 39: 255–75.

Brass, Tom, and Marcel van der Linden, eds. 1997. *Free and Unfree Labour: The Debate Continues*. Bern, Germany: Peter Lang.

Breitbart.com. 2015a. "Paul Ryan's Christmas Warning: American Companies Will Shut Down Without More Foreign Workers." December 23, 2015. http://www.breitbart.com/big-government/2015/12/23/paul-ryans-christmas-warning-american-companies-will-shut-without-foreign-workers/.

———. 2015b. "Sen. Jeff Sessions: Omnibus a 'Betrayal', Increases Foreign Workers, Fully Funds Obama Immigration Agenda." December 16, 2015. http://www.breitbart.com/big-government/2015/12/16/sen-jeff-sessions-omnibus-betrayal-increases-foreign-workers-fully-funds-obama-immigration-agenda/.

Briegel, Kaye Lynn. 1974. "Alianza Hispano-Americana, 1894–1965: A Mexican American Fraternal Insurance Society." PhD diss., University of Southern California.

Briggs, David F. 2016. *History of the Copper Mountain (Morenci) Mining District, Greenlee County*. Arizona Geological Survey Contributed Report CR-16-C. www.azgs.gov/Repository.azgs.gov. November 2016.

Brodie, Mark. 2015. "Broker: Multi-Family Housing market 'Very Hot' in Phoenix Area." KJZZ Radio, October 22, 2015. http://kjzz.org/content/209622/broker-multi-family-housing-market-very-hot-phoenix-area.

Brophy, A. Blake. 1972. *Foundlings on the Frontier*. Tucson: University of Arizona Press.

Brown, C. S. 1926. Testimony, In Seasonal Agricultural Laborers from Mexico. Hearing, Committee on Immigration and Naturalization, U.S. House of Representatives, 69th Congress, 1st Session, 32–41. January 28 and 29, February 2, 9, 11, and 23, 1926.

Brown, Malcolm, and Orin Cassmore. 1939. *Migratory Cotton Pickers in Arizona*. Washington, D.C.: Government Printing Office.

Brundage, David. 1994. *The Making of Western Labor Radicalism: Denver's Organized Workers, 1878–1905*. Urbana: University of Illinois Press.

Bulmer, M. I. A. 1975. "Sociological Models of the Mining Community." *Sociological Review* 23 (1): 61–92.

Burawoy, Michael. 1976. "The Functions and Reproduction of Migrant Labor: Comparative Material from Africa and the United States." *American Journal of Sociology* 81 (5): 1050–87.

Bureau of Labor Statistics. 2007. "Occupational Employment Statistics: Occupational Employment and Wages," 47–2181. http://www.bls.gov/oes/current/oes472181.htm.

Burrough, D. J. 1994. "Demand High for Construction Workers." *Business Journal-Phoenix and the Valley of the Sun*, April 15, 1994.

Buss, Fran Leeper. 1993. *Forged Under the Sun: The Life of María Elena Lucas*. Ann Arbor: University of Michigan Press.

Byrkit, James W. 1972. "Life and Labor in Arizona, 1901–1921: With Particular Reference to the Deportations of 1917." PhD diss., Claremont Graduate School.

———. 1977. "The IWW in Wartime Arizona." *Journal of Arizona History* 18 (Summer): 149–70.

———. 1982. *Forging the Copper Collar: Arizona's Labor-Management War of 1901–1921*. Tucson: University of Arizona Press.

———. 1992. "Land, Sky, and People: The Southwest Defined." *Journal of the Southwest* 34 (3): 257–387.

Cadava, Geraldo L. 2008. "Corridor of Exchange: Culture and Ethnicity in Tucson's Modern Borderlands." PhD diss., Yale University.

———. 2011. "Borderlands of Modernity and Abandonment: The Lines within Ambos Nogales and the Tohono O'odham Nation." *Journal of American History* (September): 362–83.

———. 2013. *Standing on Common Ground: The Making of a Sunbelt Borderland*. Cambridge: Harvard University Press.

Calavita, Kitty. 1984. *U.S. Immigration Law and the Control of Labor: 1820–1924*. Orlando: Academic Press.

———. 1992. *Inside the State: The Bracero Program, Immigration, and the I.N.S.* New York: Routledge.

Calderón, Roberto R., ed. 1984. *South Texas Coal Mining: A Community History*. Eagle Pass, TX: Ramirez Printing.

———. 2000. *Mexican Coal Mining Labor in Texas and Coahuila, 1880–1930*. College Station: Texas A&M University Press.

Calderón-Zaks, Michael Aaron. 2008. "Constructing the 'Mexican Race': Racial Formation and Empire Building, 1884–1940." PhD diss., State University of New York, Binghamton.

Camarillo, Albert. 1979. *Chicanos in a Changing Society: From Mexican Pueblos to American Barrios in Santa Barbara and Southern California*. Cambridge, MA: Harvard University Press.

Campbell, Julie. 1980. "Phoenix Women during World War II." Arizona Collection, CM MSM-40, Department of Archives and Manuscripts, University Libraries, Arizona State University.

Cardoso, Lawrence A. 1976. "Labor Emigration to the Southwest, 1916 to 1920: Mexican Attitudes and Policy." *Southwestern Historical Quarterly* 79 (4): 400–416.

———. 1979. "Labor Emigration to the Southwest, 1916 to 1920: Mexican Attitudes and Policy." In *Mexican Workers in the United States: Historical and Political Perspectives*, edited by George C. Kiser and Martha Woody Kiser, 16–32. Albuquerque: University of New Mexico Press.

———. 1980. *Mexican Emigration to the United States, 1897–1931: Socio-Economic Patterns*. Tucson: University of Arizona Press.

Carrigan, William D., and Clive Webb. 2003. "The Lynching of Persons of Mexican Origin or Descent in the United States, 1848–1928." *Journal of Social History* 37 (2): 411–38.

Carrigan, William D. 2013. *Forgotten Dead: Mob Violence against Mexicans in the United States, 1848–1928*. New York: Oxford University Press.

Casillas, Michael E. 1979. "Mexicans, Labor, and Strife in Arizona, 1896–1917." Master's thesis Arizona State University.

Casson, Mallory. 2011. "Understanding Housekeeper's Perceived Mobility and Job Satisfaction within the Hospitality Industry in Metropolitan Phoenix, Arizona, U.S.A." Master's thesis, Arizona State University.

Castañeda, Antonia I. 1990. "Gender, Race, and Culture: Spanish-Mexican Women in the Historiography of Frontier California." *Frontiers: A Journal of Women Studies* 11 (1): 8–20.

———. 1992. "Women of Color and the Rewriting of Western History: The Discourse, Politics, and Decolonization of History." *Pacific Historical Review* 61 (4): 501–33.

Castillo, Ana. 2014. *Massacre of the Dreamers: Essays on Xicanisma*. Albuquerque: University of New Mexico Press.

Celaya, Dario H. 1977. "History of the Mexican American." Chicano Research Collection, CHSM-143, Department of Archives and Manuscripts, University Libraries, Arizona State University.

Cesario, Loryn Nicolle. 2011. "Coalition Building and Cooperation between Organized Labor and Immigrant Day Laborers in Portland, Oregon." Master's thesis, University of Oregon.

Chafe, William. 1972. *The American Woman: Her Changing Social, Economic, and Political Roles, 1920–1970*. Oxford: Oxford University Press.

Chan, Sucheng. 1986. *This Bittersweet Soil. The Chinese in California Agriculture, 1860–1910*. Berkeley: University of California Press.

Chansley, Pat. 1963. *Copper Book*. Miami, AZ: Miami Copper Company.

Chauvin, Sébastien, and Blanca Garcés-Mascareñas. 2012. "Beyond Informal Citizenship: The New Moral Economy of Migrant Illegality." *International Political Sociology* 6 (3): 241–59.

Chávez, John R. 1984. *The Lost Land: The Chicano Image of the Southwest*. Albuquerque: University of New Mexico Press.

Chew-Smithart, Selfa Alejandra. 2010. "Race, Gender, and Citizenship: The Removal of Japanese and Japanese Mexicans from the United States/Mexico Borderlands during World War II." PhD diss., University of Texas at El Paso.

Chirot, Daniel, and Anthony Reid. 1997. *Essential Outsiders: Chinese and Jews in the Modern Transformation of Southeast Asia and Europe*. Seattle: University of Washington Press.

Christy, Waldo B. 1920. "American Egyptian Staple Cotton in Arizona." PhD diss., University of Chicago.

Ciuccio, Victor. 1975. "Political Change in a Mexican-American Industrial Community." PhD diss., Pennsylvania State University.

Clark, Carter Blue. 1982. "Research Tools, Guide and Bibliographies on Arizona History a Selected List." *Arizona and the West* 24 (1): 39–56.

Clark, Victor S. 1908. "Mexican Labor in the United States." *Bulletin of the U.S. Bureau of Labor, Department of Commerce and Labor* 78 (September): 466–522.

Clawson, Dan, and Mary Ann Clawson. 1999. "What Has Happened to the U.S. Labor Movement? Union Decline and Renewal." *Annual Review of Sociology* 25: 95–119.

Cleland, R. G. 1952. *A History of Phelps Dodge: 1934–1850*. New York: Alfred A. Knopf.

Clugston, Kate. 1943. *Cotton or School*. New York: National Child Labor Committee, U.S. Department of Labor. Washington, D.C.: Government Printing Office.

Cobas, José, Jorge Duany, and Joe R. Feagin, eds. 2009. *How the United States Racialized Latinos: White Hegemony and Its Consequences*. Boulder, CO: Paradigm.

Codina, G. Edward, and Frank F. Montalvo. 1994. "Chicano Phenotype and Depression." *Hispanic Journal of Behavioral Sciences* 16 (3): 296–306.

Cohen, Deborah. 2011. *Braceros: Migrant Citizens and Transnational Subjects in the Postwar United States and Mexico*. Chapel Hill: University of North Carolina Press.

Cohen, Richard. 1986. "Rehnquist: A Question of Character." *Washington Post*, September 16, 1986.

Collins, William S. 2005. *The Emerging Metropolis: Phoenix, 1944–1973*. Phoenix: Arizona State Parks Board.

Colorado Legal Services, Migrant Farmworker Division. 2010. *Overworked and Underpaid: H-2A Herders in Colorado*. http://users.frii.com/cls/Overworked%20and%20Underpaid.pdf.

Colwell-Chanthaphonh, Chip. 2003. "The Camp Grant Massacre in the Historical Imagination." *Journal of the Southwest* 45 (3): 349–69.

———. 2007. *Massacre at Camp Grant: Forgetting and Remembering Apache History*. Tucson: University of Arizona Press.

Comaroff, John L., and Jean Comaroff. 2009. *Ethnicity, Inc.* Chicago: University of Chicago Press.

Condit, Brian et al. 1998. "Construction Organizing: A Case Study of Success." In *Organizing to Win: New Research on Union Strategies*, edited by Kate Bronfenbrenner et al., 309–19. Ithaca, NY: Cornell University Press.

Congress of Industrial Organizations/Arizona Federation of Labor. 1950. Testimony. Harry S. Truman Library, President's Commission on Migratory Labor, Box 6, Phoenix Statements.

Corley, Julie A. 1992. "Conflict and Community: St. Mary's Parish, Phoenix Arizona." Master's thesis, Arizona State University.

Cortes, Carlos, ed. 1976. *The Mexican Experience in Arizona*. New York: Arno Press.

Corwin, Arthur F. 1978. "Early Mexican Labor Migration: A Frontier Sketch, 1848–1900." In *Immigrants—and Immigrants: Perspectives on Mexican Labor Migration to the United States*, edited by Arthur F. Corwin, 25–37. Westport, CT: Greenwood Press.

Corwin, Arthur F., and Lawrence A. Cardoso. 1978. "Vamos al Norte: Causes of Mass Mexican Migration to the United States." In *Immigrants—and Immigrants: Perspectives on Mexican Labor Migration to the United States*, edited by Arthur F. Corwin, 38–66. Westport, CT: Greenwood Press.

Costa, Daniel. 2016. *The H-2B Temporary Foreign Worker Program: For Labor Shortages or Cheap, Temporary Labor?* Washington, D.C.: Economic Policy Institute.

"Cotton One of Essentials for Modern War, Secretary Daniels Tells Manufacturers." 1917. *The Official Bulletin*, 8.

Coulter, Ann. 2008. "John Vincent Coulter." Human Events, Wednesday, January 9, 2008. Available at http://humanevents.com/2008/01/09/john-vincent-coulter/.

Coutin, Susan. 2000. *Legalizing Moves: Salvadoran Immigrants' Struggle for U.S. Residency*. Ann Arbor: University of Michigan Press.

Cowie, Jefferson. 2002. "Nixon's Class Struggle: Romancing the New Right Worker, 1969–1973." *Labor History* 43 (3): 257–83.

Cox, Annie M. 1938. "History of Bisbee, 1877–1937." Master's thesis, University of Arizona.

Craig, Richard B. 1971. *The Bracero Program: Interest Groups and Foreign Policy*. Austin: University of Texas Press.

Crotty, Sean Michael. 2012. "The Geographic Dimensions of Day Labor Conflict in the San Diego Metropolitan Area." PhD diss., University of California, Santa Barbara.

Cruz, Gilbert R., and James D. McBride. 2004. *Arizona Heartland of the Southwest: Handbook of History Research Materials*. Austin, TX: Eakin Press.

Cuádraz, Gloria H. 2006. *Voices from the Camps of Litchfield Park* [video]. Funded by the Arizona Humanities Council, Grant #GG05-4477-2006.

Cuádraz, Gloria H., and Yolanda Flores, eds. 2017. *Claiming Home, Shaping Community: Testimonios de los valles*. Tucson: University of Arizona Press.

Cuádraz, Gloria Holguín. 2007. "Litchfield Oral History Project." In *Using Oral History in Community History Projects*, edited by L. Mercier and M. Buckendorf. Oral History Association.

———. 2009. "Negotiating Career and Family in Arizona: Belen Soto Moreno." In *Speaking History: Oral Histories of the American Past, 1865-Present*, edited by S. Armitage and L. Mercier, 142–46. Basingstoke, United Kingdom: Palgrave MacMillan.

———. 2011. "Unearthing and Recovering Memories in a Company Town: Litchfield Park, Arizona." *Chicana/Latina Studies: The Journal of Mujeres Activas en Letras y Cambio Social* 11 (1): 9–17.

———. 2012. "Ethico-political Dilemmas of a Community Oral History Project: Negotiating the Culture of the Corporate University." *Social Justice: A Journal of Crime, Conflict, and World Order* 38 (3): 17–32.

Dambourges Jacques, Leo Michael. 1975. "The Anti-Chinese Campaigns in Sonora, Mexico, 1900–1931." PhD diss., University of Arizona.

Daniel, Cletus E. 1981. *Bitter Harvest: A History of California Farmworkers, 1870–1941*. Ithaca, NY: Cornell University Press.

———. 1991. *Chicano Workers and the Politics of Fairness: the FEPC in the Southwest, 1941–1945*. Austin: University of Texas Press.

Daniels, Fred J. 1962. "Study of Seasonal Work Force, 1956–1961, Including 1962 Spring Lettuce in Maricopa County and 1961 Winter Lettuce Harvest in Yuma County." Employment Security Commission, Arizona State Employment Service, May 1962.

Dankowski, Becky. 1997. "Women in Phoenix, 1870–1940: Daily Life and Intercultural Relations." Master's thesis, Arizona State University.

Dávila, Alene. 2008. *Latino Spin: Public Image and the Whitewashing of Race*. New York: New York University Press.

Dean, David R., and Jean A. Reynolds. 2006. "Hispanic Historic Property Survey: Final Report." City of Phoenix, Historic Preservation Office, Athanaeum Public History Group.

De Castro, Arnold, Kaori Fujishiro, Erica Sweitzer, and José Oliva. 2006. "How Immigrant Workers Experience Workplace Problems: A Qualitative Study." *Archives of Environmental and Occupational Health* 61 (6): 249–58.

DeCierdo, Margarita Arce. 1999. "The Struggle Within: The California Agricultural Labor Relations Board, 1975–1990." In *Chicano Politics and Society: In the Late Twentieth Century*, edited by David Montejano, 83–107. Austin: University of Texas Press.

De La Trinidad, Maritza. 2008. "Collective Outrage: Mexican American Activism and the Quest for Educational Equality and Reform, 1950–1990." PhD diss., University of Arizona.

De Lay, Brian. 2008. *War of a Thousand Deserts: Indian Raids and the U.S.-Mexican War*. New Haven, CT: Yale University Press.

Del Castillo, Adelaida, ed. 1990. *Between Borders: Essays on Mexicana/Chicana History*. Encino, CA: Floricanto Press.

de León, Arnoldo. 1983. *They Called Them Greasers: Anglo Attitudes Toward Mexicans in Texas, 1821–1900*. Austin: University of Texas Press.

———. 1985. *The Tejano Community, 1836–1900*. Albuquerque: University of New Mexico Press.

Delgado, Grace Peña. 2000. "In the Age of Exclusion: Race, Region, and Chinese Identity in the Making of the Arizona-Sonora Border, 1863–1943." PhD diss., University of California, Los Angeles.

———. 2005. "Of Kith and Kin: Land, Lease, and Guanxi in Tucson's Chinese and Mexican Communities, 1880–1920s." *Journal of Arizona History* 46 (1): 33–54.

———. 2012. *Making the Chinese Mexican: Global Migration, Localism, and Exclusion in the U.S.-Mexico Borderlands*. Stanford, CA: Stanford University Press.

Delgado, Hector. 1993. *New Immigrants, Old Unions: Organizing Undocumented Workers in Los Angeles*. Philadelphia: Temple University Press.

Delgado-Moreira, Juan. 1997. "Cultural Citizenship and the Creation of European identity." *Electronic Journal of Sociology* 2: 1–24.

Dershowitz, Alan. 2005. "Telling the Truth about Chief Justice Rehnquist." Huffington Post, September 4, 2005. http://www.huffingtonpost.com/alan-dershowitz/telling-the-truth-about-c_b_6844.html.

Diehl, Michel W., and Allison C. Diehl. 2001. "Economics, Ideology, and the Brick Industry in Tucson." *Journal of the Southwest* 43 (3): 423–46.

Dimas, Pete R. 1991. "Perspectives on Progress and a Mexican American Community's Struggle for Existence." PhD diss., Arizona State University.

———. 1999. *Progress and a Mexican American Community's Struggle for Existence: Phoenix's Golden Gate Barrio*. New York: Peter Lang.

———, dir. 2014. *Arizona's Mexican Heritage: An American Story*. DVD.

Dinwoodie, D. H. 1977. "Deportation: The Immigration Service and the Chicano Labor Movement in the 1930s." *New Mexico Historical Quarterly* 52 (3): 193–206.

Dorich, Thomas K. 1997. "'This is a Tough Place to Work': Industrial Relations in the Jerome Mines, 1900–1922." *Journal of Arizona History* 38 (Autumn): 233–56.

Dowell, Gregory Paul. 1978. "History of the Empire Ranch." Master's thesis, University of Arizona.

Dowling, Julie. 2015. *Mexican Americans and the Question of Race*. Austin: University of Texas Press.

Driscoll, Bárbara. 1996. *Me voy pa' Pensilvania por no andar en la vagancia: Los ferrocarrileros mexicanos en Estados Unidos durante la segunda guerra mundial*. Mexico City: Universidad Autónoma de México.

———. 1999. *The Tracks North: The Railroad Bracero Program of World War II*. Austin: Center for Mexican American Studies, University of Texas.

DuBord, Elise M. 2008. "Performing Bilingualism: An Ethnographic Analysis of Discursive Practices at a Day Labor Center in the Southwest." PhD diss., University of Arizona.

Durand, Jorge. 2006. *Programas de trabajadores temporales: Evaluación y analisis del caso mexicano*. México: Consejo Nacional de Población y Secretaría de Gobernación.

———. 2007. *Braceros: Las miradas Mexicana y estadounidense: Antología 1945–1964*. Mexico City: Miguel Ángel Porrúa.

Durham, Michael S. 1990. *The Smithsonian Guide to Historic America: The Desert States*. New York: Stewart, Tabori & Chang.

Duschiski, Haley. 2010. "Reproducing Regimes of Impunity." *Cultural Studies* 24 (1): 110–32.

Eaton, W. Clement. 1933. "Frontier Life in Southern Arizona, 1858–1861." *Southwestern Historical Quarterly* 363: 173–92.

Echeverria, Darius V. 2005. "*Aztlán* Arizona: Abuses, Awareness, Animosity, and Activism Amid Mexican-Americans, 1968–1978." PhD diss., Temple University.

Economy.com, 2002. "Arizona's Economic Future. Report for the Arizona Department of Commerce."

Economic Policy Institute. 2015. "Sen. Mikulski Wrecks Labor Standards in H-2B Guestworker Program." December 17, 2015. http://www.epi.org/blog/sen-mikulski-wrecks-labor-standards-in-h-2b-guestworker-program/.

Edelstein, Daniel. 1988. *Copper*. Available at https://minerals.usgs.gov/minerals/pubs/commodity/copper/240798.pdf. Accessed June 5, 2018.

Ehrlich, Karen Lynn. 1981. "Arizona's Territorial Capital Moves to Phoenix." *Arizona and the West* 23 (3): 231–42.

Erickson, Emily J. 2009. "Standing While Latino: Understanding Day Labor Ordinances in California Cities." Master's thesis, University of California, San Diego.

Eze, Emmanuel Chukwudi, ed. 1997. *Race and Enlightenment: A Reader*. Cambridge, MA: Blackwell.

Fantasia, Rick, and Kim Voss. 2004. *Hard Work: Remaking the American Labor Movement*. Berkeley: University of California Press.

Farmworker Justice. 2011. *No Way To Treat A Guest: Why the H-2A Visa Program Fails U.S. and Foreign Workers*. Washington, D.C. http://www.farmworkerjustice.org/sites/default/files/documents/7.2.a.6%20No%20Way%20To%20Treat%20A%20Guest%20H-2A%20Report.pdf.

Fassin, Didier. 2011. "Racialization." In *A Companion to the Anthropology of the Body and Embodiment*, edited by Frances E. Mascia-Lees, 419–34. Malden, MA: Wiley-Blackwell.

Feagin, Joe R. 2010. *Racist America: Roots, Current Realities, and Future Reparations*. New York: Routledge.

———. 2012. *White Party, White Government: Race, Class, and U.S. Politics*. New York: Routledge.

Fernández, Leah. 2012. "Race and the Western Frontier: Colonizing the Imperial Valley, 1900–1948." PhD diss., University of California, Santa Barbara.

Fernández, Raúl. 1970. "The Political Economy of Stereotypes." *Aztlán: A Journal of Chicano Studies* 12: 39–45.

Fernández-Kelly, María Patricia. 1984. *For We Are Sold, I and My People: Women and Industry in Mexico's Frontier*. Albany: State University of New York Press.

Fine, Janice 2005a. "Worker Centers: Organizing Communities at the Edge of the Dream." *New York Law School Law Review* 50: 417–63.

———. 2005b. "Community Unions and the Revival of the American Labor Movement." *Politics & Society* 33: 153–99.

Fisher, Jacob. 2006. "Streets and Work Centers: Day Labor Hiring in Phoenix Metro Area." Master's thesis, Arizona State University.

Fitzgerald, David. 2005. "State and Emigration: A Century of Emigration Policy in Mexico." Working paper no. 123, Center for Comparative Immigration Studies, University of California, San Diego.

———. 2006. "Inside the Sending State: The Politics of Mexican Emigration Control." *International Migration Review* 40 (2): 259–93.

Flake, Jeff. 2016. "Flake Introduces Bill to Establish Flexible Guest Worker Pilot Program." April 20, 2016. http://www.flake.senate.gov/public/index.cfm/press-releases?ID=A9DFF215-9FA8-4859-8D53-250D726C0513.

Fletcher, Bill, and Richard Hurd. 1998. "Beyond the Organizing Model: The Transformation Process in Local Unions." In *Organizing to Win: New Research on Union Strategies*, edited by Kate Bronfenbrenner et al., 27–53. Ithaca, NY: Cornell University Press.

Flores, John H. 2013. "Deporting Dissidence: Examining Transnational Mexican Politics, US Naturalization, and American Unions through the Life of a Mexican Immigrant, 1920–1954." *Aztlán: A Journal of Chicano Studies* 38 (1): 95–123.

Flores, Lori. 2010. "Book Review: Benton-Cohen, Katherine 2009, *Borderline Americans: Racial Division and Labor War in the Arizona Borderlands*." *Latino Studies* 8 (2): 289–91.

Flores, Raymond Johnson. 1951. "The Socio-Economic Status Trends of the Mexican People Residing in Arizona." Master's thesis, Arizona State College.

Flores, William V. and Rina Benmayor, eds. 1997. *Latino Cultural Citizenship: Claiming Identity, Space, and Rights*. Boston: Beacon Press.

Foley, Douglas et al. 1977. *From Peones to Políticos: Ethnic Relations in a South Texas Town, 1900–1977*. Austin: Center for Mexican American Studies, University of Texas.

Foley, Neil. 1997. *The White Scourge: Mexicans, Blacks, and Poor Whites in Texas Cotton Culture*. Berkeley: University of California Press.

———. 2014. *Mexicans and the Making of America*. Cambridge, MA: Belknap Press.

Fong, Lawrence M. 1980. "Sojourners and Settlers: The Chinese Experience in Arizona." *Journal of Arizona History* 21 (Autumn): 1–30.

Foo, Lora Jo. 1994. "The Vulnerable and Exploitable Immigrant Workforce and the Need for Strengthening Worker Protective Legislation." *Yale Law Journal* 103 (8): 2179–2212.

Forbes. 2000. "The World's Leading Companies." http://www.forbes.com/2010/04/21/global-2000-leading-world-business-global-2000-10_land.html.

Foster, James C., ed. 1982. *American Labor in the Southwest: The First One Hundred Years*. Tucson: University of Arizona Press.

Foucault, Michel. 2008. *The Birth of Biopolitics: Lectures at the College de France, 1978–79*. Translated by Graham Burchell. New York: Palgrave Macmillan.

Francaviglia, Richard V. 1982. "Copper Mining and Landscape Evolution: A Century of Change in the Warren Mining District, Arizona." *Journal of Arizona History* 23 (3): 267–98.

Freeman, R. B. 1972. *Labor Economics*. Englewood Cliffs, NJ: Prentice Hall.

Freire, Paulo. 1981. *Pedagogy of the Oppressed*. New York: Continuum.

Frisch, Michael. 1990. *A Shared Authority: Essays on the Craft and Meaning of Oral and Public History*. Albany: State University of New York Press.

Fuller, Roden. 1928. "Occupations of the Mexican-Born Population of Texas, New Mexico and Arizona, 1900–1920." *Journal of the American Statistical Association* 23 (161): 64–67.

Galarza, Ernesto. 1956. *Strangers in Our Fields*. Washington, D.C.: U.S. Section, Joint United States-Mexico Trade Union Committee.

———. 1964. *Merchants of Labor. The Mexican Bracero Story. An Account of the Managed Migration of Mexican Farm Workers in California, 1942–1960*. Charlotte, NC: McNally and Loftin.

———. 1977. *Farm Workers and Agri-Business in California, 1947–1960*. Notre Dame, IN: University of Notre Dame Press.

Gamboa, Erasmo. 1990. *Mexican Labor and World War II: Braceros in the Pacific Northwest, 1942–1947*. Austin: University of Texas Press.

———. 2016. *Bracero Railroaders: The Forgotten World War II Story of Mexican Workers in the U.S. West*. Seattle: University of Washington Press.

Gamio, Manuel. (1930) 1971. *Mexican Immigration to the United States: A Study of Human Migration and Adjustment*. Reprint, New York: Dover.

Gamio, Manuel 2002. *El Inmigrante Mexicano: La Historia de su vida, Entrevistas Completas, 1926–1927*. Edited by Devra Weber, Roberto Melville, and Juan Vicente Palerm. Mexico City: Miguel Ángel Porrua.

Gammage, Sarah. 2008. "Working on the Margins: Migration and Employment in the United States." In *The Gloves-Off Economy: Workplace Standards at the Bottom of America's Labor Market*, edited by Annette Bernhardt et al., 137–61. Champaign, IL: Labor and Employment Relations Association.

Gans, Judith. 2008. "Immigrants in Arizona: Fiscal and Economic Impacts." Tucson: University of Arizona, Udall Center for Studies in Public Policy. http://udallcenter.arizona.edu/immigration/publications/impactofimmigrants08.pdf.

García, Albert M. 1934. "Latin Americans in Yuma County." *El Latino Americano* 1: 6, 12.

García, John A., Theresa Córdova, and Juan R. García, eds. 1984. *The Chicano Struggle: Analyses of Past and Present Efforts*. Binghamton, NY: Bilingual Press/Editorial Bilingüe.

García, Juan Ramón. 1980. *Operation Wetback. The Mass Deportation of Mexican Undocumented Workers in 1954*. Westport, CT: Greenwood Press.

García, Justine. 2014. "Workers on the Rise." *Vimeo*, January 27. https://vimeo.com/85164509.

García, Mario T. 1981. *Desert Immigrants: The Mexicans of El Paso, Texas, 1880–1920*. New Haven, CT: Yale University Press.

———. 1984. "Mexican American Labor and the Left: The Asociación Nacional Mexico-Americana, 1949–1954." In *The Chicano Struggle: Analyses of Past and Present Efforts*, edited by John A. García, Theresa Córdova, and Juan R. García, 65–86. Binghamton, NY: Bilingual Press/Editorial Bilingue.

———. 1989. *Mexican Americans: Leadership, Ideology, and Identity, 1930–1960*. New Haven, CT: Yale University Press.

García, Matt. 2001. *A World of Its Own. Race, Labor, and Citrus in the Making of Greater Los Angeles, 1900–1970*. Chapel Hill: University of North Carolina Press.

García y Griego, Manuel. 1983. "The Importation of Mexican Contract Laborers to the United States, 1942–1964: Antecedents, Operation, and Legacy." In *The Border that Joins: Mexican Migrants and U.S. Responsibility*, edited by Peter G. Brown and Henry Shue, 49–98. Totowa, NJ: Rowman and Littlefield.

———. 1988. "The Bracero Policy Experiment: U.S.-Mexican Responses to Mexican Labor Migration, 1942–1955." PhD diss., University of California, Los Angeles.

Garcilazo, Jeffrey M. 1995. "Traqueros: Mexican Railroad Workers in the United States, 1870 to 1930." PhD diss., University of California, Santa Barbara.

———. 1998. "Chicano Labor Historiography and the Persistence of Common Labor." *Mexican Studies/Estudios Mexicanos* 142: 441–49.

———. 2001. "McCarthyism, Mexican Americans, and the Los Angeles Committee for the Protection of the Foreign-Born, 1950–1954," *Western Historical Quarterly* 3 (23): 273–95.

———. 2013. *Traqueros: Mexican Railroad Workers in the United States, 1870–1930*. Denton: University of North Texas Press.

Gardiner, C. Harvey. 1981. *Pawns in a Triangle of Hate: The Peruvian Japanese and the United States*. Seattle: University of Washington Press.

Gardner, Martha M. 2005. *The Qualities of a Citizen: Women, Immigration, and Citizenship, 1870–1965*. Princeton, NJ: Princeton University Press.

Gart, Jason H. 2006. "Electronics and Aerospace Industry in Cold War Arizona, 1945–8: Motorola, Hughes Aircraft, Goodyear Aircraft." PhD diss., Arizona State University.

General Accounting Office. 2002. *Worker Protection: Labor's Efforts to Enforce Protections for Day Laborers Could Benefit from Better Data and Guidance*. Washington, D.C.: Government Printing Office.

Ghani, Ashraf 1995. "Writing a History of Power: An Examination of Eric R. Wolf's Anthropological Quest." In *Articulating Hidden Histories: Exploring the Influence of Eric R. Wolf*, edited by Jane Schneider and Rayna Rapp, 31–48. Berkeley: University of California Press.

Gilbert, Alan. 1994. "Third World Cities: Poverty, Employment, Gender Roles and the Environment During a Time of Restructuring." *Urban Studies* 31 (4–5): 605–33.

Gillespie, William B., and Mary M. Farrell, 2002. "Work Camp Settlement Patterns: Landscape-Scale Comparisons of Two Mining Camps in Southeastern Arizona." *Historical Archaeology* 36 (3): 59–68.

Glaser, Leah. 1996. "Working for Community: The Yaqui Indians at the Salt River Project." *Journal of Arizona History* 37: 339–56.

Gleeson, Shannon. 2010. "Labor Rights for All? The Role of Undocumented Immigrant Status for Worker Claims Making." *Law and Social Inquiry* 35 (3): 561–95.

Gluck, Sherna. 1987. *Rosie the Riveter Revisited: Women, the War, and Social Change*. Boston: Twayne Publishers.

Goldberg, Anne J. 2006. "Company Town, Border Town, Small Town: Transforming Place and Identities on the U.S.-Mexico Border." *Journal of the Southwest* 483: 275–306.

Goldfield, Michael. 2006. "Achilles' Heel and the Tortoise: Race and the Labor Movement in the United States of America." In *Race and Labor Matters in the New US Economy*, edited by Manning Marable, Immanuel Ness, and Joseph Wilson, 71–95. Oxford: Rowman & Littlefield.

Goldstein, Marcy Gail. 1977. "Americanization and Mexicanization: The Mexican Elite and Anglo-Americans in the Gadsden Purchase Lands, 1853–1880." PhD diss., Case Western Reserve University.

Goldstein, Steve. 2016. "Film 'The Big Short' Shows Great Recession, Burst of Real Estate Bubble." KJZZ Radio, January 6, 2016. http://kjzz.org/content/247360/film-big-short-shows-great-recession-burst-real-estate-bubble.

Gómez, Laura E. 2008. *Manifest Destinies: The Making of the Mexican American Race*. New York: New York University Press.

Gómez-Quiñones, Juan. 1994. *Mexican American Labor, 1790–1990*. Albuquerque: University of New Mexico Press.

Gonzales, Alfonso. 2009. "The 2006 *Mega Marchas* in Greater Los Angeles: Counter-Hegemonic Moment and the Future of *El Migrante* Struggle." *Latino Studies* 7 (1): 30–59.

Gonzales, Manuel G. 2000. "Carlos I. Velasco and the Defense of Mexican Rights in Territorial Arizona." In *En Aquel Entonces: Readings in Mexican-American History*, edited by Manuel G. Gonzales and Cynthia M. Gonzales, 96–103. Bloomington: Indiana University Press.

———. 2002a. "A Rich Past: An Overview of Early Southwest and Arizona History." In *Arizona Hispanics: The Evolution of Influence. Eighty-First Arizona Town Hall*, edited by Louis Olivas, 1–17. Tempe; Arizona State University.

———. 2002b. *Mexicanos: A History of Mexicans in the United States*. Bloomington: Indiana University Press.

Gonzales, Michael J. 1994. "United States Copper Companies, the State, and Labor Conflict in Mexico, 1900–1910." *Journal of Latin American Studies* 26 (3): 651–81.

———. 1996. "U.S. Copper Companies, the Mine Workers' Movement, and the Mexican Revolution, 1910–1920." *Hispanic American Historical Review* 76 (3): 503–34.

González, Daniel. 2012. "Arizona's Illegal-Immigration Population Plunges." *Arizona Republic*, March 23, 2012.

González, Deena J. 1990. "The Widowed Women of Santa Fe: Assessments of the Lives of an Unmarried Population, 1850–1880." In *Unequal Sisters: A Multi-Cultural Reader in U.S. Women's History*, edited by Vicki L. Ruiz and Ellen Dubois, 34-50. New York: Routledge.

———. 1992. "Book Review: Thomas E. Sheridan, *Los Tucsonenses: The Mexican Community in Tucson, 1854–1941*." In *Chicano Discourse: Selected Conference Proceedings of the National Association for Chicano Studies*, edited by Tatcho Mindiola Jr. and Emilio Zamora. Houston: NACS/Mexican American Studies Program, University of Houston.

González, Gilbert Ramírez. 2004. "Strategy and Stopes: Mines, Management, and Community in Superior and Jerome, Arizona, 1900–1955." PhD diss., Arizona State University.

González, Gilbert G. 1994. *Labor and Community. Mexican Citrus Worker Villages in a Southern California County 1900–1950*. Urbana: University of Illinois Press.

———. 1999. *Mexican Consults and Labor Organizing*. Austin: University of Texas Press.

———. 2006. *Guest Workers or Colonized Labor?: Mexican Labor Migration to the United States*. Boulder, CO: Paradigm Publishers.

González, Trinidad. 2008. "The World of México Texanos, Mexicanos and México Americanos: Transnational and National Identities in the Lower Rio Grande Valley During the Last Phase of United States Colonization, 1900 to 1930." PhD diss., University of Houston.

González-Day, Ken. 2006. *Lynching in the West: 1850–1935*. Durham, NC: Duke University Press.

Goodrum, Paul. 2004. "Hispanic and Non-Hispanic Wage Differentials: Implications for United States Construction Industry." *Journal of Construction Engineering and Management* 1309: 552–59.

"Goodyear Cotton Plantation." 1917. *Arizona* 7: 3.

"Goodyear's Cotton Project near Phoenix, Arizona." 1917. *The Green Earth*, 10–11.

Gordon, Charles. 1969. "Comment: The Amiable Fiction—Alien Commuters under Our Immigration Laws." *Case Western Reserve Journal of International Law* 1: 124–30.

Gordon, Jennifer. 2005. *Suburban Sweatshops: The Fight for Immigrant Rights*. Cambridge, MA: Belknap Press.

Gordon, Linda. 1999. *The Great Arizona Orphan Abduction*. Cambridge, MA: Harvard University Press.

Governor C.C. Young's Mexican Fact-Finding Committee. 1930. *Mexicans in California*. San Francisco: California State Printing Office.

Graham, S. B. 1980. "Community, Conformity, and Career: Patterns of Social Interaction in Two Arizona Mining Towns." *Urban Anthropology* 91: 1–20.

Granger, Byrd H., ed. 1960. *Will C. Barnes' Arizona Place Names*. Tucson: University of Arizona Press.

Green, Linda. 2008. "A Wink and a Nod: Notes from the Arizona Borderlands." *Dialectical Anthropology* 32: 161–67.

Greenspan, Alan. 1996. "Remarks by Chairman Alan Greenspan at the Annual Dinner and Francis Boyer Lecture of The American Enterprise Institute for Public Policy Research." December 5, 1996. https://www.federalreserve.gov/boarddocs/speeches/1996/19961205.htm.

———. 2002. "Testimony. U.S. Senate Committee on Banking, Housing, and Urban Affairs." July 16, 2002. http://www.federalreserve.gov/boarddocs/hh/2002/July/testimony.htm.

Greenberg, Amy S. 2009. "Domesticating the Border: Manifest Destiny and the 'Comforts of Life' in the U.S.-Mexico Boundary Commission on the Gadsden Purchase, 1848–1854." In *Land of Necessity: Consumer Culture in the United States-Mexico Borderlands*, edited by Alexis McCrossen, 83–112. Durham, NC: Duke University Press.

Gressinger, A. W. 1961. *Charles D. Poston: Sunland Seer*. Globe, AZ: Dale Stuart King Publishers.

Griffin-Pierce, Trudy. 2006. *Chiricahua Apache Enduring Power: Naiche's Puberty Ceremony Paintings*. Tuscaloosa: University of Alabama Press.

Griffith, David. 2006. *American Guestworkers: Jamaicans and Mexicans in the U.S. Labor Market*. University Park: Pennsylvania State University Press.

Griswold del Castillo, Richard. 1980. *The Los Angeles Barrios, 1850–1890: A Social History*. Berkeley: University of California Press.

———. 1990a. *The Treaty of Guadalupe Hidalgo*. Norman: University of Oklahoma Press.

———. 1990b. "Chicano Historical Discourse: An Overview and Evaluation of the 1980s." *Perspectives in Mexican American Studies* 4: 1–26.

———. 2000. "Tucsonenses and Angelenos: A Socio-Economic Study of Two Mexican-American Barrios, 1860–1880." In *En Aquel Entonces: Readings in Mexican-American History*, edited by Manuel G. Gonzales and Cynthia M. Gonzales, 80–86. Bloomington: Indiana University Press.

Gritter, Matthew. 2012. *Mexican Inclusion: The Origins of Anti-Discrimination Policy in Texas and the Southwest*. College Station: Texas A&M University Press.

Grosfoguel, Ramón. 2003. *Colonial Subjects: Puerto Ricans in a Global Perspective*. Berkeley: University of California Press.

Grove, Wayne A. 2000. "Cotton on the Federal Road to Economic Development: Technology and Labor Policies Following World War II." *Agricultural History* 742: 272–92.

———. 2002. "The Economics of Cotton Harvest Mechanization in the United States, 1920–1970." *Journal of Economic History* 62 (2): 545–49.

———. 2003. "Better Opportunities or Worse? The Demise of Cotton Harvest Labor, 1949–1964." *Journal of Economic History* 63 (3): 736–67.

Grunwald, Michael. 2010. "Why the U.S. Is Also Giving Brazilians Farm Subsidies." *Time*, April 9, 2010.

Guerín-Gonzales, Camille. 1994. *Mexican Workers and American Dreams: Immigration, Repatriation, and California Farm Labor, 1900–1939*. New Brunswick, NJ: Rutgers University Press.

Guerra, Sarina, and Derick Washington, 2015. Oral History of Mr. Martínez. Phoenix, AZ.

Guevarra, Anna Romina. 2003. *Marketing Dreams, Manufacturing Heroes: The Transnational Labor Brokering of Filipino Workers*. New Brunswick, NJ: Rutgers University Press.

Guevarra, Rudy P. 2012. *Becoming Mexipino: Multiethnic Identities and Communities in San Diego*. New Brunswick, NJ: Rutgers University Press.

Guidotti-Hernández, Nicole. 2010. "Embodied Forms of State Domination: Gender and the Camp Grant Massacre." *Social Text* 28 (3): 91–117.

———. 2011. *Unspeakable Violence: Remapping U.S. and Mexican National Imaginaries*. Durham, NC: Duke University Press.

———. 2014. "Petra Santa Cruz Stevens and the Sexual and Racial Modalities of Property Relations in the Nineteenth-Century Arizona-Sonora Borderlands." *Cultural Dynamics* 26 (3): 347–78.

Gutiérrez, David G. 1993. "Significant to Whom? Mexican Americans and the History of the American West." *Western Historical Quarterly* 24 (1): 519–39.

———. 1995. *Walls and Mirrors: Mexican Americans, Mexican Immigrants, and the Politics of Ethnicity*. Berkeley: University of California Press.

———, ed. 1996. *Between Two Worlds: Mexican Immigrants in the United States*. Wilmington, NC: Scholarly Resources.

———. 2004. "Preface." In *The Columbia History of Latinos in the United States Since 1960*, edited by D. G. Gutiérrez, ix–xxiv. New York: Columbia University Press.

Gutiérrez, Gustavo. 1972. *Teología de la liberación: Perspectivas*. Salamanca, Spain: Ediciones Sigueme.

Hahamovitch, Cindy. 1997. *The Fruits of Their Labor: Atlantic Coast Farmworkers and the Making of Migrant Poverty, 1870–1945*. Chapel Hill: University of North Carolina Press.

———. 2011. *No Man's Land: Jamaican Guestworkers in America and the Global History of Deportable Labor*. Princeton, NJ: Princeton University Press.

Hale, Duane Kendall. 1981. "Mineral Exploration in the Spanish Borderlands, 1513–1846." *Journal of the West* 20 (2): 5–20.

Haley, James L. 1997. *Apaches: A History and Cultural Portrait*. Norman: University of Oklahoma Press.

Hall, Linda B., and Don M. Coerver. 1988. *Revolution on the Border: The United States and Mexico, 1910–1920*. Albuquerque: University of New Mexico Press.

Hall, Stuart. 1996. "The Question of Cultural Identity." In *Modernity: An Introduction to Modern Societies*, edited by Stuart Hall et al., 595–634. Malden, MA: Blackwell.

Hämäläinen, Pekka, and Benjamin H. Johnson, 2012. *Major Problems in the History of North American Borderlands*. Boston: Wadsworth-Cengage Learning.

Haney López, Ian F. 1996. *White by Law: The Legal Construction of Race*. New York: New York University Press.

Hannon, John James. 1982. "Power-Conflict, Cultural Preparation and Occupational Prestige: A Comparative Study of Arizona Farm Wage-Workers from Four Ethnic Categories." PhD diss., University of Arizona.

Hansen, Ronald. 2014. "Arizona Among States Where Taxes Have Climbed the Least Since 2008." *Arizona Republic*, May 20, 2014.

Haq, Husna. 2010. "Hispanics Abandon Arizona, Fleeing Economy, Immigration Law." *Christian Science Monitor*, June 10, 2010.

Hardaway, Roger. 1986. "Unlawful Love: A History of Arizona's Miscegenation Law." *Journal of Arizona History* 27: 377–90.

Harner, John P. 1993. "Patterns and Processes of Undocumented Mexican Migration to Arizona." Master's thesis, Arizona State University.

———. 1995. "Continuity Amidst Change: Undocumented Mexican Migration to Arizona." *Professional Geographer* 47 (4): 399–411.

———. 1996. "Copper Mining and Regional Identity in Sonora, Mexico." PhD diss., Arizona State University.

———. 2000. "The Mexican Community in Scottsdale, Arizona." *Yearbook, Conference of Latin Americanist Geographers* 26: 29–46.

———. 2010. "Place Identity and Copper Mining in Sonora, Mexico." *Annals of the Association of American Geographers* 91 (4): 660–80.

Harrison, Charles B. 1954. "The Development of the Arizona Labor Movement." Master's thesis, Arizona State College.

Haskett, Bert. 1935. "Early History of the Cattle Industry in Arizona." *Arizona Historical Review* 6 (1): 3–42.

———. 1936. "History of the Sheep Industry in Arizona." *Arizona Historical Review* 7 (3): 4–49.

Hatch, Heather, Karen Dahood, and Al V. Fernández. 1982. "Clifton: Photography and Folk History in a Mining Town." *Journal of Arizona History* 23: 317–40.

Hatfield, Shelley Bowen. 1998. *Chasing Shadows: Indians Along the United States-Mexico Border, 1876–1911*. Albuquerque: University of New Mexico Press.

Hayden, Carl T. 1926. Testimony. Seasonal Agricultural Laborers from Mexico, Hearing, Committee on Immigration and Naturalization, U.S. House of Representatives, 69th Congress, 1st Session, January 28 and 29, February 2, 9, 11, and 23, 190–201.

Heim, Carol E. 2001. "Urban Sprawl and Growth Management: Phoenix 1950–2000." *American Journal of Economics and Sociology* 60 (1): 245–83.

Hernández, Kathleen Anne Lytle. 2002. "Entangling Bodies and Borders: Racial Profiling and the U.S. Border Patrol, 1924–1955." PhD diss., University of California, Los Angeles.

Hernández, Kelly Lytle. 2010. *Migra! A History of the U.S. Border Patrol*. Berkeley: University of California Press.

Heyman, Josiah McC. 1991. *Life and Labor on the Border: Working People of Northeastern Sonora, Mexico, 1886–1986*. Tucson: University of Arizona Press.

———. 1993. "The Oral History of the Mexican Origin Community of Douglas, Arizona, 1901–1942." *Journal of the Southwest* 35 (2): 186–206.

———. 1995. "In the Shadow of the Smokestacks: Labor and Environmental Conflict in a Company-dominated Town." In *Articulating Hidden Histories: Exploring the Influence of Eric R. Wolff*, edited by Jane Schneider and Rayna Rapp, 156–74. Berkeley: University of California Press.

Hietter, Paul T. 2001. "A Surprising Amount of Justice: The Experience of Mexican and Racial Minority Defendants Charged with Serious Crimes in Arizona, 1865–1920." *Pacific Historical Review* 702: 183–219.

Higginbotham, Marcia, Keith Hoskins, and Steve Hall. 1978. "Survey of Federal Cases Arising in Arizona 1977–78." *Arizona State Law Journal* 2–3: 257–84.

Hill, Nancy. 2007. "The Imprint of Cotton Production on Arizona Landscapes." PhD diss., Arizona State University.

Hing, Bill Ong, and Kevin R. Johnson. 2006. "The Immigrant Rights Marches of 2006 and the Prospects for a New Civil Rights Movement." University of California, Davis, School of Law: UC Davis Legal Studies Research Paper Series, No. 96.

Hinton, Harwood. 1960. "Frontier Speculation: A Study of the Walker Mining Districts." *Pacific Historical Review* 29 (3): 245–55.

Hirtz, Frank. 1997. "Book Review: *Cotton is the Mother of Poverty—Peasants, Work, and Rural Struggle in Colonial Mozambique, 1938–1961*." *Journal of Political Ecology* 4 (1): 11–12.

Hoffman, Dennis, and Tom R. Rex. 2008. *Tax Law Changes in Arizona since 1989 and the Impact on Government Revenues and Economic Growth*. Tempe: Arizona State University.

———. 2011. *Causes of Varying Economic Performance by State.* Tempe: Arizona State University.

Hogan, Timothy. 2014. *Arizona at 100: A Look at the State's Economy Since 1987 and What the Future May Hold in Store.* https://www.researchgate.net/publication/228425115.

Holley, Michael. 2001. "Disadvantaged by Design: How the Law Inhibits Agricultural Guest Workers from Enforcing Their Rights." *Hofstra Labor & Employment Law Journal,* 182: 574–623.

Holmes, Seth M. 2013. *Fresh Fruit, Broken Bodies: Migrant Farmworkers in the United States.* Berkeley: University of California Press.

Hondagneu-Sotelo, Pierrette. 2001. *Doméstica: Immigrant Workers Cleaning and Caring in the Shadows of Affluence.* Berkeley: University of California Press.

Honey, Maureen. 1984. *Creating Rosie the Riveter: Class, Gender, and Propaganda during World War II.* Amherst: University of Massachusetts Press.

Honing, Bonnie. 2001. *Democracy and the Foreigner.* Princeton, NJ: Princeton University Press.

Howell, Frances Baseden. 1982. "A Split Labor Market: Mexican Farm Workers in the Southwest." *Sociological Inquiry* 52 (2): 132–40.

Hubbard, Howard A. 1934. "The Arizona Enabling Act and President Taft's Veto." *Pacific Historical Review* 33: 307–22.

———. 1942. "Arizona's Struggle against Joint Statehood." *Pacific Historical Review* 114: 415–23.

———. 1951. "Book Review, R. K. Wyllys, *The History of a Frontier State,* 1950." *Pacific Historical Review* 20 (3): 280–81.

Hu-DeHart, Evelyn. 1980. "Immigrants to a Developing Society: The Chinese in Northern Mexico, 1875–1932." *Journal of Arizona History* 21 (Autumn): 49–86.

Huffington Post. 2012. "Arizona Struggles to fill Construction Labor Demands." July 3, 2012. http://www.huffingtonpost.com/2012/07/03/arizona-struggles-to-fill-construction-labor-demands_n_1646109.html.

Huginnie, Andrea Yvette. 1991. "'Strikitos:' Race, Class, and Work in the Arizona Copper Industry, 1870–1920." PhD diss., Yale University.

———. 1994. "A New Hero Comes to Town: The Anglo Mining Engineer and 'Mexican Labor' as Contested Terrain in Southeastern Arizona, 1880–192." *New Mexico Historical Review* 694: 323–44.

———. 2006. "'Mexican Labour' in a 'White Man's Town': Racialism, Imperialism and Industrialization in the Making of Arizona." In *Racializing Class, Classifying Race: Labour and Difference in Britain, the USA and Africa,* edited by Peter Alexander and Rick Halpern, 32–56. London: Macmillan.

Hundley, Norris, Jr. 1972. "Clio Nods: Arizona v. California and the Boulder Canyon Act—A Reassessment." *Western Historical Quarterly* 391: 17–51.

Iber, Jorge, and Arnoldo De León. 2006. *Hispanics in the American West.* Santa Barbara, CA: ABS-CLIO.

Immigration and Naturalization Service. 2001. *Yearbook of Immigration Statistics.* Washington, D.C.: Government Printing Office.

———. 2002. *Yearbook of Immigration Statistics*. Washington, D.C.: Government Printing Office.

International Labour Organization. 2016. "ILO Data Initiative on Child Labour and Forced Labour: Standardising the Measurement of Forced Labour." http://www.ilo.org/wcmsp5/groups/public/-ed_norm/-declaration/documents/publication/wcms_534450.pdf.

Izakowitz, Pam. 1985. "Anna O'Leary: 'We Got to Battle Not the Company and the DPS, We Got to Battle the Husbands.'" *Arizona Daily Star*, June 30, 1985, C-1.

Jacobson, Matthew Frye. 1998. *Whiteness of a Different Color: European Immigrants and the Alchemy of Race*. Cambridge, MA: Harvard University Press.

Jacoby, Karl. 2008. *Shadows at Dawn: An Apache Massacre and the Violence of History*. New York: Penguin.

James, Franklin J., Betty L. McCummings, and Eileen A. Tynan. 1984. *Minorities in the Sunbelt*. New Brunswick, NJ: Rutgers University Press.

Jamieson, Stuart M. 1945. *Labor Unionism in American Agriculture*. Washington, D.C.: Government Printing Office.

Jayaraman, Saumathi, and Immanuel Ness, Eds. 2005. *The New Urban Immigrant Workforce: Innovative Models for Labor Organizing*. Armonk, NY: M. E. Sharpe.

Jenkins, J. Craig. 1978. "The Demand for Immigrant Workers: Labor Scarcity or Social Control." *International Migration Review* 12 (4): 514–35.

———. 1985. *The Politics of Insurgency: The Farm Worker Movement in the 1960s*. New York: Columbia University Press.

Jepson, Mark C. 1985. "The American Labor Movement: The Economic Structure and the Role of the State." Master's thesis, Arizona State University.

Jiménez, Tomás R. 2010. *Replenished Ethnicity: Mexican Americans, Immigration, and Ethnicity*. Berkeley: University of California Press.

Jiménez Montoya, Andrés E. 1977. "Political Domination in the Labor Market: Racial Division in the Arizona Copper Industry." Working Paper no. 103, Institute for the Study of Social Change, University of California, Berkeley.

Johnson, G. Wesley, Jr., ed. 1993. *Phoenix in the Twentieth Century: Essays in Community History*. Norman: University of Oklahoma Press.

Johnson, Susan L. 1982. "Women in Central Arizona Mining and Supply Settlements, 1863–1873." Working Paper no. 16, Southwest Institute for Research on Women, Women's Studies, University of Arizona.

———. 1984. "Women's Households and Relationships in the Mining West: Central Arizona, 1863–1873." Master's thesis, Arizona State University.

———. 1987. "Sharing Bed and Board: Cohabitation and Cultural Differences in Central Arizona Mining Towns, 1863–1873." In *The Women's West*, edited by Susan Armitage and Elizabeth Jameson, 77–91. Norman: University of Oklahoma Press.

Jones, Robert C. 1945. *Mexican War Workers in the United States: The Mexico-United States Manpower Recruiting Program and Operation, 1942 to 1944*. Washington, D.C.: Pan American Union.

Keefe, Susan E., and Amado M. Padilla. 1987. *Chicano Ethnicity*. Albuquerque: University of New Mexico Press.

Kerig, Dorothy Pierson. 1988. "Yankee Enclave: The Colorado River Land Company and Mexican Agrarian Reform in Baja California, 1902–1944." PhD diss., University of California, Irvine.

Kerr, Louise Año Nuevo. 1977. "Mexican Chicago: Chicano Assimilation Aborted, 1939–1954." In *The Ethnic Frontier: Essays in the History of Group Survival in Chicago and the Midwest*, edited by Melvin F. Holli and Peter d'Alroy Jones, 293–328, 406–10. Grand Rapids, MI: Eerdmans.

Kerry, Robert A. 1972. "A Preliminary Survey of the Arizona Farm Labor Act." *Arizona Law Review* 14: 786–810.

Kessell, John L. 1976. *Friars, Soldiers, and Reformers: Hispanic Arizona and the Sonora Mission Frontier, 1767–1856*. Tucson: University of Arizona Press.

Kilgore, B. W., L. I. Dublin, and W. S. Rossiter. 1924. "Cotton Statistics from the Department of Commerce." *Journal of American Statistical Association* 19 (146): 226–30.

Kingsolver, Barbara. 1989. *Holding the Line: Women in the Great Arizona Mine Strike of 1983*. Ithaca, NY: ILR Press/Cornell University Press.

Kiser, George C. 1973. "The Bracero Program: A Case Study of its Development, Termination, and Political Aftermath." Ph.D. diss., University of Massachusetts.

Kiser, George C., and Martha Woody Kiser, eds. 1979. *Mexican Workers in the United States: Historical and Political Perspectives*. Albuquerque: University of New Mexico Press.

Kiser, William S. 2012. *Dragoons in Apacheland: Conquest and Resistance in Southern New Mexico, 1846–1861*. Norman: University of Oklahoma Press.

Kluger, James R. 1970. *The Clifton-Morenci Strike: Labor Difficulty in Arizona, 1915–1966*. Tucson: University of Arizona Press.

Korman, Richard. 2003. *The Goodyear Story. An Inventor's Obsession and the Struggle for a Rubber Monopoly*. San Francisco: Encounter Books.

Kosack, Edward L. 2015. "Mexican Migration to the United States, 1920 to 1965: Guest Workers, Selection, and Economic Development in Mexico." PhD diss., University of Colorado, Boulder.

Kotlanger, Michael J. 1983. "Phoenix, Arizona, 1920–1940." PhD diss., Arizona State University.

Koziara, Karen S. 1977. "Agricultural Labor Relations Laws in Four States—A Comparison." *Monthly Labor Review* 100 (May): 14–18.

Kristof, N. D. 1985. "Copper's Plunge is Pushing Mining Towns to the Brink." *New York Times*, March 23, 1985.

LaBau, Jason Crabtree. 2010. "Phoenix Rising: Arizona and the Origins of Modern Conservative Politics." PhD diss., University of Southern California.

Lal, Brij V., Doug Munro, and Edward D. Beechert. 1994. *Plantation Workers: Resistance and Accommodation*. Honolulu: University of Hawaii Press.

Lamar, Howard R. 1963. "The Reluctant Admission: The Struggle to Admit Arizona and New Mexico to the Union." In *The American West: An Appraisal*, edited by Robert G. Ferris, 163–75. Santa Fe: Museum of New Mexico Press.

———. 1966. *The Far Southwest, 1846–1912: A Territorial History*. New Haven, CT: Yale University Press.

Lamb, Blaine Peterson. 1982. "Jewish Pioneers in Arizona, 1850–1920." PhD diss., Arizona State University.

Lambert, Susan. 2008. "Passing the Buck: Labor Flexibility Practices that Transfer Risk onto Hourly Workers." *Human Relations* 61 (9): 1203–27.

Lambesis, Barbara. 1976. "Memorial Hospital History." *Arizona Medicine* 33 (7): 592–97.

Lara-Valencia, Francisco, and Jacob Fisher. 2013. "Immigrant Informal Labor in Times of Anti-Immigration Rage: Insights from Greater Phoenix." In *Latino Politics and Arizona's Immigration Law SB 1070*, edited by Lisa Magaña and Erik Lee, 129–44. New York: Springer.

Larkin, Micaela Anne. 2008. "Labor's Desert: Mexican Workers, Unions and Entrepreneurial Conservatism in Arizona, 1917–1972." PhD diss., University of Notre Dame.

———. 2013. "Southwestern Strategy: Mexican Americans and Republican Politics in the Arizona Borderlands." In *Barry Goldwater and the Remaking of the American Political Landscape*, edited by Elizabeth Tandy Shermer, 66–83. Tucson: University of Arizona Press.

Lattanzi Shutika, Debra. 2011. *Beyond the Borderlands: Migration and Belonging in the United States and Mexico*. Berkeley: University of California Press.

Lause, Mark. 2018. *The Great Cowboy Strike: Bullets, Ballots, and Class Conflict in the American West*. New York: Verso.

Lee, Jennifer J. 2016. "U.S. Workers Need Not Apply: Challenging Low-Wage Guest Worker Programs." Legal Studies Research Paper Series, no. 2016–44. Temple University Beasley School of Law.

Lee, Sharon M. 1993. "Racial Classification in the U.S. Census, 1890–1990." *Ethnic and Racial Studies* 161: 75–94.

Lemus, Sergio. 2014. "Class, Labor, and Color Hierarchies: An Ethnographic Study of Mexican Yarderos/as in South Chicago." PhD diss., University of Illinois.

LeSeur, Geta. 2000. *Not All Okies are White: The Lives of Black Cotton Pickers in Arizona*. Columbia: University of Missouri Press.

Lewis, Janet, and Bill Mirand. 1998. "Creating an Organizing Culture in Today's Building and Construction Trades: A Case Study of IBEW Local 46." In *Organizing to Win: New Research on Union Strategies*, edited by Kate Bronfenbrenner et al., 297–308. Ithaca, NY: Cornell University Press.

Linder, Marc. 1987. "Farm Workers and the Fair Labor Standards Act: Racial Discrimination in the New Deal." *Texas Law Review* 65 (7): 1335–93.

———. 1999. *Wars of Attrition: Vietnam, the Business Roundtable and the Decline of Construction Unions*. Iowa City, IA: Fanpìhuà Press.

Lindquist, John H. 1969. "The Jerome Deportation." *Arizona and the West* 11 (3): 233–46.

Lipsitz, George. 2006. *The Possessive Investment in Whiteness: How White People Profit from Identity Politics*. Philadelphia: Temple University Press.

Lister, Florence C., and Robert H. Lister. 1989. "Chinese Sojourners in Territorial Prescott." *Journal of the Southwest* 31 (1): 1–111.

Litchfield, Paul W. 1945. *Autumn Leaves: Reflections of an Industrial Lieutenant*. Cleveland, OH: Corday & Gross.

———. 1954. *Industrial Voyage: My Life as an Industrial Lieutenant*. Garden City, NY: Doubleday.

———. 1956. *The Industrial Republic: Reflections of an Industrial Lieutenant*. Cleveland, OH: Corday & Gross.

London, Joan, and Henry P. Anderson. 1970. *So Shall Ye Reap*. New York: Thomas Y. Crowell

Lopes, María-Aparecida, and Paolo Riguzzi. 2012. "Borders, Trade, and Politics: Exchange Between the United States and Mexican Cattle Industries, 1870–1947." *Hispanic American Historical Review* 92 (4): 603–35.

López, Leonor. No date. *Forever Sonora, Ray, Barcelona: A Labor of Love*. [S.1]: López.

López, Steven. 2004. "Overcoming Legacies of Business Unionism: Why Grassroots Organizing Tactics Succeed." In *Rebuilding Labor: Organizing and Organizers in the New Union Movement*, edited by Ruth Milkman and Kim Voss, 114–32. Ithaca, NY: Cornell University Press.

Love, Steve, and David Giffels. 1999. *Wheels of Fortune: The Story of Rubber in Akron*. Akron, OH: University of Akron Press.

Lowe, Ronald E. 1976. "The Arizona Alien Land Law: Its Meaning and Constitutional Validity." *Arizona State Law Journal*, 253–76.

Lucio, David Drew. 2007. "Mexican Suburbanization in the Salt River Valley: Resurrecting the Memory of Litchfield Park." Master's thesis, Arizona State University.

Luckingham, Bradford. 1989. *Phoenix: The History of a Southwestern Metropolis*. Tucson: University of Arizona Press.

———. 1994. *Minorities in Phoenix: A Profile of Mexican American, Chinese American, and African American Communities, 1860–1992*. Tucson: University of Arizona Press.

Luey, Beth, and Noel J. Stowe, eds. 1987. *Arizona at Seventy-Five: The Next Twenty-Five Years*. Tucson: University of Arizona Press.

Lukens, Patrick D. 2012. *A Quiet Victory for Latino Rights: FDR and the Controversy over "Whiteness."* Tucson: University of Arizona Press.

Lukens Espinosa, Patrick. 1999. "Mexico, Mexican Americans and the FDR Administration's Racial Classification Policy: Public Policy in Place of Diplomacy." PhD diss., Arizona State University.

Lyon, Cherstin M. 2012. *Prisons and Patriots: Japanese American Wartime Citizenship, Civil Disobedience, and Historical Memory*. Philadelphia: Temple University Press.

Magaña, Rocío. 2011. "Dead Bodies: The Deadly Display of Mexican Border Politics." In *A Companion to the Anthropology of the Body and Embodiment*, edited by Frances E. Mascia-Lees, 157–71. Malden, MA: Wiley-Blackwell.

Maines, Rachel. 1993. "Twenty-Nine Thirty-Seconds or Fight: Goal Conflict and Reinforcement in U.S. Cotton Policy, 1933–1946." In *The Sinews of War: Essays on the Economic History of World War II*, edited by Geofrey T. Mills and High Rockoff, 199–218. Ames: Iowa State University Press.

Majka, Linda, and Theo J. Majka. 1982. *Farm Workers, Agribusiness, and the State*. Philadelphia: Temple University Press.

Malavé, Idelisse, and Esti Giordani. 2105. *Latino Stats: American Hispanics by the Numbers*. New York: New Press.

Maldonado, Edwin. 1979. "Contract Labor and the Origin of Puerto Rican Communities in the United States." *International Migration Review* 13 (1): 103–21.

Maldonado, José A. "¡Si Se Puede! The Farm Worker Movement in Arizona 1965–1979." Master's thesis, Arizona State University.

Maldonado, Marta María. 2009. "'It is Their Nature to do Menial Labour: The Racialization of 'Latino/a Workers' by Agricultural Employers." *Ethnic and Racial Studies* 326: 1017–36.

Malos, Ellen, ed. 1980. *The Politics of Housework*. London: Allison & Busby.

Manney, O. W. 1950. Testimony. Harry S. Truman Library. President's Commission on Migratory Labor, Box 6, Phoenix Statements.

Marez, Curtis. 2001. "Signifying Spain, Becoming Comanche, Making Mexicans: Indian Captivity and the History of Chicana/o Popular Performance." *American Quarterly* 53 (2): 267–307.

Marin, Christine. 1981. "Mexican Americans on the Homefront: Phoenix in World War II." Hayden Arizona Collection (CM MSM-134), Department of Archives and Manuscripts, University Libraries, Arizona State University, Tempe.

———. 1987. "The First Mexican Americans in Central and Salt River Valleys." Paper presented at the Third Annual Lecture Series of the Arizona Historical Society, Phoenix.

———. 1993. "Mexican Americans on the Home Front: Community Organizations in Arizona during World War II." *Perspectives in Mexican American Studies* 4: 75–92.

———. 1997. "They Sought Work and Found Hell: The Hanigan Case of Arizona." *Perspectives in Mexican American Studies* 6: 96–122.

———. 2000. "The Union, Community Organizing, and Civil Liberties: Clinton Jencks, Salt of the Earth, and Arizona Copper in the 1950s." *Mining History Journal* 7: 64–70.

———. 2001. *LULAC and Veterans Organize for Civil Rights in Tempe and Phoenix, 1940–1947*. Tucson: Mexican American Studies and Research Center, University of Arizona.

———. 2005. "Always a Struggle: Mexican Americans in Miami, Arizona, 1909–1951." PhD diss., Arizona State University.

Marquez, Benjamin. 1993. *LULAC: The Evolution of a Mexican American Political Organization*. Austin: University of Texas Press.

Martín, Carlos, and Stephen Whitlow. 2012. *The State of the Residential Construction Industry*. Washington, D.C.: Bipartisan Policy Center.

Martín, Patricia Preciado. 1992. *Songs My Mother Sang To Me: An Oral History of Mexican American Women*. Tucson: University of Arizona Press.

———. 2004. *Beloved Land: An Oral History of Mexican Americans in Southern Arizona*. Tucson: University of Arizona Press.

Martinelli, Phyllis Cancilla. 2006. "Negotiating Boundaries of Place and Identity, 1900–1930: European Spaniards, a Split Labor Market, Whites, or Latinos?" Paper presented at the American Sociological Association.

———. 2009. *Undermining Race: Ethnic Identities in Arizona Copper Camps, 1880–1920*. Tucson: University of Arizona Press.

Martínez, Daniel, Robin C. Reineke, Raquel Rubio-Goldsmith, and Bruce O. Parks. 2014. "Structural Violence and Migrant Deaths in Southern Arizona: Data from the Pima County Office of the Medical Examiner, 1990–2013." *Journal on Migration and Human* Security 2 (4): 257–86.

Martínez, John (1957) 1971. "Mexican Emigration to the U.S., 1910–1930." PhD diss., University of California, Berkeley. Reprinted by R & E Research Associates.

Martínez, Oscar J. 1987. "Hispanics in Arizona." In *Arizona at Seventy-Five: The Next Twenty-Five Years*, edited by Beth Luey and Noel J. Stowe, 87–122. Tucson: University of Arizona Press.

———. 1988. *Troublesome Border*. Tucson: University of Arizona Press.

———. 1994. *Border People: Life and Society in the U.S.-Mexico Borderlands*. Tucson: University of Arizona Press.

———. 2001. *Mexican-Origin People in the United States: A Topical History*. Tucson: University of Arizona Press.

Martínez-Matsuda, Verónica. 2009. "Making the Modern Migrant: Work, Community, and Struggle in the Federal Migratory Labor Camp Program, 1935–1947." PhD diss., University of Texas.

Matheny, Robert L. 1976. "Lumbering in the White Mountains of Arizona, 1919–1942." *Arizona and the West* 18 (3): 237–56.

Mattison, Ray H. 1946. "Early Spanish and Mexican Settlements in Arizona." *New Mexico Historical Review* 21 (4): 273–327.

Mauck, Jeffrey Gordon. 1991. "The Gadsden Treaty: The Diplomacy of Transcontinental Transportation." PhD diss., Indiana University.

Mawn, G. P. 1979. "Phoenix, Arizona: Central City of the Southwest, 1870–1920." PhD diss., Arizona State University.

Mbembe, Achille. 2003. "Necropolitics." *Public Culture* 15 (1): 11–40.

McBride, James D. 1974. "The Development of Labor Unions in Arizona Mining, 1884 to 1919." Master's thesis, Arizona State University.

———. 1975. "The Liga Protectora Latina: A Mexican American Benevolent Society in Arizona." *Journal of the West* 14 (October): 82–90.

———. 1978. "Deportation at Jerome: The Reaction to Militant Unionism in a Western Mining Camp." *Scottsdale Corral of the Westerners*. Tempe, AZ: Publications Services.

———. 1999. "The Bisbee Deportation in Words and Images." *Mining History Journal* 6: 63–76.

McCartin, Joseph A. 2006. "Professional Air Traffic Controllers Strike (1981)." In *Encyclopedia of U.S. Labor and Working-Class History*, ed. Eric Arnesen, 1123–26. New York: Routledge.

McClintock, Jas A. 1918. "The Crowning Production of a Royal Valley." *Arizona: The State Magazine* 8: 3–4, 4–7.

McCombs, Brady. 2006. "With 5,000 Building Jobs Open Here, Illegal Workers Heed Call." *Arizona Daily Star*, June 12, 2006.

McCombs, Brady, and Thomas Stauffer. 2006a. "Overhaul Must Break the Culture that Encourages Illegal Work Force." *Arizona Daily Star*, June 11, 2006.

———. 2006b. "Work Done More Cheaply by Undocumented. Undocumented Keep Prices Down and Wait Times Less." *Arizona Daily Star*, June 14, 2006.

———. 2006c. "Illegal Labor Helps Put Tucsonans Into Homes." *Arizona Daily Star*, June 14, 2006.

McConnell, Eileen Díaz. 2013. "Latinos in Arizona: Demographic Context in the SB 1070 Era." In *Latino Politics and Arizona's Immigration Law SB 1070*, edited by Lisa Magaña and Eric Lee, 1–18. New York: Springer.

McCrossen, Alexis, ed. 2009. *Land of Necessity: Consumer Culture in the United States-Mexico Borderlands*. Durham, NC: Duke University Press.

McGinnis, Anthony. 1930. "The Influence of Organized Labor on the Making of the Arizona Constitution." Master's thesis, University of Arizona.

McGirr, Lisa. 2001. *Suburban Warriors: The Origins of the New American Right*. Princeton, NJ: Princeton University Press.

McGowan, Joseph C. 1961. "History of Extra Long-Staple Cotton." Master's thesis, University of Arizona Press.

McKinnon, Shaun. 2011. "Roosevelt Dam Is the Cornerstone of Phoenix-Area Growth." *Arizona Republic*, March 18, 2011.

McWilliams, Carey. 1940. *Factories in the Field: The Story of Migratory Farm Labor in California*. Boston: Little, Brown and Company.

———. (1941) 1967. *Ill Fares the Land: Migrants and Migratory Labor in the United States*. Reprint, New York: Barnes & Noble.

———. (1949) 1968. *North from Mexico: The Spanish-Speaking People of the United States*. Reprint, New York: Greenwood Press.

Meeks, Eric V. 2001. "Border Citizens: Race, Labor, and Identity in South-Central Arizona, 1910–1965." PhD diss., University of Texas.

———. 2006. "Protecting the 'White Citizen Worker': Race, Labor, and Citizenship in South-Central Arizona, 1929–1945." *Journal of the West* 48 (1): 91–113.

———. 2007a. *Border Citizens: The Making of Indians, Mexicans, and Anglos in Arizona*. Austin: University of Texas Press.

———. 2007b. "The Tohono O'odham, Wage Labor, and Resistant Adaptation." *Western Historical Quarterly* 34 (4): 469–89.

Meier, Matt S., and Feliciano Rivera. 1981. *Dictionary of Mexican American History*. Westport, CT: Greenwood Press.

Melcher, Mary S. 1994. "Tending Children, Chickens, and Cattle: Southern Arizona Ranch and Farm Women, 1910–1940." PhD diss., Arizona State University.

———. 1999. "'This Is Not Right': Rural Arizona Women Challenge Segregation and Ethnic Divisions, 1925–1950." *Frontiers: A Journal of Women Studies* 20 (2): 190–214.

———. 2004. "Planning for Survival: Civil Defense and Anti-Communism in Arizona, 1950–1975." *Journal of Arizona History* 45 (2): 167–92.

Mellinger, Phil. 1992. "'The Men Have Become Organizers': Labor Conflict and Unionization in the Mexican Mining Communities of Arizona." *Western Historical Quarterly* 23 (3): 323–47.

———. 1995. *Race and Labor in Western Copper: The Fight for Equality, 1896–1918*. Tucson: University of Arizona Press.

Members of the Faculty of the University of Arizona. 1972. *Arizona: Its People and Resources*. Tucson: University of Arizona Press.

Menjívar, Cecilia. 1995. "Kinship Networks Among Immigrants: Lessons from a Qualitative Comparative Approach." *International Journal of Comparative Sociology* 36 (3–4): 219–32.

———. 1997. "Immigrant Kinship Networks: Vietnamese, Salvadoreans and Mexicans in Comparative Perspective." *Journal of Comparative Family Studies* 28: 1–24.

Mexican American Studies and Research Center. 2002. *The Arizona Report, 1999–2002*. Tucson: University of Arizona.

Mesa Day Labor Task Force (*Mesa Grupo de Trabajo Sobre Jornaleros*). 2000. "Final Report/ *Informe Final*, Mesa Day Labor Task Force." Mesa Day Labor Task Force.

Meyer, Jacob, and Robert Greenleaf. 2011. "Enforcement of State Wage and Hour Laws: A Survey of State Regulators." Columbia Law School, National State Attorneys General Program. https://web.carpenters.org/Libraries/AApril_Merlo/Enforcement_of_State_Wage_and_Hour_Laws-Columbia_Univ.sflb.ashx.

Meyers, William K. 1994. *Forge of Progress, Crucible of Revolt: The Origins of the Mexican Revolution in La Comarca Lagunera, 1880–1911*. Albuquerque: University of New Mexico Press.

———. 1998. "Seasons of Rebellion: Nature, Organisation of Cotton Production and the Dynamics of Revolution in La Laguna, Mexico, 1910–1916." *Journal of Latin American Studies* 30: 63–94.

Mignolo, Walter. 2000. *Local Histories/Global Decisions: Coloniality, Subaltern Knowledge, and Border Thinking*. Princeton, NJ: Princeton University Press.

Milkman, Ruth. 2006. *L.A. Story: Immigrant Workers and the Future of the US Labor Movement.* New York: Russell Sage.

———. 2008. "Putting Wages Back into Competition: Deunionization and Degradation in Place-Bound Industries." In *The Gloves-Off Economy: Workplace Standards at the Bottom of America's Labor Market*, edited by Annette Bernhardt et al., 65–90. Champaign, IL: Labor and Employment Relations Association.

Milkman, Ruth, and Kim Voss. 2004. *Rebuilding Labor: Organizing and Organizers in the New Union Movement.* Ithaca, NY: Cornell University Press.

Milkman, Ruth, and Kent Wong. 2000. "Organizing the Wicked City: The 1992 Southern California Drywall Strike." 168–98. In *Organizing Immigrants: The Challenge for Unions in Contemporary California*, edited by Ruth Milkman, 65–90. Ithaca, NY: Cornell University Press.

Miller, Joseph, ed. 1972. *The Arizona Rangers.* New York: Hastings House.

"Miners Organized." 1973. *Labor Journal* 1 (2): 3.

Mitchell, Don. 2012. *They Saved the Crops. Labor, Landscape, and the Struggle Over Industrial Farming in Bracero-Era California.* Athens: University of Georgia Press.

Mitchell, Pablo. 2005. *Coyote Nation: Sexuality, Race, and Conquest in Modernizing, 1880–1920.* Chicago: University of Chicago Press.

Miura, Junko. 2011. "Ethnic Mexicans' Labor Activity in Texas: Class, Citizenship, and Americanization in the 1930s." Master's thesis, California State University, Chico.

Mize, Ronald L. 2013. "Critically Interrogating the Elusive Sign: The New 'Race' Theories and a Plausible Alternative for Understanding Cultural Racializations of Latino/a Identities." *Latino Studies* 11 (3): 341–65.

Mize, Ronald L., and Alicia C. S. Swords. (2010) 2011. *Consuming Mexican Labor: From the Bracero Program to NAFTA.* Toronto: University of Toronto Press.

Mohapatra, Prabhu. 2005. "Regulated Informality: Legal Constructions of Labour Relations in Colonial India 1814–1926." In *Workers in the Informal Sector: Studies in Labour History*, edited by Sabyasachi Bhattacharya and Jan Lucassen, 65–95. India: Macmillan.

Mohl, Raymond. 1987. "Black Immigrants: Bahamians in Early Twentieth-Century Miami." *Florida Historical Quarterly* 65 (3): 271–97.

Molina, Natalia. 2006. *Fit to Be Citizens? Public Health and Race in Los Angeles, 1879–1939.* Berkeley: University of California Press.

———. 2010a. "In a Race All Their Own': The Quest to Make Mexicans Ineligible for U.S. Citizenship." *Pacific Historical Review* 79 (2): 167–201.

———. 2010b. "The Power of Racial Scripts: What the History of Mexican Immigration to the United States Teaches Us about Relational Notions of Race." *Latino Studies* 8 (2): 156–75.

Montejano, David. 1979. "Frustrated Apartheid: Race, Repression, and Capitalist Agriculture in South Texas, 1920–1930." In *The World-System of Capitalism: Past and Present*, edited by Walter L. Goldfarb, 131–68. Beverly Hills, CA: SAGE.

———. 1987. *Anglos and Mexicans in the Making of Texas, 1936–1986*. Austin: University of Texas Press.

Montoya Zavala, and Erika y Ofelia Woo Morales. No date. "Participación laboral y autoempleo de las mujeres mexicanas en Phoenix, Arizona. El caso de las estilistas." Typescript.

Moody, Kim. 1988. *An Injury to All: The Decline of American Unionism*. London: Verso.

Moore, Colleen A. 1980. "The Educational Ideas of P. W. Litchfield: Early Corporate Education at the Goodyear Tire and Rubber Company, 1913–1930." Master's thesis, University of Akron.

Mora, G. Cristina. 2014a. *Making Hispanic: How Activists, Bureaucrats, and Media Constructed a New American*. Chicago: University of Chicago Press.

———. 2014b. "Cross-Field Effects and Ethnic Classification: The Institutionalization of Hispanic Panethnicity, 1965 to 1990." *American Sociological Review* 79 (2): 183–210.

Morin, Richard. 1977. "Illegal Aliens Have Been Striking in Arizona Citrus Groves." *Washington Post*, October 27, 1977.

Morrow, Carson. 1950. Testimony. Harry S. Truman Library, President's Commission on Migratory Labor, Box 6, Phoenix Statements.

Mulligan, Raymond A. 1964. "New York Foundlings at Clifton-Morenci: Social Justice in Arizona Territory, 1904–1905." *Arizona and the West* 6 (2): 104–18.

———. 1970. "New York Foundlings at Clifton-Morenci: Social Justice in Arizona Territory, 1904–1905." In *The Mexican-Americans: An Awakening Minority*, edited by Manuel P. Servín, 54–67. Beverly Hills, CA: Glencoe Press.

Muñoz, Laura. 2006. "Desert Dreams: Mexican American Education in Arizona, 1870–1930." PhD diss., Arizona State University.

Musoke, Moses D., and Alan L. Olmstead. 1982. "The Rise of the Cotton Industry in California: A Comparative Perspective." *Journal of Economic History* 42 (2): 385–412.

Mydans, Seth. 1995. "A Building Boom Transforms the Phoenix Desert." *New York Times*, February 25, 1995.

Myrick, David. 1981. *Railroads of Arizona*. Vol. 1. San Diego: Howell-North Books.

Nader, Laura. 2002. *The Life of the Law: Anthropological Projects*. Berkeley: University of California Press.

Nash, Gerald D. 1985. *The American West Transformed: The Impact of the Second World War*. Bloomington: Indian University Press.

———. 1987. "Reshaping Arizona's Economy: A Century of Change." In *Arizona at Seventy-Five: The Next Twenty-Five Years*, edited by Beth Luey and Noel J. Stowe, 123–47. Tucson: University of Arizona Press.

———. 1990. *World War II and the West: Reshaping the Economy*. Lincoln: University of Nebraska Press.

Navin, Thomas R. 1978. *Copper Mining and Management*. Tucson: University of Arizona Press.

Ness, Immanuel. 2005. *Immigrants, Unions and the New US Labor Market*. Philadelphia: Temple University Press.

———. 2011. *Guest Workers and Resistance to U.S. Corporate Despotism*. Urbana: University of Illinois Press.

New York Times. 1964. "Goldwater Statements." August, 4, 1964.

Nickell, Naaman. 1998. "Severe Labor Shortage Threatens Prosperity Across Phoenix Area." *Arizona Republic*, January 12, 1998.

Noel, Linda Carol. 2006. "'The Swinging Door': U.S. National Identity and the Making of the Mexican Guestworker, 1900–1935." PhD diss., University of Maryland.

———. 2011. "'I Am an American': Anglos, Mexicans, Nativos, and the National Debate over Arizona and New Mexico Statehood." *Pacific Historical Review* 80 (3): 430–67.

Nordlund, Willis. 1997. *The Quest for a Living Wage: The History of the Federal Minimum Wage Program*. Westport, CT: Greenwood Press.

North, Diane. 1984. "'A Real Class of People' in Arizona: A Biographical Analysis of the Sonora Exploring and Mining Company, 1856–1863." *Arizona and the West* 26 (3): 261–74.

Northrup, Herbert. 1990. "Arizona Construction Labor: A Case Study of Union Decline." *Journal of Labor Research* 11: 161–79.

Oberle, Alex Paul. 2005. "*Se Venden Aquí*: Phoenix Latino Retail Landscape, Urban Change, and Hispanic Identity." PhD diss., Arizona State University.

O'Bannon, Patrick W. 1979. "Railroad Construction in the Early Twentieth Century: The San Diego and Arizona Railway." *Southern California Quarterly* 61 (3): 255–90.

Oboler, Suzanne. 2002. "The Politics of Labeling: Latino/a Cultural Identities of Self and Others." In *Transnational Latina/o Communities: Politics, Processes, and Cultures*, edited by Carlos G. Vélez-Ibáñez and Anna Sampaio, 73–89. Lanham, MD: Rowman & Littlefield.

Office of Immigration Statistics, Department of Homeland Security. 2003–2016. *Yearbook of Immigration Statistics*. Washington, D.C.: Government Printing Office.

Officer, James E. (1987) 1989. *Hispanic Arizona, 1536–1856*. Tucson: University of Arizona Press.

Olivas, Louis, ed. 2002. *Arizona Hispanics: The Evolution of Influence*. 81st Arizona Town Hall, Tempe, Arizona State University.

O'Leary, Anna Marie Ochoa 1993. "The Bureaucratic Model of Industrial Organization and the Emergence of a Class and Cultural Identity in Borderland Mining Communities." Master's thesis, University of Arizona.

———. 1985. *Bringing Home the Spirit of Nairobi. The Copper Era*. Clifton, AZ: New Horizons.

Omi, Michael, and Howard Winant. 1986. *Racial Formation in the United States: From the 1960s to the 1980s*. New York: Routledge.

O'Neal, Bill. 1987. *The Arizona Rangers*. Austin, TX: Eakin Press.

O'Neill, Colleen. 1993. "Domesticity Deployed: Gender, Race, and the Construction of Class Struggle in the Bisbee Deportation." *Labor History* 34: 256–73.

Ong, Aihwa. 1991. "The Gender and Labor Politics of Postmodernity." *Annual Review of Anthropology* 20: 279–309.

———. 2010. *Spirits of Resistance and Capitalist Discipline: Factory Women in Malaysia*. 2nd ed. Albany: State University of New York Press.

O'Reilly, Maurice. 1983. *The Goodyear Story*. Elmsford, NY: Benjamin Company.

Orozco, Cynthia E. 1992. "The Origins of the League of United Latin American Citizens LULAC and the Mexican American Civil Rights Movement in Texas With an Analysis of Women's Political Participation in a Gendered Context, 1910–1929." PhD diss., University of California, Los Angeles.

Orth, Samuel P. 1907. "The Alien Contract Labor Law." *Political Science Quarterly* 22 (1): 49–60.

Osborn, Sidney Preston. 1942. Letter from Governor Osborn to C. H. Nelson, March 4, 1942. http://azmemory.azlibrary.gov/cdm/ref/collection/archgov/id/329.

Otero, Lydia. 2010. *La Calle: Spatial Conflicts and Urban Conflict in a Southwest City*. Tucson: University of Arizona Press.

Overmyer-Velásquez, Mark. 2011. *Beyond La Frontera: The History of Mexico-U.S. Migration*. New York: Oxford University Press.

Overstreet, Daphne. 1977. "On Strike! The 1917 Walkout at Globe, Arizona." *Journal of Arizona History* 18 (2): 197–218.

Padfield, Harland, and William E. Martin. 1965. *Farmers, Workers and Machines: Technological and Social Change in Farm Industries of Arizona*. Tucson: University of Arizona Press.

Palmer, David J. 1986. "The Arizona Agricultural Employment Relations Act: First Amendment v. Legitimate State Interest." Class paper, Brigham Young University.

Palsson, Mary Dale. 1974. "The Arizona Constitutional Convention of 1910: The Election of Delegates in Pima County." *Arizona and the West* 16 (2): 111–24.

Paredes, Raymund. 1978. "The Origins of Anti-Mexican Sentiment in the United States." In *New Directions in Chicano Scholarship*, edited by Ricardo Romo and Raymund Paredes, 139–65. La Jolla: Chicano Studies Monograph Series, University of California, San Diego.

Park, Joseph F. 1961. "The History of Mexican Labor in Arizona during the Territorial Period." Master's thesis, University of Arizona.

———. 1977. "The 1903 'Mexican Affair' at Clifton." *Journal of Arizona History* 18: 119–48.

Parrado, Emilio, and William Kandel. 2008. "New Hispanic Migrant Destinations: A Tale of Two Industries." In *New Faces in New Places: The Changing Geography of American Immigrants*, edited by Douglas Massey, 99–123. New York: Russell Sage Foundation.

Parrish, Michael E. 1979. *Mexican Workers, Progressive, and Copper: The Failure of Industrial Democracy in Arizona during the Wilson Years*. La Jolla: Chicano Studies Monograph Series, University of California, San Diego.

Passel, Jeffrey S. 2006. "The Size and Characteristics of the Unauthorized Migrant Population in the U.S." Pew Hispanic Center. http://www.pewhispanic.org/files/reports/61.pdf.

Passel, Jeffrey, Randy Capps, and Michael Fix. 2004. "Undocumented Immigrants: Facts and Figures." Urban Institute Immigration Studies Program. http://www.urban.org/Uploaded PDF/1000587_undoc_immigrants_facts.pdf.

Peck, Gunther. 2000. *Reinventing Free Labor: Padrones and Immigrant Workers in the North American West, 1880–1930*. New York: Cambridge University Press.

Pendleton, Edwin Charles. 1950. "History of Labor in Arizona Irrigated Agriculture." PhD diss., University of California, Berkeley.

Peña, Devon. 1997. *The Terror in the Machine: Technology, Work, Gender, and Ecology on the U.S-Mexico Border*. Austin: Center for Mexican American Studies, University of Texas.

Perales, Monica. 2010. *Smeltertown: Making and Remembering a Southwest Border Community*. Chapel Hill: University of North Carolina Press.

Pérez, Ana Celia. 1997. "Los Hijos de Los Mineros: Crossing the Line." PhD diss., Arizona State University.

Perry, Charles R., Andrew M. Kramer, and Thomas J. Schneider. 1982. *Operating during Strikes: Company Experience, NLRB Policies, and Governmental Regulations. Unit Wharton School. Industrial Research*. Vol. 23. Philadelphia: Industrial Research Unit, University of Pennsylvania.

Peterson, Helen Palmer. 2008. "Landscapes of Capital: Culture in an Industrial Western Company Town, Clarksdale, Arizona, 1914–1929." PhD diss., Northern Arizona University.

Peterson, Herbert B. 1974. "Twentieth-Century Search for Cíbola: Post–World War I Mexican Labor Exploitation in Arizona." In *An Awakening Minority: The Mexican Americans*, 2nd ed., edited by Manuel Servín, 113–32. Beverly Hills, CA: Glencoe Press.

———. 1975. "A Twentieth Century Journey to Cíbola: Tragedy of the Bracero in Maricopa County, Arizona, 1917–21." Master's thesis, Arizona State University.

Peterson, John. 1981. *Minimum Wages: Measures and Industry Effects*. Washington D.C.: American Enterprise Institute.

Pettis, Mildred K. 1965. "A Study of Employment Trends in Arizona's Farm Labor Market from 1954–1962." Master's thesis, Arizona State University.

Pew Hispanic Center. 2008. "Arizona: Population and Labor Force Characteristics, 2000–2006." http://pewhispanic.org/files/factsheets/37.pdf.

———. 2012. "When Labels Don't Fit: Hispanics and Their Views of Identity." http://www.pew hispanic.org/2012/04/04/when-labels-dont-fit-hispanics-and-their-views-of-identity/.

Pew Research Center. 2015. "More Mexicans Leaving Than Coming to the U.S." http://www .pewhispanic.org/2015/11/19/more-mexicans-leaving-than-coming-to-the-u-s/

Pickering, George. 1950. Testimony. Harry S. Truman Library, President's Commission on Migratory Labor, Box 6, Phoenix Statements.

Pisani, Michael J., and David W. Yoskowitz. 2005. "Grass, Sweat, and Sun: An Exploratory Study of the Labor Market for Gardeners in South Texas." *Social Science Quarterly* 86 (1): 229–51.

Pitt, Leonard. (1970) 1999. *Decline of Los Californios: A Critical History of Spanish Speaking California, 1846–1890*. Berkeley: University of California Press.

Plascencia, Luis F. B. 2009. "The 'Undocumented' Mexican Migrant Question: Re-examining the Framing of Law and Illegalization in the United States." *Urban Anthropology* 38 (2–4): 375–434.

———. 2011. "Racialized Labeling of Mexican-origin Persons." In *Anti-Immigration in the United States: A Historical Encyclopedia*, vol. 1, edited by Kathleen Arnold, 420–24. Santa Barbara, CA: Greenwood Press.

———. 2012. *Disenchanting Citizenship: Mexican Migrants and the Boundaries of Belonging*. New Brunswick, NJ: Rutgers University Press.

———. 2013a. "Alien Contract Labor Law of 1885: The Foran Act." Unpublished.

———. 2013b. "Attrition Through Enforcement and the Elimination of a 'Dangerous Class.'" In *Latino Politics and Arizona's Immigration Law SB 1070*, edited by Lisa Magaña and Erik Lee, 93–127. New York: Springer.

———. 2016. "State-Sanctioned Coercion and Agricultural Contract Labor: Jamaican and Mexican Workers in Canada and the United States, 1909–2014." In *On Coerced Labor: Work and Compulsion after Chattel Slavery*, edited by Marcel van der Linden and Magaly Rodríguez García, 225–66. Leiden, Netherlands: Brill.

———. 2017. "Where Is 'the Border'?: The Fourth Amendment, Boundary Enforcement, and the Making of an Inherently Suspect Class." In *The U.S.-Mexico Transborder Region: Cultural Dynamics and Historical Interactions*, edited by Carlos G. Vélez-Ibáñez and Josiah Heyman, 244–80. Tucson: University of Arizona Press.

Pluth, Edward John. 1970. "The Administration and Operation of German Prisoner of War Camps in the United States during World War II." PhD diss., Ball State University.

Poole, Kenneth, et al. 2005. "A Workforce Needs Assessment of the Arizona Construction Trades Industry." Phoenix: Arizona Department of Commerce, Office of Workforce Development.

Popov, Boris Jakob. 1972. "Black and Mexican-American Enrollees' Perceptions of the Concentrated Employment Program in Phoenix." Master's thesis, Arizona State University.

Popovich, Marcos A. 2006. "Chicanos Por La Causa: Political and Economic Empowerment in South Phoenix, 1969–1980." Master's thesis, Arizona State University.

Posadas, Carlos Ezequiel. 2007. "Mexican Immigrant Women and their Social Networks in Phoenix, Metro, AZ." PhD diss., Arizona State University.

Powell, Lawrence Clark. 1976. *Arizona: A Bicentennial History*. New York: W. W. Norton.

Powers, Jeanne M. 2008. "Forgotten History: Mexican American School Segregation in Arizona, 1900–1951." *Equity & Excellence in Education* 41 (4): 467–81.

Powers, Jeanne M., and Lirio Patton. 2008. "Between Méndez and Brown: *Gonzales v. Sheely* (1951) and the Legal Campaign against Segregation." *Law & Social Inquiry* 33 (1): 127–71.

Preisler, Dennis. 1992. "Phoenix, Arizona during the 1940s: A Decade of Change." Master's thesis, Arizona State University.

President's Commission on Migratory Labor. 1950. *Migratory Labor in Agriculture: Report of the President's Commission on Migratory Labor*. Washington, D.C.: Government Printing Office.

Prichard, Nancy Lee. 1992. "Paradise Found? Opportunity for Mexican, Irish, Italian, and Chinese Born Individuals in Jerome Copper Mining District, 1890–1910." PhD diss., University of Colorado.

Pry, Mark E., comp. 1997. *Historic Resources Survey. Miami, Arizona*. Phoenix: State Historic Preservation Office, Arizona State Parks.

Pugsley, Andrea. 2003. "'As I Kill this Chicken So May I Be Punished If I Tell an Untruth': Chinese Opposition to Legal Discrimination in Arizona Territory." *Journal of Arizona History* 44 (2): 171–90.

Quijano, Anibal. 2000. "Coloniality of Power, Eurocentrism, and Latin America." *Nepantla: Views from the South* 1: 533–80.

Quiros, Victor A. 2009. "Notions of Home: Implications for Neighborhood Transformation & Gentrification in Tucson, Arizona." PhD diss., Nova Southeastern University.

Radbourne, Allan. 2005. "The Education of Mickey Free: Conflict and Acculturation in the Arizona-Sonora Borderlands." *Journal of Arizona History* 46 (3): 249–68.

Rak, Mary Kidder. 1921. *A Social Survey of Arizona*. University of Arizona Bulletin no. 11, University Extension Series no. 10, Tucson, University of Arizona.

Ramos, Juan. 1968. "Spanish-Speaking Leadership in Two Southwestern Cities: A Descriptive Study." PhD diss., Brandeis University.

Ranches, Dude. 1935. *Guest Ranches on Lines of Southern Pacific*. San Francisco and Houston, TX: Southern Pacific, System Passenger Traffic.

Rasmussen, Wayne D. 1951. *A History of the Emergency Farm Labor Supply Program, 1943–47*. Washington, D.C. U.S. Department of Agriculture.

Raymer, Robert G. 1935. "Early Copper Mining in Arizona." *Pacific Historical Review* 4 (2): 123–30.

Reagor, Catherine. 1996. "Arizona Developers Looking for Skilled Labor." *Arizona Republic*, July 29, 1996.

Reed, Allen C. 1952. "Goodyear Farms. Laboratory in the Desert." *Arizona Highways*, April 1952, 28–39.

Reisler, Mark. 1973. "Passing Through Our Egypt: Mexican Labor in the United States, 1900–1940." PhD diss., Cornell University.

———. 1976a. *By the Sweat of Their Brow: Mexican Immigrant Labor in the United States, 1900–1940*. Westport, CT: Greenwood Press.

———. 1976b. "Always the Laborer, Never the Citizen: Anglo Perceptions of the Mexican Immigrant during the 1920s." *Pacific Historical Review* 45 (2): 231–54.

Reynolds, Jean. 1998. "'We Made Our Life as Best We Could with What We Had': Mexican American Women in Phoenix, 1930–1949." Master's thesis, Arizona State University.

Reynolds, Jean A. 1986. "Farm Labor Camps Turn to Dust, Employees Move On." *Westsider*, May 20, 1986.

Rex, Tom. 2013. "New Population Projections for the United States, Arizona, and Arizona Counties: A Report from the Office of the University Economist." Phoenix: Arizona State University.

Rios-Bustamante, Antonio. 1998. "'As Guilty as Hell': Mexican Copper Miners and their Communities in Arizona, 1920–1950." In *Border Crossing: Mexican and Mexican-American Workers*, edited by John Mason Hart, 163–83. Wilmington, DE: SR Books.

Rivera, José A. 1987. "Self-Help as Mutual Protection: The Development of Hispanic Fraternal Benefit Societies." *Journal of Applied Behavioral Science* 23: 387–96.

Roberts, Shirley. 1973. "Minority Group Poverty in Phoenix: A Socio-Economic Survey." *Journal of Arizona History* 14 (4): 347–62.

Robinson, Robert S. 2007. "Creating Foreign Policy Locally: Migratory Labor and the Texas Border, 1943–1952." PhD diss., Ohio State University.

———. 2010. "Taking the Fair Deal to the Fields: Truman's Commission on Migratory Labor, Public Law 78, and the Bracero Program, 1950–1952." *Agricultural History* 84 (3): 381–402.

Roca-Servat, Denisse. 2009. "Justice for Roofers: Toward a Comprehensive Union Organizing Campaign Involving Latino Construction Workers in Arizona." *Labor Studies Journal* 35: 343–63.

Rockel, Stephen J. 1997. "Book Review: *Cotton is the Mother of Poverty—Peasants, Work, and Rural Struggle in Colonial Mozambique, 1938–1961*. By Isaacman, Allen F. Canadian." *Journal of African Studies* 31 (1): 180–82.

Rodda, Jeanette 1992. "'A Little Bit Better': William Andrews Clark and Welfare Work in Arizona." *Montana: The Magazine of Western History* 42 (4): 34–47.

Roddy, Dennis. 2000. "Just Our Bill." PostGazette.com, December 2, 2000. http://old.post-gazette.com/columnists/20001202roddy.asp.

Rodengen, Jeffrey L. 1997. *The Legend of Goodyear: The First 100 Years*. Fort Lauderdale, FL: Write Stuff Syndicate.

Rodríguez, Chantel R. 2013. "Health on the Line: The Politics of Citizenship and the Railroad Bracero Program of World War II." PhD diss., University of Minnesota.

Rodríguez, Dylan. 2014. "Goldwater's Left Hand: Post-Raciality and the Roots of the Post–Racial Racist State." *Cultural Dynamics* 26 (1): 29–51.

Rodríguez, Joseph A. 1998. "Becoming Latinos: Mexican Americans, Chicanos, and the Spanish Myth in the Urban Southwest." *Western Historical Quarterly* 29 (Summer): 165–85.

Rodríguez, Néstor. 2004. "'Workers Wanted': Employer Recruitment of Immigrant Labor." *Work and Occupations* 31 (4): 453–73.

Rodríguez, Robyn Magalit. 2010. *Migrants for Export: How the Philippine State Brokers Labor to the World*. Minneapolis: University of Minnesota Press.

Roll, Jarod. 2010. *Spirit of Rebellion: Labor and Religion in the New Cotton South*. Urbana: University of Illinois Press.

Romero, Mary, and Marwah Serag. 2004–2005. "Violation of Latino Civil Rights Resulting from INS and Local Police's Use of Race, Culture, and Class Profiling: The Case of the Chandler Roundup in Arizona." *Cleveland State Law Review* 52: 75–96.

Romero, Mary. 1992. *Maid in the U.S.A*. New York: Routledge.

Romo, Ricardo. 1983. *East Los Angeles: History of a Barrio*. Austin: University of Texas Press.

Roniger, Luis, and Marío Sznajder, eds. 1998. *Constructing Collective Identities and Shaping Public Spheres: Latin American Paths*. Portland, OR: Sussex Academic Press.

Rork, James, and Richard Sutter. 1951. *Arizona Cotton Harvest: A Study of Hand and Machine Picking in Cotton in Arizona*. Phoenix: Arizona State Employment Service.

Rosales, F. Arturo. No date. "Lost Lands: Origins of Mexicans in the Salt River Valley of Arizona, 1865–1910." Unpublished manuscript.

———. 1993. "A Historical Overview." In *The Hispanic American Almanac*, edited by Nicolás Kanellos, 1–53. Detroit: Gale Research.

———. 1996. *Chicano!: The History of the Mexican American Civil Rights Movement*. Houston: Arte Publico Press.

———. 1999. *¡Pobre Raza! Violence, Justice, and Mobilization among Mexico Lindo Immigrants, 1900–1936*. Austin: University of Texas Press.

———. 2000. *Testimonio: A Documentary History of the Mexican American Struggle for Civil Rights*. Houston: Arte Publico Press.

———. 2007. "Report: Civil Rights History of Mexicans in Arizona." Typescript.

Roseberry, William 1988. "Political Economy." *Annual Review of Anthropology* 17: 161–85.

Rosenberg, Mica, Ryan Mcneil, Megan Twohey, and Michelle Conlin. 2015. "Exclusive: Donald Trump's Companies Have Sought Visas to Import 1,100 Workers." Reuters, August 2, 2015.

Rosenblum, Jonathan D. 1995a. *Copper Crucible: How the Arizona Miners; Strike of 1983 Recast Labor-Management Relations in America*. Ithaca, NY: Industrial Labor Relations Press.

———. 1995b. "How Arizona's 'CIA' Helped Phelps Dodge Destroy the Unions." *Tucson Weekly*, June 29–July 5, 1995.

Roth, Wendy D. 2009. "'Latino before the World': The Transnational Extension of Panethnicity." *Ethnic and Racial Studies* 32 (6): 927–47.

———. 2102. *Race Migration: Latinos and the Cultural Transformation of Race*. Stanford, CA: Stanford University Press.

Rubio-Goldsmith, Raquel et al. 2006. *The 'Funnel Effect' & Recovered Bodies of Unauthorized Migrants Processes by the Pima County Office of the Medical Examiner, 1990–2005*. Tucson, AZ: Binational Migration Institute.

Rubio Goldsmith, Raquel. 1987. "Shipwreck in the Desert: A Short History of the Mexican Sisters of the House of the Providence in Douglas, Arizona, 1927–1949." In *Women on the U.S.-Mexico Border*, edited by Vicki L. Ruiz and Susan Tiano, 177–96. Boston: Allen & Unwin.

———. 1990. "Oral History: Considerations and Problems for its Use in the History of Mexicanas in the United States." In *Between Borders: Essays on Mexican/Chicana History*, edited by Adelaida Del Castillo, 161–73. Encino, CA: Floricanto Press.

Rudy, Preston. 2004. "Justice for Janitors, Not Compensation for Custodians. The Political Context and Organizing in San Jose and Sacramento." In *Rebuilding Labor: Organizing and Organizers in the New Union Movement*, edited by Ruth Milkman and Kim Voss, 133–49. Ithaca, NY: Cornell University Press.

Rugg, O. W. 1950. Testimony. Harry S. Truman Library, President's Commission on Migratory Labor, Box 6, Phoenix Statements.

Ruha, William. No date. "William Rehnquist is Unfit to Judge Florida's Recount." Democrats .com. http://archive.democrats.com/view.cfm?id=698.

Ruiz, Vicki L. 1987. *Cannery Women, Cannery Lives: Mexican Women, Unionization, and the California Food Processing Industry, 1930–1950*. Albuquerque: University of New Mexico Press.

———. 1988. "'And Miles to Go. . . .': Mexican Women and Work, 1930–1985." In *Western Women: Their Lives, Their Land*, edited by Lillian Schlissel, Vicki Ruiz, and Janice Monk, 113–50. Albuquerque: University of New Mexico Press.

———. 1993. "'Star Struck': Acculturation, Adolescence, and the Mexican American Woman, 1920–1950." In *Building with Our Hands: New Directions in Chicana Studies*, edited by Adelita de la Torre and Beatriz Pesquera, 109–29. Berkeley: University of California Press.

———. 1998. *From Out of the Shadows: Mexican Women in Twentieth-Century America*. New York: Oxford University Press.

———. 2001. "South by Southwest: Mexican Americans and Segregated Schooling, 1900–1950." *OAH Magazine of History* 15 (2): 23–27.

Ryan, Paul. 2015. Radio interview, *The Michael Medved Show*, December 17, 2015. http://www .michaelmedved.com/highlight/speaker-paul-ryan-discusses-budget-deal/.

Sain, Wilma Gray. 1944. "A History of the Miami Area, Arizona." Master's thesis, University of Arizona.

Saito, Natsu Taylor. 1998. "Justice Held Hostage: US Disregard for International Law in the World War II Internment of Japanese Peruvians—A Case Study." *Boston College Third World Law Journal* 19 (1): 275–348.

Salinger, Sharon V. 1997. "Labor, Markets, and Opportunity: Indentured Servitude in Early America." *Labor History* 38 (2): 311–38.

Sánchez, George J. 1993. *Becoming Mexican American: Ethnicity, Culture, and Identity in Chicano Los Angeles, 1900–1945*. New York: Oxford University Press.

Sánchez, George J. 2000. "Race and Immigration History." In *Immigration Research for a New Century*, edited by Nancy Foner, Rubén Rumbaut, and Steven J. Gold, 54–57. New York: Russel Sage Foundation.

Sangster, J. 2000. "Feminism and the Making of Canadian Working-Class History: Exploring the Past, Present and Future." *Labour/Le Travail* 46: 127–65.

Sanidad, Cristina. 2011. "Stories from Immigrant Workers in the Valley of the Sun: Status, Wage Theft, Recourse, and Resilience." Master's thesis, Arizona State University.

Santa Ana, Otto. 1999. "'Like an Animal I was Treated': Anti-Immigrant Metaphor in US Public Discourse." *Discourse & Society* 10 (2): 191–224.

———. 2002. *Brown Tide Rising: Metaphor of Latinos in Contemporary Public Discourse*. Austin: University of Texas Press.

Santillán, Richard. 1989. "Rosita the Riveter: Midwest Mexican American Women during World War II, 1941–1945." *Perspectives in Mexican American Studies* 2: 115–47.

Sassen-Koob, Saskia. 1988. "New York City's Informal Economy." Paper presented at the Institute for Social Science Research, Los Angeles.

———. 1989. "New York City's Informal Economy." In *The Informal Economy: Studies in Advanced and Less Developed Countries*, edited by Alejandro Portes, Manuel Castells, and Laura Benton, 60–77. Baltimore, MD: Johns Hopkins University Press.

Saunders, Robert T. 1871. *Cotton and Immigration: Address by Robert T. Saunders, of Mobile Alabama, Before the British Association in Liverpool*. New York: Cowan & Co.

Sayre, Nathan. 1999a. "The Cattle Boom in Southern Arizona: Towards a Critical Political Ecology." *Journal of the Southwest* 41 (2): 239–71.

———. 1999b. "Species of Capital: An Anthropological Investigation of the Buenos Aires Ranch, Pima County, Arizona and its Transformation into a National Wildlife Refuge, Volume 1 and 2." PhD diss., University of Chicago.

Schell, Greg. 2002. "Farmworker Exceptionalism Under the Law: How the Legal System Contributes to Farmworker Poverty and Powerlessness." In *The Human Cost of Food: Farmworkers' Lives, Labor, and Advocacy*, edited by Charles D. Thompson Jr. and Melinda F. Wiggins, 139–66. Austin: University of Texas Press.

Schetter, Clyde E. 1976. *Story of a Town: Litchfield Park*. Litchfield Park, AZ: Litchfield Park Library Association.

Scheuer, John Dominic. 2004. "Discrimination in the Desert: Contesting Jim Crowism in Phoenix, Arizona." Master's thesis, Arizona State University.

Schiavone Camacho, Julia María. 2012. *Chinese Mexicans: Transpacific Migration and the Search for a Homeland, 1910–1960*. Chapel Hill: University of North Carolina Press.

Schmidt Sr., Ronald. 2013. "Racialization and the Unauthorized Immigration Debate." Paper presented at the American Political Science Association's annual meeting, Chicago.

Schneider, Anna E. 2011. "The Racial Hierarchy of Labor in Bisbee, Arizona, 1880–1917." Senior paper, Colorado College.

Schnurr, Matthew. 2010. "Breeding for Insect-Resistant Cotton across Imperial Networks, 1924–1950." *Journal of Historical Geography* 372: 223–31.

Schwartz, Harry. 1942. "Agricultural Labor in the First World War." *Journal of Farm Economics* 24 (1): 178–87.

Scote, Dinae Marie. 2003. "Race, Class, and Chemicals: The Political Ecology of Environmental Injustice in Arizona." PhD diss., Arizona State University.

Scott, James C. 1992. *Domination and the Art of Resistance: Hidden Transcripts*. New Haven, CT: Yale University Press.

Scruggs, Otey M. 1960. "The First Mexican Farm Labor Program." *Arizona and the West* 28 (2): 319–26.

———. 1988. *Braceros, "Wetbacks," and the Farm Labor Problem. Mexican Agricultural Labor in the United States 1942–1954*. New York: Garland Publishing.

Servín, Manuel Patricio. 1966. "The Pre-World War II Mexican-American: An Interpretation." *California Historical Society Quarterly* 45 (4): 325–38.

Servín, Manuel P., ed. 1970. *The Mexican-Americans: An Awakening Minority*. Beverly Hills, CA: Glencoe Press.

———. 1979. "California's Hispanic Heritage: A View into the Spanish Myth." In *New Spain's Far Northern Frontier: Essays on Spain in the American West, 1540–1821*, edited by David J. Weber, 117–33. Albuquerque: University of New Mexico Press.

Servín, Manuel P., and Robert L. Spude. 1975. "Historical Conditions of Early Mexican Labor in the United States: Arizona—A Neglected Story." *Journal of Mexican American History* 5: 43–56.

Settlement of the Salt River Valley. 2015. "Chapter IV in the History of Arizona." University of Arizona Library. http://southwest.library.arizona.edu/hav6/body.1_div.4.html.

Shapiro, Erik-Anders. 1989. "Cotton in Arizona: A Historical Geography." Master's thesis, University of Arizona.

Sharpe, Teresa. 2004. "Union Democracy and Successful Campaigns: The Dynamics of Staff Authority and Worker Participation in an Organizing Union." In *Rebuilding Labor: Organizing and Organizers in the New Union Movement*, edited by Ruth Milkman and Kim Voss, 62–87. Ithaca, NY: Cornell University Press.

Sheridan, Thomas E. (1986) 1992. *Los Tucsonenses: The Mexican Community in Tucson, 1854–1941*. Reprint, Tucson: University of Arizona Press.

———. 1994. "The Other Arizona." *Journal of the Southwest* 36 (3): 255–86.

———. 1995a. *Arizona: A State History*. Tucson: University of Arizona Press.

———. 1995b. "Arizona: The Political Ecology of a Desert State." *Journal of Political Ecology* 2: 41–57.

———. 2001. "Cows, Condos, and the Contested Commons: The Political Ecology of Ranching on the Arizona-Sonora Borderlands." *Human Organization* 6 (2): 141–52

———. 2006. "Rio Rico and the Great Arizona Land Rush." *Journal of the Southwest* 48 (1): 1–36.

———. 2007. "Embattled Ranchers, Endangered Species, and Urban Sprawl: The Political Ecology of the New American West." *Annual Review of Anthropology* 36: 121–38.

———. 2012. *Arizona: A History*. Revised edition. Tucson: University of Arizona Press.

Shermer, Elizabeth Tandy. 2008. "Origins of the Conservative Ascendancy: Barry Goldwater's Early Senate Career and the De-Legitimization of Organized Labor." *Journal of American History* 95 (3): 678–709.

———. 2009a. "Counter-Organizing the Sunbelt: Right-to-Work Campaigns and Anti-Union Conservatism, 1943–1958." *Pacific Historical Review* 78 (1): 81–118.

———. 2009b. "Creating the Sunbelt: The Political and Economic Transformation of Phoenix, Arizona." PhD diss., University of California, Santa Barbara.

———. 2013a. *Sunbelt Capitalism: Phoenix and the Transformation of American Politics*. Philadelphia: University of Pennsylvania Press.

———. 2013b. *Barry Goldwater and the Remaking of the American Political Landscape*. Tucson: University of Arizona Press.

Shindo, Charles J. 1997. *Dust Bowl Migrants in the American Imagination*. Lawrence: University Press of Kansas.

Silverstein, Paul A. 2005. "Immigrant Racialization and the New Savage Slot: Race, Migration, and Immigration in the New Europe." *Annual Review of Anthropology*, 363–84.

Simkins, Larry Dean. 1989. "The Rise of the Southeastern Salt River Valley: Tempe, Mesa, Chandler, Gilbert, 1871–1920." PhD diss., Arizona State University.

Smith, Adrian. 2013. "Law, Resistance, and Pathways of Exit from Agrarian Labor Regimes." Paper presented at the Global History of Agrarian Labor Regimes, 1750–2000 Conference, April 25–27, 2013, Harvard University, Cambridge, MA.

Smith, Dean. 1967. *La Gloria Escondida: The Guerrero Story*. Phoenix: Sims Publishing.

Smith, Karen L. 1982. "The Magnificent Experiment: Building the Salt River Reclamation Project, 1890–1917." PhD diss., University of California, Santa Barbara.

Smith, Rebecca, Ana Avendaño, and J. M. Ortega. 2009. *ICEd out: How Immigration Enforcement has Interfered with Workers' Rights*. New York: National Employment Law Project.

Smith, Rebecca, Amy Sugimori, Ana Avendano, and Marielena Hincapié. 2007. *Undocumented Workers: Preserving Rights and Remedies after Hoffman Plastic Compounds v NLRB*. New York: National Employment Law Project.

Smith, Susan. 1948. "Litchfield Park and Vicinity." Master's thesis, University of Arizona.

Solliday, Scott W. 1993. "The Journey to Rio Salado: Hispanic Migrations to Tempe, Arizona." Master's thesis, Arizona State University.

Solorzano, Armando, and Jorge Iber. 1997. "Digging the 'Richest Hole on Earth': The Hispanic Miners of Utah." *Perspectives in Mexican American Studies* 7: 1–27.

"Some Cotton Patch." 1917. *Arizona* 7: 14.

Sotelo, Joe. 2006. *Burro Alley*. Mesa, AZ: Hispanic Institute of Social Issues.

Southern Poverty Law Center. 2013. *Close to Slavery: Guestworker Programs in the United States*. https://www.splcenter.org/20130218/close-slavery-guestworker-programs-united-states.

Spicer, Edward H. (1962) 1967. *Cycles of Conquest: The Impact of Spain, Mexico, and the United States on the Indians of the Southwest, 1533–1960*. Reprint, Tucson: University of Arizona Press.

———. 1984 *Pascua: A Yaqui Village in Arizona*. Tucson: University of Arizona Press.

Spicer, Edward H., and Raymond H. Thompson, eds. 1972. *Plural Society in the Southwest*. Albuquerque: University of New Mexico Press.

Spickard, Paul, ed. 2012. *Race and Immigration in the United States: New Histories*. New York: Routledge.

Spude, Robert L. 1975. "The Walker-Weaver Diggings and the Mexican Placero, 1863–1864." *Journal of the West* 14: 64–74.

———. 1976. "Swansea, Arizona: The Fortunes and Misfortunes of a Copper Camp." *Journal of Arizona History* 17: 375–96.

Standing, Guy. 2008. "Migration and Modes of Exploitation: Social Origins of Immobility and Mobility." *Journal of Peasant Studies* 8 (2): 173–211.

Star Publishing. No date. "Law of Necessity as Applied in the State of Arizona, Bisbee I.W.W. vs. Deportation Case H.E. Wootton." http://www.library.arizona.edu/exhibits/bisbee/docs/lawnec.html.

Stauffer, Thomas. 2006. "Worker Shortfall, Immigrant Laws Put Construction Firms in Squeeze." *Arizona Daily Star*, June 16, 2006.

Steedman, M. 2000. "The Red Petticoat Brigade: Mine Mill Women's Auxiliaries and the Threat from Within, 1940s–70s." In *Whose National Security? Canadian State Surveillance and the Creation of Enemies*, edited by G. Kinsmen, D. K. Buse, and M. Steedman, 55–72. Toronto: Between the Lines.

Stensvaag, James T. 1981. "Seeking the Impossible: The State Histories of New Mexico, Arizona, and Nevada—An Assessment." *Pacific Historical Review* 504: 499–525.

St. John, Rachel. 2011. *Line in the Sand: A History of the Western U.S.-Mexico Border*. Princeton, NJ: Princeton University Press.

St. Petersburg Times. 1977. "Goldwater's Brother Hired Illegal Aliens, Article Says." March 21, 1977.

Stepick, Alex, et al. 1994. "Brothers in Wood." In *Newcomers in the Workplace: Immigrants and the Restructuring of the U.S. Economy*, edited by Louise Lamphere, Alex Stepick, and Guillermo Grenier, 145–63. Philadelphia: Temple University Press.

Sterba, James P. 1977. "Dollar Drain Laid to Illegal Aliens Estimated in the Billions Annually." *New York Times*, May 27, 1977.

Stewart, Susan. 1984. *On Longing: Narratives of the Miniature, the Gigantic, the Souvenir, the Collection*. Baltimore, MD: John Hopkins University Press.

Stone, Stephanie. 2015. "Undercover Sting Targets Illegal Contractors." *ABC15 News*, March 13, 2015.

Stowell, Jay S. 1921. *The Near Side of the Mexican Question*. New York: George H. Doran. Reprinted in *Perspectives on Mexican-American Life*, edited by Carlos Cortés. New York: Arno Press, 1974.

Street, Richard S. 2004. *Beasts of the Field: A Narrative History of California Farmworkers, 1769–1913*. Stanford, CA: Stanford University Press.

Stucki, Larry R. 2009. *Copper Miner, Company Towns, Mexicans, Indians, Mormons, Masons, Jews, Muslims, Gays, Womb, McDonalds, and the March of Dimes: 'Survival of the Fittest' in and Far Beyond the Deserts of Arizona, New Mexico, and Utah*. Victoria, British Columbia, Canada: Trafford Publishing.

Stuesse, Angela, and Mathew Coleman. 2014. "Automobility, Immobility, Altermobility: Surviving and Resisting the Intensification of Immigrant Policing." *City & Society* 261: 51–72.

Stuesse, Angela. 2016. *Scratching Out a Living: Latinos, Race, and Work in the Deep South*. Berkeley: University of California Press.

Sugimori, Amy. 2008. "State and Local Policy Models Promoting Immigrant Worker Justice." In *The Gloves-Off Economy: Workplace Standards at the Bottom of America's Labor Market*, edited by Annette Bernhardt et al., 217–42. Champaign, IL: Labor and Employment Relations Association.

Sutton, Shan C. 2005. "Bringing the Borderlands to the Web: The Arizona-Sonora Documents Online Project." *Western Historical Quarterly* 36 (2): 201–7.

Sweeney, E. S. 1950. Testimony. Harry S. Truman Library, President's Commission on Migratory Labor, Box 6, Phoenix Statements.

Swenson, Helen D. 1988. *We Remember Humboldt and Dewey Arizona*. Humboldt, AZ: Humboldt and Advertising.

Tafoya, Onofre. 2006. *Mother Magma: A Memoir of Underground Life in the San Manuel Copper Mine*. Apache Junction, AZ: Hispanic Institute of Social Issues.

Takaki, Ronald. 1992. "The Tempest in the Wilderness: The Racialization of Savagery." *Journal of American History* 79 (3): 892–912.

Tapia, Nick. 1998. "Cactus in the Desert: The Chicano Movement in Maricopa County, Arizona 1968–1976." Master's thesis, Arizona State University.

Taylor, ed. 1993. "Valley Builders Face Skilled Labor Shortage." *Scottsdale Progress*, September 22, 1993.

Taylor, Paul S. (1931–1932) 1968. *Mexican Labor in the United States*. Vol. 2. New York: Johnson Reprint Corporation.

———. 1934. *American-Mexican Frontier: Nueces County, Texas*. Chapel Hill: University of North Carolina Press. "Desert Dreams: Mexican American Education in Arizona, 1870–1930."

———. 1970. *Mexican Labor in the United State*. Vol. 1. New York: Arno Press.

Téllez, Michelle, Cristina Sanidad, and Nicolas de la Fuente. 2011. "Immigration and the State of Labor." *Latino Studies* 9 (1): 145–54.

Tetreau, E. D. 1939. "Arizona's Farm Laborers." *Agriculture Experiment Station Bulletin* 163: 294–336.

———. 1940a. "Arizona's Agricultural Population." Technical Bulletin No. 88, Agricultural Experiment Station, College of Agriculture, University of Arizona.

———. 1940b. "Social Aspects of Arizona's Farm Labor Problem." *Sociology & Social Research* (July–August): 550–57.

———. 1944. "Wartime Changes in Arizona Farm Labor." *Sociology & Social Research* 28: 384–96.

Thompson, E. P. 1964. *The Making of the English Working Class*. New York: Vintage Books.

Tinker Salas, Miguel. 1997. *In the Shadow of the Eagles: Sonora and the Transformation of the Border during the Porfiriato*. Berkeley: University of California Press.

Titcomb, Mary Ruth. 1984. "Americanization and Mexicans in the Southwest: A History of Phoenix's Friendly House, 1920–1983." Master's thesis, Arizona State University.

Toepel, Edor John. 1971. "A Migrant Town in Transition: El Mirage, a Case Study." Master's thesis, Arizona State University.

Tomasek, Robert D. 1957. "The Political and Economic Implications of Mexican Labor in the United States under the Non-Quota System, Contract Labor Program, and Wetback Movement." PhD diss., University of Michigan.

———. 1961. "The Migratory Problem and Pressure Group Politics." *Journal of Politics* 23 (2): 295–319.

Torres, David L. 1990. "Dynamics Behind the Formation of a Business Class: Tucson's Hispanic Business Elite." *Hispanic Journal of Behavioral Sciences* 12 (1): 25–49.

Torres, José Ignacio. 1974. "The Globe Strike Lockout? Of 1896." Unpublished manuscript, CHSM-263, Chicano Research Collection, Department of Archives and Special Collections, Hayden Library, Arizona State University.

Torres, Rebecca et al. 2013. "Building Austin, Building Justice: Immigrant Construction Workers, Precarious Labor Regimes and Social Citizenship." *Geoforum* 45: 145–55.

Trail, Mary Patricia 1970. "Arizona Population, 1860- 1870: An Empirical Examination of Leyburn's Hypothesis." Master's thesis, Arizona State University.

Trimble, Marshall. 1986. *Roadside History of Arizona*. Missoula, MT: Mountain Press.

———. 1988. *Diamond in the Rough: An Illustrated History of Arizona*. Norfolk, VA: Donning Company.

———. 1989. *Arizona: A Cavalcade of History*. Tucson: Treasure Chest Publications.

Trouillot, Michel-Rolph. 1995. *Silencing the Past: Power and the Production in History*. Boston: Beacon Press.

Truett, Samuel Jefferson. 1997. "Neighbors by Nature: The Transformation of Land and Life in the U.S.-Mexico Borderlands." PhD diss., Yale University.

———. 2004. "Transnational Warrior: Emilio Kosterlitzky and the Transformation of the U.S.-Mexico Borderlands, 1873–1928." In *Continental Crossroads: Remapping U.S.-Mexico Borderland History*, edited by Samuel J. Truett and Elliott Young, 241-70. Durham, NC: Duke University Press.

———. (2006) 2008. *Fugitive Landscapes: The Forgotten History of the U.S.-Mexico Borderlands*. New Haven, CT: Yale University Press.

Truett, Samuel, and Elliott Young, eds. 2004. *Continental Crossroads: Remapping U.S.-Mexico Borderland History*. Durham, NC: Duke University Press.

Turner, Sylvia D. 2010. "The Kingdom Come: The Intersection of King Cotton and Immigration Policy." PhD diss., Emory University.

Underwood, Kenneth Dale. 2009. "Mining Wars: Corporate Expansion and Labor Violence in the Western Desert, 1876–1920." PhD diss., University of Nevada, Las Vegas.

Unemployment Compensation Division. 1951. *Arizona's Agricultural Workers: An Analysis of Arizona's Year-Around and Migratory Agricultural Employment, with Long-Range Cost Estimates for Unemployment Insurance Coverage of Agricultural Workers*. Phoenix: Employment Security Commission of Arizona.

United Nations. 2000. "Protocol to Prevent, Suppress and Punish Trafficking in Persons Especially Women and Children, Supplementing the United Nations Convention against Transnational Organized Crime." http://www.ohchr.org/EN/ProfessionalInterest/Pages/ProtocolTraffickingInPersons.aspx.

United Nations Human Rights. 2010. *Migrant Labor Rights*. Geneva, Switzerland: United Nations Human Rights.

Urtuzuastegui, Frank. 1972. "The Farmworkers Conditions in Arizona During the 1930s." Chicano Research Collection, CHSM-127, Department of Archives and Manuscripts, University Libraries, Arizona State University.

U.S. Bureau of Labor Statistics. 2013. "Union Membership in Arizona. BLS-11-26." http://azmemory.azlibrary.gov/digital/collection/feddocs/id/2527/rec/1.

———. 2014. "Union Membership in Arizona." http://www.bls.gov/regions/west/news-release/unionmembership_arizona.htm.

U.S. Bureau of National Affairs. 1944. *War Labor Reports: Wage & Salary Stabilization*. Vol. 14. Washington, D.C. Office of Economic Stabilization and Bureau of Internal Revenue.

———. 1945. *Miami Copper Company, et al.—Decision of the National Board*. Vol. 18. Washington, D.C. Office of Economic Stabilization and Bureau of Internal Revenue.

U.S. Bureau of the Census. 1870. "Schedules: Maricopa County."

———. 1880a. "Schedules: Widman, Arizona." Hayden Library, Arizona State University.

———. 1880b. "Schedules: The Life of a Pioneer Woman." Hayden Library, Arizona State University.

———. 1913. *Thirteenth Census of the United States Taken in the Year 1910*. Washington, D.C.: Government Printing Office.

———. 1922. *Fourteenth Census, 1920 Census, Arizona Compendium*. Washington, D.C.: Government Printing Office.

———. 1924. *Fourteenth Census of the United States: State Compendium, Arizona*. Washington, D.C.: Government Printing Office.

———. 1931–1933. *Fifteenth Census of the United States Population*. Vol. 4, *Occupations by State: Arizona*. Washington, D.C.: Government Printing Office.

———. 1940. *Sixteenth Census of the United States. Population Schedule*. Washington, D.C.: Government Printing Office.

———. 1993. *1990 Census of Population: Social and Economic Characteristics, United States Summary*, Table 115. Available at www.census.gov.

———. 2006. Fact Sheet: Arizona. http://factfinder.census.gov/servlet/ACSSAFFFacts?_event=Search&geo_id=&_geoContext=&_street=&_county=&_cityTown=&_state=04000US04&_zip=&_lang=en&_sse=on&pctxt=fph&pgsl=010.

———. 2015. "Population by Race, Race and Ethnicity Selections, 1980–2000." Census Scope, Social Science Data Analysis Network SSDAN.

U.S. Commissioner General of Immigration. 1919. *Annual Report of the Commissioner General of Immigration Fiscal Year Ended June 30, 1919. Bureau of Immigration, U.S. Department of Labor*. Washington, D.C.: Government Printing Office.

U.S. Department of Agriculture. 2014a. 2012 Census of Agriculture, Arizona, State and County Data, Volume 1. Geographic Area Series, Part 3. AC-12-A-3. Washington, D.C.

———. 2014b. 2012 Census of Agriculture, United States, Summary and State Data, Volume 1. Geographic Area Series, Part 51. AC-12-A-51. Washington, D.C.

U.S. Department of Labor. 1917. *Department of Labor Bulletin*. Washington, D.C.: Government Printing Office.

———. 2010a. "2010 Arizona Economic Profile." http://www.doleta.gov/programs/2008reportsandplans/economic_analysis_reports/az.pdf.

———. 2010b. *Strategic Plan: 2011–2016*. Washington, D.C.: U.S. Department of Labor.

———. 2014. "Wage and Hour Division Administrator David Weil on Strategic Enforcement." https://www.youtube.com/watch?v=ejB6yE3tLAw&feature=youtu.be&t=8m32s.

U.S. House of Representatives, Select Committee Investigating National Defense Migration 1942. *National Defense Migration*. 77th Congress, 2nd Session. Washington, D.C.: Government Printing Office.

U.S. House of Representatives. 1871. *Survey of Pima and Maricopa Reservation*. 41st Congress, 3rd Session, 1–17.

U.S. House of Representatives, Committee on Immigration and Naturalization. 1920. *Hearing. Temporary Admission of Illiterate Mexican Laborers*. 66th Congress, 2nd Session, January 26, 27, 28, 30, and February 2, 1920. Washington, D.C.: Government Printing Office.

———. 1926. *Hearing. Seasonal Agricultural Laborers from Mexico*. 66th Congress, 1st Session, January 28 and 29, and February 2, 9, and 11, 1926. Washington, D.C.: Government Printing Office.

U.S. House of Representatives, Subcommittee on Equipment, Supplies, and Manpower. Committee on Agriculture. 1958. *Hearings, Farm Labor*. 85th Congress, 2nd Session, February 28, and March 1 and 3, 1958. Washington, D.C.: Government Printing Office.

———. 1960. *Hearings, Extension of Mexican Farm Labor*. 86th Congress, 2nd Session, March 22–25, 31, 1958. Washington, D.C.: Government Printing Office.

U.S. House of Representatives, Subcommittee on Immigration and Policy Enforcement, Committee on the Judiciary, Senate. 2012. *Hearing. Regional Perspectives on Agricultural Guestworker Programs*. 112th Congress, 2nd Session, February 9, 2012. Washington, D.C.: Government Printing Office.

U.S. House of Representatives, Subcommittee on Immigration, Border Security, and Claims. 2004. *Hearing. How Would Millions of Guest Workers Impact Working Americans and Americans Seeking Employment?* 108th Congress, 2nd Session 24 March. Washington, D.C.: Government Printing Office.

U.S. Immigration Commission. 1911. "Mexicans." In *Abstract of Reports of the Immigration Commission: Report of the Immigration Commission*, vol. 1, 61st Congress, 3rd Session, Senate Doc 747, 682–94. Washington D.C.: Government Printing Office.

U.S. Library of Congress. 1989–2016. Congress.gov database. https://www.congress.gov/advanced-search/legislation.

U.S. Senate, Committee on Agriculture and Forestry. 1965. *Hearing. Importation of Foreign Agricultural Workers*. 89th Congress, 1st Session, January 15 and 16, 1965.

U.S. Senate, Committee on Immigration. 1921. *Hearing. Emergency Immigration Legislation*. 66th Congress, 3rd Session, January 3–26, 1921. Washington, D.C.: Government Printing Office.

U.S. Senate, Subcommittee of the Committee on Education and Labor. 1940. *Violations of Free Speech and Rights of Labor*. 76th Congress, 2nd Session. Washington, D.C.: Government Printing Office.

Valdéz, Armando, Albert Camarillo, and Tomás Almaguer, eds. 1983. *The State of Chicano Research on Family, Labor, and Migration*. Stanford, CA: Stanford Center for Chicano Research.

Valdéz, Dennis Nodín. 1984. "From Following the Crops to Chasing the Corporations: The Farm Labor Organizing Committee, 1967–1983." In *The Chicano Struggle: Analyses of Past and Present Efforts*, edited by John García, Theresa Cordova, and Juan R. García, 42–64. Binghamton, NY: Bilingual Press/Editorial Bilingüe.

———. 1989. "Betabeleros: The Formation of an Agricultural Proletariat in the Midwest, 1897–1930." *Labor History*, 30 (4): 536–62.

———. 1991. *Al Norte: Agricultural Workers in the Great Lakes Region, 1917–1970*. Austin: University of Texas Press.

———. 1995. "Legal Status and the Struggle of Farmworkers in West Texas and New Mexico, 1942–1993." *Latin American Perspectives* 22 (1): 117–37.

———. 2000. *Barrios Norteños*. Austin: University of Texas Press.

Valenzuela, Abel et al. 2006. "On the Corner: Day Labor in the United States." Chicago: University of Illinois at Chicago. https://cued.uic.edu/wp-content/uploads/onthecorner_daylaborinUS_39p_2006.pdf.

Valle, Maria Eva. 1996. "MEChA and the Transformation of Chicano Student Activism: Generational Change, Conflict, and Continuity." PhD diss., University of California, San Diego.

Vander Meer, Philip R. 2010. *Desert Visions and the Making of Phoenix, 1860–2009*. Albuquerque: University of New Mexico.

van der Linden, Marcel, and Magaly Rodríguez García, eds. 2016. *On Coerced Labor: Work and Compulsion After Chattel Slavery*. Leiden, Netherlands: Brill.

Vargas, Nicolas. 2015. "Latina/o Whitening? Which Latina/os Self-Classify as White and Report Being Perceived as White by Other Americans?" *Du Bois Review* 12 (1): 119–36.

Vargas, Zaragosa. 1991. "Armies in the Fields and Factories: The Mexican Working Classes in the Midwest in the 1920s." *Mexican Studies/Estudios Mexicanos* 7 (1): 47–71.

———. 1993. *Proletarians of the North: A History of Mexican Industrial Workers in Detroit and the Midwest, 1917–1933*. Berkeley: University of California Press.

———. 1997. "Citizens, Immigrants, and Foreign Wage Workers: The Chicana/o Labor Refrain in U.S. Labor Historiography." Occasional Paper no. 19, Julian Samora Research Institute, Michigan State University.

———. 1999. *Major Problems in Mexican American History*. Boston: Houghton Mifflin.

———. 2005. *Labor Rights Are Civil Rights: Mexican American Workers in Twentieth-Century America*. Princeton, NJ: Princeton University Press.

———. 2011. *Crucible of Struggle: A History of Mexican Americans from Colonial Times to the Present Era*. New York: Oxford University Press.

Vélez-Ibáñez, Carlos G. 1983. *Bonds of Mutual Trust: The Cultural Systems of Rotating Credit Associations among Urban Mexicans and Chicanos*. New Brunswick, NJ: Rutgers University Press.

———. 1996. *Border Visions: Mexican Cultures of the Southwest United States*. Tucson: University of Arizona Press.

———. 2010. *An Impossible Living in a Transborder World: Culture, Confianza, and Economy of Mexican-origin Populations*. Tucson: The University of Arizona Press.

———. 2017. "Continuity and Contiguity of the Southwest North American Region: The Dynamics of a Common Political Ecology." In *The U.S.-Mexico Transborder Region: Cultural Dynamics and Historical Interactions*, edited by Carlos G. Vélez-Ibáñez and Joe Heyman, 11–43. Tucson: University of Arizona Press.

Vélez-Ibáñez, Carlos G., and Anna Sampaio, eds. 2002. *Transnational Latina/o Communities: Politics, Processes, and Cultures*. Lanham, MD: Rowman & Littlefield.

Vest, Marshall. 2000. "Outlook for the 'New Economy.'" *Arizona's Economy*, November 2000.

———. 2002. "2002–2003 Economic Outlook." *Arizona's Economy*, January 2002.

———. 2003. "2003–2004 Outlook: A Recovery for All to See." *Arizona's Economy*, January 2003.

———. 2004. "Buckle Your Seat Belts. . . . Prepare for Takeoff." *Arizona's Economy*, January 2004.

———. 2005. "2005–2006 Economic Outlook." *Arizona's Economy*, January 2005.

———. 2006a. "2006–2007 Outlook: Continued and More Balanced Growth Ahead." *Arizona's Economy*, January 2006.

———. 2006b. "Forecast for Arizona in 2036: A Top 5 State?" *Arizona's Economy*, October 2006.

———. 2007. "Economic Outlook for 2007–2008." *Arizona's Economy*, January 2007.

———. 2008. "Economic Impacts of Homebuilding." *Arizona's Economy*. Report for 93rd Arizona Town Hall, University of Arizona.

———. 2009. "Economic Outlook for 2009–2010: Riding out the Storm." *Arizona's Economy*, January 2009.

Wacquant, Loïc J. D. 1996. "The Rise of Advanced Marginality: Notes on its Nature and Implications." *Acta Sociologica* 39: 121–39.

Wade, Michael S. 1976. *The Bitter Issue: The Right to Work Law in Arizona*. Tucson: Arizona Historical Society.

Wagoner, Jay J. 1949. "History of the Cattle Industry in Southern Arizona, 1540–1940." Master's thesis, University of Arizona.

Waldinger, Roger et al. 1998. "Helots No More: A Case Study of the Justice for Janitors Campaign in Los Angeles." In *Organizing to Win: New Research on Union Strategies*, edited by Kate Bronfenbrenner et al., 102–19. Ithaca, NY: Cornell University Press.

Waldinger, Roger, and Michael Lichter. 2003. *How the Other Half \ Works: Immigration and the Social Organization of Labor*. Berkeley: University of California Press.

Walker, E. J. 1926. Testimony. In *Seasonal Agricultural Laborers from Mexico*. Hearing, Committee on Immigration and Naturalization, U.S. House of Representatives, 69th Congress, 1st Session, January 28 and 29, February 2, 9, 11, and 23, 148–54.

Walker, Helen W. 1928–1929. "Mexican Immigrants as Laborers." *Sociology & Social Research* 13: 55–62.

Walker, Henry P., and Don Bufkin 1979. *Historical Atlas of Arizona*. Norman: University of Oklahoma Press.

Walker, Scott 2012. "Making the Desert Bloom: Mexicans and Whites in the Agricultural Development of the Salt River Valley, 1867–1930." PhD diss., Arizona State University.

Wallace, Anthony F. C. 1978. *Rockdale: The Growth of an American Village in the Early Industrial Revolution*. New York: Knopf.

Walsh, Casey. 2001. "Development in the Borderlands: Cotton Capitalism, State Formation, and Regional Political Culture in Northern Mexico." PhD diss., New School University

———. 2008. *Building the Borderlands: A Transnational History of Irrigated Cotton along the Mexico-Texas Border*. College Station: Texas A&M University Press.

War Labor Reports. 1944. *Reports of Decisions of the National War Labor Board with Headnotes and Index-Digest,* Vol. 14, *Wage and Salary Stabilization*. Washington, D.C.: Bureau of National Affairs.

———. 1945. *Reports of Decisions of the National War Labor Board with Headnotes and Index-Digest,* Vol. 14, *Wage and Salary Stabilization*. Washington, D.C.: Bureau of National Affairs.

Warren, Robert, and Donald Kerwin. 2017. "The 2,000 Mile Wall in Search of a Purpose: Since 2007 Visa Overstays have Outnumbered Undocumented Border Crossers by Half Million." *Journal on Migration and Human Security* 5 (1): 124–36. http://cmsny.org/publications/jmhs-visa-overstays-border-wall/.

Webb-Vignery. 1985. "Jacome's Department Store: Business and Culture in Tucson, Arizona, 1896–1980." PhD diss., University of Arizona.

———. 1992. "A Grande Dame Stripped of Her Jewels: The Last Days of Jacome's Department Store." *Perspectives in Mexican American Studies* 3: 53–72.

Weber, David J. 1973. *Foreigners in Their Native Land: Historical Roots of the Mexican Americans*. Albuquerque: University of New Mexico Press.

———. 1979. "'Scarce More than Apes,' Historical Roots of Anglo-American Stereotypes of Mexicans in the Border Region." In *Spain's Far Northern Frontier: Essays on Spain in the American West, 1540–1821*, edited by David J. Weber, 296–307. Albuquerque: University of New Mexico Press.

———. 1982. *The Mexican Frontier, 1821–1846: The American Southwest under Mexico*. Albuquerque: University of New Mexico Press.

———. 2009. *The Spanish Frontier in North America*. New Haven, CT: Yale University Press.

Weber, Devra. 1994. *Dark Sweat, White Gold: California Farm Workers, Cotton, and the New Deal*. Berkeley: University of California Press.

Weber, John. 2013. "Homing Pigeons, Cheap Labor, and Frustrated Nativists: Immigration Reform and the Deportation of Mexicans from South Texas in the 1920s." *Western Historical Quarterly* 44 (Summer): 167–86.

Weil, David. 2010. "Improving Workplace Conditions through Strategic Enforcement." Report for the Wage and Hour Division. Boston: Boston University.

———. 2011. "Protecting Workers in Fissured Workplaces." *Perspectives on Work* (Summer/Winter): 38–42.

Weise, Julie M. 2015. *Corazón De Dixie: Mexicanos in the U.S. South since 1910*. Chapel Hill: University of North Carolina Press.

Weisiger, Marsha L. 1995. *Land of Plenty: Oklahomans in the Cotton Fields of Arizona, 1933–1942*. Norman: University of Oklahoma Press.

Welch, Frank, and D. Gray Miley. 1950. "Cotton Labor Requirements." *Journal of Farm Economics* 32 (4): 752–58.

Welch, Nancy. 2008. *AZ Workforce: Latinos, Youth, and the Future*. Tempe: Morrison Institute for Public Policy, Arizona State University.

Wells, Miriam J. 1984. "What is a Worker: The Role of Sharecroppers in Contemporary Class Structure." *Politics Society* 13: 295–320.

Whitaker, Matthew C. 2003. "'Creative Conflict': Lincoln and Eleanor Ragsdale, Collaboration, and Community Activism in Phoenix, 1953–1965." *Western Historical Quarterly* 34 (Summer): 165–90.

———. 2005. *Race Work: The Rise of Civil Rights in the Urban West*. Lincoln: University of Nebraska Press.

White, Harold C. 1973. "The Labor Unions in the Fields: The Arizona Farm Labor Laws." *Arizona Business*, October 1973, 17–26.

White, Harold C., and William Gibney. 1980. "The Arizona Farm Labor Law: A Supreme Court Test." *Labor Law Journal* 31 (2): 87–99.

White House. 2011. "Building a 21st Century Immigration System." ttp://www.whitehouse.gov/sites/default/files/rss_viewer/immigration_blueprint.pdf.

White, Richard. 1991. *The Middle Ground: Indians, Empires, and Republics in the Great Lakes Region, 1650–1815*. New York: Cambridge University Press.

———. 2012. *Railroaded: The Transcontinentals and the Making of Modern America*. New York: W. W. Norton.

Winegarten, Ruthe Lewin, and Teresa Palomo Acosta. 2003. *Las Tejanas: 300 Years of History*. Austin: University of Texas Press.

Winter, Jay, and Emmanuel Sivan. 1999. *War and Remembrance in the Twentieth Century*. Cambridge: Cambridge University Press.

Wolf, Eric R. 1997. *Europe and the People without History*. Berkeley: University of California Press.

Wolff, David A. 1996. "Book Review: *Race and Labor in Western Copper: The Fight for Equality, 1896–1918*, by Philip J. Mellinger." *Western Historical Quarterly* 27 (1): 104–5.

Wollenberg, Charles. 1969. "*Huelga*, 1928 Style: The Imperial Valley Cantaloupe Workers' Strike." *Pacific Historical Review* 38 (1): 45–58.

———. 1973. "Working on *El Traque*: The Pacific Electric Strike of 1903." *Pacific Historical Review* 42 (3): 358–69.

Work Projects Administration. 1989. *The WPA Guide to 1930s Arizona*. Tucson: University of Arizona Press.

Woznicki, Robert. 1977. *History of Arizona*. Glendale, AZ: Bernard Publications.

Wrenn, Rob. 1985. "The Decline of American Labor." *Socialist Review* 15: 89–117.

Wyllys, Rufus Kay. 1950. *Arizona, the History of a Frontier State*. Phoenix: Hobson & Herr.

Yang, Fang. 2002. "Recent Trends in Occupational Segregation for White and Hispanic Women in the Greater Phoenix Area, 1983–1998." Master's thesis, Arizona State University.

Yantis, John. 2004. "Arizona OSHA Encourages Spanish-language Safety Training for Hispanic Workers." *East Valley Tribune*, March 27, 2004.

Ynfante, Charles. 1997. "Arizona during the Second World War, 1941–1945: A Survey of Selected Topics." PhD diss., Northern Arizona University.

Zamora, Emilio. 1993. *The World of the Mexican Worker in Texas*. College Station: Texas A&M University Press.

Zatz, Noah. 2008. "Working Beyond the Reach or Grasp of Employment Law." In *The Gloves-Off Economy: Workplace Standards at the Bottom of America's Labor Market*, edited by Annette Bernhardt et al., 31–64. Champaign, IL: Labor and Employment Relations Association.

Zavella, Patricia. 1987. *Women's Work and Chicano Families: Cannery Workers of the Santa Clara Valley*. Ithaca, NY: Cornell University Press.

Zlolniski, Christian. 2006. *Janitors, Street Vendors, and Activists: The Lives of Mexican Immigrants in the Silicon Valley*. Berkeley: University of California Press.

LEGAL CASES, COURT OPINIONS, AND STATUTES

1862. Homestead Act. P. L. 37–64, 12 Stat. 392.

1877. Desert Land Act. P. L. 44–1877, 19 Stat. 377.

1885. Alien Contract Labor Act (Foran Act). Session II, Chap. 164, 23 Stat. 332.

1902. Reclamation Act. P. L. 57–161, 32 Stat. 388.

1915. *Truax v. Raich*, 239 U.S. 33.

1917. Immigration Act. P. L. 65–301, 39 Stat. 874.

1920. *U.S. v. Wheeler*. 254 U.S. 281.

1924. Indian Citizenship Act. P. L. 68–175, 43 Stat. 253.

1948. *Harrison v. Laveen*, 67 Ariz. 337.

1950. President H. Truman, Executive Order No. 10129.

1951. To Amend the Agricultural Act of 1949, P. L. 82–78, 65 Stat. 119.

1952. McCarran-Walter Immigration and Nationality Act. P. L. 82–414, 66 Stat. 163.

1966. *Miranda v. Arizona*, 384 U.S. 436.

1979. *Babbitt v. United Farm Workers National Union*, 442 U.S. 289.

1986. Immigration Reform and Control Act (IRCA), P. L. 99–603, 100 Stat. 3359.

2000. *Bush v. Gore*, 531 U.S. 98.

2006. *Juárez, et al. v. CC Services, Inc.* 434 F.Supp.2d 755.

2007. State of Arizona, House HB 2779. Fair and Legal Employment Act (FLEA; subsequently renamed Legal Arizona Workers Act, LAWA).

2008. State of Arizona, Senate, SB 1482 (Arizona Temporary Worker Program).

2012. AZ Rev. Stat. Sec. 23–356.

2013. U.S. Senate, S.744, Border Security, Economic Opportunity, and Immigration Modernization Act.

2015. Consolidated Appropriations Act for 2016 (H.R. 2029). http://docs.house.gov/billsthisweek/20151214/CPRT-114-HPRT-RU00-SAHR2029-AMNT1final.pdf.

2016. U.S. Senate, S. 2827, Willing Workers and Willing Employers Act.

NEWSPAPERS

Arizona Citizen. 1873.

Arizona Daily Star. June 30, 1985.

Arizona Gazette. January 21, 1882; February 26, 1941.

Arizona Republic. August 8, 1914a; August 9, 1914b; August 10, 1914c.

Arizona Republican. June 25, 1896; May 26, 1917; September 5, 1917; January 22, 1921.

Arizona Producer.

Arizona Sentinel. April 4, 1874a; April 14, 1874b; November 23, 1878; February 14, 1880; July 23, 1883.

Arizona Silver Belt. January 24, 1941.

Arizona Weekly Miner. January 7, 1871a; March 25, 1871b; April 27, 1872a; July 1, 1872b; June 15, 1872c; September 14, 1872d; November 16, 1872e; November 30, 1872f; August 10, 1875.

El Latino Americano. 1934.

El Mensajero. October 17, 1936; June 13, 1936; August 8, 1936; March 7, 1941; April 4, 1941; August 8, 1941; October 24, 1941; January 16, 1942; February 10, 1944; July 12, 1944.

El Observador. October 2, 1897a; October 16, 1897b; November 27, 1897c; February 5, 1898a; October 15, 1898b.

El Observador Mexicano. April 23, 1898a; March 19, 1898b; October 1, 1898c; October 15, 1898d; March 19, 1898e.

El Ocasional. February 25, 1898a; April 1, 1898b; October 1, 1898c; October 23, 1898d; October 30, 1898e; November 6, 1898f; November 20, 1898g.

El Sol. March 10, 1942; August 18, 1942; August 25, 1942; January 21, 1943; January 28, 1943; February 11, 1943; February 18, 1943; April 2, 1943; April 16, 1943; May 2, 1943; May 5, 1943; September 10, 1943; January 21, 1944; February 4, 1944; February 10, 1944; February 18, 1944; April 4, 1944; May 5, 1944; June 30, 1944; August 18, 1944.

El Universal. June 5, 1925.

The Labor Journal (Arizona). April 23, 1937.

Los Angeles Times. April 23, 1903.

Phoenix Gazette. January 21, 1881; February 26, 1941.

Phoenix Herald. February 2, 1882a; June 24, 1882b; June 30, 1882c; August 3, 1882d; June 24, 1897.

Tempe News. October 20, 1895; January 23, 1897.

Union (Denver, CO). February 14, 1944.

Westsider. May 20, 1986.

Weekly Arizona. November 30, 1872.

SPECIAL COLLECTIONS, ARCHIVES, AND INTERVIEWS

Arizona Cotton Growers Association. 1950–1987. MS FM MSS 30. Records and Correspondence. University Libraries, Arizona State University.

Arizona Industrial Congress Bulletin. 1931. RG 1, Office of the Governor, SG 8, George W. P. Hunt, Box 5, Folder 11, Phoenix, AZ. July 8, 1931. Arizona State Archives, Department of Library, Archives and Records.

Axsom, Karen. 2012. Interview by Cristina Sanidad. Phoenix, Arizona, July 25, 2012.

Balsz, David. No date. Biography Packet. Department of Archives and Special Collections. Hayden Library, Arizona State University.

Balsz, Joseph. 1939. Biography Section. Obituary, January 2, 1939. Hayden Library, Arizona State University.

Campbell Papers. "Servicio Consular Mexicano, Feb. 5, 1921." Arizona State Library, Archives & Public Records, Phoenix.

Clayton, Roberta F. No date. "Pioneer Women—Juanita González Fellows." WPA Writers Project Files, Hayden Library, Arizona State University.

Duckett, Michael. "Seeds of Growth: Phoenix, Arizona, 1942–1943." 1977. Arizona Collection CM MSM-67, Department of Archives and Manuscripts, University Libraries, Arizona State University.

Durán, Josefina. 1989. "Memories of 707 East Jefferson." Chicano Research Collection, ME CHI H-62, Department of Archives and Manuscripts, University Libraries, Arizona State University.

Eligio, José. No date. Amabisca Family. Buckeye Centennial. Arizona Collection. Hayden Library, Arizona State University.

García Redondo, Annie. 1997. Interview by Jean Reynolds. Phoenix, Arizona, March 18, 1997, and November 13, 1997.

García Smith, Plácida Elvira. No date. "Autobiographical Resume: Placida Elvira Garcia Smith." Hayden Arizona Collection, CB BIO, SMI PLA, Department of Archives and Manuscripts, University Libraries, Arizona State University.

Goldman, Charles, and Pedro Sotelo. 1901–1904. Arizona Reports. 8. Arizona State University.

Goodyear Tire & Rubber Company. Records. 1898–1993. Regional History Collections. University Libraries. University of Akron Archives, Akron, Ohio.

Hayden, Carl T. Collection-MSS, University Libraries, Arizona State University.

Hudson Cotton Company Collection-MSS 120, University Libraries, Arizona State University. Huerta, Guadalupe Verdugo. 1997. Interview by Jean Reynolds. Phoenix, Arizona, November 12, 1997.

Kupel, Douglas. 1992. History Consultant. Interview by F. Arturo Rosales.

Lamb, Blaine. 1870–1930. *Historical Overview of Tempe, Arizona, 1870–1930*. Hayden Library, Arizona State University.

Litchfield Park Collection. Department of Archives & Special Collections. University Libraries, Arizona State University.

López García, Mary. 1997. Interview by Jean Reynolds. Phoenix, Arizona, March 3, 1997.

López Rogers, Marie. 2007. Interview by Elizabeth Martínez, Mexican Americans of Litchfield Park Oral History Project, April 17.

Maricopa County. No date. Deeds, Book 14. Arizona State Archives. 1876, 1894. Great Registers, Arizona State Archives.

Marin, Christine. 2015. Interview by Jaime R. Águila. Tempe, Arizona, May 4, 2015.

McWilliams, Carey Collection 1243, Box 12, "Migratory Labor-Arizona" folder. Special Collections, University of California Los Angeles.

McWilliams, Carey Collection 1243, Box 12, McKeehan, Noel. 1939. "The Sanitarian's Role in Maricopa County's Transient Labor Problem." Special Collections, University of California Los Angeles.

McWilliams, Carey Collection 1243, Box 12, McWilliams, Carey. 1939. "A Survey of the Migratory Agricultural Labor Population and the Program of the Agricultural Worker's Health and Medical Association in Maricopa and Pinal Counties, Arizona." Special Collections, University of California Los Angeles.

Miami Copper Company. 1909. *Annual Report of Miami Copper Company for Fiscal Year Ending December 31, 1909.*

Paredes, Américo. 1992. Interview by F. Francisco Rosales.

Peralta, Miguel. 1870. United States, Ninth Census Schedules. Biography Collection, Hayden Library, Arizona State University.

Pérez, Pedro. 1938. Interview by Ernest Mendívil. August 7, 1938. WPA Writers Project. Hayden Library, Arizona State University.

Phoenix City Directories. 1895, 1905–1906, 1914, 1918, 1928, 1930, 1931, 1939.

Pamphlet. No date. "A Saga of the Vulture Road or: Whatever Became of Marinette, Arizona?" Hayden Library, Arizona State University.

Rabinowitz, Richard, Nancy Dallett, and Chris Malczewski. 1991. "Community of Vision and Persistence, Phase II: Curatorial and Conceptual Plan." Report submitted to the Arizona Historical Society, 27–28.

Ramírez Díaz, Esther. 1997. Interview by Jean Reynolds. Phoenix, Arizona, March 14, 1997.

Rangel Martínez, Minnie. 1998. Interview by Jean Reynolds. Phoenix, Arizona, January 23, 1998.

Records of the National Youth Administration, Records of the Service Products Section, Field Inspection Reports and Related Correspondence, 1941–1943. "Verda W. Barnes, Regional Girls' Work Officer, Arizona Report," January 23, 1942, RG 119, Box 1, National Archives, Washington, D.C.

Report of the Governor's Unemployment Relief Bureau. 1932. RG1, Office of the Governor, SG 8, George W. P. Hunt, Box 5, Folder 11, Arizona State Archives, Department of Library Archives and Public Records, Phoenix, Arizona.

Rojas, Arnold. 1999. Interview by Christine Marin. Tempe, Arizona, October 12, 1999.

Ruiz Saldate, Ernestina. 1997. Interview by Jean Reynolds. Chandler, Arizona, March 12, 1997.

Salas, Miguel Tinker. 1992. Interview by F. Francisco Rosales.

Seiberling Collection. "Southwest Cotton Company, 1917–1921." MSS 342, 347, Box 36, 42, 46. Ohio Historical Society, Columbus, Ohio.

Smith, John (Pseudonym). 1999. Interview by Christine Marin. Tempe, Arizona, March 2, 1999.

Solliday, Scott W. Personal Files.

Solliday, Scott W. Files. 1894–1900. M. G. Lavelle, Tempe City Council, 1894–1900. Hayden Library, Arizona State University, Tempe Historical Society.

Sotelo, Joe. 2002. Interview by Christine Marin. Tempe, Arizona, February 25, 2002.

Sotelo Miller, María. No date. *The Life of a Pioneer Woman*. Arizona Collection. Department of Archives and Special Collections. Hayden Library. Arizona State University.

"The Story of Goodyear Farms." No date. Litchfield Park Collection, MS MSS, Box 124, Folder 2, Department of Archives and Special Collections, University Libraries, Arizona State University.

St. Mary's Church. 1882–1926. Parish Records.

Stuart Family Papers. 1935. "1935 Employees and Salaries." Stuart Family Papers, Box 7, Folder 4. Arizona Collection CM MSS-77, Department of Archives and Manuscripts, University Libraries, Arizona State University.

Verdugo Huerta, Guadalupe. 1998. Interview by Jean Reynolds, Phoenix, Arizona, March 5, 1998.

Villa, Judi Ann. 1988. "The Carrillo Women: Past and Present." Chicano Research Collection CHSM-439, Department of Archives and Manuscripts, University Libraries, Arizona State University.

Widman, Theron T. No date. *Arizona—Prehistoric, Aboriginal, Modern*. WPA Writers Project Files. Hayden Library, Arizona State University.

Working Together at AiResearch. 1944. Pamphlet, Hayden Arizona Collection (CE EPH WI-117), Department of Archives and Manuscripts, University Libraries, Arizona State University, Tempe.

Yaqui Indians. No date. WPA Writers Projects Files. Hayden Library, Arizona State University.

CONTRIBUTORS

CO-EDITORS

Luis F. B. Plascencia, PhD, Social Anthropology, University of Texas at Austin, 2005, is an adjunct professor at the Center for Mexican American Studies at the University of Texas at Arlington. He is the author of *Disenchanting Citizenship: Mexican Migrants and the Boundaries of Belonging* (Rutgers University Press, 2012). His expertise encompasses scholarship and public policy analyses in the areas of Latina/o migration, citizenship, agricultural workers, federal and state laws regarding migrants and migration, public assistance, and others. Recent book chapters and journal articles include: "Where is 'the Border'?: The Fourth Amendment, Boundary Enforcement, and the Making of an Inherently Suspect Class" (2017), "State-Sanctioned Coercion and Agricultural Contract Labor: Jamaican and Mexican Workers in Canada and the United States, 1909–2014" (2016), "The Military Gates to U.S. Citizenship: Latina/o 'Alien and Noncitizen Nationals' and Military Work" (2015), and "Attrition Through Enforcement and the Elimination of a 'Dangerous Class'" (2013). He has held positions of associate director with the Tomás Rivera Policy Institute; assistant professor, Southwest Borderlands Scholar, and affiliated scholar in the School of Transborder Studies at Arizona State University; project coordinator/research associate at the Public Policy Institute at the University of Texas at Austin; and policy and budget analyst in the Texas Office of the Governor. He has also served as president of the Association of Latina and Latino Anthropologists (2013–2014), a section of the American Anthropological Association, and presented testimony as an expert to international and federal agencies regarding migration and agricultural workers.

Gloria H. Cuádraz, PhD, Sociology, University of California, Berkeley, 1993, is an associate professor of sociology in the School of Humanities, Arts, and Cultural Studies at Arizona State University. Cuádraz's research and publications are in the interdisciplinary study of Chicana/os and higher education, theory and method of oral history, qualitative methods, *testimonio*, and Arizona Chicana/o labor history. She is co-editor, with Dr. Yolanda Flores, of *Claiming Home, Shaping Community: Testimonios de los Valles* (University of Arizona Press, 2017). She is a member of the Latina Feminist Group, coauthors of *Telling to Live: Latina Feminist Testimonios* (Duke University Press, 2001). Based on oral history and archival research of the Mexican community of Litchfield Park, Arizona, she is currently working on a manuscript titled *Negotiated Belonging: Mexicans and the Making of Community in Arizona*. In 2013 she was awarded the Dan Shilling Public Humanities Scholar of the Year Award by the Arizona Humanities Council. From 2014 to 2017 she served as co-lead editor of *Chicana/Latina Studies: The Journal of Mujeres Activas en Letras y Cambio Social.* She is a lifetime member of the Oral History Association and Mujeres Activas en Letras y Cambio Social, an organization dedicated to the advancement of Chicana/Latina and Indigenous women's feminist scholarship, creative, and artistic work.

CONTRIBUTORS

Jaime R. Águila is an associate professor of history at Midland College. Previously, he held tenure-track appointments at Arizona State University and the University of Texas of the Permian Basin. His scholarship focuses on the evolution of Mexican emigration policy and Mexican-U.S. relations. He is a former México-Norte transnationalism fellow, a NEH summer research fellow, and has been published in *Diplomatic History*, the *Journal of American Ethnic History*, *Teaching Ethics*, and *Aztlán*. He also co-edited a special edition of the *Organization of American History Magazine of History*, which focused on immigration to and from North America.

In 2000 Jaime earned his doctorate from Arizona State University; his dissertation was titled "Protecting México *de afuera*, 1876–1928." He is a native of Fresno, California, a former farmworker, and the son of former undocumented immigrants. He earned his bachelor's and master's degrees from the University of California, Davis, and an associate's degree from Fresno City College.

Cristina Gallardo-Sanidad graduated from Arizona State University's Social Justice and Human Rights master's program and worked for six years as a labor rights promoter and, later, director of the Arizona Interfaith Alliance for Worker Justice, a nonprofit Worker Rights Center (WRC). Her scholarship focuses primarily on topics she learned about firsthand at the WRC and explored through her thesis: wage theft and other employment law violations, Mexican immigrant and undocumented workers in Arizona, and U.S.-Mexico cross-border organizing. Gallardo-Sanidad currently works for Lubin & Enoch, PC, a socially progressive labor and employment law firm.

Christine Marin is professor emerita and archivist-historian at Arizona State University. Dr. Marin is the founder of the prestigious archival repository, the Chicano/a Research Collection and Archives at the Hayden Library in Tempe, Arizona. As adjunct faculty associate in the College of Liberal Arts and Sciences, she taught courses on the history of Mexican Americans for the former History Department and the School of Transborder Studies, and the history of Mexican American women and Latinas for the Women and Gender Studies Department. The National Association for Chicana and Chicano Studies awarded Dr. Marin its Community Award in recognition of her commitment to the Latino community as an archivist and historian in the field of Chicano and Chicana studies. Her recent publications include three books of Latina biographies and stories called *Latina Trailblazers: Stories of Courage, Hope, and Determination*, published by the Raul Castro Institute at Phoenix College. Her recent articles include "'Get Rid of the Shacks': West Live Oak Street Redevelopment in Miami, Arizona, 1946–1952," (*Journal of Arizona History*, Summer, 2015) and "Courting Success and Realizing the American Dream: Arizona's Mighty Miami High School Championship Basketball Team, 1951" (*International Journal of the History of Sport*, June 2009).

Anna Ochoa O'Leary is an associate professor, head of Mexican American Studies, and co-director of the Binational Migration Institute at the University of Arizona. She received her PhD in cultural anthropology from the University of Arizona. Her dissertation research, supported by a National Science Foundation dissertation improvement award, examined how Mexican-origin households invested in the education of its members, and women in particular. Dr. O'Leary's current research focuses on immigration policy, the U.S.-Mexico border, gender issues, and the culture and urban politics of Mexican American and Mexican-origin populations in the United States. As a 2006 Garcia-Robles Fulbright scholar, she researched repatriated migrant women and their interaction with U.S. Border Patrol. She has developed a textbook, *Chicano Studies: The Discipline and the Journey* (Kendall-Hunt, 2007), and is editor of a two-volume work, *Undocumented Immigrants in the United States Today: An Encyclopedia of Their Experience* (ABC-CLIO, 2014), and co-edited *Unchartered Terrain: New Directions in Border Research Method and Ethics* (University of Arizona Press. 2013). During the 1983–1986 copper miners' strike against the Phelps Dodge Corporation, she served as one of the presidents of the Morenci Miners Women's Auxiliary, an organization of women historically dedicated to support efforts of striking copper miners. She resigned that position when the strike ended and resumed her studies at the University of Arizona.

Jean Reynolds is the cultural affairs coordinator and former public history coordinator for the City of Chandler. She received her master's in public history from Arizona State University and her bachelor's in American studies from ASU's West campus. As a member of the Athenaeum Public History Group, in 2006 she co-authored, with David R. Dean, the *Hispanic Historic Property Survey: Final Report*, sponsored by the City of Phoenix. Her public history expertise has positioned her to oversee a number of community-based projects, including the Chandler Hispanic Heritage Photo Exhibit and the Chandler Museum WWII Veterans History Project; in 2012 as project director and centennial coordinator, she oversaw the production and publication of *Southside Neighborhood: 100 Years of Recipes and Stories* for the Chandler Museum of Culture, History, and Art, for the City of Chandler.

F. Arturo Rosales (1942–2016) was professor emeritus of history at Arizona State University. He passed away peacefully on December 22, 2016. He was born in Fresno, California, where his family labored as migrant agricultural workers. Nonetheless, he proudly considered himself a native Arizonan. His ancestry dates back to the Tubac, Arizona, area before Mexico became independent from Spain. He is survived by his wife, son, daughter, and two grandchildren.

Arturo joined the history faculty at Arizona State University in 1980, after five years at the University of Houston. In 1978 he earned his PhD from Indiana University upon completing his dissertation, "Mexican Immigration to the Urban Midwest during the 1920s." He published over forty articles and essays and six books concerning the Mexican immigrant experience and Latino civil rights. His book *Chicano! A History of the Mexican American Civil Rights Movement* (Arte Público Press, 1996) accompanied a PBS documentary of the same name. His most influential work, *¡Pobre Raza!: Violence, Crime, Justice, and Mobilization Among Mexico Lindo Immigrants, 1900–1936* (University of Texas Press, 1999), examined the response of Mexican immigrants to Anglo American prejudices and violence in the early twentieth century.

INDEX

Abbott, H. S.: member of National Farm Labor Advisory Committee, 145; testimony of, 145
Acuña, Rodolfo, 22n17, 25, 98, 167, 255; and scholarship on Mexicans in Arizona, 25
African Americans, 20n7, 45, 106, 203, 213, 223, 228, 235, 239–40, 244
Águila, Jaime, 15, 16, 61–89, 311, 372
AiResearch, 236; and employment of women, 238
Alamillo, José, 22n17, 34, 56n15, 167
Alianza Hispano Americana, 79, 81, 86, 216
Alien Contract Labor Law (1885), 48, 104, 105, 128–29, 132, 135, 170n27, 171n33, 207, 224, 367. *See* Foran Act
Aluminum Company of America (ALCOA), 238; and employment of women, 238
Anderson, Henry P., 126, 135, 146, 172n36, 172n40, 173n47, 174n48, 175n54, 177n71; observation that no full study of the Bracero Program has been carried out, 135
Apaches: diversity, 89. *See also* indigenous communities
Arau, Sergio: *Un Día sin Mexicanos* (A Day Without a Mexican), 23
Arizona: and promotion of low-wage jobs, 277; anti-union positions in, 277; as cattle paradise, 29; demographic growth between 1980 and 2000, 6; denial of suffrage to Native Americans in, 21n10; and five Cs, 5; and six Cs, 15, 27–59; and largest native American population, 7; granting women the vote, 8; Great Depression in, 18; historical diversity, 7; importance of military expenditures in, 7; Japanese internment in, 7, 20n5; limits in child labor protections in, 9; Right-to-Work law in, 39, 277; wage hierarchies/dual wage in, 17; water and federal role in, 45
Arizona Citrus Growers Association (ACGA), 35
Arizona Cotton Growers Association (ACGA), 4, 5, 12, 16, 47, 48, 93, 105, 107–18, 122n34, 123n34, 128, 129, 131, 133, 134, 139, 171, 230; and *enganchadores* (labor recruiters), 48. *See also* cotton

Arizona Humanities Council, 120n4, 313, 372
Arizona Worker Rights Center (WRC), 285, 291, 294, 296, 297, 372
Arpaio, Joseph M., 5, 293; and *Ortega Melendres et al.* racial profiling case, 303; convicted of contempt of court, 303; implementation of Arizona's employer sanctions law, 305
Asians, 66, 77, 223, 228, 240. *See also* Chinese
Aulette, J., 249, 250, 260,262, 263, 269n11; women's challenge to male-centered norms, 250–51. *See also* Mills, T.
Avondale (Arizona), 38, 115, 116. *See also* Rogers, Marie López

Babbitt, Bruce (Governor), 41, 367; involvement in 1983 copper strike, 248, 254
Bakhtin, Mikhail M., 15; and no neutral words, 15
Balsz family, 71, 79, 80, 81, 82, 84, 86
Benton-Cohen, Katherine, 12, 57n28, 108, 122n32, 206, 207, 216, 222, 251, 252
biopolitics, 27, 55n7, 125, 281; defined, 167n6; and Agamben, 167n6; eugenics as, 167n6; and Foucault, 167n6; and Mbembe, 167n6; and Pioneer Fund, 167n6
Bisbee, 206, 207, 216, 222, 223, 251, 269n8; Deportation from (1917), 40, 41, 53, 251–52. *See also* Phelps Dodge Corporation; Jerome (Arizona)
Bonacich, Edna, 205; and ethnic antagonism, 205; and racialization of global labor, 205; and split labor market, 205
Boswell, Terry E., 42, 44, 58n32; and company stores, 44; and debt peonage, 44
bracero: dehumanizing use of term, 169n16; early uses of the term, 169n16, 169n17; problems in use of term, 169n17
Brown, Malcom, 3, 58n39, 59n45, 122n30
Burnett, John L., 170n23; and challenge to William B. Wilson's authority, 170n23; proposed H.R. 4852, 170n23
Byrkit, James W., 250, 251; and Bisbee Deportation (1917), 251

Cadava, Geraldo L., 22n19
Calderón, Roberto R., 11, 22n17, 58n31
Campbell, Thomas E. (Governor), 41, 92, 112, 115, 123n37, 123n44, 132
Cananea (Sonora), copper strike in, 251; Green Copper Company in, 251
Cassmore, Orin, 3, 58n39, 59n45, 122n30
Castañeda, Antonia I., 22n14, 80
Castillo, Ana, 259
cattle (first C), 28–33; British Royal Commission and, 30; and collapse of cattle boom, 31; and ecological impact of, 32; introduction in Arizona, 29–30; sources of capital in, 29–30; and state entitlements provided to, 29; Wagoner's estimates of, 31
Chandler (Arizona), 100, 101, 107, 112, 115, 192, 193, 312, 374; Improvement Company, 116; police and immigration service roundup, 306
Chinese labor, 16, 22, 34, 43–44, 89, 125, 203, 206, 213, 234; Chinese Exclusion Act (1882), 34; railroads and, 73; exclusion from U.S., 34, 106; and cotton harvesting in Baja California, 165; recruitment from California, 72. *See also* Colorado River Land Company
citrus (second C), 33–36; description of commodity and harvesting of, 33, 35; Goldwater family employment of undocumented workers, 35, 36
Clark, Victor, 46, 55, 102, 119, 171, 203, 224; and description of wage hierarchies, 203; and erroneous view of Foran Act, 171n33
Clifton-Morenci, 13, 40, 41, 58n32, 216, 223, 248–69; and company town, 206; and dual wage system, 251; as Mexican camp, 206. *See also* wage hierarchies
climate (third C), 36–39; link to low wages, 39. *See also* tourism

coloniality of power, 55, 125, 132, 162, 167–68n7, 205. *See also* racialization of Mexicans
Colorado River Land Company (Baja California), 165–66; cotton production by, 165–66; preference for Chinese labor, 166
Comité por Trabajadores en General: See Miami
construction (sixth C), 49–53, 56n21, 124, 148–49, 161, 203, 270–99; and planned retirement communities, 51; and President Hoover's views of house ownership, 50; impact of interstate highway system on, 51; post-WWI stimulus of, 51; price impact of undocumented labor in, 51–52. *See also* wage theft; flexible labor regimes; elastic supply of labor
contract labor: and coercion, 125, 127, 159, 164–65; and exploitation, 140–41; as indentured labor, 17, 44, 111, 124–66, 168n13, 169n14, 171n31, 171n34, 173n41, 173n47, 174n51, 176n62, 178n77, 307, 308; and elastic labor supply, 125; as unfree workers, 93, 103, 120n5, 126–27, 132, 135, 147, 156, 158, 161, 163, 167n4, 169n14, 169n15; as labor trafficking, 164–65; demand for (1917–2016), 124–78; regime, 55n7, 125, 128, 136, 158–59, 167n5, 172n36. *See* Ninth Proviso; WWI; WWII
Cook, Judy, 120, 312
copper (fourth C), 39–44; and dual wage, 40, 42, 43; and gender, masculinity, race, and class, 40; and Globe strike (1896), 40; and "Mexican" and "White man's" camps, 41, 44; classification of skilled/unskilled in, 42; sources of capital in, 250; strikes during WWI, 251. *See also* Bisbee Deportation (1917); Great Arizona Copper Strike; Jerome
cotton (fifth C), 3, 4, 5, 6, 9, 12, 15, 16, 21n12, 26, 27, 28, 33, 35, 37–38, 40, 44–49, 50, 53, 58n39, 58n40, 59n47, 59n48, 71, 87, 90–123, 125, 128–34; and collapse of price of, 115; and recruitment of families, 90, 102, 109, 134, 230; experiments in use Jamaican and Puerto Rican workers, 162–63; most lucrative field crop in 2012, 46; plantations in Arizona, 5, 47, 101, 113, 121, 122, 132–35, 162; producers as empire builders, 134, 135; wage payment to families, 134
Crouch, Celeste, 120
Cuádraz, Gloria H., 16, 90–123, 128, 129, 372. *See also* Voices from the Camps of Litchfield Park

Department of Labor, General Order 86 (1927), 34, 56n17, 173n44; and creation of commuter labor, 34. *See also* Yuma
Desert Land Act (1877), 47, 66, 100
Díaz, Porfirio (*Porfiriato*), 59n42, 63, 71–73, 98
Díaz-Taft contract labor agreement (1909), 59n42. *See also* contract labor
Dillingham Commission (1907–1911), 46, 94, 102, 119n3; and Mexicans, 46. *See* U.S. Immigration Commission
Dimas Pete, 22n18, 53, 65, 100, 101, 120n7, 228, 238, 311
dual wage hierarchy. *See* wage hierarchies

elastic supply of labor, 3–5, 16, 17, 18, 19, 38, 44, 47, 87, 103, 108, 110–11, 124–25, 135, 139, 147, 157, 163–64, 204, 209, 223–24, 230, 246, 274–75, 278, 298, 301–4, 307, 308, 313; and alleged labor shortages, 17, 26; and construction, 274, 275, 278; and gender, 17, 110; and links to debt peonage, 44; concept discussed, 26–27; women as part of, 18, 110, 246. *See also* flexible labor regimes; racialization of Mexicans

Fair Employment Practices Committee (FEPC), 214, 217–19, 222, 225n12

Fair Labor Standards Act (FLSA, 1938), 9; child labor protections in, 9; state limitations in protections, 9
Fannin, Paul Jones (Governor/Senator), 146, 147, 174–75
Flagstaff (Arizona), 13, 28, 37, 62; limited published research on Mexican labor in, 13
Flake, Jeff, 8, 124, 148, 149, 151–56, 161; Gang of Eight member, 8, 152; and H-2C visa, 124, 151, 154–56; and labor trafficking, 166; and proposed indentured labor bill (S. 2827), 124, 151, 154–56, 162, 166
flexible labor regimes, 275, 276, 278, 280, 297, 298. See also elastic supply of labor
Foley, Neil, 45, 58, 22n17
Foran Act (1885). *See* Alien Contract Labor Law

Gadsden Purchase (Venta de la Mesilla), 62, 66, 68, 206
Galarza, Ernesto, 127, 141, 144, 146, 168n8, 172n36, 172n40, 173–74n47, 174n48, 178n78
Gallardo-Sanidad, Cristina, 19, 50, 270–99, 311, 372–73
Gamio, Manuel, 98, 203
Gang of Eight (2013), 8. *See also* Flake; McCain
García Redondo, Annie, 231, 237, 239, 242, 243, 245, 246
García Smith, Plácida, 219, 225n14, 233, 245; and Phoenix LULAC Council, 219; and struggle against dual wage, 219
García y Griego, Manuel, 59n42, 172n36, 172n40, 174n47
Garcilazo, Jeffrey, 22n17, 25, 94, 120n7; and importance of Mexican labor (*traqueros*) in U.S. railroads, 25
General Order 86 (1927). *See* Department of Labor
Gifford, Gabrielle, 5; and Tucson shooting, 5
Glendale (Arizona), 13, 100, 115, 230, 238, *La Purísima* Bakery in, 199; sugar-beet processing plant in, 13; and Goldwater Arrowhead Ranch, 36. *See also* Goldwater
Globe (Arizona), 40, 117, 197, 205, 207, 208, 215, 238, 251; and Old Dominion Copper Company, 205; 1896 copper strike in, 40
gloves-off economy, 276
Goldwater, Barry M., 8, 20n6; and racialization, 20; and employment of undocumented citrus workers, 35, 36; argument for an open border, 145; political views of, 8; support of bracero program, 145
Gómez-Quiñones, Juan, 22n17, 89n3, 98, 113
González, Gilbert G., 11, 22, 34, 58n31,167, 169n18, 172n36, 172n40, 174n47, 174n48, 175n54, 210, 216, 223
Goodyear Tire & Rubber Company, 16, 37, 38, 47, 90, 92, 93, 95–97, 99, 100–2, 104–5, 107, 113, 115, 118–19, 119n1, 120n6, 121n14, 121n17, 121n20, 122n29, 123n47, 191, 312; abandonment of contract labor, 115, 118–19; and aircraft, 236, 238; and Historic Cemetery, 91, 312; entry in Arizona, 93. *See also* Legally Imported Aliens; Southwest Cotton Company (SWCC)
Gordon, Linda, 22n18, 43, 56n17
Great Arizona Copper Strike, 248–269; women confront male-centered positions, 257–58. *See also* Morenci
Great Depression, 18, 37, 48, 50, 72, 171, 213, 227, 229, 230, 232, 233, 235, 239, 246
Great Recession, 19, 49, 53, 151, 157, 160
Greenspan, Alan: and infectious greed within capitalism, 53; and irrational exuberance within capitalism, 56
Grosfoguel, Ramón, 167n7
Guerin-Gonzales, Camille, 22n17, 98, 120, 167n4

Guerra, Sarina E., 10, 91, 195, 196, 197, 198, 199, 200, 201, 312. *See also* Washington, Derick D.
guest worker: as euphemism, 127; first use by Congress, 128. *See also* contract labor; H-2 visas

H-2 (H-2A, H-2B) visas, 4, 34, 48, 124, 126, 140, 142, 146, 147, 148, 150, 153, 154, 156, 157, 158, 159, 160, 161, 162, 164, 165, 166n1, 166n3, 167n5, 168n10, 168n12, 172n39, 173n41, 174n49, 174n50, 175n55, 175n56, 178n77, 178n79, 307, 308; H-2 visa overlap with Bracero Program, 142; H-2 visa limited use before 1964, 143; temporary visas and undocumented migration, 162. *See* McCarran-Walter Act
Hahamovitch, Cindy, 172n36
Hall, Stuart: and identification, 22n20
Haney López, Ian F., 15; and legal court cases on defining who is white, 15
Hayden, Carl T., 8, 74, 92, 122n34, 123n37, 130, 131, 132, 134, 171n31, 175n53, 312, 373; and changing position on the need for Mexican workers, 171n31; Senate terms, 8
Hendrick, Sonja, 120
Hernández, Kelly Lytle, 22, 129, 224n4; and boundaries of whiteness, 224n4
Heyman, Josiah McC., 16, 22, 58, 72, 167, 251, 253, 255, 269n6
Hill, Nancy, 38, 58n39, 102, 121n17
Homan, Sara, 120
Homestead Act (1862), 66, 67, 100
Huginnie, Andrea Yvette, 42, 54n3, 167n4
Hunt, George P. (Governor), 41

Immigration Act of 1917, 16, 34, 47, 50, 59n44, 59n45, 92, 105, 106, 121n19, 122n30, 128, 131, 133, 302, 367; aims of, 47. *See also* World War I; Ninth Proviso
Immigration Reform and Control Act (1986), 147, 367; and employer sanctions, 52, 147, 176n67; enactment by President Reagan, 147; and amnesty/legalization, 287
immobilization, 16, 26, 44, 90–123, 167; and labor repression, 93. *See also* mobilization
indigenous communities: American Indian, 240; and lynching, 89n7; Apaches, 20n4, 58n36, 65, 66, 67, 71, 72, 78, 89n6, 210; Diné (Navajo) 7; disenfranchisement in Arizona, 21n10; Gila River, 210; *Harrison v. Laveen* (1948), 21n10; Indian Citizenship Act (1924), 21n10; Maricopa, 68, 210; Native Americans, 7, 16, 21n10, 29, 43, 89n7, 203, 206, 210, 223, 303; Pima, 65, 68, 72, 210; Tohono O'odham, 210; Yoéme/Yoéme Noki (Yaqui), 73, 78, 85, 100, 119n3
International Union of Mine, Mill and Smelter Workers (IUMMSW), 213, 214, 215, 217, 219, 221–22, 224n7, 225n14, 225n16, 249
International Workers of the World (IWW), 112, 123n37, 212, 252; inclusiveness of, 212

Jerome (Arizona), 41, 251, 252; Deportation from (1917), 53; Miners Union in, 43; United Verde Copper Company in, 41. *See also* Bisbee Deportation (1917)
Jiménez Montoya, Andrés, 42, 58n32, 203, 208; and race in copper production, 42

Kingsolver, Barbara, 249, 250, 262, 269n2
Knox, William H., 115, 132, 133, 134, 171. *See also* Arizona Cotton Growers Association
Korean War, 17, 136, 142, 161

Larkin, Micaela A., 20n6, 35, 55n8, 56, 108, 114, 123n41, 123n45
Larson, Orville, 214, 217, 219, 224n7, 225n14

League of United Latin American Citizens (LULAC), 214–17, 219, 224n10, 224n11, 225n14, 237; and President Plácida García Smith, 219, 225n14; and struggle against dual wage, 215–17, 219
Legally Imported Aliens, 16, 103, 118, 119. *See also* Goodyear Tire & Rubber Company
LeSeur, Geta, 45; and African American cotton harvesters in Arizona, 45–46; and Oklahoman cotton workers in Arizona, 45–46. *See also* Weisiger
Liga Protectora Latina, 54, 113. *See* McBride
Litchfield Federal Labor Union, 114
Litchfield Park (Arizona), 37, 38, 90, 91, 92, 95, 100, 115, 118, 119, 120, 121, 122n29, 123n47, 238, 313, 372; and Oral History Project, 57n23, 120n4; Collection, 92; Historical Society of, 92, 120, 190, 191, 312, 313
Litchfield, Paul W., 90, 97, 105, 121n21. *See also* Goodyear Tire & Rubber Company
Lost Land, 12, 15, 61, 62, 63, 64, 87; and identity, 62, 65; esthetics, 88; evolution to México Lindo, 87; overlap with México Lindo, 88; scholars using concept of, 63. *See also* México Lindo
Lucas, María Elena, 9; and scholarship on female Mexican farmworkers, 9
lynching, 75, 89n7; in Arizona, 75, 76, 253; of Frank Little, 252; of Mariano Tisnado, 76

Maricopa (County): citrus production in, 36
Marin, Christine, 17, 61, 65, 99, 120, 121n13, 203–25, 236, 237, 311, 313, 373
Martinelli, Phyllis Cancilia, 58n33
Martínez family shoe business, 10; family migration to Phoenix, 10; daughters' shoe and leather skills, 10
Mawn, G. P., 55, 56n19, 99
McBride, James, 53–54
McCain, John, 8; terms in the Senate, 8; Gang of Eight member, 8, 152, 153
McCarran–Walter Act (Immigration Act, 1952), 49, 140, 142, 146, 173n46, 367. *See* H2 (H-2A, H-2B) visas
McWilliams, Carey, 14; and difficulties in defining the Mexican community, 14–15; and difficulty in defining the Anglo community, 15
Meeks, Eric, 11, 12–13, 22n17, 43, 44, 58n39, 59n41, 59n45, 67, 88n1, 101, 122n30, 210, 223; and limitations of dual wage concept, 210
Mellinger, Phil, 42, 43, 57n30, 89n4, 122n30, 210, 216, 223, 251; and Italians earning Mexican wage, 210
Mesa (Arizona), 34, 61, 100, 107, 215
Mexicana(o)/Mexican labor: active recruitment of (1917–2017), 17, 124–78; alleged labor shortage and recruitment of, 17; biopolitical argument for, 27; and Chinese Exclusion Act (1882), 34; and family wage, 108; and inclusion in the 1921 and 1924 Quota Acts, 133–34; and limited scholarship on Mexicana unpaid work, 21n11; challenge to dual wage, 211–22; day labor, 52; employment in laundry firms, 244; employment in retail stores, 242–43; gender, class, and race and, 42; greater scholarship in California and Texas than in Arizona, 5; links to Chicana/o labor history in the Southwest, 12; occupations (1870–1900), 70; political paradox, 3–4, 125, 301, 303; recruitment of men, women and children, 45; relative invisibility of, 8–9; transnational nature of, 57. *See also* elastic supply of labor
Mexico: anti-Chinese movement in, 58n36, consul intervention with displaced cotton workers, 115–17; recruitment of Chinese by, 165; report on agricultural

workers in Phoenix–area, 228. *See also* Chinese labor
México Lindo, 15, 62, 63, 64, 65, 87, 374; consciousness, 63; evolution from Lost Land, 87; overlap with Lost Land, 88. *See also* Lost Land
Miami (Arizona), 13, 17, 40, 203–25; and segregation in Catholic Church, 207; demographic diversity in 1940, 213; Inspiration Consolidated Copper Company, 206, 211, 212, 213, 217, 218, 219, 220, 222, 224n7, 224n9, 225n13, 254; International Smelter and Refining Company, 206, 217, 249; Iron Cap mine, 224n3; Miami Copper Company, 206, 207, 211, 212, 213, 217, 218, 219, 220, 222, 224n3; Miami Miners Union (MMU), 211, 212; Old Dominion Copper Company, 205, 206. *See also* Globe
Miami Copper Company, and destruction of payroll records, 222
Mignolo, Walter, 167n7
migrant rights, 53; protest rallies/marches (2006–2007), 53, 304; protest rallies/marches (1983), 249, 260, 262, 263
Mikulski, Barbara A., 161, 178n77; support for indentured H-2B crab pickers, 161
Mills, T., 249, 250, 260,262, 263, 269n11; women's challenge to male-centered norms, 250–51. *See also* Aulette, J.
Miranda, Ernesto Arturo (*Miranda v. Arizona*), 7, 367
Mize, Ronald L., 22n17, 89n3. *See also* Swords, Alicia C. S.
mobilization, 16, 26, 45, 93; and labor repression, 93. *See also* immobilization
Montejano, David, 22n17, 93, 102, 103, 120n5, 121, 167n4; and labor repression, 167n4; and web of labor controls, 167n4
Morenci (Arizona), 18, 40; and Great Arizona Copper Strike, 18, 248–269. *See also* Phelps Dodge Corporation
Morenci Miners Women's Auxiliary (MMWA), 18, 248–269. *See also* Morenci
Moreno, Belen Soto, 120n4
Morgan, E. S., labor shortage as a shortage in surplus labor, 163

Napolitano, Janet, 5; and enactment of 2007 Arizona employer sanctions law, 5
National Labor Relations Act, 21n13; and exclusion of agriculture from coverage, 21n13
Ninth Proviso, 16,47, 48, 50, 59n44, 59n45, 92, 106, 108, 109, 110, 111, 112, 113, 114, 121n18, 122n27, 128, 129, 133, 135, 164, 170n23, 170n28, 171, 302, 312; and indentured labor, 135; predecessor to H-2 visa, 48; text, 170n25; use after WWII, 48; use during WWII, 48; used by Army to build barracks, 50. *See also* H-2 (H-2A, H-2B) visas
Non-Ferrous Metals Commission, 219, 221
North Carolina Growers Association (NCGA), 168n12
Northrup, Herbert, 252, 266, 269n6, 269n9; and anti-union manual, 252

Obama, Barack H., 157, 309; and H-4 visa, 157
O'Connor, Sandra Day, 8, 21n8, 21n9
Officer, James, 64, 65, 66, 67, 80
O'Leary, Anna Ochoa, 18, 41, 248–269, 311, 312, 373–74
O'Leary, Jorge, 249, 257, 258, 260, 269n9; and Morenci People's Clinic, 257
Ong, Aihwa, 58n31, 276, 278
Operation Eagle Eye, 20n7. *See also* Rehnquist, William Hubbs
Ortega, Daniel, 284

Padfield, Harland, 33, 56n15, 58n37, 59n41
Park, Joseph F., 54n3, 101, 167n4, 206, 208

Parker, Edward E., 105, 112, 115, 121n22, 121n23; and lobbying for contract labor from Mexico, 105. *See also* Arizona Cotton Growers Association
Parrish, Michael E., 42, 57n30
Pendleton, Edwin C., 54n3, 55n8, 59n45, 101, 102, 108, 117, 121, 122n30, 230
Peña, Devon, 22n17, 58n31
Peonage Abolition Act (1867), 168–69n13
Perales, Monica, 11, 22, 58n31, 167
Pérez, Thomas: efforts to improve the work conditions of contract labor, 166n3; strategies to block his efforts, 166–67n3
Peterson, Herbert B., 45, 58n39, 102, 107, 113, 114, 115, 117, 119, 121n17, 122n30, 123n41, 123n46
Phelps Dodge Corporation, 18, 40, 41, 251, 252, 253, 254, 257, 258, 260, 261, 262, 263, 266, 267, 268, 268n4, 269n6, 269n8, 269n9, 269n10, 269n12, 312, 373; acquired by Freeport-McMoRan, 57n27; Copper Queen mine, 41. *See also* Clifton-Morenci
Phoenix, 7, 10, 16, 18, 28, 34, 227–47; G. Wesley Johnson Jr.'s book on, 23, 25
Pinal (County): citrus production in, 36
Plascencia, Luis F. B., 17, 48, 58n35, 59n44, 104, 111, 120n5, 121n19, 122n27, 122n31, 124–78, 203–25, 298n2, 305, 306, 313, 371; and web of coercion, 125, 167
Poston, Charles D., 44; and debt peonage, 44; and purchase of worker debts from hacienda in Sonora, 44
Prescott (Arizona), 62, 80, 238
Proposition 206 (2016), 57n24; Goldwater Institute and others opposition to, 57

Quijano, Anibal, 55n7, 125, 167n7, 205. *See also* coloniality of power

racial profiling, 5, 284, 303. *See also* Arpaio, Joseph M.; SB1070
racialization of Mexicans: 12, 13, 17, 19n1, 27, 34, 35, 40–43, 46, 58n32, 58n33, 93, 95, 102, 103, 106, 109, 162, 168, 205, , 210–13, 221, 260, 292, 302. *See also* coloniality of power; elastic supply of labor; racial profiling
Rasmussen, Wayne D., 173n42
Ray (Arizona): WWI copper strike, 251
Reagan, Ronald, 3, 7, 8; and decertification of air traffic controllers, 253; and enactment of 1986 IRCA employer sanctions
Reclamation Act (1902), 20n4, 47, 100
Redondo, José María and family, 71, 79; Delores, 79
Rehnquist, William Hubbs, 8, 20n7, 21n8; and role in Operation Eagle Eye (1964), 20n7; and voter suppression, 20–21n7
Reisler, Mark, 22n17, 45, 59n41, 59n44, 98, 102, 104, 106, 120, 121, 122, 167, 168, 170
Reynolds, Jean, 18, 101, 121n15, 227–47, 311, 374
Right-to-Work, 39, 277, 299
Roca-Servat, Denisse: study of roofers in Phoenix, 52
Rogers, Marie López, 38, 57n23; Avondale mayor, 38
Rojas, Arnold, 214, 219, 220, 224n6, 225n14
Romero, Mary, 22n15, 22n17
Roosevelt Dam (1905–1911), 20n4, 47; and importance to large-scale agriculture, 47, 100–1; part of the Salt River Project, 100. *See also* Reclamation Act
Roosevelt, Franklin D., 222; enactment of Fair Employment Practice Committee. *See* Fair Employment Practice Committee
Roosevelt, Theodore: views of whiteness, 170n24
Rosales, F. Arturo, v, 15, 16, 61–89, 228, 311, 374
Rosenblum, Jonathan, 250, 252, 253, 254, 266, 268n4
Ruiz, Vicki L., 22n15, 22n17, 56, 98, 167, 232, 240, 242, 244

Ryan, Paul D., 161, 174n50; and tiny provision, 174n50

Salt of the Earth (video), 260, 263
Salt River Valley (*El Salado*), 3, 13; 15–16, 18, 27, 35, 45, 47, 60, 61–89, 90, 94, 95, 97, 99, 100, 101, 104, 105, 106, 107, 108, 112, 113, 115, 117, 119, 121n15, 121n17, 128, 131–34, 162, 228, 229–30, 245; as altogether valueless, 94; Cotton Company, 132. *See also* Valley of the Sun
Sanidad, Cristina. *See* Gallardo-Sanidad, Cristina
Sayre, Nathan, 29, 30, 55n9, 55n10
SB 1070 (2010), 5, 285, 287, 295, 296, 299n8, 303, 304, 305, 306, 309. *See also* racial profiling
Seiberling, Frank A., 92, 95, 105, 112, 113, 115, 118, 121n23, 123n39, 123n40, 123n43; and lobbying for contract labor from Mexico, 105; and need to exclude U.S. workers, 105, 118. *See also* Goodyear Tire & Rubber Company; Southwest Cotton Company
Servín, Manuel P., 22n17, 23, 25; and study of Mexicans in Arizona, 23
Sheridan, Thomas E., 16, 22n22, 28, 32, 55n8, 55n9, 59n43, 62, 65, 94, 100, 120n7, 250–51, 255; and ecological impact of cattle, 32
skilled/unskilled labor: arbitrary classification, 42
Smith, John (pseudonym), 222, 225n18; and Miami Copper Company destruction of payroll records, 222
Sonora (Mexico), 22n16, 22n19, 29, 30, 31, 35, 42, 44, 56n17, 57n26, 58n36, 65, 66, 67, 69, 70, 71, 72, 73, 74, 75, 76, 78, 84, 98, 102, 107, 120n9, 207, 228, 229; and Arizona as Pimería Alta, 29; anti-Chinese ferment in, 58n36; Cananea, 57n26; Desert, 38, 61, 67; migration from, 68, 99
Sotelo, Joe, 215, 224n8, 224n9
Sotelo family, 72: María, 78, 80; Pedro, 68–69, 72, 87; Tiburcio, 66, 67, 78
Southwest Cotton Company (SWCC), 90, 93, 101, 102, 104, 112, 118, 121n23, 122n24, 122n25, 123n39, 123n43, 238. *See also* Goodyear Tire & Rubber Company
Southwest North American Region, 12. *See also* Vélez-Ibáñez, Carlos G.
Spicer, Edward H., 55n9
Spude, Robert L., 42, 58n30, 206; and Walker-Weaver mining district, 42, 206; marginalization of Mexicans, 42, 206
St. Mary's Catholic Church, 66, 77, 78, 79, 81, 85
Superior (Arizona), 215
Swords, Alicia C. S., 22n17, 89n3. *See also* Mize, Ronald L.

Taylor, Paul S., 22n17, 58n31, 98
Tempe (Arizona), 61, 67, 68, 69, 71, 72, 73, 74, 76, 78, 80, 81, 83, 84, 85, 86, 87, 100, 107, 180, 181, 186, 215, 224n6, 224n8, 225n18, 312, 373; Canal, 67, 78; San Francisco Canal, 72
Texas Proviso (1952), 173. *See* McCarran-Walter Act
Thirteenth Amendment (1865), 44
Thompson, E. P., 13
tourism (hospitality), 5, 18, 36, 37, 38, 39, 56n19, 148, 149, 151, 157, 161, 271, 284, 307, ; and link to seasonal low-wage service work, 38; and production of sanitized representations of Mexican past, 37; omission of negative factors, 39. *See also* climate; elastic supply of labor
Truman, Harry S., 137, 140, 142, 173n45, 367; and Commission on Migratory Labor, 137–40; enactment of P.L. 82–78, 172n35; enactment of P.L. 82–414 (McCarran-Walter Act), 142; failed to enact Commission's recommendations, 140

Trump, Donald J., 3, 4, 8, 160, 178n76, 298, 303, 307, 308, 309; and Border Wall, 19; and Make America Great Again, 4. *See also* Trump Organization, The
Trump Organization, The, 4, 125, 157, 307; and use of H-2A visa workers at Trump Winery, 4, 307; and use of H-2B visa workers at Mar-a-Lago Resort, 4, 307; and use of undocumented construction workers, 4
Tucson, 5, 14, 28, 65, 66, 67, 68, 73, 80, 87, 88, 137, 186, 205, 216, 228, 251, 259, 263, 273, 280, 303

unfree worker paradox, 125, 158
United Verde Copper Company (Jerome), 41; the Big Hole, 41; owned by William A. Clark, 41, 43
U.S. Immigration Commission, 46, 102, 120n8. *See also* Dillingham Commission
U.S. workers: defined, 20n3

Valley of the Sun, 19, 33. *See also* Salt River Valley
Van Dyke, Clete W., 207, 208; and Miami Flats, 207; Miami Land and Development Company, 208; Miami Trust, 208
Vargas, Zaragosa, 11, 22n17, 167
Vélez-Ibáñez, Carlos G., 12, 22n16. *See also* Southwest North American Region, 12
Voices from the Camps of Litchfield Park (video), 120. *See also* Cuádraz, Gloria H.

wage fixing, 111, 144, 155, 162, 174n52
wage theft, 272, 277, 278, 279, 281, 282, 283, 284, 285, 291, 293, 294, 295, 299n7, 372; and Arizona Industrial Commission low priority in enforcing wage payments, 282, 283; and classification of successful investigation, 283–84. *See also* construction
wage hierarchies: and boundary of whiteness, 209; and copper mining, 204; and peon wages, 206; and race as explanation, 208; as racialized systems, 203; association between lower-wage work and work performed by Mexicans, 204; discussion by scholars, 203; in multiple sectors in the Southwest, 203; limits in dual wage categorization, 203; limits in understanding of articulation with gender, class, and race, 204
Walker, Scott, 58n39, 59n45, 102, 111, 114, 121n17, 123n36, 123n37
Walsh, Casey, 94, 95, 97, 98, 99, 120n9, 120n11; and integration of cotton into a global system, 94; and federal irrigation as state formation, 95
Washington, Derick D., 10, 91, 195, 196, 197, 198, 199, 200, 201, 312. *See also* Guerra, Sarina E.
Watsonville Women's Strike, 259
web of coercion, 125, 167. *See also* Plascencia, Luis F. B.
Weber, Devra, 22n17, 45, 109; and study of cotton, 45
Weise, Julie, 168n8
Weisiger, Marsha L., 45, 48, 59, 99, 100, 107, 122n30; and African American cotton harvesters in Arizona, 45–46; and Oklahoman cotton workers in Arizona, 45–46. *See also* LeSeur, Geta
Western Federation of Miners (WFM), 42, 43, 211, 212
Wharton School anti-union handbook. *See* Northrup, Herbert
White, Richard: problems in cattle accounting (book cattle), 30, 39
Wickenburg (Arizona), 67, 71, 74, 79, 228
Wilson, William B., 106, 128, 129, 130, 133, 135, 170n23, 170n30
Wilson, Woodrow: investigation of Arizona copper companies, 252
Women, Mexican: and agriculture, 229, 230, 231;and Americanization, 233–-35; and cotton, 45, 107–10; and domestic work, 233; and elastic supply of labor,

17, 107–10, 302; and employment in Phoenix, 227–47; and families as units of production, 21n12, 34, 107–10; and gender roles, 257–58; and Great Depression, 234–35; and Howell Code, 79; and intermarriage, 63, 64, 68, 78, 80,86; and organizing, 53, 243, 248–69; and seafood industry, 178n77; and service industry, 232–33, 244–45; and trafficking of, 165; and unpaid labor, 110, 122n33; and wage labor, 9, 12, 233, 234; and Morenci Miners Women's Auxiliary, 248, 259–65, 268; and western history, 22n14; and white collar and service occupations, 241; and women's auxiliaries, 249; work in mining towns, 220, 211, 225n15, 229, 258; and WWII, 235–40, (mobility) 246; labor force participation of, 18, 231–32, 245

World War I, 5, 12, 16, 17, 34, 35, 47, 48, 50, 64, 96, 97, 106, 124, 128, 129, 130, 131, 132, 133, 134, 136, 139, 161, 162, 164, 170n22, 171n31, 172n41, 173n41, 173n43, 211, 251, 312; temporary contract labor during, 12; copper strikes during, 251; as first motorized war, 97. *See also* Immigration Act of 1917; Ninth Proviso

World War II, 7, 17, 49, 50, 51, 61, 161, 166n3, 213, 222, 227, 235, 244, 245, 246, 312; and contract labor, 34, 47, 48, 127, 128, 135, 136, 137, 139, 140, 142, 143, 145, 156, 162, 169n16, 171n31, 171n35, 172n36, 172n37, 172n38, 172n39, 172n41, 173n41, 173n43, 173n44, 173n47, 174n47, 174n48, 176n62, 177n72; and Luke Air Force Base, 20n4; and Mexican women, 235–40, 246; integration of Basque, Canadian, Caribbean, Mexican, Newfoundland labor, 136; use of contract labor for railroads, 136–37; U.S. integration of natural resources and labor during, 136. *See* contract labor

Yaqui (Yoéme). *See* indigenous communities

Yuma (Arizona), 3, 13, 20, 27, 28, 62, 65, 68, 69, 71, 77, 79, 129, 132, 137, 138, 162, 173n44, 228, and citrus, 35, 36; Mexican commuter labor in, 13, 34, 35, 56n17, 173n44; Proving Grounds health hazards in, 39; vegetable production in, 27, 28, 35, 137

Zamora, Emilio, 22n17, 98, 113, 167

Zavella, Patricia, 22n15, 22n17, 56n16, 167n4

Zlolniski, Christian, 167n4, 278; and critique of formal/informal economy binary, 278